W9-AHF-599

# Popular China

## Unofficial Culture in a Globalizing Society

Edited by
Perry Link, Richard P. Madsen,
and Paul G. Pickowicz

ROWMAN & LITTLEFIELD PUBLISHERS, INC.
*Lanham • Boulder • New York • Oxford*

ROWMAN & LITTLEFIELD PUBLISHERS, INC.

Published in the United States of America
by Rowman & Littlefield Publishers, Inc.
4720 Boston Way, Lanham, Maryland 20706
www.rowmanlittlefield.com

12 Hid's Copse Road, Cumnor Hill, Oxford OX2 9JJ, England

Copyright © 2002 by Rowman & Littlefield Publishers, Inc.

*All rights reserved.* No part of this publication may be reproduced, stored in a retrieval
system, or transmitted in any form or by any means, electronic, mechanical,
photocopying, recording, or otherwise, without the prior permission of the publisher.

British Library Cataloguing in Publication Information Available

**Library of Congress Cataloging-in-Publication Data**

Popular China : unofficial culture in a globalizing society / edited by Perry Link, Richard
P. Madsen, and Paul G. Pickowicz.
    p.   cm.
    Includes bibliographical references and index.
    ISBN 0-7425-1078-6 (alk. paper)—ISBN 0-7425-1079-4 (pbk. : alk. paper)
    1. Popular culture—China.  I. Link, E. Perry (Eugene Perry), 1944–   II. Madsen,
Richard, 1941–   III. Pickowicz, Paul.
DS727 .P67   2001
306′.0951—dc21                                                          2001041864

Printed in the United States of America

∞ ™ The paper used in this publication meets the minimum requirements of American
National Standard for Information Sciences—Permanence of Paper for Printed Library
Materials, ANSI/NISO Z39.48-1992.

# Popular China

# Contents

# Tables and Illustrations

## TABLES

## FIGURES

## PHOTOS

# Acknowledgments

We are grateful to the National Endowment for the Humanities for a generous grant in support of meetings held at Princeton University in October 1999 and at the University of California at San Diego a year earlier that produced the intellectual ferment from which this book has sprung. We are grateful as well to the Program in East Asian Studies at Princeton University for supplying meeting space, equipment, and other items at no charge; to Claire Sutherland, Princeton '01, for her superb work as coordinator and bookkeeper; to Sigrid Schmalzer, Ph.D. candidate at UC-San Diego, for skillfully editing our papers into a uniform, readable style; and to Susan McEachern, our enthusiastic editor, who has been supporting our collaborative projects for more than ten years.

Many people whose work is not included in the present volume contributed importantly to the intellectual exchange. We cannot name them all, but we note the substantial contributions of Ian Buruma, Lizhu Fan, Sheldon Lu, and Anna Szemere.

The Editors

# Introduction

*Perry Link, Richard P. Madsen, and Paul G. Pickowicz*

This is a book about the people of China, not the abstract People as defined by the government of the People's Republic, not the imagined subjects of a socialist state, but actual living, desiring, struggling people trying to make sense of who they are and how they should act in the rapidly globalizing economy and culture of the early twenty-first century. We assume that this search for meaning is connected with, but is not the same as, China's century-long search for wealth and power. Thus neither the laws of economics nor the structures of politics can fully determine how Chinese history will unfold. To understand the forces driving the transformation of Chinese society, we need to know what people think and feel about their economic, political, and social situations, and how their thoughts and feelings are evolving.

This kind of understanding requires theories and methods different from those commonly cultivated in mainstream economics or political science. It requires a deep knowledge of linguistic structures and rhetorical styles and of the legacies of ideas and values (including late imperial, republican, and socialist) that help constitute the cultural environment of China today. It requires theoretical frameworks that can make us sensitive to the ways in which that environment makes it relatively hard for people to express some thoughts and feelings and relatively easy to express others. It requires methods to gain access to a variety of relatively uncensored forms of expression and communication. We have produced this book (based on papers presented at a conference sponsored by the National Endowment for the Humanities at Princeton University in the fall of 1999) not only to provide a fresh look at popular culture in China, but to encourage scholars to develop better theories and methods for studying it.

The book is a follow-up to our *Unofficial China*, published in 1989, just a few

1

months after the rise and fall of the huge demonstrations in Beijing and many other Chinese cities, and it documents how much Chinese popular culture has changed since then and how much our capacity to understand and misunderstand China has developed. The demonstrations in spring 1989 came as a tremendous surprise to most foreign observers of China, who had little inkling of the powerful currents of thought and feeling that had begun to move under the more obvious economic and political changes of the 1980s. The chapters included in *Unofficial China* were pioneering attempts to fathom those currents. Even though they had been written before the events at Tiananmen Square, we argued that they could help scholars acquire the kind of knowledge necessary to understand the crucial contribution of popular culture to such events.

Since then, China has continued to undergo enormous transformations. Although China scholars have become much more aware of the importance of cultural changes than they were in the 1980s, and although some are doing increasingly sophisticated research on such changes, it is still the case that their collective understanding of popular Chinese culture lags well behind their knowledge of China's economic and political developments. In this book, we try to push the scholarly understanding of cultural change in China to a new level, one that can show us how changes in popular culture—in categories of thinking, textures of feelings, horizons of aspiration, patterns of resignation—have been intertwined with and are shaping the direction of China's momentous economic and political changes.

Part of the challenge of understanding contemporary Chinese culture arises from an embarrassment of riches. In a word, the information revolution has arrived in China. In contrast to an era when all public media were under the tight control of the Communist Party and when most ordinary people were afraid to express their real thoughts (especially to foreigners), the contemporary Chinese scene is awash in a bewildering proliferation of new media—all sorts of serious and frivolous, sophisticated and crude, earnest and crass magazines, newspapers, books, advertisements, radio and television shows, "hotlines," and Internet sites. Although Party and government officials still exercise supervision and censorship, the vigorous proliferation of such forms of expression and communication has greatly loosened state control. Meanwhile, ordinary citizens are increasingly outspoken. Although they have to steer clear of shifting, rather indistinct boundaries established by changing coalitions of political powers, they can find plenty of ways to express their opinions and prejudices, hopes and fears. And often enough, they are willing to express them to sympathetic observers, Chinese and foreigners alike. The scholar of Chinese culture now has to develop methods for interpreting all of these different modes of expression, for determining which are more or less important, and for fitting them, in all of their fragmentation and contradictoriness, into a coherent mosaic of Chinese life. The chapters in this book make creative leaps forward in locating, interpreting, and explaining the larger significance of newly accessible expressions of popular Chinese sense and sensibility.

Of course, no single volume can present a comprehensive picture of Chinese popular culture. Like any living culture, Chinese popular culture is a chaotic mix of contradictory ideas, symbols, and practices, all of which are constantly changing in the cacophony of popular conversation. But even in chaos underlying patterns may appear, and even in cacophony certain resonances emerge. At different times, the conversations driving a particular culture tend to focus on different themes, and the lines of disagreement tend to cluster along certain axes. The foci in this book are importantly different from those represented in *Unofficial China* a decade ago. New shared concerns and new poles of disagreement have evolved in popular Chinese culture.

All of the chapters in *Unofficial China* were concerned, at least implicitly, with the tension between state and society. Echoing distinctions commonly made by ordinary Chinese citizens, the "popular" was equated with the "unofficial"—with realms of life that grew up outside of the formal structures of the Party and the state. But in this new book, the tension between state and society, although it does not completely disappear, loses its centrality. The new central tension is between different aspects of globalization.

China has entered what some of our contributors call a "postsocialist," "market socialist," or "late socialist" world. The socialist state has by no means disappeared, and many important legacies of the socialist era endure, but the state does not have the power that it once had to dominate the popular imagination. Market reforms have given citizens unprecedented levels of economic independence. Loosening of the system of household residence permits (*hukou*) has made it possible for citizens to evade many of the structures of state surveillance and control. The emergence of a consumer culture has given people paths other than the political through which to seek social status. And, as mentioned above, new media of communication have broken the government's monopoly over information. While it is still an intrusive presence, the state is not looming as large in Chinese people's lives as it once did.

What is looming ever larger, on the other hand, are the exciting new opportunities and terrifying new pressures of a global market economy and the models of aspiration conveyed by a global popular culture. China's economy is still only partly integrated into the global economy. But throughout the 1990s increasing levels of foreign investment and trade were powerful stimulants to Chinese industry, and this process will accelerate as China enters the World Trade Organization (WTO). Meanwhile, parts of China have undergone a "consumer revolution," driven by commercial advertising, pleasure seeking, and entertainment, which, even when domestically produced, take their lead from the global "infotainment" industry. These processes of globalization affect, directly or indirectly, almost everyone portrayed in the chapters of this book, even people in remote rural areas who seem to be still living a very traditional sort of life. To understand this dynamic, it is important to locate the phenomena associated with present-day globalization in the broader context of the social, cultural, political, and economic legacies of the recent and even the distant past.

Depending on their social situations, people experience globalization in very different ways and they bring different cultural resources to the task of making sense out of this experience. For the basketball fans described in chapter 1, "I Believe You Can Fly: Basketball Culture in Postsocialist China," by Andrew Morris, globalization has linked them imaginatively to a world of flashy NBA players, whose dramatic, individualistic exploits (contrasted with the older, team-oriented play of Chinese basketball culture) inspire Chinese fans to "believe [they] can fly." The belief is not just about jumping high on the basketball court but about sailing through life with the flamboyant, aggressive self-expressiveness of the slam dunk star. This is an enormous shift in popular aspiration from the culture of state socialism in which people warned one another that "the bird that sticks its head out gets it shot off." It goes along with visions of big money available to resourceful entrepreneurs and professional managers in an expanding urban market economy driven by multinational investors.

For the migrant factory workers described in chapter 7, "The Culture of Survival: Lives of Migrant Workers through the Prism of Private Letters," by Anita Chan, however, globalization has manufactured a cage. Sometimes literally locked within the walls of their factories (and perhaps producing the very basketball shoes that enable players to "fly"), they often earn less than one American dollar a day producing goods for export to the global economy. Although they may earn more than they could have in their home villages, most of their earnings do not go toward their self-development but to help their families pay off debts incurred because of the low price of agricultural products (which will be even lower with China's accession to the WTO). Such rural women workers, Chan argues, are trapped in a "culture of survival" that tends to reinforce rather than break down customary family bonds.

Most of the contributors to this volume see the emerging new world either from the perspective of the globalization that gives you wings to fly or from the one that puts you in a cage. But, to a greater or lesser degree, the perspectives partially overlap. In chapter 12, "Urban Experiences and Social Belonging among Chinese Rural Migrants," for example, Li Zhang describes how alienating the urban world is for the migrants, but she reports that some of her informants are getting a good deal of personal benefit out of the experience. They are forging new forms of multifaceted identity and, in spite of the hardships of their existence, are often finding real satisfaction in this. In chapter 8, "The Chinese Enterprising Self: Young, Educated Urbanites and the Search for Work," Amy Hanser describes the new, open labor market, which gives them an exciting realm for autonomy and self-development. Nonetheless, they often come to realize that "in reality there are lots of limitations, imposed by society," although they rarely give up on their aspirations for self-development.

Faced with these ambiguous experiences, the people portrayed in this book struggle to make sense out of them—to name the experiences, locate them in a cognitive universe, and render a moral verdict on them. To achieve such understanding, they apply the various implements of a bulging cultural toolkit that contains both old and new resources.

Depending on their circumstances, they deploy mixtures of ideas and symbolic practices drawn from old cultural traditions, the various approaches to modernity debated during the early twentieth-century republican era, the more recent cultural legacies of Maoist socialism, and contemporary global culture. Here the global meets the local. Almost no people portrayed in this book see local culture in opposition to globalizing forces. Instead they employ aspects of their local traditions to interpret that culture and to negotiate their way through it. They engage with globalization in a variety of distinctively Chinese styles.

For instance, because of the dissolution of the socialist redistributive economy, it has now become possible for urban residents to purchase their own homes (indeed the government is encouraging it). The dream of home ownership is given color and shape by a new array of home decorating magazines. International merchandisers (including Ikea) establish immensely popular stores in such metropolises as Beijing and Shanghai and set an international standard for the home furnishings that define the good life. In chapter 10, "When a House Becomes His Home," Deborah Davis asserts that "within the confines of newly privatized residential settings, socialist lifestyles have been replaced by a transnational global reference group that at first glance looks suspiciously 'bourgeois.' " Yet, according to Davis, this globalized ideal of a bourgeois lifestyle has taken on a distinctively Chinese character. In the West, interior decorating and furnishing is more likely to be the province of women, but in the privatized homes of China today it is more likely to be dominated by men and to reflect male interests and tastes. Davis argues that this results from long traditions of male privilege, which are given new opportunities to reassert themselves in the market economy.

At the same time, urban Chinese women are reading Chinese versions of *Cosmopolitan* and *Elle* as well as the home-grown *How*, which imitates much of the style of the foreign glamour magazines. In image and word, such publications portray a "new Chinese woman," characterized by Julia Andrews and Kuiyi Shen in chapter 6, "The New Chinese Woman and Lifestyle Magazines in the Late 1990s," as a "strong yet elegant educated lady" who "occupies almost as central a part in the popular mentality as did the cheerful, muscular farm girl of Mao's utopian China a quarter century ago." Yet the Chinese magazines, especially *How*, also give plenty of (often contradictory) advice about how to reconcile these new feminine ideals with a real world that is not especially hospitable to them—for instance, how to deal with unreliable lovers or with an "overconfident boss," a "suspicious boss," a "foreign boss," or an "unreasonable boss."

Not every kind of emergent or reemergent identity can appear in print—at least not yet. The proximate models for contemporary gay and lesbian identities among urban professionals, as portrayed by Robert Geyer in chapter 11, "In Love and Gay," are communicated orally and seem related to current practices in the West. But even these are played out on the deep structure of Chinese culture. Gays and lesbians in China today are confronted with enormously powerful expectations, deriving from the legacy of Confucianism, that they must eventually marry and have children. Most do so, sometimes at the cost of great anguish for their homosexual lovers and their heterosexual spouses.

Some of our contributors attest to an uneasy mixture of new ideals and old patterns of behavior in the context of a rapidly expanding array of new opportunities and constraints. The mixture becomes all the more volatile when it crosses the urban-rural divide. This is illustrated by Paul Pickowicz and Liping Wang in chapter 3, "Village Voices, Urban Activists: Women, Violence, and Gender Inequality in Rural China." Much of their discussion is based on a close reading of the journal *Rural Women Knowing All*, published by Beijing feminists with the support of the Ford Foundation. The magazine contains stories written by rural women themselves—including terrible narratives of abuse and rape. Without the intervention of the Beijing intellectuals, the rural authors perhaps never would have been able to tell their stories or never would have known that they had stories worth telling. Thus the magazine introduces ideals of women's empowerment, developed through globalized feminist movements, into the Chinese countryside. There they enable rural women to speak in an authentic local voice about age-old problems that have taken on new forms and may have been exacerbated during the recent opening up of opportunities for labor mobility in the socialist market economy.

Tensions result not only when urban patterns of thought and value travel to the countryside but also when rural patterns enter the city. In chapter 9, "Beggars in the Socialist Market Economy," Leila Fernández-Stembridge and Richard Madsen show that some of the increasing numbers of beggars now found in major Chinese cities conduct themselves in accordance with a premodern conception of the beggar's role, which gives a certain order and even a modicum of dignity to their craft. However, especially in places (like Shenzhen) that are closely tied in to the global economy, they face a harsh world that sees them as useless losers in a competitive market.

When the ideals of a global market culture intersect with the interests of entrepreneurs and officials, the result is a truly explosive tension, for this mixture manifests itself as political corruption. As seen in the ideals of the earnest young urban job seekers described in Amy Hanser's chapter or in the lifestyle magazines studied by Andrews and Shen, the legitimately successful man or woman is one who has achieved wealth and status through hard work and talent in a fair market competition. In the absence of a stable, impartial rule of law, however, much of Chinese business is carried out through personal connections. The way to accumulate enough money to live the lifestyle idealized by global consumer culture is for business entrepreneurs to work in collusion with government officials to secure special advantages. Transparency International has rated China as one of the most corrupt economies in the world. In chapter 2, "Corruption in Popular Culture," Richard Levy analyzes popular understandings of corruption. The popular consciousness, he finds, is full of contradictions. People are angry about corruption but also cynically accepting of it, and even proud of knowing how to play the system to get some benefits for themselves. The battle lines in the struggle over corruption are not drawn between good citizens and dishonest officials, but penetrate the hearts and minds of citizens themselves.

How are we to untangle the knotted strands of thought and feeling through which people in different parts of a globalizing Chinese society render verdicts on their situations? All of our contributors make creative use of new or newly accessible media, but two of them focus deeply on such media and grapple explicitly with how to interpret them. In chapter 5, "The Rich, the Laid-off, and the Criminal in Tabloid Tales," Yuezhi Zhao studies tabloid newspapers. They were banned during most of the Maoist period for being "politically suspicious and morally decadent" but have now returned in such force that "China may well be the world capital of tabloids." Like Western tabloids, these Chinese newspapers aim for commercial success by catering to popular demands for the sensational, scandalous, and bizarre. Although at first glance they seem to represent the populist sentiments of the lower classes, in reality they cater to the tastes of "the beneficiaries of the economic reforms, the professional and managerial elite and the urban middle-class consumers who are invited to indulge themselves in the pleasure of consumption and relate themselves horizontally to middle-class lifestyles in the West." In the worldview of the tabloids, the rich have extravagantly luxurious lifestyles, but they have earned those lifestyles through hard work and talent. Tabloids present workers who are being laid off in droves from state-run enterprises with exciting new opportunities to gain fame and fortune in the market. Peasants and migrant workers, on the other hand, are backward and dangerous, responsible for most sex and property crimes. Crime stories, including those about official corruption, celebrate the bravery and efficiency of the police. The ideology of the tabloids is captured nicely in a quote from Karl Marx placed at the top of a "layoff special page": "Life is an ocean. Only those with a strong will can reach the other side." Marx now becomes the prophet of the social Darwinist neoliberalism that is the dominant ideology of the global market economy.

With belief in anything like an authentic Marxism having long since collapsed, this pseudo-Marxist neoliberalism is the closest thing to an official ideology that exists in China today, and the chapters in this volume demonstrate that many Chinese people, especially the successful urbanites who have learned to "fly" in the new globalized economy, truly believe in it. But what about those trapped in a cage? As they are described in this volume, they express ambivalent reactions to the dominant ideology. They do not completely reject it, even as they acutely see its downside. In chapter 4, "*Shunkouliu*: Popular Satirical Sayings and Popular Thought," Perry Link and Kate Zhou show us a powerful tool for gaining access to the spirit of social criticism boiling beneath the surface of China today. Mostly in the traditional form of snappy jingles, these sayings, *shunkouliu*, circulate by word of mouth among all strata of society. Link and Zhou write that such sayings "reflect genuine popular ideas, values, and attitudes with extraordinary vividness." As one retrospection on the course of the Chinese revolution puts it:

> For forty-some years, ever more perspiration,
> And we just circle back to before liberation,
> And speaking again of that big revolution,
> Who, after all, was it for?

# 1

## "I Believe You Can Fly": Basketball Culture in Postsocialist China

*Andrew Morris*

> My greatest desire in this life is to truly make a real dunk, and to experience just once the feeling of being "the flier" [*feiren*, i.e., Michael Jordan]. . . . I am 1.75 meters [5′9″] tall, my arms spanning 1.77 meters [5′10″]. . . . I am not blessed with the best physical qualifications. Please suggest some training program for me.
>
> —Wang Qiang[1]

During the summer of 1998, more than half a million basketball fans all over China purchased copies of the magazine *Lanqiu* (Basketball), published by the Chinese Basketball Association (CBA), the Chinese official state basketball bureaucracy.[2] The magazine's flashy covers promised details on such subjects as "Can Utah Strum Some 'Jazz' and Again Become an NBA Power?" "An Illuminating Record of the PLA [People's Liberation Army] Capturing the Men's Championship," "The CBA's Flaws and Future Hopes," and "Conversations with the Flier [Jordan]."[3] Thus drawn in, fans gladly paid ¥4.20 for the forty-eight-page issues full of photos and news of basketball leagues—professional and amateur, men's and women's, Chinese and international.

As readers eagerly opened the magazine to get to the heart of these issues, they saw on the front inside cover a tempting advertisement for Beijing-based Handsun Footwear, which teased in bold print, "Do you dream of slam-dunking [a basketball]? Maybe you could."[4] What Handsun offered, for ¥623 (plus ¥30 shipping and handling, for a total of some U.S.$80), was a "revolutionary" new training shoe that would strengthen the wearer's calf muscles so dramatically that he would be able "to casually do things on the basketball court that before could only flash across your mind." This company prepared to fulfill the dreams of millions of Chinese young people—for a lower price than even a new pair of

Nike Air Jordans and their English-language corporate slogan that said it all: "I believe you can fly."

This Handsun slogan was of course a play on R. Kelly's hit theme song, "I Believe I Can Fly," from the Michael Jordan-Warner Brothers film *Space Jam*, widely screened in China in the summer of 1997. Any young Chinese basketball fan who had seen this film or had heard the omnipresent theme music played on CCTV basketball highlight shows would surely be able to connect personal desires for achievement, fame, and dunking a basketball with the charisma, superhuman basketball skills, and globalized commercial force that are Michael Jordan.

Yet Handsun's tweaking of Kelly was significant in other ways as well. Kelly's anthem invited the properly inspired listener to imagine himself or herself succeeding in life in the smooth, seemingly effortless way in which Jordan dominated the basketball court. Handsun's "I believe you can fly," however, was a direct challenge to the reader. (Much like the state's unofficial new mantra, "I believe you can find a job and health care"?) Here "flying" was linked directly to the purchase of these ¥653 training shoes, and the challenge, the dare even, that the truly committed basketball player/consumer would spare no expense to achieve these Jordanesque dreams. Where their parents heeded Deng Xiaoping's summons to get rich in the 1980s, youth all over China are now answering this updated clarion call—the call of globalized desire, capitalism, and modernity, the call that teaches us all to believe that we too can fly.

## GLOBALIZED CHINESE BASKETBALL

Handsun Footwear's "revolutionary" training shoe and savvy advertising campaign represent much that is fascinating about youth basketball culture in the postsocialist PRC. The aspects of basketball culture mentioned above—the commercialized basketball media, broad exposure to American professional basketball, the availability of specialized training equipment and other paraphernalia for the player and avid fan—make this realm more than just sport, fitness, sportsmanship, or competition. Basketball culture has become an important mode of understanding and negotiating Chinese modernity, desires, and this fin-de-siècle postsocialist moment.

Today's Chinese basketball culture reflects the language of globalization. Fredric Jameson's recent essay on globalization is quite useful here. On its best days, the globalizing NBA (National Basketball Association) culture can bring the "tolerant contact" between peoples and the "immense cultural pluralism" that Jameson cites. And the other side of this physical culture—the destruction of "traditional cultural systems, which extend to the way people live in their bodies and use language"—is just as indisputably a cornerstone of basketball culture.[5]

Yet a model of globalization like Jameson's ignores the often more complicated and subtle process by which recipients of these global cultures can use them to understand or shape their identities and communities. If world basketball culture indeed destroys many indigenous cultural norms (and it is a safe bet, just for starters, that notions of the body, leisure, race, class, gender, and education are just several among many that it substantially impacts wherever it lands), it is also true that this culture is just as subject to corruption, transformation, and displacement by its recipients as they are by it. This is the purpose of this chapter—to understand how it is agents like Wang Qiang, desiring and yearning to dunk a basketball, much more than Michael Jordan or David Stern, who make this culture a truly globalizing one.

Recent studies of other transnational, or "globalizing," cultures offer some strategies for understanding this aspect of local processing of these forms of knowledge, behavior, and discipline. James Watson has tried to challenge the stereotype of a brutally hegemonic "McDonaldization" of East Asia, instead seeing the Golden Arches as providing "local" cuisine that holds and creates local significances anywhere and everywhere it is served up.[6] Aviad Raz has written on Tokyo Disneyland, the institution feared in Japan as a cultural "black ship," the very "shock troops of American capitalism." The globalizing culture that Watson calls "multilocal," Raz describes with his own term "glocalization," coined to describe the tension between global cultural production and local acquisition. He suggests that a newer, more sophisticated model is necessary to clearly show "the more colorful and playful themes characterizing the (usually ingenious) local practices of consumption."[7]

John Van Maanen uses another violent metaphor to describe Tokyo Disneyland: "a cultural bomb dropped on perfect strangers." He also urges the researcher to investigate how "the local core may even be recharged, reinvigorated" by contact with these commercialized word cultures.[8] Eric Zolov, in his work on *rocanrol* music in Mexico, has recently asked important questions about capitalism and its ability to create subversive, if still wholly commodified, popular memories out of such globalizing cultures as American rock music.[9]

The globalized NBA/basketball culture as received in urban China today, I would argue, is certainly a presence that disrupts and corrupts previous norms and assumptions. At the same time, once on the ground in China, basketball culture has quickly become subject to redefinition and reconstitution at the hands of its Chinese recipients and practitioners. This is the problem in which I am most interested: How has basketball culture become an instrument for questioning, testing, and working out notions about China and modernity in the postsocialist age?[10]

This research began as an investigation of Chinese men's professional basketball—the CBA and its vanquished competitor league, the Chinese New Basketball Alliance (CNBA).[11] The CBA professional league, inaugurated in 1995, is funded totally by the International Marketing Group and its sponsors, among them Hilton Tobacco, Nike, and Motorola.[12] Each of the league's twelve teams is managed by the appropriate provincial or municipal sports commission. These are the same bureaucratic units (under the State Sports Commission) that managed the teams during the forty-plus previous years of socialist-style organization, which consisted of yearlong training for a single, almost annual national tournament. The difference in the postsocialist "professional" age is the source of team funding for salaries and training expenses—now local corporations that grace the team name with their corporate moniker, for example, the Shanghai Oriental Sharks or the Zhejiang Wanma Cyclone.[13] The teams are concentrated almost exclusively along the coastal provinces; the PLA Rockets (previously based in Xi'an and Chongqing, now in Ningbo) and the Sichuan Blue Sword Beer Pandas are the only squads from west of Guangzhou or Beijing that have joined the league.

Upon arriving in Beijing in July 1998, I learned that the CBA hardly occupies the center of the Chinese basketball universe. Fan support around the league is spotty—ranging from the fanatic (the Guangdong boom city Dongguan and its South China Hongyuan Tigers)[14] to the enthusiastic (Hangzhou, home of the Cyclone) to the fantastically apathetic (Beijing and its two teams, the Capital Steel Ducks and Beijing Vanguard Olympian). In fact, in China's capital, CBA action ranks a distant third behind the two leading sources of basketball culture production—the NBA and the Japanese animation series *Slam Dunk* (Guanlan gaoshou), both widely televised in Chinese cities. Given such a state of affairs, the focus of this research quickly evolved into a new project—an attempt to understand the larger cultural meanings of the Chinese leagues and of basketball culture as a whole.

While the Chinese Basketball Association is still trying to define and situate itself as a major cultural and commercial force, the larger globalizing basketball culture is already an important part of youth culture in China today. This game, which has become a way of life for so many Chinese youth, has come to represent a significant and meaningful way of interrogating their society and polity, as well as their role in a new globalizing China. Training shoes and dunking a basketball are hardly the only concerns of this realm. Modernity, global markets, consumption, individualism, gender, class, race, corruption, mobility, inequity, nationalism—all these crucial concepts become fair game in virtually any discussion of this new world sport.

## BACKGROUND

The history of basketball in China situates the game in a liminal space between essentialized dichotomies of the West and China, of capitalist and socialist, of imperialist and revolutionary. It always has been impossible to characterize basketball as simply a legacy of Western capitalist cultural imperialism, or of Chinese revolutionary nationalism. Basketball was brought to China by YMCA instructors in Tianjin, depending on whose account one believes, sometime between 1895 and 1898.[15] By the 1920s the game had taken hold in urban centers and school physical education curricula, and in 1935 it was voted (along with soccer) as China's "national pastime" *(guomin youxi)*.[16] Basketball teams, made up mostly of college stars, were among the most successful representatives of the Chinese Olympic delegations of 1936 and 1948.

If basketball was a national pastime of Old China, introduced by the hated and hegemonic American imperialists, this did not damage the game's utility in the new PRC state; until the soccer boom of the 1990s, basketball was clearly the most popular sport, at elite and popular levels, in China. The PRC's international sports debut was in the basketball competition at the Tenth World University Summer Games held in Budapest in August 1949 (several weeks before the People's Republic was actually inaugurated). National men's and women's championships were established in 1951 and 1952 and, except for several years during the Great Leap Forward famine and the Cultural Revolution, have been held annually ever since.[17] Even in periods of great political radicalism, the game's revolutionary credentials were unquestionably red. Xie Jin's 1957 film *Woman Basketball Player No. 5* showed how hardworking players and coaches transformed the game, once defiled by Guomindang-era capitalism and corruption, into a symbol of Communist sportsmanship and will.[18] In 1962 *New Sport* magazine published pictures of a Beijing nightsoil carriers' work unit engaged in a healthy basketball game with high school students, another revolutionary alliance unthinkable in Old China.[19] And Liang Heng, in his memoir *Son of the Revolution*, discusses the great emphasis placed on, and the great amount of material and bureaucratic resources devoted to, basketball teams from factory through provincial levels even during the Cultural Revolution.[20]

In the 1970s, Chinese basketball culture was defined by its military and rural contexts, its "popular" quality by the Maoist or any other definition. By the 1990s, however, the domination of this culture by the globalizing commercial forces of the NBA and Nike had displaced the center of the Chinese basketball world. If the sport is still universally popular in China, urban sporting goods and department stores are clearly seen as a more crucial arena than the crowded dirt courts of the inland provinces. The state sports bureaucracy supports fully the infusion of Chinese basketball with Jordan's soaring presence; long gone are the days when the Party might have labeled Jordan and his NBA a cultural weapon imperializing the minds of the people, like the eastern bloc's understanding of Elvis Presley in the 1950s.[21] And the loyalty dance performed for Chairman Mao by youth all over China now has been replaced by a different choreography— one of stutter steps and leaps, legs kicked out wide and tongue thrust forward— performed in tribute to a different red idol, not in Beijing but in Chicago, Illinois. Yet the game clearly remains a cornerstones of the PRC's march toward international sporting glory.

Soccer is truly a world sport, making the efforts of Michael Jordan and David

Stern's NBA to conquer the world seem at times quaintly quixotic. Though soccer culture in China is more spectator-based than participatory, and therefore
counter to the spoken state goals of popular sport and fitness, the PRC and its
sports bureaucracy work hard to achieve a Chinese presence on the glorious
world soccer stage. Yet world soccer offers little of the dynamic tension that the
U.S.-dominated global basketball culture carries. To be a soccer fan in China, to
follow teams not only in the Chinese A-League but in several European leagues
as well, to stay up until dawn watching World Cup matches, is indeed to engage
in the multiculturalism and "tolerant contact" that Jameson cites. Participation
in the new global basketball culture, however, is a much more loaded and liminal
experience. It entails, almost by definition, dangerously flirting with the American cultural and economic hegemony that forms the basis of this sphere. Yet for
all the exciting and menacing globalized (here read American) connotations
that this basketball enterprise carries, it is still a culture that, in many ways,
could not be more Chinese.

## AN APPROACH TO POSTSOCIALIST
## CHINESE BASKETBALL

Basketball has become a form of engagement with modernity and globalizing
forces on several different levels. The state invests in, and profits from, the dominant performances by Chinese basketball teams in Asian and world competitions. (Nevertheless, the state is roundly criticized for its "gold medal strategy"
that deemphasizes basketball and other team sports and favors individual events
such as swimming, track, and gymnastics that can produce a higher and more
efficient gold medal count.) One level down, those in the official basketball
bureaucracy have found their profit-making niche via the professional CBA
league and its deep-pocketed sponsors. Even with its sub-par fan base, the league
has become quite remunerative for the basketball bureaucracy. In 1998 the
league's main sponsor, the International Marketing Group, was forced to fend
off the Adidas-funded International Sports and Leisure agency in a bidding war
for CBA marketing rights through 2002.[22] However, where the national and
bureaucratic investment in the new world basketball culture is important, it is
the popular-level engagement (mostly through the force of the American NBA)
with the world, with modernity, and with the issues that face postsocialist Chinese society, that I address in this chapter.

The data that I use here come mainly from three sources: personal interviews,
a survey by mail conducted in Beijing during the summer of 1998,[23] and the
popular magazine *Basketball* (Lanqiu), official publication of the CBA and an
important source of NBA news for Chinese readers.[24] There is no doubt that
much of the material in *Basketball*, especially the articles on the Chinese game,
is self-serving Party-line pap. Among the least worthwhile reading presently

available in the PRC are the pieces submitted by China's future cadres and bureaucrats for essay contests on such topics as "Chinese Professional Basketball Reform for the Socialist Market Economy." Yet in some ways this magazine provides a view of the common reader and basketball fan. Besides several articles each month on Chinese and American star players and standout teams, *Basketball* also includes several monthly features that put the spotlight squarely on the fan/reader. The columns "Fan Mailbox," "Rules Q & A," "Making Connections and Building Bridges" (in which fans and amateur players can place personal advertisements), and "Fan Gauntlet" (in which readers debate issues important to the Chinese and world basketball scene) allow hundreds of thousands of *Basketball* readers to participate in shaping China's new basketball culture.[25]

These contemporary discussions of basketball are hardly ever limited to basketball. Whether they touch on the importance of fan participation in the 1990s professional game (the odd yet oft repeated mantra is that "The fan is God"), crooked or heavily biased officiating during games, or the pros and cons of recruiting foreign players into the league, other larger topics pertinent to Chinese society, politics, and economics are never far from the surface. For the Chinese multitudes who consider basketball an important part of their lives at the turn of the century, a conversation about basketball can well provide many vantage points for examination and critique of contemporary life. The conversations I had with basketball fans in Beijing and the responses I received from my mailed survey, as well as readers' contributions to *Basketball*, were loaded with commentary on the China and the world that they are inheriting.

## BASKETBALL AND THE MARKET

One of the central themes of popular basketball discourse ties the new game to the workings of the capitalist market system. The basketball public has no monopoly on this language; "marketization" and "professionalization" are two important cornerstones of the Chinese basketball bureaucracy's standard justification for the sport's new direction. Beginning with the new CBA format unveiled in 1995, the language of "marketization" and "professionalization" has consistently been used to bless the new enterprise.

Few would argue against the centrality of these new tenets of the postsocialist world, but it is interesting to see how these official terms are put to use in daily practice. On one hand, this language can be used to justify tacky and tawdry elements of the market, such as the presence of scantily clad cheerleader squads at games during the 1996–1997 season. On the other hand, this terminology is used to justify the other side of the "Market-Leninist" logic that rules Chinese society today, the modern disciplining effects that are so easy to forget in these liberating and "multicultural" times. The official CBA perspective on "the market" reminds the reader of how quickly the invisible hand can be clenched into an iron fist. For example, the Liaoning Shenfei Passenger Car Hunters, perpetual CBA runners-up to the powerful PLA Rockets, are praised for their front office formulas of "strict management" and "strict punishment" in running their top-level club.[26] "The market" and the elusive concept of "professionalization" can validate other authoritarian visions as well. One editorial writer concerned with the "basketball market" praised the enthusiasm and even the craziness of Chinese fans but added that these qualities could be admirable only if properly rational, market-trained fans "also work to cultivate a civilized politeness, and refrain from disturbing the order of the arena."[27] In the age of the expanding, modernizing, and bureaucratizing People's Liberation Army, the term "professional" can even become code for "militaristic." One official observer proclaimed that only a larger proportion of military teams in the CBA (besides just the PLA Rockets and Ji'nan Army Doublestar Pegasus) could provide a truly "professional" and patriotic spirit in Chinese basketball.[28]

At the same time, this elite use of the language of capitalism is deftly countered at a popular level by young basketball fans skilled in the art of market-speak and critical of the state of the Chinese game. Readers write regularly to *Basketball* with critiques of the CBA, often grounded in concepts of "the market." Dong Weihua of Tianjin, citing the NBA precedent of fan-pleasing rule changes, suggested sweeping changes for the CBA, such as awarding three points for a successful dunk, a shorter (eighteen-second) shot clock to encourage more scoring, and dunking contests before games, all as a means of enlarging the basketball market.[29] A *Basketball* reader from Xiamen University suggested another NBA-tested practice, the sales of licensed team merchandise, as another means of increasing the CBA's market potential.[30] But even when nationalism trumps market considerations, "professionalism" remains the lingua franca of late-1990s Chinese basketball. Xing Desheng, a native of Heze, Shandong, was able to cite the league's weak and immature commercial structure as a way of registering his disapproval of the CBA foreigner allowance of two non-Chinese players per team.[31] The basketball bureaucracy's use of the language of "the market" and "professionalization" to explain its new format and approach has thus opened up a new avenue for popular and original critiques of the CBA via the creative use of this very same terminology.

This explicit language of capitalism is used often in official and popular narratives of China's new basketball culture, even as the implications of China's new postsocialist market economy are discussed in more veiled terms in the new basketball discourse.

One such context involves the realization and negotiation of the new inequities that shape postsocialist Chinese society. The Dengist reforms take it for granted that some people and regions will "get rich first." Official CBA discourse explicitly shuns, and also ridicules as pathetically antiquated, the old Maoist-tinged policies of egalitarianism in favor of the brave new capitalist world. One dogmatic winner of the Chinese basketball reform for the socialist market economy essay contest urged the total abolition of the old state-subsidized basketball structure, in which "everyone ate but no one got full."[32] The Jiangsu Nanjing Steel Dragons were likewise praised for "destroying the 'big rice pot' egalitarianism of the past," when they instituted a bonus system and acquired new players from outside the Jiangsu province basketball pipeline.[33] But this departure from the egalitarian commitment, regardless of its Maoist inconsistency, has brought just as much anxiety as self-congratulation. One joke published in *Basketball* in 1995 touched on the selfish, dog-eat-dog ways of the new China:

A.  Ah, today's society—public morals and manners just get worse by the day!
B.  What do you mean?
A.  Just look at those people—adults—surrounding a little leather ball, swiping and grabbing; it's really indecent!
B.  Indeed! And what's worse is that all those people around them just clap and cheer—no one goes down to try and settle the issue.[34]

Less humorous and more jarring are the quiet commentaries made by many respondents to the questionnaire I distributed to readers of *Basketball* all around China. In many of the returned surveys, I see respondents utilizing understandings of space and social inequity that echo Xin Liu's work on new social meanings of space, as well as the ways in which geography can serve as a signifier for socioeconomic differentiation in today's China.[35] The last of thirty-four questions on my questionnaire asked what type of basketball shoes the recipient wore. Many of these respondents, fully aware of the new socioeconomic hierarchies and how central even basketball shoes can be to these calculations, answered my question by citing the relative status of their home region. Wang Fei, a Shaquille O'Neal fan from Shanxi, answered that he wears Huili brand, only because "Huili shoes are the best shoes in Qixian county."[36] Li Li, a student in Yuechi county, Sichuan, explained that she wears Li Ning shoes because "the area where we live has its economic limitations."[37] And an anonymous respondent from the Ili Kazak autonomous prefecture, Xinjiang, wrote that he wears Huili because "our place here only has this type of shoe."[38] I read these responses as reflecting a sophisticated understanding of China's new hierarchy of place and the distribution of modern goods like Nike or Converse sneakers. Clearly, readers like these, who are bombarded with advertisements for these absolutely unaffordable trappings of market modernity, have learned—if in no other way than through the hierarchy of basketball sneakers—where "their place here" ranks in the new postegalitarian PRC.

Other respondents with the good fortune to be located higher up on national hierarchies discuss the material culture of their basketball lives in very different terms that mark them as proud and capable participants in globalized consumer culture. Chu Ye, a Phoenix Suns fan from Wuxi, wrote that he wears Nike shoes simply because "I trust this brand."[39] Meng Chao from Shijiazhuang felt that

Nike shoes "are perfect for me *(shihe ziji)*."⁴⁰ Wang Zhaogang of Gongyi city, Henan, had a different but equally cosmopolitan reason for choosing Nike— "They created the myth of Michael Jordan the flier."⁴¹ Nike, author of this seamless Jordan mythology and modern sporting goods marketing as we know it, is such a unanimous choice among these basketball players/fans that its swoosh, not the PRC's five gold stars, has perhaps become the most enduringly hegemonic symbol in China today.

The swoosh has become an unquestionably superior sign of all that is good and right in any Nike-infiltrated society, as demonstrated by the imitation Nike swooshes plastered on so many types of Chinese-made consumer goods. Ex–student leader Urkesh Döulät (Wuerkaixi) remarked that what students wanted in the 1989 Beijing spring was "Nike shoes."⁴² Indeed, even Pan Jinjin, a student from Qinhuangdao who played basketball "on a court on the side of the road" and a faithful wearer of more affordable Chinese-made Huili sneakers, could deliver on command a convincing argument for Nike superiority. Pan wrote to me, "If I had more money, I would wear Nikes because they protect the foot, provide strong traction, allow one to exhibit speed and jumping ability, and are comfortable, shockproof, and good-looking."⁴³ Discussions of the new hegemonic basketball material culture, then, end up telling us much about young Chinese people's imagination of space and status, as well as of the new market of culture and desire that has displaced or reinforced so many older Chinese and socialist hierarchies.

While I was in Beijing in July 1998, I watched and participated in the Third Annual Beijing Municipal Three-on-Three Basketball Challenge, an all-day affair held at the Beijing Children's Palace and sponsored by *Basketball*. The tournament attracted 165 teams in five divisions: boys' and girls' junior high and high school teams and men's at-large teams. Stakes were high, with championship teams in each division winning top-of-the-line Nike and Spalding paraphernalia. More interesting than the fabulous prizes were the ways in which these Beijing youth sought to represent themselves to the world of their peers via their team names. Many of the team names were roughly what one would expect, especially from the schoolboy teams—Cobra, The Wild Men, The Bombs, Super, The Zeros, The Virgin Boys, The All-Stars, Assassin, The Charming Boys, Burning Sun, Super Sensation, The Dream Stars, UFO, ZOOM, Big Foot, and Super Man (the last four in English). Yet many of the team names showed a consumer savvy that would have been unheard of in decades past. Among the teams that came to compete that day at the Children's Palace were Barbie Girls (in English), Sanling (i.e., Mitsubishi), The Wild "555" (after the cigarette brand), Aladdin, Garfield, E.T., and The Ever-Victorious Guests (Bishengke, the official transliteration for "Pizza Hut").⁴⁴ Such a lineup would be hard to imagine in many areas of China, where youth are less plugged in to these Madison Avenue buzzwords. That Beijing youth are able to identify with symbols of globalized capitalist power clearly and consciously sets them apart from the lower, Chinese-sneaker-wearing, dirt-court playing orders of the Chinese basketball scene.[45]

One young man whom I met at this all-city tourney was an unforgettable example of China's new globalized basketball culture. Wang Liang, seventeen years old that summer, was captain of a team called (in English) Bloody Mary. Not quite understanding my shock at this moniker, he explained to me matter-of-factly that he just liked the name of this popular cocktail. He was familiar with it through his job as a bartender at the Beijing Hotel (although he was hoping to move up to the Shangri-La or the China World Hotel soon). His ease in talking to me was certainly a product of working in such a multicultural atmosphere, and we talked for quite a while between games about basketball. Foremost on his mind was whether Michael Jordan would return to play in the 1998–1999 season—a question into which he had put a great deal of thought. When I asked him about his basketball-related consumer habits, he estimated that he spent about ¥300 a month on the game. This amount did not include the two ¥23 bottles of Michael Jordan Cologne that Wang had recently bought at the Sogo Department Store. (He bought one extra because each bottle came with a free Jordan model basketball.) It did include an expensive and thoroughly unnecessary-looking Nike elbow band. When I asked why he wore it, he answered that it was for protection but then smiled and admitted, "Because Jordan wears one—it's just my blind worship (*mangmu de chongbai*) [of Jordan]."

Besides being a charming and delightful (and before long probably very successful) young man, Wang also taught me more about the role of basketball in postsocialist China than any of the experts, writers, or bureaucrats who work to shape an official Chinese basketball discourse. In his study of Tokyo Disneyland Raz suggests that the "playful" local variations on global culture are the important sites to examine.[46] Sherry Ortner's thoughts on "social games" are relevant as well, her point being that social life requires that we actors "play with skill, intention, wit, knowledge, intelligence" at social "games," which, if sometimes playful, can also carry very high stakes.[47] Young Wang's negotiation of globalized culture through his hotel bartending job (which surely sits in the eye of the globalizing hurricane in China), as well as his self conscious "blind worship" of MJ and all products Jordan, is nothing if not contagiously "playful." Yet it must surely will prove, in his case, to be a genius strategy for shaping a cosmopolitan future that would have been unthinkable in China less than a decade earlier. In Wang's future, globalization will work just as efficiently for him as it does for Michael Jordan, Jack Valenti, or Tommy Hilfiger. Globalization is serious business, but these hegemonizing cultures, no matter how hard they try, are still far from brutal juggernauts that flatten native cultures like so many screaming apartment dwellers under Godzilla's heels. They win and hegemonize via the efforts of actors like Wang Liang, who has skillfully shaped his future according to the fun and liberating possibilities that hotel bars and NBA telecasts open up and come together perfectly in playing on a basketball team called "Bloody Mary."

The advantages of life in the capital and rewarding jobs in flashy hotels are obviously open to only a minuscule percentage of the youth I surveyed or read about in the pages of *Basketball*. Much more common were the respondents who said they could spend ten, twenty, thirty yuan a month on basketball supplies, those who were conscious of the real economic limitations of "their place there" in the provinces. The opportunities that globalized basketball culture has provided them likely have little to do with world-class consumer goods. Yet concepts of the market are understood as part of new basketball culture, as youth in far-off towns and villages feel comfortable writing on "professionalization" or dreaming of a comfortable pair of Nikes, even though they know that these things are simply not for them. What is left for them is another type of "playful" use of basketball culture, which can be utilized in the creation of a new individual self.

## BASKETBALL AND THE INDIVIDUAL

Basketball is a team sport, yet, thanks to recent trends in the NBA, perhaps the team sport most dominated by the individual megastar. The old debate over the team versus the individual, as much a part of modern sports history in China as it is anywhere else, has been rendered almost moot by the relentless worldwide NBA marketing of stars like Jordan, Penny Hardaway, Shaquille O'Neal, and Kobe Bryant. Jiang Zemin's "core" Party leadership's recent efforts to develop a new cult of personality for Deng Xiaoping and Jiang himself look like the work of some tinhorn dictator occupying an AM radio station when compared with the truly awe-inspiring star marketing projects achieved by Nike, Sprite, Converse, and Fila.

"The individual" is a central concept in Chinese basketball culture today, and one that its Chinese subjects wear well. The surveys returned to me were full of observations about what basketball meant to all these "selves" across China— that the game is "my choice" or that it "shows my skills." Many respondents' parents support their interest in basketball because it is "my interest" or "my ideal" or "my life's goal." Others explained that through basketball they could "show my own individual style" or simply "make more and more people know who I am."[48] The creation of this new space of discourse on individual and inherent talents and skills by the new me-generation is at the very heart of the basketball realm in China.

This theme of the individual in the new world basketball culture is closely related to the discourse, described above, of the global market in Chinese basketball. The unanimous acceptance that Nike shoes "perfectly fit me" or that an Adidas shoe "when worn over one's real foot, feels as comfortable as if it was just another foot"[49] betrays an understanding of the real self that can only be truly fulfilled through the market and consumer desires. I will address separately the individual and individualism that permeates popular and official discussions of Chinese basketball today.

Official CBA publicity, just like American popular sports media, includes paeans to teamwork and the team spirit. In China teamwork is located in the traditions of Lei Feng or Lee Kuan Yew as a Chinese quality, as opposed to an American-style individualistic game. This is a predictable move, one that attempts to occidentalize "individualism" as a distinctly un-Chinese mode and ignores the ways in which global market forces can grip individual Chinese "selves" much more vividly than any Politburo proclamation. But there is also an understanding at the bureaucratic level that the flashy "individualistic" game is what works in the basketball market that now justifies all.[50] Thus a writer for *Beijing Youth Report* can call for "an individualization of fundamental skills" in the CBA, another commentator can identify the cultivation of real individualism as one of three tasks facing the league, and another can suggest that the league begin keeping and publishing more individual statistics that are ignored by the league's team-centered statistical approach.[51] This "market discourse" is surely popular among China's basketball-playing and basketball-consuming youth, but it may already be too late for the CBA. In the NBA and its awesome propaganda machine, young Chinese have found the most potent and attractive model of this individualist spirit imaginable.

One important expression of this spirit in basketball discourse is that most thrilling and individualistic staple of the modern game, the slam dunk (in Chinese *koulan*, "strike the basket," or *guanlan*, "throw down the basket"). Beijing's Handsun Company's exploitation of the now universal desire to "fly" and dunk like Mike or Kobe has already been noted. Indeed, probably few goals occupy as many Chinese minds today as this great challenge. The most common letter to the editors of *Basketball* seems to be one that goes, as Wang Qiang from Linfen city, Shanxi, wrote, "My greatest desire in this life is to truly make a real dunk."[52] Another fan submitted an essay titled "I Have a Dream" on his similarly consuming desire to dunk a basketball like Julius Erving, Shaquille O'Neal, or Patrick Ewing.[53] The physical mastery that goes into a slam dunk—the flying, the momentary transcendence of any team or group concept—have made this feat not just a focus for consumer desires but the ultimate life goal of many youth in China today. Among these young people of postsocialist China, the point is no longer to serve the people but to dunk in an opponent's face.

The slam dunk is a site where fans' desires converge with the basketball bureaucracy's marketing quest. Since the 1995 CBA season, when this exciting technique was first encouraged, slam dunks have been tabulated as an official league statistic (although this is not the case in the American game). In 1996 *Basketball* printed several articles by fans imploring CBA players to dunk the basketball for the sake of the Chinese game. "Please courageously dunk," pleaded one, who lamented the disappointment of CBA fans when fast breaks were concluded by less impressive means and suggested that a successful dunk be worth three points. Pei Yongli from Hebei testified that the slam dunk was the most efficient way to uplift a player's confidence and thrill a crowd. Zhou You from Jiangxi turned his appeal into a moral challenge to CBA players, opining that the scarcity of CBA dunks proved that Chinese players simply were not physically fit and, moreover, were afraid of failing in front of an audience.[54]

Lisa Rofel, in her work on women silk workers, explains that in the postsocialist era capitalist desire has become "a sign of daring, the site of risk, glory, individual achievement, and masculine strength."[55] This is exactly the significance that is imagined in the slam dunk, a desire that the enterprising basketball bureaucracy has tried to flame. In 1997, to encourage players to meet and master this stiff challenge, the CBA/Nike All-Star Game ceremonies included the first Nike slam dunk contest. However, CBA fans' fears about Chinese dunking inferiority were reinforced when the dunk title was captured by Liaoning's James Hodges, whose 360-degree slam showed why he was known as "the Shawn Kemp of the CBA."

Producing Chinese CBA heroes to rival the American stars depends on the league's ability to integrate these fan-pleasing but team-denying moves. Xiaomei Chen's term "Occidentalism" describes the practice in which "constructing its Western Other [allows] the Orient to participate actively and with indigenous creativity in the process of self-appropriation."[56] The Chinese fans who hold out these precedents of the thrilling NBA Other as the only acceptable standard for their CBA are participating in what Chen calls "anti-official Occidentalism," in which Chinese design powerful discourses "using the Western Other as a metaphor" for liberation.[57] Although Chinese basketball discourse holds little of the subversive, antistate connotations that Chen describes, the dunk can certainly be seen as a form of liberation from what youth see as the older, provincial, and "backward" forms of their parents' age. The fans' challenge to the CBA and its players clarified the stakes in this popular desire for the transcendent individualism of the dunk.

Another important site for discussion of the individualist element is on the person of erstwhile NBA star Dennis Rodman. Rodman's antics, self-mutilation, or even as John Hoberman has suggested, black self-hatred, have provided a perfect forum for American discussion of the team versus the individual in modern sport and society. In the United States, Rodman is marketed (by himself, as well as by the usual corporate suspects) "as spectacle to white America, which has always embraced variations of the black jester."[58] However, his wild personal life and showmanship have made him a different type of household name among China's basketball population, a Bart Simpson– or Andre Agassi–like figure who serves as a virtual synonym for the disobedient yet market-friendly individualist spirit. Although it is no longer right to rebel in most ways in postsocialist China, "Rodman" has become a code for this safely carnivalesque esprit.

This Chinese-commodified Rodman image (i.e., the Chinese commodification of Rodman's own commodified "rebellion" against traditional modes of commercialized sport) first appeared on the Chinese scene in 1997 in a series of print advertisements for the new Converse Chuck Taylor All-Star shoe. The first featured a close-up of Rodman's stud- and ring-pierced mien, with the English-language print, "I've got the Vibe. Get it." The second was a self-conscious (if tired and market-tested) tweaking of conventional ideals of the American "individualist" spirit—a shot of Rodman's bared and tattoo-covered back superimposed over a giant American flag and a Converse symbol.[59] However, by the second ad, the basketball establishment had already begun to coopt the image of the Worm (as Rodman is known in the United States and China). Baoyuan Shoes, national Converse agent and (at the time) official sponsor of the CBA's Shandong Flaming Bulls, announced the Rodman Strange Image Creativity Contest. Readers sending in photos of themselves in Rodman-style "strange and weird costume" would be eligible to win Rodman shoes, jerseys, backpacks, and even adhesive body tattoos. The only entry pictured in *Basketball* was that of a third-place winner from Inner Mongolia. He and his young daughter posed in T-shirts and shorts, wearing sunglasses and do-rags, both holding basketballs against their hips, in a touched-up photo clearly taken in a professional studio.[60] The photo was cute, but far from the dangerous threat to sporting, sexual, and sartorial mores that the "real" Rodman can constitute on even his more understated days. And this was the very point of the contest—to recast Rodman's own potentially menacing commodified image in more G-rated and marketable shades.

Although Michael Jordan's popularity in China is overwhelming (73 percent of my respondents named him as their favorite player), the Worm's "individualist" image also captures the imagination of many Chinese youth. One can get a more specific picture of what Rodman signifies in China through images submitted by artistic readers/fans to *Basketball*'s occasional "Cartoon Page" feature. His flashy, controversial demeanor and lifestyle have made him a favorite among China's aspiring cartoonists in very interesting and unlikely ways. In one cartoon, captioned " 'Playboy' Rodman," the reader is presented with a figure that looks more like Axl Rose or a *West Side Story* extra than it does the NBA star (fig 1.1). In one of the few such cartoons in which African American players' features are not grotesquely exaggerated and transformed, Rodman the "playboy" is imagined here as a cheesy white hoodlum, only his partially visible Bulls number 91 jersey and oversized Nike bandanna marking his NBA status.[61] The Nike swoosh even manages to trump dark skin—no small feat in China (or anywhere else for that matter). That Rodman is under contract with Converse and contractually could never don the Nike bandanna pictured here is beside the point; what matters is how smoothly his "individualist" spirit can translate into a purely commercial identity.

In another amateur rendering of Rodman, he is drawn thrusting forward a basketball on which is written (in English), "Do you know me?" This happens to be an appropriate question because the artist has portrayed Rodman squarely within

"花花公子" 罗德曼

作者／沈毅

**Figure 1.1**   *Basketball* reader Shen Yi's drawing of "Playboy Rodman" (1997)

another commercial style—the hugely popular Japanese comic book/cartoon series *Slam Dunk* (see below). Rodman's posture, loose fitting jersey, facial expression, and body lines mirror perfectly those in the Shōhoku High stars of *Slam Dunk*.[62] Thus the reader "knows" Dennis Rodman only through the commercial and cosmopolitan medium of Japanese youth culture. If Rodman is celebrated as the ultimate basketball "individualist," it is significant that he can only be known in China through these wholly commercialized forms of knowledge and brand identification. The young Chinese self that the Dengist reforms liberated from political and ideological obligations has been firmly embraced by a new atomizing market community in which individual identities can be freely bought and sold.

One reason I include these examples of basketball fan/reader contributions is to illustrate the centrality of the sport to the lives and identities of so many Chinese youth. Their relationship to basketball culture is another element of the new imagination of the individual. Many who responded to my mailed survey commented, "Basketball has become a part of my life." Some are very passionate about what basketball means to them. Wei Wei, captain of a Whirlwind basket-ball team in Wujiangpuchen town, Hexian county, Anhui, included with his completed survey an unsolicited letter to me in which he explained what his eight years of playing basketball had taught him. Wei wrote that basketball now meant much more to him than just physical exercise; it was an enterprise that had taught him how to live—how to have a strong will and a steady spirit, how to banish vanity and pride from his heart, and how to fight to the end. Wei told me that, despite being 170 centimeters (5'7") tall, he had skills that were the equal of anybody's. Like the diminutive NBA star Muggsy Bogues, he would never give up basketball no matter how much others insulted him. He con-cluded, "To me, basketball is my life."[63]

*Basketball* has printed similar testimonies from readers, some going beyond the constraints of mere prose. Jin Xin, a Beijing student, wrote, "I've discovered that basketball has entered my life; I can't separate myself from it for a single day." He included a short poem to help express his deep and complicated, even strangely erotic, feelings:

Ball, I respect you, I want to hold you;
Basket, I gaze at you, I want to fly to you;
Court, I draw near you, I want to be inside you.[64]

Another basketball poet named Huang Jun submitted a more substantial effort, a sonnet entitled "Gently You Come to Me," which included the two lines: "Brimming with the powerful scent of the basketball season; / Ever after there is no trace of boredom in my heart."[65]

Not just basketball players but enthusiasts of a myriad hobbies and pastimes, from stamp collecting to foreign language study to Falun Gong, can now reflect that "X is my life," a concept impossible to imagine when flows of information and market were still subject to political command. In this way, then, basketball becomes just one more destabilizing force that enables Chinese people to forget about rigid political commitments and participate in global communities, loyal-ties, and ideologies.

However, I argue that few of these globalized realms have the power of the new basketball culture to create truly globalized selves and identities. I have already mentioned Wang Liang, the young Beijing bartender who spoke so frankly about his "blind worship" and imitation of Michael Jordan. Other teams entered in the same Beijing three-on-three tournament used team names that showed their identification with NBA stars: MJ, Team 23, The Fliers (all after Jordan), The Little Worms (after Rodman's nickname), LA, and Dream Team IV.[66] Two respondents explained that they loved Stephon Marbury and Dennis Rodman because they shared similar playing styles and skills with these NBA stars.[67] Zheng Yi from Guizhou wrote of his friend whose obsession with Houston Rockets veteran Charles Barkley was so hopeless that his friends finally had to give in and just start calling him "Ba-ke-li."[68]

Other youth in China now live their lives through *Slam Dunk*, the Japanese comic book/television animation series based on the sporting and social exploits of an improbably skilled and ethnically diverse basketball team from Shōhoku High School. Long a favorite in Taiwan, *Slam Dunk* is now sweeping through the PRC as television stations in many large cities rush to show years' worth of old episodes during prime time. One team at the Beijing three-on-three tournament took the name Shōhoku (Xiangbei). *Basketball* also published a picture of a Chongwen Elementary School second-grade "Shōhoku" team, whose five members now go by the "Japanese" names of the show's main characters—Yingmu Huadao, Liuchuan Feng, Chimu Gangxian, and so on.[69] Young Li Ping from Qionglai county, Sichuan, wrote to *Basketball* to testify that he enjoyed *Slam Dunk* even more than NBA basketball because the Shōhoku schoolboys' lives were so much more like his own.[70]

The cosmopolitan basketball culture to which many Chinese youth are now exposed has become much more than just a sport; it and the market forces that it brings to China have become avenues for the very creation and redefinition of personal identities. From original and creative imaginations of basketball "individualism" and its icons to the impulse and ability to identify personally with representations of American or Japanese basketball culture, the loaded role of the individual in today's basketball discourse is one more factor that makes this realm important in understanding Chinese youth culture. In many ways the discussion of the individual in Chinese basketball is as hard to separate out from the market as it was for Jin Xin (mentioned above) to separate himself from his basketball for a day. These understandings of the "self" and the individual clearly are a product of the capitalist mission, here perfected by Nike and David Stern's NBA, to seek out and identify the unique identities and needs of each and every consumer. However, in China there is a force that can triumph over the destabilizing and unsettlingly diverse desires and loyalties that these youth are manufacturing, redefining, buying, and selling. It is, of course, the nation.

## BASKETBALL AND THE NATION

Of the powerful globalizing market forces that shape Chinese postsocialist culture today, basketball is one of the few that are strongly grounded in ideas of the nation and nationalism. Basketball's history in modern China—its status as a national pastime in the republican era, a marker of revolutionary fitness and endeavor in the Maoist era, and a sport in which Chinese men's and women's teams have traditionally done quite well in international competition—has provided the game with a national resonance that, while certainly not uncomplicated, serves as an easy reference point for both popular and official basketball discourse. Although young basketball fans neglect their own CBA for the more glamorous American NBA, they seem to care passionately about "Chinese basketball" as a whole, whatever that is.

The narrative of the nation in Chinese basketball is one that official bureaucratic structures work to keep very prominent, even (and especially) as the game acts as a destabilizing force in Chinese youth culture. Almost any issue of *Basketball* includes reminders that, after all, national glory and status is the real reason for this basketball enterprise. This commitment then serves as the standard against which any member of the basketball community—players, referees, fans—can be evaluated.

The ways in which the nation figures in popular basketball discourse today are far more interesting than this clunky rhetoric because, for all of the consciousness of globalized market forces and a globalized individual self that China's basketball youth share today, the nation really does matter. One question on my mailed survey asked whether "winning glory for the nation" was a motivation for the respondent's participation in basketball; twenty-two of sixty (37 percent) answered that it was. These results are more interesting when paired with those of another question, one that asked the highest-level team the respondent hoped to join in his or her basketball career—school, county, provincial, (W)CBA, national, or (W)NBA.[71] The results are in table 1.1.

The fact that twenty of sixty, or a full third, of my respondents hope someday to play in the NBA is surely an important sign of an unprecedented range of individual ambitions and goals. But we also see that the higher one's basketball career goals are, the more the nation seems to figure in one's notion of the very meanings of the game![72] Basketball nationalists would also have been comforted to see several of the Beijing three-on-three tournament team names that, far from betraying a soft spot for things American and capitalist, referenced familiar PRC and Maoist images, such as Red Star, The Masses, and The East Is Rising.[73]

**Table 1.1   Survey Respondents' Basketball Goals and National Commitment**

| Basketball Career Goal | Number Hoping to Reach Goal | Respondents for Whom Nation Is Significant | |
|---|---|---|---|
| | | Number | Percentage |
| School team | 5 | 0 | 0 |
| County team | 5 | 1 | 20 |
| Provincial team | 6 | 1 | 17 |
| (W)CBA team | 12 | 4 | 33 |
| National team | 8 | 4 | 50 |
| (W)NBA team | 20 | 10 | 50 |
| No answer | 4 | 2 | 50 |
| Total | 60 | 22 | 37 |

Despite fears that the globalizing forms of knowledge and behavior which basket-ball culture brings to China will destabilize notions of the nation as the center, the nation does still remain an important focus for many Chinese basketball youth.

I have already explained that most young basketball fans and players focus more on the American NBA in terms of their identities and desires than on their own CBA. Although young Chinese seem to invest more in the performance of certain NBA players and teams, many of them retain strong national attach-ments to the idea and even the structure of the CBA, if not to the actual com-petitive affairs of the league itself.

The notion that the PRC has to have its own uniquely Chinese professional basketball league, even if no one pays attention to it, is a powerful one. A com-mon concern of fans writing in to *Basketball* relates to the appropriate level of Chineseness maintained by the CBA. Liu Shichao, a junior high student from Ji'nan, asked why all the CBA players wore "foreign" shoe brands instead of sup-porting Chinese-made goods and the Chinese market.[74] A fan from Shandong submitted an essay to the magazine in which he asked why players' names were stenciled on the backs of their jerseys in romanized *pinyin*, such as "Z. Z. Wang" or "X. B. Gong," instead of in China's own character script.[75]

Proving the uncanny success of the Jiang-era "patriotic education" program, and also the ingenuity of these educated patriots, the inevitable notion of "pro-fessional basketball with Chinese characteristics" is commonly cited by fans. It and the term *guoqing* ("national characteristics") are used frequently to articu-late a uniquely Chinese basketball enterprise that need not always follow Ameri-can or NBA precedents in its development. One reader even coined the remarkable term *qiuqing* (basketball characteristics) in warning against the dan-gers of "total westernization" (*quanpan xihua*) in the Chinese basketball project.[76] Indeed, as two fans explained, to support a CBA rule that the worst two teams each year face possible demotion to Division B, diverging from NBA precedent, is justification enough for many Chinese league policies.[77] Thus, if fans' use of the NBA Other sometimes serves as an "Occidentalist" critique of the Chinese polity, here it works in an opposite direction. Fans like these are now more nationalistic than the state basketball bureaucracy that has sold this patriotic line. The power of their critique is in their ability to reference the Otherized "Occident" as a means of presenting their self-Orientalizing appeal for a CBA tied more closely to Chinese culture and "characteristics."

Another significant subject of nationalist basketball discourse relates to the recruitment of foreign players to supplement CBA rosters. Each team is allowed two foreign players, although their play is limited to four "player quarters" per game.[78] The first *waiyuan* (literally, "foreign aid") player was an Uzbek who joined the old Zhejiang Zhongxin Squirrels for the 1995–1996 season, and other early *waiyuan* included several Russian players. Now, however, the foreigners are overwhelmingly American, a fact that elicits national (and often racial) sentiments about the CBA and its relationship to the hegemonic forces of American basketball culture.

Those in the basketball bureaucracy seem to take a very ambivalent stand on the role of the CBA's foreign players. In the lead article of the January 1998 issue of *Basketball*, "To Fire Up the Basketball Market, We Need More Foreign Players," the author told of the players' contributions to the CBA game and attempted to defuse narrow nationalistic arguments by pointing out even that the American NBA itself employed many foreign players.[79] At the same time, *Basketball* reporters regularly praise such teams as the PLA Rockets or the Shandong Wing On Flaming Bulls that, because of military regulations or nationalistic pride, have not employed foreign players.[80] Yet the careful ambivalence that the official basketball world maintains on this issue does not spill over into the popular realm. In fact, few questions about the CBA are debated more fiercely than this issue of *waiyuan* players' role in the league.

One aspect of the popular debate is fairly straightforward and revolves around how foreign players help or hinder the development of Chinese basketball. Some argue that the *waiyuan* presence acts as a catalyst for the CBA, pushing Chinese players to their limits, while others worry that these foreign players take up roster spots that could accommodate China's future stars. Yet for all these very practical considerations voiced by CBA fans, it is never long before purely nationalist narratives emerge in this space. Such nationalist lines obviously allow little room for those who like their *waiyuan* players, but many fans are able to show great creativity in justifying a foreign presence in the CBA. They maintain a national focus by explaining, as Zhang Long from Beijing did, that without this *waiyuan* catalyst, Chinese basketball would fall farther and farther behind the rest of the world. Hou Zhongwei from Daqing, Heilongjiang, called the inclusion of these foreign players an important step on "the road to national strength and widespread prosperity *(qiangguo fumin)*." And Qi Guangming from the Houma Electrical Cable Factory in Shanxi held out the tempting possibility that someday Chinese players would be desired as *waiyuan* in pro leagues in other foreign lands.[81]

The nationalist constraints of this debate clearly favor opponents of the foreign presence, however. Fans writing in to oppose the *waiyuan* policy—and its inherent implication that the Chinese game is merely a local variation of a global American standard—do an effective job of laying out their arguments. Chen Yan from Fuxin Mongol autonomous county, Liaoning, testified that these foreigners could not truly help the development of Chinese basketball because they were only in the CBA to "sell tricks" and make money. He also noted that although the NBA did include many foreign players, all the biggest stars were American. Zhang Shuping of Wujin county, Jiangsu, was disgusted, as were many other readers, that their CBA was becoming just "a place for foreign athletes to make money." Zhang Lei of Urumchi brought up another point—that the simple presence of foreigners brought chaos to any team—and he asked why these "second- and third-rate European and American players" were worth the disruption.[82] One fan was even more explicit in his dislike of the CBA's foreign players, vowing that the CBA would not serve as "the NBA's reject stand." He also employed sensitive historical references to remind the community that "[this] is Chinese basketball. The ones winning glory for the nation in international competition are the men of China, not these 'eight-nation allied forces.' "[83]

The tensions present in this nationalist narrative coalesced at the CBA All-Star Game in Shenyang in April 1998, a contest that for the first time used an ill-advised "Chinese versus foreigner" format. The game was marred by what *Basketball* euphemized "patriotic officiating," the referees' blatant pro-Chinese favoritism that even this official publication decried as shameful and "corrupt." Even worse, however, was the scene after the game, won 83–80 by the Foreign All-Stars on a last-second three-point shot by Ray Kelly of the Sichuan Blue Sword Beer Pandas. As the victorious *waiyuan* celebrated at midcourt, the bitter Shenyang crowd showered them with cans and bottles, a barrage so heavy and prolonged that CCTV was forced to cut off its broadcast.[84] The sight of China's national all-star team losing to these third-rate American "rejects" was evidently too much for these proud fans, whose own Shenyang Army Lions were one of the few CBA squads that did not employ foreign players. Their spontaneous demonstration against the *waiyuan* presence in the CBA was a clear statement against American hegemony in the Chinese basketball world.

This kind of hard, literal nationalism comes out in the basketball world in other ways as well. One is a seeming impatience among fans for the 1997 Hong Kong handover to have some real effect on their lives, and for teams from Hong Kong's professional league to join the CBA. Fans write in to *Basketball* regularly with this query. I read it as a challenge to the PRC's stated mission to "reunify" all of the Qing dynasty's lost territories, a challenge that this official nationalism produce some real tangible result for all the 1.3 billion Chinese, who will never personally set foot in Hong Kong, to truly enjoy nonetheless.[85]

Sometimes the state provides answers to these nationalist challenges, even if they are not the ones that people want. In 1999 Chinese basketball fans who were accustomed to watching the NBA playoffs and championship series on CCTV had to find new, more appropriate entertainments. Among the measures taken in the aftermath of the May 1999 NATO bombing of the Chinese embassy in Belgrade was a ban on Chinese television broadcasts of the NBA playoffs.[86] The logic of these reactions in the cultural sphere seems unclear—are they meant to punish the Western cultural producers of entertainment like the NBA, or are they supposed to shelter the Chinese population from exposure to poisonous Western culture, which could produce such violence as the Belgrade bombing?

Yet the Chinese urbanites who rose as one to condemn this latest example of American hegemonism and imperialism are probably just as ambivalent about the position of the NBA, again an extremely liminal one in these days of the new détente. American media reports hoping to discredit with irony the anti-U.S. protests in Beijing, Chengdu, and other cities were careful to point out the number of demonstrators wearing NBA and Michael Jordan T-shirts and shoes. All irony aside, however, it would be very interesting to know how many of these anti-American protesters, before this decision was made for them by proper authorities, would have been moved enough by their reflections on national humiliation to sacrifice watching the 1999 NBA playoffs. When push comes to shove in postsocialist China, how much does the nation matter? Could Jiang Zemin and his carefully crafted message of nationalism have defeated the grace and appeal of Michael Jordan's NBA? And which anthem's lyrics would have rung out the loudest—"Arise, ye who refuse to be slaves" or "I believe I can fly"?

## CONCLUSION

Of the sixty respondents to my mailed survey, one stood out from all the rest. Li Jinsheng, a seventy-four-year-old retired cadre from Yulin city, Guangxi, was among those *Basketball* readers who received my questionnaire. Li was the only respondent to answer that he did not watch NBA or CBA games on television, that he was not a basketball fan, that he did not spend money on basketball merchandise, and that he did not prefer any particular brand of athletic shoe.[87] As I read his replies, I began thinking that I had finally located a basketball enthusiast who, despite admitting to an admiration for the Chicago Bulls, somehow had managed to avoid the great globalizing sweep of this new hegemonic basketball culture.

But I was wrong, and I realized this when I read the six-page letter he mailed to me along with his completed questionnaire, telling the story of his basketball life. An avid basketball player since elementary school in the 1930s, Li became even more dedicated after he retired in the mid-1980s, practicing free throws and three-point shots for three hours every single day. Li told me that on 2 April 1997, this hard work paid off, as he became the proud owner of a new official Guinness world record, making 4,691 of 5,795 free throws over a twelve-hour span, breaking the old record by 821 baskets![88] Next on Li's list was the world record for three-point shooting, which he broke later that year by making 475 of 577 shots in a single hour. If Li, perhaps only by virtue of his age and his six decades of basketball experience, had managed to withstand the global onslaught in some ways, other facets of this basketball culture had clearly drawn him in just as deeply as any of my NBA-clone teenage respondents.

Yet Li is certainly no dupe for this global culture, on which he made his mark from inside an old dusty gym in southeast Guangxi. His letter to me included a photograph of him posing, basketball in hand, outside his front door. His doorway is graced by a large calligraphic couplet, reading "Setting another Guinness world record, greatly undertaking this grand enterprise and soaring into the heavens," complemented by a "Loving my China" above. There is no doubt that Li's great enterprise has brought him more renown and reward than his long career in the Yulin Party branch ever could have—and this is exactly the logic of the forces of globalization in which Li is now forever engaged.

Each of my survey respondents, every *Basketball* reader and letter writer, every participant in the tournament I attended and others like it all around China, and every Chinese fan of teams from the Shandong Wing On Flaming Bulls to the Chicago Bulls, have done the same thing—corrupting, transforming, and displacing these new forms of knowledge, behavior, and desire to carve out one more piece of their own identities. The postsocialist moment in China promises exactly these unprecedented freedoms—to define one's own individual identity, to explore the West of Michael Jordan and Nike, to see how this world could exist in their China, to make their contributions to a strong China (and for once) on their own unique terms.

I have discussed three segments of the new basketball narrative—ideas of the market, the individual, and the nation—which allow these imaginations of postsocialist China. There are surely many more—notions of gender, regionalism, race, class, fitness, sportsmanship—that are not addressed here at length but are no less meaningful to China's basketball-playing millions.

The sport has been played in China for more than one hundred years now, and at each moment during the last century has been taken to represent different aspects of a Chinese drive for modernity and parity with the strong nations of the world. Now the absolute and irrevocable link that has been created between Chinese basketball and the hegemonic NBA/world basketball culture has loaded that much more capitalist import and bounce to the game. In China's postsocialist age, basketball has become a site not only for strategy and skills but also for sonnets, dreams, playful ingenuity, profits, and desire. Perhaps today basketball is truly worthy of being called a "national pastime," a realm as useful and important as any other for Chinese people busy theorizing, shaping, and negotiating Chinese modernity and the world around it.

## NOTES

1. "Qiumi xinxiang" (Fan mailbox), *Lanqiu* (Basketball), April 1995, 28.

2. Chinese Basketball Association (CBA, *Zhongguo lanqiu xiehui*) is technically the name of the state basketball bureaucracy, not the professional league that it cosponsors (see below). However, these initials are too close to NBA for the league to pass up.

3. *Lanqiu* was established in 1981 but did not adopt its current market-friendly format of color photos and advertisements and NBA feature stories until 1995, the same year as the CBA's first professional season.

4. Advertisement for Handsun Footwear (*Beijing xin hengxin tiyu yongpin youxian gongsi*), *Lanqiu* (Basketball), June-August 1998, inside front covers.

5. Jameson cites the Indian filmmaker dismayed at the effects of American television programs on the very gestures and postures of his teenage son; how much more the parents of the young Chinese basketball fanatic? Fredric Jameson, "Notes on Globalization as a Philosophical Issue," in *The Cultures of Globalization*, ed. Fredric Jameson and Masao Miyoshi (Durham, N.C.: Duke University Press, 1998), 56–63.

6. James L. Watson, "Introduction: Transnationalism, Localization, and Fast Foods in East Asia," in *Golden Arches East: McDonald's in East Asia*, ed. James L. Watson (Stanford, Calif.: Stanford University Press, 1997), 2–14, 35–37.

7. Aviad E. Raz, *Riding the Black Ship: Japan and Tokyo Disneyland* (Cambridge: Harvard University Asia Center, 1999), 6, 14–15.

8. John Van Maanen, "Displacing Disney: Some Notes on the Flow of Culture," *Qualitative Sociology* 15, no. 1 (1992): 8–9.

9. Eric Zolov, *Refried Elvis: The Rise of the Mexican Counterculture* (Berkeley: University of California Press, 1999), 258.

10. Susan Brownell uses the term "public culture" to describe this same idea of engaging in national debates via the supposedly "depoliticized" realm of sports in 1980s China. Susan Brownell, *Training the Body for China: Sports in the Moral Order of the People's Republic* (Chicago: University of Chicago Press, 1995), 67–98.

11. Note the convenient connotations that come with this league's abbreviated name as well. The CNBA, managed by Hong Kong's Jingying Company, was later forced to change its name to the Chinese Men's Basketball Alliance after the American NBA threatened legal action over infringement of these three powerful initials. Before the league's second season (1997–1998), the league folded; several teams and players have been incorporated into the CBA.

12. The formal name of the league is the Hilton Chinese Men's Basketball First Division (*Xi-er-dun nanzi lanqiu jia a liansai*), but the snappier "CBA" is almost universal usage.

13. Besides this twelve-team first division, the CBA also operates a seventeen-team Division B, a minor league of sorts whose top two teams each year are eligible to replace Division A's eleventh- and twelfth-place finishers.

The CBA also manages the WCBA, a far less publicized women's "league" consisting of a yearly tournament for about twenty Division A and B teams. Much like the CBA, WCBA propaganda attempts to link their league to its American WNBA counterpart. However, the postsocialist moment seems to have made women's basketball much less relevant to national goals than it was even a few years ago; male basketball players (see below) are apparently more deserving and capable with regard to the capitalist impetus that now justifies Chinese basketball culture. My concentration on men's basketball in this chapter parallels, but does not explicitly question, the gross disparity in emphasizing men's basketball over women's basketball in today's PRC.

14. The Guangdong team regularly sells out its ultramodern 5,000-seat stadium and has been officially praised for its marketing skills and its adaptability in switching from a passive/consumptive to an active/productive mode. Hao Ying, "Bian 'gong xue' tizhi wei 'zaoxue' jizhi—Guangdong Hongyuan Lanqiu Julebu de jingying celüe" (The Guangdong Hongyuan Basketball Club's marketing strategy: Changing the "supplied blood" structure to a mechanism for "creating blood"), *Lanqiu* (Basketball), January 1998, 12–13.

15. The first basketball game in China was the earliest YMCA-sponsored sporting

competition in China. Andrew Morris, "Cultivating the National Body: A History of Physical Culture in Republican China" (Ph.D. diss., University of California, 1998), 76.

16. " 'Guomin youxi' xuanshang da'an jiexiao" (Announcing the prizes and results of the 'national pastime' contest), *Qinfen tiyu yuebao* (The Chin Fen sports monthly), February 1936. For a discussion of the 1930s concern/obsession with creating a "national pastime" to rival American and Japanese baseball, British soccer, and German gymnastics, see Morris, "Cultivating the National Body," 303–309.

17. This tournament has historically been dominated by the People's Liberation Army team; through 2001 the PLA men's team had won thirty-five of forty national championships. Li Fucai, Wen Fuxiang, Dong Erzhi, Shen Enlu, and Zhong Tianfa, *Zhongguo lanqiu yundongshi* (The history of the Chinese basketball movement) (Wuhan: Wuhan chubanshe, 1991), 92, 110, 113.

18. Xie Jin, *Nü lan wu hao* (Woman basketball player no. 5) (Beijing: Tianma dianying zhipianchang, 1957).

19. Shi Chuanxiang, "Women taofen gongren ye you le tiyu huodong" (We nightsoil carriers also take part in athletic activities now), *Xin tiyu*, February 1965, 24.

20. Liang Heng and Judith Shapiro, *Son of the Revolution* (New York: Vintage, 1983), 211–21.

21. Timothy W. Ryback, *Rock around the Bloc: A History of Rock Music in Eastern Europe and the Soviet Union* (New York: Oxford University Press, 1990), 25–28.

22. Hu Yeping, " '98 Zhongguo lanqiu shichang di yi zhan" (The first battle over the Chinese basketball market, 1998), *Lanqiu* (Basketball), July 1998, 6–7.

23. I mailed out one hundred surveys of thirty-four questions each to readers who had written in to *Basketball* with their name and address in the April 1998 through July 1998 issues. Each copy of my survey was accompanied by a stamped return envelope addressed to the People's Sporting Press in Beijing. Of these one hundred, I received sixty surveys back.

24. *Basketball*, with a circulation between 150,000 and 200,000, is the third most popular of the twelve magazines published by the People's Sporting Press in Beijing, behind *Soccer World* and *Chinese Fishing*. The magazine's NBA concentration is clearly a marketing strategy; through January 1999, thirty-three of the last thirty-seven *Basketball* covers featured photos of NBA stars.

25. Of course, there is the important question of the authenticity of these submissions from "readers." I learned that in the magazines published by the People's Sporting Press, a reliable rule of thumb is that submissions which come with full names and addresses are authentic communications from real fans, while those that include only a name are "plants" used by the editors to address certain issues.

26. Mao Aimin, "Yan'ge guanli qiudui, jiji gaohuo qiushi" (Strictly manage the team, energetically fire up the basketball market), *Lanqiu* (Basketball), February 1998, 10.

27. Liang Xiyi, "Zhenxi qiushi" (Cherish the basketball market), *Lanqiu* (Basketball), March 1998, 1.

28. Sun Yuanyuan, "Lanqiu gaige ying fuhe guoqing" (Basketball reforms should accord with national characteristics), *Lanqiu* (Basketball), December 1998, 37. In past seasons, the CBA has featured other military teams such as the Chinese Air Force Eagles, the Shenyang Army Lions, the Nanjing Army Unicorns, and Guangzhou Army.

29. Dong Weihua, "Mianxiang shichang gai guize" (Face up to the market and change the rules), *Lanqiu* (Basketball), October 1996, 4.

30. Shen Zhiyu, "CBA de qian zai shichang" (CBA's potential is in the market), *Lan-qiu* (Basketball), April 1997, 8.

31. "Qiumi Leitai: CBA yinjin waiyuan li da yu bi" (Fan gauntlet: Do the benefits of CBA's use of foreign players outweigh the negatives?), *Lanqiu* (Basketball), November 1997, 17.

32. Li Jianjun, "Zhongguo lanqiu de chanyehua yu zhiyehua" (Productionizing and professionalizing Chinese basketball), *Lanqiu* (Basketball), March 1998, 18.

33. Hao Guohua, "Tiandi guangkuo, jingying youfang" (Broadening earth and sky with effective management), *Lanqiu* (Basketball), April 1998, 11.

34. Kang Wenxiong, "Qiumang" (Sports blind), *Lanqiu* (Basketball), October 1995, 23.

35. Xin Liu, "Space, Mobility, and Flexibility: Chinese Villagers and Scholars Negotiate Power at Home and Abroad," in *Ungrounded Empires: The Cultural Politics of Modern Chinese Transnationalism*, ed. Aihwa Ong and Donald Nonini (New York: Routledge, 1997), 96–99.

36. Survey respondent 22.

37. Survey respondent 36.

38. Survey respondent 28. This respondent tore off the top part of the survey on which I had written his name. (I received back two of the six surveys I sent to Xinjiang readers, so I do not know whose this was.) This respondent was also the only one of sixty to name A-de-jiang, the Xinjiang native and starting point guard for the PLA Rockets, as his favorite player—another likely indication of this reader's identification with Xinjiang's place in national hierarchies.

39. Survey respondent 23.

40. Survey respondent 6.

41. Survey respondent 43.

42. Richard Gordon and Carma Hinton, *The Gate of Heavenly Peace* (Brookline, Mass.: Long Bow Group, 1995).

43. Survey respondent 32.

44. " 'Lanqiu zazhi bei' Beijing shi di san jie sanren lanqiu tiaozhansai zhixuce" (The "*Basketball* Cup" Beijing Municipal Three-on-Three Basketball Challenge Program), 1998.

45. That is not to say that this three-on-three tournament was purely a festival of materialist excess; in fact, opposite bottom-up expressions of class difference were utilized as well. One young man, furious with the officiating that he felt cost his team a championship, was almost inconsolable with dramatic rage during and after the final awards ceremony. When tournament organizers tried to calm him, he repeatedly, between curses, brought up the fact that both his parents had recently been "stood-down" (*xiagang*) from their state jobs. His notion that he thus deserved additional considerations was never challenged; however, organizers dismissed his claims as simply untrue, since he had been able to afford the tournament entrance fee and a nice pair of leather basketball sneakers.

46. Raz, *Riding the Black Ship*, 14.

47. Sherry Ortner, *Making Gender: The Politics and Erotics of Culture* (Boston: Beacon, 1996), 12.

48. Survey respondents 1 (Yin Ming, Zoucheng city, Shandong), 4 (Ma Jia, Hohhot, Inner Mongolia), 11 (Zeng Raofeng, Huizhou, Guangdong), 54 (Dong Bin, Pingba

county, Guizhou), 38 (Tan Weisen, Kaiping, Guangdong), 52 (Xiong Xueyou, Chafang village, Yunxian county, Yunnan), and 47 (Wang Zhiqiang, Baotou, Inner Mongolia).

49. Survey respondent 35 (Wang Xin, Beijing).

50. Again, the importance of the market is explained as "the fan is god"—an easy signifier for market forces as an omniscient "god" (or at least as the god's invisible hands).

51. Jinyan, "CBA xuyao xuannian" (The CBA has to be concerned), *Beijing qingnian bao* (Beijing youth news), reprinted in *Lanqiu* (Basketball), August 1998, 33; Ma Hongguan, "CBA yonghan" (The CBA calls), *Lanqiu* (Basketball), December 1998, 30; Yan Jiashun, "Ye tan CBA de shuju" (A discussion of CBA statistics), *Lanqiu* (Basketball), September 1997, 10.

52. "Qiumi xinxiang" (Fan mailbox), *Lanqiu* (Basketball), April 1995, 28.

53. He referred to Ewing by the nickname that the Knicks star has picked up in China, the "Big Gorilla." (Some of Ewing's fans go even further with this unfortunate riff and affectionately call him the "African gorilla.") Yang Jianbin, "Wo you yi ge meng" (I have a dream), *Lanqiu* (Basketball), April 1998, 25.

54. Song Zhongyi, "Qing dadan koulan" (Please courageously dunk), *Lanqiu* (Basketball), February 1996, 5; Pei Yongli, "Koulan—qiuyuan gongjili de zui jia tixian" (The dunk: A player's most effective means of exhibiting offensive power), *Lanqiu* (Basketball), October 1996, 5; Zhou You, "Xiwang CBA qiuyuan duo koulan" (Hoping that more CBA players will dunk), *Lanqiu* (Basketball), September 1996, 8–9.

55. Lisa Rofel, *Other Modernities: Gendered Yearnings in China after Socialism* (Berkeley: University of California Press, 1999), 54.

56. Xiaomei Chen, *Occidentalism: A Theory of Counter-Discourse in Post-Mao China* (New York: Oxford University Press, 1995), 5.

57. Chen, *Occidentalism*, 8.

58. John Hoberman, *Darwin's Athletes: How Sport Has Damaged Black America and Preserved the Myth of Race* (Boston: Houghton Mifflin, 1997), xviii, 39.

59. Advertisements for Converse All-Stars, *Lanqiu* (Basketball), August-September 1997, inside front covers.

60. " 'Luo-de-man Guaizaoxing Chuangyi Dasai' pingjiang jiexiao" (Announcing the prize winners of the Rodman strange image creativity contest), *Lanqiu* (Basketball), March 1998, 43.

61. Shen Yi, " 'Huahua gongzi' Luo-de-man" ("Playboy" Rodman), *Lanqiu* (Basketball), September 1997, 37.

62. Gu Wei, "Luo-de-man" (Rodman), *Lanqiu* (Basketball), January 1999, 16.

63. Survey respondent 17.

64. "Qiumi xinxiang" (Fan mailbox), *Lanqiu* (Basketball), October 1995, 22.

65. Huang Jun, "Qingqing di, nin zou jin wo" (Gently you come to me), *Lanqiu* (Basketball), April 1998, 25.

66. " '*Lanqiu* zazhi bei.' "

67. Survey respondents 10 (Tan Ke, Nanning, Guangxi) and 40 (Wu Raomin, Suzhou city, Anhui).

68. Zheng Yi, "Wo de pengyou 'Ba-ke-li' " (My friend "Barkley"), *Lanqiu* (Basketball), September 1998, 31.

69. "Zhuizong 'Guanlan Gaoshou' " (Catching up with *Slam Dunk*), *Lanqiu* (Basketball), November 1998, 34–35.

70. *Lanqiu* (Basketball), December 1998, 36.

71. Of the sixty returned surveys, only four were from women. Their basketball career goals closely matched those of their male counterparts. One each said she hoped to reach the provincial women's team, the WCBA, the women's national team, and the WNBA, and two of these four felt that national considerations were relevant to their basketball career. Liu Liwei, from Shuangyashan city, Heilongjiang, gave a tantalizing response that spoke to a women's sphere in basketball that I have not been able to cover here, explaining that the significance of Chinese basketball on the world stage lies in the fact that in China "women's basketball has developed faster than men's basketball." This is a forceful response to the male-centered nature of China's new basketball culture, and to official critiques of the low-scoring women's "cosmetics basketball" circuit. Survey respondent 39; Yang Xiaoyang, " 'Zhifen' lanqiu" ("Cosmetics" basketball), *Lanqiu* (Basketball), November 1998, 41.

72. Even among the twenty respondents who hope to join the NBA, there is a clear correlation between their confidence in themselves and their national commitment. The ten who cited national glory gave themselves an average 37 percent chance to make the NBA (mean value = 30 percent), as compared with an average 13 percent chance (mean 0.5 percent) for the ten who did not cite the nation!

73. " '*Lanqiu* zazhi bei.' "

74. "Qiumi xinxiang" (Fan mailbox), *Lanqiu* (Basketball), July 1996, 14.

75. Wang Hai, "CBA de yi xie xijie" (Some CBA details), *Lanqiu* (Basketball), April 1997, 9. This concern with the representation of players' personal names is in itself an important departure from past PRC basketball norms; see, for example, Xie Jin's dutiful 1950s take on team sports and the absence of any personal names in *Woman Basketball Player no. 5*.

76. Sun Yuanyuan, "Lanqiu gaige," 37.

77. Deng Min (Zhongjiang county, Sichuan) and Zhang Xinrui (Jalaid Banner, Inner Mongolia), "Qiumi xinxiang" (Fan mailbox), *Lanqiu* (Basketball), November 1998, 40; December 1998, 33.

78. That is, a team can use one foreign player per twelve-minute game quarter or both foreigners in a single quarter. Both must be rested for another whole quarter.

79. "Qiushi yao huo, waiyuan yao duo" (To fire up the basketball market, we need more foreign players), *Lanqiu* (Basketball), January 1998, 1.

80. However, Shandong, desperate to improve on its third-place finish of the previous season, went against its nationalistic principles and employed two Russian (read: not American) players for the 1998–1999 season.

81. "Qiumi Leitai: CBA yinjin waiyuan li da yu bi" (Fan gauntlet: Do the benefits of CBA's use of foreign players outweigh the negatives?), *Lanqiu* (Basketball), December 1997, 8. Indeed, as this volume goes to press, PLA Rocket center Wang Zhizhi has made history by joining the NBA's Dallas Mavericks for the team's playoff run.

82. "Qiumi Leitai: CBA yinjin waiyuan li da yu bi" (Fan gauntlet: Do the benefits of CBA's use of foreign players outweigh the negatives?), *Lanqiu* (Basketball), November 1997, 17.

83. Sun Yuanyuan, "Lanqiu gaige," 37.

84. Hao Guohua, " 'Aiguo xiao' chuyi" (A modest proposal on "patriotic officiating"), *Lanqiu* (Basketball), June 1998, 12.

85. Some fans, even less patient with Jiang Zemin's "reunification" project, ask when a team from Taiwan would join the CBA. Taiwan's own six-team professional Chinese Basketball Alliance folded in April 1999, but there are no plans for a Taiwan team to join China's CBA. Wei Guanzhong, "Dalu jia a liansai Taiwan zhibu" (No admittance for Taiwan into the mainland's basketball first division), *Huaxun xinwenwang* (Taiwan Today News Network), 1 April 2000. www.ttnn.com/cna/000401/sp06.html. Accessed 2 May 2000.

86. "No U.S. Basketball, No Music, after Belgrade Embassy Bombing," *Inside China Today*, 13 May 1999. www.insidechina.com. Accessed 13 May 1999.

87. Survey respondent 42.

88. This record was confirmed by Du Nengbin, a national-class basketball official. "Zhongguo dazhong lanqiu Ji-ni-si jilubang" (List of Guinness records from Chinese popular basketball), *Lanqiu* (Basketball), June 1997, 35.

# 2

# Corruption in Popular Culture

*Richard Levy*

> Revolution is not a dinner party.
> —Mao Zedong (1927)

> Revolution is a dinner party!
> —1990s folk saying

Corruption is a topic on the lips of people in all walks of life in contemporary China. It was a central focus of the 1989 Tiananmen demonstrations. Throughout the 1990s, Transparency International[1] evaluated China as one of the world's most corrupt countries. Corruption continues to be recognized by observers inside and outside China as a serious threat to China's economy and the regime's legitimacy. As the contemporary folk saying goes, "If we don't root out corruption, the country will perish; if we do root out corruption, the Party will perish."

But will it? Does corruption really threaten China's economic development and political stability? The answer partly depends on how angry the Chinese public is about corruption, and what the public realistically thinks can be done about it. It is misguided, however, to seek an articulate public opinion about corruption, the kind of public opinion found in an open, pluralistic civil society, where citizens have many forums in which to openly discuss sensitive public issues and begin to reach some coherent conclusions about them. Ordinary citizens in China have half-formed, ambiguous ways of talking, thinking, and feeling about the subject. These relatively inchoate sentiments are mostly political potential, not political actuality. They could probably be pulled and shaped in different directions by different factions of elites. But to get some sense of how the potential might someday turn into actuality, we ought to know (1) the category systems in terms of which people at the grass roots define the phenomenon,

(2) the intensity of feelings they have about it, and (3) the rhetorical strategies they use to discuss how to balance the prevalence of corruption with more positive elements in current society. I explored these issues by interviewing ordinary citizens and collecting popular magazines in Taishan county, Guangdong, in the summer of 1998.

Because of the sensitivity of the topic, I conducted these interviews informally in a spontaneous and flexible but nonetheless structured way. In order to allow the individuals to frame the topic, I asked no preset questions, instead using questions that stimulated a discussion of corruption in each individual's own terms. The interviews lasted anywhere from fifteen minutes to more than four hours and were conducted in a wide range of settings, including motorcycle taxis, stores and restaurants, the streets, bars, and people's homes. Since the nature of the interviews prevented tape-recording, quotations from these interviews are approximate quotations based on note taking that immediately followed the interviews. I interviewed some twenty-five individuals in this way—eighteen men and seven women ranging in age from mid-twenties to early seventies, including workers, retired workers, taxi drivers (auto and motorcycle), *getihu* (self-employed small-scale businesspeople) and other businessmen, street hawkers, clerks, lower-level government workers, unemployed individuals, and the wife of a man jailed for swindling. In order to both expand the database and address the issue of people's relative unwillingness to discuss this issue in China, I supplemented the interviews listed above with interviews of twelve recent Cantonese emigrants (six male, six female) in Boston Chinatown in December 1999. These interviews, though still informal, were recorded, allowing for direct quotations. Although the interviews were done in mostly Cantonese, where Romanized Chinese is provided, I have used the Mandarin versions in *hanyu pinyin*.

The analysis of popular magazine culture on corruption is based on an examination of thirteen magazines on corruption purchased from private booksellers in Taishan—the vast majority in Taicheng, the urban center of Taishan. I chose these magazines because they were either special issues dedicated to corruption or had cover-page leaders on corruption or economic crime, including swindling.[2]

## DEFINING CORRUPTION

In Chinese law, corruption (*fubai*) is a subset of economic crime (*jingji fanzui*). Although the exact definition of corruption is constantly changing as a result of both the rapidly changing economic structure and elite struggles over the definition, corruption is consistently defined as economic crime committed by public officials.[3] Thus graft (*tanwu*) and bribery (*xing hui shou hui*) are specific, punishable acts of corruption, but punishment is normally levied only on the official who receives the bribe, not on the person who offers it. Corruption, conceived of in this restricted way, receives far more publicity in the official media than do important forms of economic crime committed mostly by entrepreneurs—crimes such as swindling (*qipian*), speculation and profiteering (*toujidaoba*), producing fake or counterfeit products, and tax evasion. This official way of framing corruption is reflected in popular discourse.

"I was a worker, but my husband is a public security official," said a middle-aged woman interviewed in 1996. She continued:

> Everything is *guanxi* (connections). When the reforms began, I got a job in a joint enterprise; then I became an assistant manager in a hotel. Now I have five private enterprises and a restaurant. Of course I have to spend a lot of money, entertain officials from out of town a lot and help their children in various ways. I do lots of things to make business work. . . . I can't talk about [kickbacks (*huikou*)] in public. . . . I wouldn't want to leave China because I would never be able to have as good a living standard anywhere else.

There is no sense of guilt or shame here. Rather, there is a measure of pride in knowing how to make the system work for her. Pride is even more evident in the following braggadocio from a businessman/smuggler interviewed in 1999:

> I had a speedboat for smuggling. We were a clique (*jituan*). We worked with the state to smuggle. . . . I bought a hotel . . . through a company run by a friend in the county government. . . . It was on the coast. . . . In the basement was a secret storage facility. . . . The police station was on the top floor, so we knew them and bought them off. . . . We had lookout boats all along the coast so we knew when it was safe to make our runs [to Macao]. . . . We were only afraid of getting arrested when we were loading. That's when they get you. . . . If [the boat] were half loaded and we saw the police, we would just take off. . . . They couldn't catch us because our boat was too last. . . If you were caught and were a small fish, they'd fine you ¥50,000–60,000 and let you go. That's nothing. If you knew someone, they'd let you out for ¥20,000 and then you'd get it back and could use it again. They were really corrupt!

Not surprisingly, he is also unashamed of tax evasion. "There's no one to manage [the tax system]. . . . If you get paid ¥4,000 a month [in a private enterprise] . . . you report ¥800 . . . to avoid taxes . . . Everyone does it. China is like that. There's no way to deal with it."

Slightly more surprising, though, was that most people interviewed, from most walks of life, agreed with his attitude toward tax evasion. Even a Grain Bureau official admits, "If you make . . . money, you should pay taxes. There are tax laws. . . . but the issue is enforcing them. . . . If I'm an official I won't have to pay taxes. Everything is dependent on the individual, not the law, so I won't tax myself."

## INFLAMING FEELINGS ABOUT CORRUPTION

Most interviewees discussed corruption in a matter-of-fact way, without strong expressions of outrage. They are constantly exposed, however, to a flow of tabloid magazines that compete to sensationalize corruption. These publications are widely available at bookstands down to the county level (see photo 2.1).[4] The writing is frequently quite stylized, exaggerated, crude, and/or prurient.

The first example is from an article supposedly written by the mistress of Wang Baosen, the vice mayor of Beijing who committed suicide when his role in a major bribe-taking scandal was exposed (photo 2.1). "Whenever I don't feel comfortable or in the mood, Wang [Baosen] turns to Yang Qing for fun and plea-sure. . . . For a while, he even took turns having sex with Yang and me. When one is done, the other enters the room."[5] Other magazines ran similar accounts: "She not only did not protest, but even gave him a charming smile. He became even more daring and touched her inside thigh with his hands. Her whole body tingled so much that she nearly collapsed onto his chest." "In ten minutes, this old cadre felt limp, numb, and swollen in his private parts."[6]

The magazines that report such behavior are not independent muckrakers. Most are officially registered with the government and are often semilegal "spe-cial editions" or "supplements" put out by money-losing literary and specialized

*Photo 2.1   Popular magazines on corruption in Taishan, July 1998.*
*(Photograph by Lenore Balliro)*

**Table 2.1  Magazines Reporting on Corruption**

| Title | Responsible Department | Cover and Contents |
|---|---|---|
| *Fazhi xinwenbao* (Legal system news) | Qingnianbao Publishers | Special issue, "Wang Baosen's Lover: Zhao XX's Own Story" (photo 2.2) |
| *Fazhi fengyun* (Instability in the legal system) | None (Fazhi fengyun)[a] | Special issue, "Murders by Corrupt Cadres"[b] (photo 2.1) |
| *Jiating shijie* (Family world) | Inner Mongolia Publication Workers Association | Special issue, "Contemporary Chinese Swindler Kings" (photo 2.3) |
| *Keji yu qiye* (Science and technology and enterprises) | Anhui Science and Technology Association | Focused almost entirely on "Chen Xitong and His Women" (photo 2.1) |
| *Qingnian wenhua* (Youth culture) | None (Qingnian wenhua Publishing House) | Special issue, "The New Black Way" (photo 2.1) |
| *Shichang fazhi daokan* (Market law herald) | PRC Legislative Bureau | Special issue, "Mainland Capital Swindler Mou Qizhong" |
| *Zuojia tiandi* (Writer's world) | Ma'anshan Literature and Arts Federation | Special issue, "1998 Anticorruption in Action"[c] |
| *Huangtudi* (Yellow earth) | None (Huangtudi Publishers) | Headlines such as "Exposé: Wholesaling of Officialdom," "Million-Yuan Buying of Assistant District Chief," and a limerick satirizing corruption |
| *Minzhu yu fazhi* (Democracy and the legal system) | Chinese Chemistry Society | Headlines such as "Number 1 Anticorruption Case in Southern Sichuan," "How Large-Scale Graft in a Bank Succeeded," with a picture of an arrest on the cover |

[a]If no responsible department is listed, this is indicated by "none" and the publisher is listed in parentheses.

[b]This magazine was laced with pictures of guns. Seventeen of the twenty-two stories included pictures of guns, and nineteen of forty-four pictures in the magazines are of guns, not including additional pictures of mortars, military airdrops, armored personnel carriers, and a phalanx of riot police.

[c]This magazine focuses on Shen Taifu's Great Wall Machinery and Electronics Corporation scam in a very progovernment tone.

trade magazines to increase their income (table 2.1).[7] Although they make money by catering to a market that demands ever more lurid stories (whether true or not), they do not engage in a political analysis of the systemic origins of the behavior. However, while adhering to the official line that defines corruption, strictly speaking, as something that only officials engage in, they also cover entrepreneurial and private sector economic crime, often quite provocatively (photo 2.2). In summer 1998, entire issues of magazines focused on such nationally known multimillionaire businessmen as Shen Taifu and Mou Qizhong[8] as well as such lesser known swindlers as Zhang Xiaoping (accused of reaping over ¥1 million in a *qigong* scam) and Wang Hongcheng (accused of having caused losses of over ¥40 million with a scam for changing water into oil). There were also numerous stories of fake products, one involving a scandal in Shanxi, reported in two different magazines, in which 161 people were poisoned and nine died as a result of improperly made wine. Others covered patent and trademark infringement as well as a wide range of other incidents of private sector swindling and economic crime.

The message on the significance of corruption in these magazines is mixed. On the one hand, the wide and spectacular coverage, ranging from rather minor issues to cases involving more than ¥1 billion, reinforces the significance of the issue and evokes powerful emotions (ranging from righteous anger to lustful envy) about the subject. Whether or not readers believe every detail of the stories of corruption reported in the tabloids (they probably do not), we can infer from the popularity of these lurid stories that ordinary people are prone to think the worst about the rich and powerful and to harbor intense passions toward them. This could provide the fuel for populist social movements. If there ever were a Maoist resurgence, one could imagine the tabloid images being used to whip up mass emotions during struggle sessions. Indeed, in some ways the stories in the tabloids continue the Maoist tradition of character assassination against privileged people. Only now the stories are produced for commercial rather than political reasons (photo 2.3).

On the other hand, as Yuezhi Zhao has suggested in her chapter in this volume, the tabloid stories usually focus on corrupt individuals who have been arrested by heroic investigators and police, thus conveying the message that the system works. Do ordinary people believe this? Let us turn to an analysis of the interviews.

## TALKING ABOUT CORRUPTION

Although these interviews do not constitute a representative sample that can accurately depict public opinion on corruption, they demonstrate the rhetorical strategies that ordinary people use in evaluating corruption and in looking for solutions for it. Most discourse about corruption starts from the assumption that

*Photo 2.2* Title reads, "Wang Baosen's Lover: Zhao XX's Own Story." Notice the small-print magazine title at the bottom. (Photograph by Lenore Balliro)

the system does not work. But it does not usually lead to a conclusion that the system can or should be fundamentally changed. When talking about corruption, most interviewees focused on how ordinary people like themselves could survive within—and if possible benefit from—an inevitably corrupt system.

When people contrasted the significance and extensiveness of corruption in contemporary China with that in the Mao period, they implicitly linked the difference to changes in the political and economic system. The emergence of corruption is seen not simply as a result of moral failure by individuals, but as a result of systemic pressures and temptations. For example, as several interviewees

*Photo 2.3 "Contemporary Chinese Swindler Kings." Notice barely visible magazine title in white outline characters in bottom left corner. (Photograph by Lenore Balliro)*

said in a discussion: "[Now] even if someone [who's an official] doesn't want to be corrupt, it's really hard. People will still make demands on him since he has power." They are also concerned with how the corrupt system engulfs everyone, including themselves. "If someone is righteous or honest, what use is it? . . . If one person is honest . . . she or he ends up at the bottom. . . . She or he simply gets harassed and ends up 'having to wear tight shoes.' " The present system, they remark frequently, is in sharp contrast to that of the Cultural Revolution period. Back then, "there was no corruption! . . . You didn't have to pay to get things done."

This does not necessarily mean, however, that the Mao era was better than the present. Interviewees talk of the Maoist period not as a golden age but as a period in which low crime and corruption, safety, and some degree of social spirit and collectiveness were combined with severe poverty and strict control of daily life, such that no one would "dare engage in bribery." Said a fifty-year-old nurse,

> When a society opens up and reforms, there will definitely be some people who seek personal gain. . . . Before 1978, we never heard that Guangzhou had prostitutes, drugs, or those kinds of things. At that time we were very pure. . . . [No one locked doors]; no one stole things; no one sold guns [illegally]; there was no smuggling. Really. The whole society was very peaceful, but . . . we were very poor. . . . After the reforms, these types of things entered society.

She does not suggest, however, that she would want to go back to Mao's time. Her views are echoed and succinctly summarized by a fifty-year-old male farmer. "In Mao's time, there was no corruption. But we were very poor."

Although the interviewees started with the assumption that they did not want to go back to the Maoist system, they recognized the complexity of the trade-offs between increasing affluence and decreasing public morals. Some of their increased income goes toward paying bribes for essential services. Medical care is a special focus of their complaints. Several interviewees, for instance, discussed the bribes necessary for a surgical procedure on the mother of a thirty-year-old female garment worker from Taicheng:

> This is really bad. . . . If you don't pay, there's no way! (*Bugei buxing*) . . . A big operation costs over ¥1,000 [in bribes]. . . . You even have to pay about ¥50 to make an appointment. . . . There's no reason for them to be taking this kind of money, I feel. It's totally unreasonable (*buheli*). . . . I have a friend who ended up sitting there all day . . . because she wasn't paying enough . . . so her husband put ¥500 in a red envelope with the money sticking out and then they helped her with her baby's delivery.

Some also feel a moral disgust at having to get along by participating in webs of corruption.

> I'm an accountant in a state-owned enterprise. To keep my job, I have to maintain good relations with my superiors or they'll just get someone else. My boss regularly brings in bills for ¥3,000 for lunch for four, which I have to sign off on. We constantly rotate the bills through the different units so they aren't too obvious. Other accountants and I get together to exchange stories about how corrupt our bosses are, but there's nothing we can do about it. Even if you oppose it, all that happens is that you lose your job and nothing changes. I do things that make me sick. Sometimes I can't sleep at night. But I don't have any other choice.

Despite expressing anger at such widespread corruption, very few people mentioned it as a threat to the regime. Many saw it as virtually inevitable. "Every country has it," said a farmer hawking vegetables on the street. At the same time, they devoted considerable intellectual energy into gathering what benefits they could from the system. The accountant quoted above is a forty-year-old woman living in an exquisite apartment that is hardly affordable on her stated combined salary and consultant incomes.

Some interviewees devoted considerable energy to mastering the complicated etiquette of giving bribes. Said a businessman/smuggler:

> If you don't know the official, first you give him a cigarette, then you take him out to eat, then go for a massage to start an opening. Later on you go for another massage until you get to know him, then you slowly start to pay him. Officials don't just take the money at once. It can take a year or two of *guanxi* at least. . . . A lot of them use one-way contacts [that can't be traced back to them] or get payoffs through indirect channels. They're not that stupid. The newspapers publish cases that come out [of those who were caught] and some of the specifics, so people read it and learn what works. . . . They have good techniques.

As for combating corruption, many of those interviewed said that the issue was too big for a "little person (*xiaoren*) such as myself." The remedies they did suggest were mainly a combination of raising salaries for officials, tightening surveillance, and meting out strict punishment on severe offenders. The businessman/smuggler said,

> An important reason for corruption is low officials' salaries. For example, the state pays mayors about fifteen hundred a month. . . . So if you're not corrupt, where do you get money? . . . You can't even smoke, since cigarettes cost over ten yuan a pack. You can't even pay your own utilities. . . . A peddler makes more than an official. It's ridiculous.

A fifty-year-old nurse told a similar story:

> A governor makes less than a hairdresser [hair salons often double as brothels]. It's the same for us medical personnel. There's really no way to deal with it.

According to a twenty-year-old male judicial translator,

> The U.S. consulate in Guangzhou does a good job of anticorruption by paying salaries of ¥8,000–10,000 per month, so people have no need to take bribes. . . . In addition, the very limited advancement opportunities for officials force people to be corrupt to increase their incomes.

Another commonly cited measure for fighting corruption was increased supervision of cadres, usually by establishing direct supervision structures within governmental organizations. Finally, there were calls for more severe punishment, ranging from making the penalties more directly proportionate to the gains to executing greater numbers of corrupt people. Despite some comments that anti-corruption efforts had improved recently, however, there were very considerable doubts about the possibility of significantly reducing corruption.

Popular thinking about corruption is thus a bundle of contradictions. On the one hand, there is deep anger about corruption, a profound suspicion of those in power, and a willingness to believe the most scandalous tales about China's elites. Moreover, there is an awareness that corruption pervades the whole system. Yet corruption is seen as inevitable and as part of a system that has brought more positive benefits than negative liabilities. Attention is directed more toward how to get along in a corrupt world and how, if possible, to benefit from it than toward how to change it. There is little realistic hope of fundamentally rooting out corruption. But ordinary people do take pleasure in seeing the downfall of some seriously corrupt individuals.

## POLITICAL IMPLICATIONS

If this description of the way ordinary people think and feel about corruption is basically correct, what are its political implications? The level of anger connected with corruption renders it a potentially explosive issue. As a forty-year-old female accountant put it:

> Corruption is really bad. Older people say it's worse than under the Nationalists. There is so much corruption while street hawkers who have been pushed out of their jobs and are struggling to keep themselves and their families going are constantly hassled by the police. It's all going to explode.

However, the anger is sufficiently diffused by the resigned, cynical pragmatism portrayed above[9] and the limited anticorruption reforms undertaken by the regime[10] that it will probably not become politically explosive without either manipulation by elites or a significant environmental change.

Currently there are vigorous debates among elite intellectuals and policy formulators about the causes and consequences of and potential solutions to corruption. There are basically three positions. At one extreme, the "neoconservatives" argue that corruption is the result of abandoning national state socialism in favor of participation in a globalized market economy. The solution would be a return to the collectivism (and perhaps some of the political campaigns) of the Maoist era (although not of the Cultural Revolution) and a tightening of control of the Communist Party over all aspects of life. At another extreme, "democracy activists" (made up predominantly of individuals outside of China) argue that corruption is the result of not having pushed market reforms far enough and not having coupled them with political reforms, such as a multiparty political system, a "just" legal system, civil liberties, an independent military, and limits on the privileges and rights of officials. In the middle, reformers advocate a steady withdrawal of the government from the economy, development of a more professionalized (and better paid) civil service, increased supervision of officials, and increased punishment of offenses. If elite debates about corruption lead to serious splits in the top leadership, the result could be social unrest among masses at the bottom of society. The nature of the unrest would depend on how the contending elite factions mobilized the masses on the basis of their grievances about corruption. It would be easier for a faction to mobilize a mass following if its way of framing the corruption issue resonated with the common sense of ordinary people.[11]

The practical wisdom of ordinary people seems to resonate most strongly with the middle-of-the-road reformers. Like the moderate reformers, they see no need for (or at least no hope for) any fundamental change in the political and economic structures of China. They think that the higher standard of living brought by this system outweighs the evils of corruption. They assume that corruption can be ameliorated through better salaries and improved administrative measures. The ordinary people with whom I spoke differ from elite policy theorists in that ordinary people do not envision a supervisory system as complex as seems necessary to many members of the reformist elite. Elite discussions of supervision focus on various forms of "mass supervision," such as strengthening the *jubao* system (in which citizens have structured avenues to report corruption), audits of officials' assets, increased press coverage of corruption, restricting officials' involvement in business, and in some cases increased local democracy. With the exception of two calls for an independent anticorruption organ (as opposed to the present organs, which are seen as controlled by the Party), interviewees did not mention such supervision methods. Although ordinary people would like to see someone supervise dishonest officials, they do not want to participate in this themselves. If unsuccessful (and most people seem resigned to a low success rate in efforts to combat corruption), such activities could get them in serious trouble.

Ordinary people did not talk about the more abstract prescriptions advocated by moderate elite reformers, such as deepening the reforms, reducing government intervention in the economy, improving the legal system, improving education and upholding moral values, and increasing transparency in government dealings. Embedded within these abstract prescriptions, however, may be measures that could someday affect popular evaluations of corruption. Particularly important is how and with what degree of speed the reforms will be deepened and government intervention reduced. Deepening the reforms leads to widespread unemployment and the reduction of many benefits for urban workers, as does membership in the World Trade Organization. Economic polarization has also increased exponentially during the reforms.[12] If many people begin to feel that their standard of living is plummeting, their passions about corruption and increasing inequality may prevail over their practical, cynical resignation.[13] Where reformers see a painful transition to a better macroeconomy—at least for some—ordinary people often see corrupt manipulation by the powerful. *And both may be right.* Many of our interviewees saw the collapse of state-owned enterprises and the ensuing unemployment largely as a result of officials draining the resources from these enterprises for themselves and fleeing abroad. Some also see their economic distress in zero-sum terms. As a rural motorcycle-taxi driver put it, officials' siphoning off of wealth has made it impossible for farmers to improve their economic status.

If there is widespread economic distress, anticorruption anger may indeed be mobilized by neoconservatives to attack the current political establishment in the name of a return to a purer form of socialism. The anger could lead to considerable violence. "I'm very friendly with a judge," said one interviewee. "He said that if you executed all the Communist officials above the section level, there wouldn't even be one mistake." This maxim is echoed in many similar folk sayings in China today. If passions about corruption were inflamed in mass movements, it would not be difficult to persuade many ordinary people that almost any high official was guilty enough to die.

Such populist mobilization of anticorruption outrage by China's neoconservatives is less likely than the containment of outrage both by appeals to pragmatic resignation by China's moderate reformist establishment and by structuring the discourse to eliminate the concept of an alternative road.[14] What is least likely of all is a mobilization of ordinary citizens around the vision of democratic activists. Among the ordinary people whom I interviewed there was no realistic hope that corruption could be contained by introduction of political pluralism.

## IDEOLOGICAL HEGEMONY

For all of the differences within popular and elite discourse, they share a common horizon, limited by a common definition of corruption. Corruption, as we have seen, is defined in terms of bribe taking by officials, not bribe giving by people seeking official favors or seeking to avoid laws designed, at least nominally, to protect workers and/or consumers. When I asked one lower-level official in Taishan, who was very focused on methods of supervision and punishment, about punishing bribe givers as well as bribe takers, he answered that the law does not call for arresting bribe givers. Were they all arrested, he added, there would be no one left.

In fact, China's bribery law specifies that bribe giving is illegal only if the bribe is given in pursuit of "inappropriate interests" (*bu zhengdang liyi*). But the absence of a definition of "inappropriate interests" again highlights the importance of who gets to define legitimate interests and play a significant role in legitimizing many a bribe. In legal discussions about the definition of bribery, the argument is made that if citizens are forced to pay bribes in order to attain something to which they are legally entitled, they are not in fact bribing someone but being extorted and should not be punished for bribe giving.[15] Moreover, in many elite analyses, a crackdown on bribe givers would be detrimental to the economy, since the bribe givers are either foreign investors or the movers and shakers of economic development, despite the fact that in a stunning number of cases, the major beneficiaries of corruption are private entrepreneurs functioning as bribe givers.[16] Despite the development of increasingly integrated strata of officials and entrepreneurs, in popular culture official wealth is seen as dirty wealth, while entrepreneurial wealth—despite the fact that much of it is garnered at or over the edge of legal, or even moral, practices—is seen as clean.

Excluding bribe givers from definitions of corruption makes it difficult to discuss the creation of new forms of class stratification within China and the development of a new "bureaucratic capitalist" ruling class of officials and entrepreneurs who help one another get rich and stay rich. An article in *Science and Technology and Enterprises* (Keji yu qiye), citing *Forbes* magazine, stated that in 1995 China had over a million millionaires, including seventeen of the world's wealthiest five hundred individuals, that less than 0.1 percent of China's population had 33 percent of all its financial capital, and that this economic polarization had developed more quickly than in Singapore, Japan, and other countries because of the role of illegal methods.[17] Although universally lamenting the prevalence of corruption, the persons I interviewed had little interest in focusing on the moral or social implications of such developments.

In my interviews, only a few people mentioned economic polarization. "In 1996, a lot of people in Guangdong had never seen a one hundred-yuan bill," said one. Another alleged, "Polarization is very serious now. The difference between a worker's income and a manager's is 1:100. That's really big!" "Ten people went out for dinner at the White Swan Hotel in Guangzhou," recounted another. "It cost ¥138,000! . . . The poor can't make that much in a lifetime!" But when pressed, most explicitly rejected a linkage between corruption and class polarization, or if they acknowledged one, they almost always referred to official corruption. The newly created wealthy entrepreneurial strata, when referred to at all, were usually discussed as beneficiaries of an unfair system rather than as corrupt individuals, or as "people who have accomplished what many others would like to be able to do."

Within this framework there is no way of imagining a more egalitarian society, open to genuine talent from all social levels, in which investment capital might be morally, rationally, and fairly channeled to meet public needs. It would not be in the interests of any of China's privileged elites to encourage such popular imagination, and they seem to have established an ideological hegemony that stifles it.

This ideological hegemony, however, rests on a foundation of contradictions.

The regime promotes such slogans as "To get rich is glorious" and "Some get rich first" while occasionally criticizing and even curbing some of the behaviors necessary to get rich quick. Meanwhile, the regime's anticorruption policies are seriously flawed (although in ways not necessarily unique to China). First, intra-elite divisions have negatively influenced both the design and implementation of the policies. Second, focus on anticorruption efforts risks exposing the regime's weaknesses to its opponents and to the general population. Third, anticorruption policies are enforced by agencies under the control of the Party-state (and perhaps under the control of corrupt elements in that structure). This, plus the protective networks of cadres and entrepreneurs that has arisen, makes enforcement of any anticorruption policies extremely difficult. Finally, and most significantly, the goals of the regime are contradictory. On the one hand, it seeks to control corruption (largely through administrative reforms), reduce the size of government,[18] and deepen the reforms themselves. Contradictorily, its strategies and policies for reform and economic growth have structural implications that encourage a competitive ideology of short-term, individual, material self-interest that promotes corruption and creates strata (if not classes) likely to challenge the regime—since, as the Grain Bureau official stated, "These policies are cutting the CCP (Chinese Communist Party) off at its base."

Its imagination confined within this dominant paradigm, popular consciousness is likely to continue to reflect the contradictions of official policy. Ordinary people like those I interviewed in Taishan are likely to continue to separate their anger at the growth of corruption from a critique of the radical social, economic, and political transformations taking place in China today. As a result the public will continue to oscillate between a cynical, resigned, passive acceptance of corruption and bursts of emotional resistance targeted at the manifestations of corruption rather than its roots.

## NOTES

I would like to thank Richard Madsen for his insight and help in editing this chapter.

1. See Transparency International's Internet Corruption Perception Index. www.transparency.de/documents/cpi/index.html. Retrieved 21 June 1999.

2. The magazines were *Beiyue feng* (Wind from the north hills), June 1998; *Fazhi xinwenbao* (Legal system news), February 1998; *Fazhi fengyun* (Instability in the legal system), April 1998; *Huang tudi* (Yellow earth), July 1998; *Jiating shijie* (Family world), October 1997; *Jin qiao* (Golden bridge), August 1998; *Jizhe yu tianxia* (Reporters and the world), May 1998; *Keji yu qiye* (Science and technology and enterprises), June 1998; *Mingpin xiaofei* (Consumption of name brands), January 1998; *Minzhu yu fazhi* (Democracy and the legal system), 10 April 1998; *Qingnian wenhua* (Youth culture), December 1997; *Shichang fazhi daokan* (Market law herald), 10 September 1997; and *Zuojia tiandi* (Writer's world), July 1998. According to booksellers, the magazines generally sold well, although several interviewees stated that they rarely, if ever, read such magazines.

3. In contrast, public opinion definitions, frequently incorporating a public official–based definition, focus on acts that contradict public morality—although this morality is frequently quite difficult to define. Market-based definitions focus on contravention of government-sanctioned rules of economic behavior, regardless of the agent. The constantly changing definition of corruption—and the potential to define it out of existence—is apparent in the 1997 *Criminal Law* (chap. 8), in which "the definition of corruption was further clarified so that employees in collective enterprises were no longer subject to the control of the anti-corruption law." Kin-man Chan, "Corruption in China: A Principal-Agent Perspective," in *Handbook of Comparative Public Administration in the Asia-Pacific Basin*, ed. Hoi-kwok Wong and Hon S. Chan (New York: Marcel Dekker, 1999), 300.

4. In contrast, during the Cultural Revolution (1966–1976), very few magazines were available. All were directly controlled by the Party-state and focused on politics, economics, technology, culture, and so on. They were very stylized and were laced with quotations from Chairman Mao. No hint of sexuality or erotica appeared. Truly popular magazines, to say nothing of tabloids, did not exist.

5. *Fazhi xinwenbao*, 55. (Reprinted from *Jiating* [Household] magazine.)

6. *Jin qiao*, 57; *Qingnian wenhua*, 5.

7. In most cases, in parallel to the tabloid practices noted by Yuezhi Zhao, the actual names of the magazines were deemphasized or consciously hidden so that buyers or inspectors would be unlikely to notice them (see photos 2.1, 2.2, 2.3). For an excellent analysis of magazine and tabloid culture and related issues, see Yuezhi Zhao, *Media, Market, and Democracy in China: Between the Party Line and the Bottom Line* (Urbana: University of Illinois, 1998), particularly 72–93, 118–52; also her chapter 5, "The Rich, the Laid-off, and the Criminal in Tabloid Tales," in this volume. My thanks to Yuezhi Zhao for her input to this section of my chapter.

8. Originally praised by Party and government officials as a model entrepreneur, Shen's Great Wall Machinery and Electronics Corporation raised over ¥1 billion, about 50 percent of which was recovered after it was exposed as a scam (see Zhao, *Media, Market and Democracy*, 80–81). Mou was one of China's "ten best private entrepreneurs" and a "reform hero" in 1995, but he was jailed for life in May 2000 for business fraud.

9. In *Streetlife China* (New York: Cambridge University Press, 1998), Michael Dutton suggests that the commodification of politics its transformation from a reality to a desirable commodity such as a sensationalist tabloid—also tends to defuse anger and reinforce the growing capitalism in China.

10. In research that is yet to be published, Professor He Zengke of Beijing found considerably greater anger at the corruption of local officials than did this research but also more interest in local democracy, competitive elections, and transparency as at least partial remedies for corruption than appears in my analysis. Professor He, personal correspondence with author.

11. For discussions of these elite positions on corruption, see Richard Levy, "Corruption, Economic Crime, and Social Transformation since the Reforms: The Debate in China," *Australian Journal of Chinese Affairs*, January 1995, 1–25; Richard Levy, "*Fubai*: Differing Chinese Views on Corruption since Tiananmen," *International Journal of Public Administration*, January 2001.

12. In her controversial book, *Zhongguo de xianjing* (China's pitfall) (reviewed by Liu

Binyan and Perry Link in *New York Review of Books*, 8 October 1998) economist He Qing-lian, who posited a more direct link between corruption and the reforms than is usually permitted in public discourse, stated: "The Gini coefficient is a standard measure of income disparity. A coefficient of 0.3 indicates substantial equality; 0.3 to 0.4 indicates acceptable equality, and 0.4 or higher is considered too large. 0.6 or higher is predictive of social unrest." In two different 1994 surveys, China had Gini coefficients of 0.45 and 0.59.

13. While elite discourse frequently portrays polarization as a negative and potentially explosive consequence of corruption, some reformists argue that corruption plays a posi-tive role in assisting the primitive accumulation of capital necessary for economic devel-opment. Moreover, both elite and popular discourse have tended to understate the polarizing consequences of corruption by portraying the proceeds of corruption as being spent predominantly on consumption instead of being reinvested.

In "Corruption and the Transition from Socialism in China," in *The Corruption of Poli-tics and the Politics of Corruption*, ed. Michael Levi and David Nelken (Cambridge, Mass.: Blackwell, 1996), Gordon White suggests that much of the indignation is not actually against corruption per se but against accelerating inequalities and the emergence of a new class incorporating elements of the old political and new economic elites.

14. According to a relatively high-ranking cadre in Beijing, the boundaries for legiti-mate elite debate allow discussion of new "strata" but not new classes, since these would imply the reconstitution of a class society in "socialist" China. Despite endless euphe-misms for classes and class struggle, the notion of class is rejected while the differential access to wealth, power, and life options for those at different locations in the political-economic-social structure is recognized. Such discredited language and concepts of the Mao period as class, class struggle, exploitation, capitalism, the proletariat, and the bour-geoisie are replaced with the language and concepts of the isolated and independent indi-vidual.

15. See "Quanguo renda changweiyuan guanyu chengzhi tanwuzui huiluzui de buchong guiding" (Supplementary regulations on tanwu and bribery of the standing com-mittee of the NPC), 21 January 1988, articles 7–9. In "Subsistence Crisis, Managerial Corruption, and Corruption Protest in China," *China Journal*, July 2000, Feng Chen argues that managerial corruption only tends to become a topic of political protest when workers' ability to subsist is threatened.

16. For example, the banking officials who allowed the bribe givers to exceed their credit limits to the tune of over ¥1 billion themselves only received ¥400,000 in bribes. See "Shiyiyi jinrong da'an de zhuizong" (Tracing a major financial case of 1.1 billion yuan), *Zuojia tiandi*, 108–12. See also *Minzhu yu fazhi*, 32–33 (in which officials wrote up false tax bills that cost the state ¥120 million while they received a 5 percent kickback); *Minzhu yu fazhi*, 20–23; "Guanchang dapifa" (Wholesaling officialdom), *Huang tudi*; *Jizhe yu tianxia*, 38ff.; "Yangman tawang qianse hanghuilu" (Record of Eel King's bribe giving), *Beiyue feng*, 95–97; and *Zuojia tiandi*, 24–74, on Shen Taifu and how he benefited from corruption at the expense of both the bribed officials and large numbers of common people.

17. "Fanfu ge 'yongju,' guoren chang 'da feng'—quanzhu xiandai fantan xinminyao" (Anticorruption cuts out "ulcers," people sing about the current "big wind"—Notes and commentary on contemporary anticorruption "new folk rhymes") *Keji yu qiye* (Science and technology and enterprises), 92–99.

18.  Numerous analysts, however, have criticized the notion that smaller government will mean less corruption rather than a relocation or transmogrification of the form of corruption. See, for example, Bardhan Pranab, "Corruption and Development: A Review of Issues," *Journal of Economic Literature*, September 1997, 1320–46; White, "Corruption and the Transition"; and Susan Rose-Ackerman, *Corruption: A Study in Political Economy* (New York: Academic Press, 1978), 207. Moreover, the size of the government bureaucracy has increased significantly under the reforms. The *China News Digest* for 22 September 2000, on the other hand, highlights a case in which the prosecution of six private entrepreneurs who had allegedly offered large bribes to senior officials in Jiangxi was widely publicized to serve as a warning against such practices.

# 3

# Village Voices, Urban Activists: Women, Violence, and Gender Inequality in Rural China

*Paul G. Pickowicz and Liping Wang*

Few would dispute the assertion that much of rural China witnessed phenomenal economic growth after decollectivization in the early 1980s. But relatively little is known about the lives of ordinary people during the economic boom. For instance, how have rural women fared in the brave new world of market socialism? How do women talk about their experiences? We began field research on this topic in 1995 by focusing on two communities we had visited often in connection with earlier projects. One village is a remote and historically poor community in central Hebei, a place where most peasants depend on farming for a modest income. The second site is located in central Jiangsu, an historically prosperous region. Thanks to rural industrialization, peasants there have incomes comparable to those of urban workers. Our preliminary research in these two places included interviews with three dozen rural women.

The complex social world of rural China became apparent at once in an initial meeting with a dozen women in the Hebei village.[1] One young woman, twenty-four-year-old Li Meidu, made a particularly strong impression. Like most brides in the region, Meidu was an outsider. Her parents arranged for her to marry into the village in 1993. Meidu stood out from the others we met that night not only because she was tall and quite attractive by local standards, but also because she was well educated. She was the only high school graduate in the group. Meidu's gold ring, gold necklace, and fashionable clothing also set her apart from the other women.

We wondered how she could afford such luxuries on a part-time teacher's salary of only ¥200 per month. Would she not prefer to make more money working in one of the small factories in the village? "My job is easier and requires more skill," she said. "My in-laws aren't really counting on this tiny sum." The other women then informed us that Meidu's new family was the richest in the village. Her father-in-law had been running a local factory for a decade.

Suddenly someone said, "Here comes Meidu's man!" The young man who appeared at the door was very different from Meidu. He was short and plain. There was something odd about his eyes. Meidu was clearly annoyed at the sight of the intruder. She questioned her husband, Nine Happinesses Wei, in an uneasy voice, "Who told you to come? What do you want?" Wei mumbled, "Mother told me to come and take you home." Further agitated, Meidu replied, "Get out! I'm not going with you!"

After Wei retreated, the village director of women's affairs (*funü zhuren*) felt compelled to explain away the obvious tension in the couple's relationship. Meidu's in-laws, she said, were especially concerned about her activities these days because she was three months pregnant.

But other village women made it clear that the incident was far more complicated. The oldest son of the prosperous Wei family, Nine Happinesses was widely believed to be retarded. His parents had arranged a marriage for him once before, but the union soon ended in divorce (an increasingly common phenomenon in rural China). The woman demanded her freedom on the grounds that life with Nine Happinesses was unbearable. The Weis, in turn, accused the woman of being barren and then approached Meidu's parents to arrange a second marriage.

Meidu was known for her good looks, but her family was rather poor. Her father, an accountant in a nearby village, earned only ¥200 a month. According to local people, the family was desperate to support Meidu's younger brother, who was studying in a professional school. It was hoped Meidu could help out, but her family lacked the connections necessary to get her a high-paying job. The Weis told the Lis that they would pay not only a handsome bride price for Meidu but also the entire cost of Meidu's bridal dowry, an obligation normally assumed by the bride's family. A respectable dowry cost ¥8,000–9,000. Furthermore, the Lis were told that Meidu would get enough cash each month to help out with her natal family's basic expenses.

The problem was that Meidu did not like Nine Happinesses and protested the arrangement right up until the wedding day. In the end, however, she complied with her parents' decision. This background information, we were told, explained the confrontation we had witnessed. Meidu made no secret of the fact that she considered Wei an undesirable mate, and some villagers predicted that she too would eventually seek a divorce. In the meantime, Meidu's in-laws showered her with money, and Meidu, for her part, seemed determined to make them pay dearly for the arrangement. When Meidu's mother-in-law gave her ¥500 for "lucky money" (*ya sui qian*) on the occasion of the lunar new year, a sum ten times the amount village brides expect to receive, Meidu demanded an additional ¥50, saying that she did not want to break the nice ¥100 bills when it came time to give smaller cash gifts to youngsters in her natal family. Her father-in-law donated ¥10,000 to the village primary school so that Meidu could be hired as a part-time teacher. Meidu also expected her in-laws to pay the ¥9,000 tuition bill for a teacher training certificate she hoped to earn. This course would qualify her for a full-time teaching job.

We visited Li Meidu's house several times to learn more about her experiences with marriage and rural family life. Why did she agree to the arranged marriage? What did she think about her situation? Meidu spent plenty of time grumbling, but she appeared to be willing to go along with the arrangement.

Our encounter with Li Meidu and others taught us many things. First, while it is true that the dynamism of the reform-era economy is appreciated by almost everyone, the individual experiences of rural people often vary according to such factors as gender and age. We also learned that rural women have an exceedingly keen sense of the interplay between family life and commercial life. Indeed, given the demographic imbalance that is responsible for a shortage of women in the Chinese countryside, we were tempted for a time to see people like Meidu as capable, even wily, negotiators who have been empowered by the commercialization of rural society. This, we soon learned, was an exceedingly premature judgment.

Convinced that there was no way to understand the experiences of rural women without gaining access to the voices of rural women, we had looked forward to doing systematic field research. The interviews with Li Meidu and the others were most informative, but there are definite limits to what people will say to strangers. In China, as elsewhere, it is extremely difficult for outsiders to discover what happens in rural families when tensions escalate.

At this point in our research we were able to benefit from the information revolution that was sweeping through China. Seeking to dig deeper than interviews could take us, we were advised by many people to take a close look at new monthly entitled *Rural Women Knowing All* (Nongjia nü bai shi tong), first published in Beijing in January 1993.[2] Claiming to be the "first magazine solely for rural women," this remarkable publication had achieved a circulation of 150,000 copies in less than two years.[3] Led by the vivacious Xie Lihua, a deputy editor of *Chinese Women's News* (Zhongguo funü bao), *Rural Women* has an informal connection to the official national Women's Association (Fu lian), which plays a key role in the distribution of the magazine in the rural sector. But, we noted with interest, *Rural Women* has also received crucial nongovernmental support in the form of significant financial assistance from both the Ford Foundation and such quasi-independent corporations in China as the Beijing Peony Electronic Group (Beijing shengdan dianzi jituan). The magazine also sells advertising space.

Dedicated to the task of "helping rural women surmount obstacles and resolve difficulties," *Rural Women* targets rural girls and women between the ages of sixteen and forty who have received nine years of schooling and have "a strong desire to acquire knowledge, skills and information that will help them change their lot." The magazine is easy to read and includes regular sections, "Letters from Young Women," "Laws and Lawsuits," "Love and Marriage," "Reproduction and Health," and "Sex Education," among its regular offerings.

Xie Lihua and her staff have a complex relationship with rural women. On one hand, the urban women believe they know more about the needs of rural women than rural women themselves know. They preach and write patronizing editorials in order to raise the consciousness of their rural sisters. They plead with rural women to "go public" in order to create political pressure for urgently needed law enforcement and legal reforms. The urban women see themselves as a lobby and often act like lobbyists who have an agenda surprisingly independent of the program of the state and Party.

But the crusading urban women also listen to rural women and are passionate about publishing their stories in the magazine. As a result, the voices of rural women are heard in ways that are unknown in other publications and that go well beyond what is said in field interviews with women like Li Meidu. Apparently these wrenching firsthand accounts of marriage and family problems in village China are published in *Rural Women* without much editing. The stories written by rural women are certainly quite different in language and style from the professional reports written by the journal's own staff.

The narratives contain exaggerations and partial truths, but, taken as a whole, they seem authentic. It is important to remember, however, that it is the urban women, not the rural women, who determine which stories will be published. The editorial decisions of the urban women reflect their own political and legislative agendas, which may or may not resonate with the concerns of rural women themselves.

In 1997 *Rural Women* initiated a policy aimed at generating a steady flow of detailed reports from the countryside. Each year the journal invites about ten of its rural contributors, mainly those who have reported on cases that are in tune with the reform agenda of urban advocates, to gather in Beijing for a week. These people are given further journalistic training and hold discussions with the journal's staff regarding social and political priorities.

The reports that rural women send in are refreshing in that they do not repeat the usual general condemnations of "feudal remnants" identified time and again during the republican and Maoist periods as the culprits most responsible for the sufferings of village women. Instead, they provide the details of women's personal experiences, including compelling accounts of the emotional agony endured by those who suffer from physical and verbal abuse. Indeed, the rural women who speak out in the magazine leave the clear impression that men in rural China routinely employ coercion, force, and violence to impose their will in matters related to the arrangement of marriages, household discipline, sexuality, and other sensitive areas.

*Rural Women* is an especially interesting source. It provides rich data that were unavailable in quantity in earlier materials and seeks to mobilize rural women largely outside the framework of ineffective or discredited state and Party institutions. Its political agenda includes a determination to influence mainstream urban writers, who pay almost exclusive attention to urban issues. A handful of sympathetic urban intellectuals agree with editor Xie Lihua that rural women have been largely ignored by influential publications.[4] The few writers who work on gender inequality in rural China are inclined to focus on theoretical debates. Is the "feminization of agriculture," they ask, a function of rural-urban migration and the rise of rural industry? Such discussions rarely consider the details of individual cases, and issues of domestic violence are almost never mentioned.[5]

When mainstream publications turn to practical matters, they do little more than recycle information that can be found in *Rural Women*. For instance, *Chinese Women* (Zhongguo funü), an official journal, published an article in 1998 that highlighted the difficulties facing rural wives when their husbands join the ranks of migrant workers in the cities. In this case, the author was an editor of *Rural Women*, and her article merely summarized several firsthand reports that had appeared in her own journal during the previous two years.[6]

The unusual data in *Rural Women* convinced us to make violence against women in contemporary rural China the focus of this chapter. What started out as an open-ended effort to learn more about the concerns of rural women in reform-era China has ended up as an inquiry on women and violence. In this chapter we define violence broadly to include hitting, beating, battering, sexual assault, rape, murder, and suicide, as well as verbal abuse, psychological torture, intimidation, stalking, harassment, threats, and other extreme forms of coercion and domination. Rural women have testified that violence occurs in many contexts. For the sake of discussion, however, this study looks at women and violence under four broad categories: the problem of arranged marriages that are forced on rural daughters, the explosive tensions associated with failing rural marriages, the phenomenon of domestic violence, and, finally, the agonies associated with sexual crimes committed within the framework of marriage and outside it. We do not mean to suggest that these problems can only be understood as the byproducts of market socialism. There can be no doubt that they have been around for a long time in China and throughout the world. What we are saying is that the accounts in *Rural Women* allow us a rare opportunity to get a detailed look at social practices that are normally hidden from view. The challenge is not to label the problems as "old" or "new" but to account for patterns of continuity and change in the broad context of post-Mao decollectivization and commercialization.[7]

## ARRANGED MARRIAGES

The phenomenon of parental arrangement of marriages in post-Mao China, clearly a primary concern of contemporary rural women, is certainly nothing new. While female resistance to arranged marriage is by no means easy to mount, thanks to the efforts of the *Rural Women* group, village women seem somewhat more aware now that they have legal rights in such matters and that they can appeal to sympathetic supporters outside the family. Part of what rural women express is the familiar and age-old refrain about tyrannical parents who are driven by old-fashioned values. But they also recognize that in contemporary China the desire to arrange marriages is motivated as well by the sorts of distinctively commercial considerations that have come to prevail in postsocialist society. To put it bluntly, many rural women understand that cashing in on arranged marriages is an important way for families to meet postsocialist financial needs.

Zhang Zhenlan, a resident of Ningjin county in Shandong, wrote to *Rural Women* about her own arranged marriage in the early 1990s. "I was only eighteen when I was engaged," she lamented. "As much as the terms of the engagement sounded nice," she recalled, "I went through the day of the engagement in tears. I felt like I was being sold." The youngest child in the family, Zhang had no doubt that her mother loved her. But she could not help wondering how her mother "had the heart to sell her own daughter."

Efforts were made to convince the teenager that the primary factor in the arrangement was the political and social status of the young man, the son of a village official. The head of the village committee, who served as the matchmaker in this arrangement, insisted that it was an honor for Zhang's family to be singled out in this way. Other young women were said to be eager to marry the young man. Her mother asserted that the family should not "miss the opportunity to be honored in this way," but Zhang claims that she saw through this rhetorical facade.

The story behind the story is that Zhang had a twenty-four-year-old brother who was not yet married. Village women had been gossiping for some time about the brother because it was rare to be that old and lack a marriage prospect. Deeply concerned about the family's reputation, Zhang's mother was exceedingly anxious to locate a marriage partner for him and a daughter-in-law for herself. Despite the shortage of eligible women in many villages, the mother was on the verge of finalizing a match for the son in the weeks just before Zhang's own arrangement was announced. The problem was that Zhang's family did not have the money for the bride price and the son's arrangement was in jeopardy.

As Zhang tells it, she realized at once that the news of her own engagement a few days later was a case of "getting wool from a donkey," that is, getting something of real value from an unlikely source. The parents told the village official that the bride price for Zhang Zhenlan would be ¥800. As soon as an agreement was reached, a second understanding was worked out to pay the same sum, ¥800, to the family of the prospective daughter-in-law. Zhang, commenting on the inhumanity of the process, later wrote, "This was like trading a sack of sorghum for a sack of millet." On her engagement day she hid in her room staring at the ceiling as tears rolled down her face.[8]

Liu Mei, a resident of Hanlou village in Mengcheng county, Anhui, reported a variation of the same story. The parents of an eighteen-year-old named Xiaosan were tempted to marry her to a twenty-five-year-old butcher in Maji township. The man, said to be attracted to Xiaosan's beauty and obedient temperament, had offered a whopping ¥8,000 bride price. The parents accepted the proposal without consulting Xiaosan because the offer came at a time of urgent financial need. Xiaosan's younger brother and sister (twins) had been admitted to a trade school that promised opportunities for jobs in a large city. But in the reform era higher education was no longer free, and the family needed to come up with ¥10,000. Xiaosan's bride price solved the problem. "Big sister, your sacrifice has made the whole family happy!" the twins said. But not everyone was happy. Xiaosan ran away from home, an increasingly common occurrence these days. She left a note saying she would not return until she had earned enough money to pay back the bride price.[9]

In a third case in which grinding poverty was not the source of family financial difficulties, Zhou Hongyun of Nanzhang county in Hubei wrote to *Rural Women* about the sad story of her cousin, Honger. Honger's mother died when Honger was five years old. Her father remarried. By 1996 Honger's father had produced three more children with his new wife and had been fined ¥4,000 for grossly violating family planning codes. According to her cousin, the fifteen-year-old Honger was then sold off to an unattractive "bare stick" in a nearby village for precisely the sum of ¥4,000. Because Honger was too young to be legally recognized as the man's spouse, she was forced to get an abortion when she became pregnant.[10]

The disturbing accounts described above came to light only because the victim, a friend, or a relative wrote to *Rural Women*. It is important to recognize, however, that public complaints about arranged marriages are, in all probability, relatively rare, in large part because resistance involves serious risks. Many women, perhaps most, agree to arranged marriages, even in cases in which initial unhappiness was registered. The story of a person such as Chen Ying, a resident of our field research site in Jiangsu, is more likely to be encountered in interviews than on the pages of a crusading publication like *Rural Women*.[11]

Chen Ying's mother, Huizhen, is in her late fifties. Better educated than most rural women, she worked as a primary school teacher for a couple of years. Thus she is referred to in the village as "laoshi" rather than in the usual way as "the wife of so-and-so." Chen Ying graduated from high school and was among the few village women qualified to hold a better-paying managerial position in a rural enterprise. At the time of her arranged marriage she was an accountant in a township construction company. Her older brother left the village to start a new life in a city. Her younger brother is a gambling addict whose habits caused his parents to doubt his ability to care for them in their later years.

In 1989 Huizhen said that she wanted Chen Ying to marry Xiaoping, a truck driver who lived in a nearby village. At first Chen Ying objected to the match, in part because she was fond of a coworker who, like herself, was a high school graduate. Chen Ying complained that she had little in common with Xiaoying because he never finished primary school. But the mother insisted that Chen Ying go through with the arranged marriage.

Even though the marriage would be a step down in cultural terms for both Chen Ying and the family, Huizhen frankly acknowledged that the main purpose of the arrangement was to keep Chen Ying close to her natal family. And once again the main consideration was economic. "I thought Xiaoping was a good match because his house is very close to ours; it takes only ten minutes by bike," Huizhen remarked. "This way," she continued, "Chen Ying can come home every weekend, and I won't be so lonely after she gets married. The other guy lived too far away, so if they were married I wouldn't see her very often. Also, Xiaoping's family is well-off and has a new house. The other guy's family is poor and still lives in an old house. I figured that if Chen Ying married Xiaoping, she'd always have some money to help me. But if she went with this other guy, all the money she made would be used to build their new house."

Short-term financial gain was not what motivated Huizhen. Chen Ying's job paid well, and the family would have no difficulty returning the bride price of ¥3,000 if that became necessary. Huizhen eventually persuaded Chen Ying to agree to the arrangement, but not before Chen Ying's father (a worker in Shanghai) threatened to disown the young woman if she insisted on breaking the engagement.

Chen Ying married Xiaoping in 1990, when she was twenty-five. She later attributed her change of heart to the pleas of her mother and her own concern about her moral standing in the community. She said that "people would talk" because breaking off a marriage agreement still reflects poorly on a rural woman. After the marriage Chen Ying did indeed visit her mother every weekend. Huizhen realized that Xiaoping was no match for Chen Ying in matters related to education, job status, and income, but she appreciated Xiaoping's willingness to help with farm work and other tasks requiring hard physical labor. After the marriage Huizhen worried far less about her security in later years.

Contributors to *Rural Women* report that many rural families seek to avoid the problem of resistance to arranged marriages by committing daughters to engagements when they are still very young, in some cases between the ages of thirteen and eighteen. Teenage girls, they reason, have less education and experience and thus are more likely to listen obediently to parents. Furthermore, teenage girls are more likely to be attracted to the gifts and money offered by matchmakers.[12] But many other accounts, including autobiographical narratives, reveal that stubborn resistance, even for slightly older and better educated women, violates deeply rooted rural ethical norms. Loyalty to one's natal family is highly valued and quite often causes women to willingly accept unwanted arranged marriages. They know that by rejecting current standards of filial conduct, and thus endangering the old-age security of parents, they risk being cut off from the natal family. A rural primary school teacher from Sichuan wrote to *Rural Women* to say that when she tried to resist an arranged marriage to an illiterate farmer, her father, a village official concerned about his welfare in later years, said "You can just get the hell out of the house then!"[13]

The story of Shang Jianling, a member of a family of modest means in Dali county, Shanxi, is rather typical. When her father fell ill in 1992 and family medical expenses began to mount, Shang allowed herself to be engaged to a deaf-mute whose parents were well-to-do. The bride price received was used to pay for her father's medical care. She was eighteen at the time. Shang's father soon died, and she became suicidal when she contemplated the upcoming marriage. In the end, however, she concluded, "My mother couldn't lose her only daughter after having suffered her whole life and after having lost her husband." Looking ahead to the wedding day, she "felt no happiness, only the pressure of force." After four years of marriage, she wrote, she was torn between her desire to seek a divorce and her guilt about bringing pain and unhappiness to her husband, her daughter, and her in-laws.[14]

Active and stubborn resistance to arranged marriages seems to be more common among rural women who have already found a partner on their own. But when resistance is more determined, the perceived threat to parental authority is more pronounced. The outcome can be quite violent. In the early 1990s a rural primary school teacher named Liu Xiurong from Xiushan county outside Chongqing in Sichuan met a young carpenter. He agreed to stay in her family's house for two days to help make a coffin for Liu's father. Such things are done far in advance in much of rural China. The two got along very well, but when Liu accompanied the young man on a visit to his aunt, who lives in the same village, Liu's father exploded. When the couple returned to Liu's house, the old man grabbed a knife and chased the young carpenter out of the compound. A few days later Liu's father harshly rebuffed a matchmaker sent by the young man's family.

Even though the patriarch threatened to break her legs if she continued to see the carpenter, Liu carried on a secret relationship for nearly a year in hopes that the father would change his mind. Several times she thought about running off with the young man, but the thought of her mother gave Liu pause each time. Eventually Liu's mother told her why the father would never change his mind. Apparently the old man was criticized by Liu's elder brother and sister-in-law for failing to discipline the young woman and allowing her to run wild. The father regarded this criticism as a serious challenge to his authority and was determined to prevent neighbors and villagers from talking about him in such humiliating terms. Seeing that it was a hopeless cause, Liu stopped seeing her boyfriend.[15]

The loosening up of the family registration (*hukou*) system in postsocialist China has led to new and sudden opportunities for mobility, and, not surprisingly, increasing numbers of rural women have chosen to run away with their boyfriends when they encounter intractable parental disapproval. The case of Wang Xianxiu may not be typical, but it demonstrates in vivid terms that women can now consider multiple options when it comes to matters of the heart. Wang is from Yaoping township in Fangxian county, Hubei. In 1996 she fell in love with a young man from her village named Xiao Liu. The bond between the two was said to be very strong: they had grown up together and attended school together.

Wang's father staunchly opposed the marriage, however, on the grounds that he did not want his daughter to be trapped in their remote village forever. Wang protested, saying, "There is freedom of marriage. Parents have no right to interfere!" Her father replied, "You are my daughter. You'll have freedom when I give it to you. You must obey me when I deny you this freedom!" When Wang defiantly insisted on marrying Xiao Liu, her father beat her several times and threatened to kill both Wang and her boyfriend. Family members, including some women, closely monitored Wang's activities in order to prevent her from seeing Xiao Liu. Nevertheless, on 16 March 1997 Wang and Xiao Liu slipped away to the township to register their marriage according to the law. After the ceremony Wang and her new husband stood outside the government building crying, fearful that Wang's father would seek retribution. They decided at once to move to another community.[16]

Not surprisingly, the official Women's Association is reluctant to encourage this form of resistance to parental authority, even though it is entirely consistent with the law. According to Xu Jidong, an official in charge of defending women's rights in the city of Jizhou in Hebei, elopement is now a common method of resisting arranged marriages. She reported that in 1996–1997 instances of resistance to parental interference in matters related to marriage accounted for nearly 42 percent of rural runaway cases handled by the local Women's Association. In most of these incidents rural women ran away together with their self-selected boyfriends. Reflecting the perspective of the Party-state, Xu wrote to *Rural Women* to warn rural women about the dangers associated with running away. The government frowned on illegal marriages and unapproved childbirths, and running away heightened tensions within the larger family and stiffened parental opposition to the union. By running away, officials said, women cut off their ties to their natal families and effectively closed off the option of returning home if the marriage of their own choice did not work out.[17]

Urban women who lobby on behalf of rural women make a different point. The problem is that the law is unacceptably vague. According to the letter of the law, young men and women are free to choose their own marriage partners. It is illegal for parents to force a daughter into a marriage. The difficulty is that officials do not enforce the law that is already on the books. Courts and lawyers rarely exist at the village level. Complaints are typically handled by village leaders, usually males, who are not at all inclined to "interfere" in family life in ways that undermine customary parental authority. Parents can simply deny that force has been used. Young women have nowhere to turn, even if they understand their rights. Increasingly, they opt to run away.

## BROKEN MARRIAGES

Flight is even more difficult for married women. Decollectivization gave rural people the right to travel outside the village to earn cash and to engage in various commercial activities. But the pattern of rural migration for married people since the 1980s is for husbands to venture out to the cities to find work and for wives to remain at home to tend to farming and household matters, including child and elder care. In other words, married women have benefited far less than married men from the new and liberating mobility of the reform era. To make matters worse, farmwork and housework are undervalued these days, while earning cash on the outside is valued in ways that were unthinkable in the Mao era. Men who achieve economic success away from home (where village ethical norms cannot be enforced) are often tempted to engage in extramarital affairs and even to abandon their wives in favor of other women.

In the mid-1990s *Rural Women* made frequent use of the term "women who stay behind" *(liu shou nü)* to refer to this aspect of the division of labor under market socialism. The magazine openly sympathized with rural women between the ages of twenty and fifty whose marriages were in ruins because of new patterns of mobility and power. While virtually all *liu shou nü* welcomed decollectivization, many began to complain that the fruits of the economic reforms were being distributed unfairly, according to gender. In short, the new mobility encouraged new patterns of gender inequality. Men who made money outside the village controlled the earnings. Their resources gave them more leverage in family matters and made it easier for them to abuse and oppress their wives.

Lin Meihua, a resident of Fujian, wrote to *Rural Women* about her own plight and asked whether she had the right to sue her husband for bigamy. "My husband is the head of a construction team from our village and has been working in cities since 1983," Lin stated. "He made a lot of money but never gave me much of it. He rarely came home. There were rumors among villagers about my husband having another woman who is pretty, sexy, and more than ten years younger than he. It was said that he shared a house with the woman."

Lin's husband denied the rumors, so Lin hired someone to follow him. "The result of the investigation," Lin wrote, "was that my husband and the woman do indeed have a nice multistory house in a suburb of the city. He goes there four times a week. Furthermore, he and that woman have a son who is about three years old. Once I learned about the actual situation, I had a big fight with my husband. He put his cards on the table and demanded a divorce. I didn't agree to it because I couldn't swallow my anger. Can I sue my husband for bigamy (*chonghun*)?"[18]

In one important sense, Lin Meihua's story is atypical of those involving wives who have been abandoned by prosperous husbands. Apparently most rural women in such situations do not consider legal action. Most feel helpless in the face of adulterous spouses, and most would rather maintain a hollow married status than agree to a divorce. Once again, a principal reason is that the husband working outside the village controls both money and property. It is also true that many, perhaps most, rural women are not aware of their legal rights or have no faith in the willingness of male-dominated local courts to defend their interests. There is confusion about the law and how it should be enforced in such cases.

Ye Chunling, a thirty-one-year-old resident of Yichuan county, Henan, exemplifies the type of rural woman who eventually stops protesting. In the mid-1990s Ye and her husband opened a fast food restaurant in Luoyang. "Because I was honest and I was able to make several good snack foods," she wrote, "our business went very well." Problems arose when the eatery was expanded into a more formal restaurant (*jiu lou*) and a couple of attractive waitresses were hired to help out. "In the beginning," Ye recalled, "he treated me okay, but later he began finding fault with everything I did. It was then that I discovered his disloyalty. One day I found him making out with a waitress in broad daylight! I was so angry I slapped her face." The waitress shot back, "He likes me and I love him. I'm already pregnant with his child!"

Despite Ye's many contributions to the enterprise, her husband controlled the assets. It was from this position of considerable strength that he gave Ye two options: "If you continue to make a fuss, you'll end up divorced. But if you calm down, I'll give you our house back home along with some pocket money each month." Ye told *Rural Women*, "I hate his guts when I think of these things, but I have no way to deal with him. I'll just make do this way."[19] With the offending couple residing outside the village environment, community opinion mattered very little. Under such circumstances rural women are forced to handle the issue of infidelity on their own.

In fact, in cases of male adultery, rural women cannot count on the support of their natal families and their in-laws, including women relatives. Chen Jianping of Jinta county in Gansu wrote to tell the sad story of her elder sister, who married into a poor family in the late 1980s. After the marriage her husband worked as a driver and made good money. As is often the case in post-Mao rural China, the mobility and success of the husband was made possible by the back-breaking labor of the wife back home. While her husband made money outside the village, the wife farmed more than ten *mu* of land and took complete care of their two sons. The husband did not send any money back home, spending it instead on another woman. When the wife confronted the husband about his philandering, she received a beating. Desperate for help, she returned to her natal family and began to talk about divorce. But her own father said, "A good woman would never marry more than once." When she returned to her husband's home, her mother-in-law told her to forget about the infidelity: "It's nothing for men to be involved in that kind of thing on the outside."[20]

According to *Rural Women*, many abandoned rural women develop mental health problems. A surprising number resort to suicide. For instance, twenty-nine-year-old Xu Fengzhi of Dongshan village in Longhua county, Hebei, committed suicide by ingesting poison on 19 June 1997. In this case the husband was involved in a sexual liaison with a woman in Dongshan village itself, an important factor that compounded Xu's sense disgrace and shame.

Xu had entered into an arranged marriage with her husband when she was twenty. Initially the two got along well. Xu was not well educated but was known as a hard worker and a filial wife. Moreover, she gave birth to a son one year after the marriage.

According to Wang Lixia, a resident of a nearby village who reported this story, the troubles began in 1994 when Xu's husband joined two others from the village (a man named Huang and his wife) on a trip to south China, where they had arranged for jobs in a brick factory.

Huang's wife was a good talker, was stylish, and had a reputation for being "loose." Xu's husband soon entered into a sexual relationship with Huang's wife. Xu made a fair amount of money but spent most of it on Huang's wife and gambling. A year later he returned to the village with little to show for his labor. Xu learned about the affair but expressed a willingness to forgive her husband if he changed his ways. But he failed to do so. Secret liaisons with the woman gave way to an open relationship. In fact, Xu's husband began to take care of all the farming work for the Huang household and even moved in with Huang's wife whenever Huang was away working.

The case was regarded as a major scandal in the village. Xu's approach was to work alone to win back her husband's affections. She took great pride in being a good wife. "What is the value of being a woman," she once said, "if you can't have a husband and kids?" Xu pleaded with her husband, shed many tears, and followed him around the village. Her husband beat her up. Xu then worked quietly to keep the house tidy and take care of her blind mother-in-law. But in June 1996, when she learned that her husband planned to go out to work again with Huang's wife, Xu begged her husband to stay. On 19 June she prepared a feast of tasty dishes and tried to remind her husband of the joys of their earlier days. But he turned a deaf ear, knocked over the table, and stormed out. When he returned a few hours later, he discovered that his wife had taken poison and was on the verge of death. Villagers gathered at the house, but it was too late to save her life.[21]

Wang Lixia, the twenty-eight-year-old peasant woman who reported this tale, commented that rural women her age often wonder whether there is any meaning to life. Many feel their future is shaped by factors almost totally beyond their control. Some say, "Luckily, my husband is good to me. My life is not so bad after all since I have a good man." In Wang's view, the plight of rural women has much to do with their enormous burdens in the domestic sphere in the new market socialist era. Comparing urban and rural women, she points out, "Women in the cities have jobs and careers in addition to having a husband and kids. They have their work to focus on when frustrations come along in family life. Their spiritual world cannot fall apart so completely, and they would not end their lives so easily. But in poor and remote mountain villages like ours, peasant women have no way to gain spiritual sustenance and cannot find a career outside the family. Therefore, they feel empty spiritually and their only desire is to maintain the family and to try to live a good life."[22]

Many of the cases of suicide reported in *Rural Women* involve broken marriages. Victims in such cases usually feel a profound sense of isolation. The state, conspicuously absent in accounts of their stories, is perceived as irrelevant to the most important things in women's lives. Village leaders are disinclined to mediate in matters related to family life and gender relations. In some cases, including one brought to light by Yao Junying in Heilongjiang province, suicide is seen both as the only way out and as a form of protest. Yao tells the story of Yang Xiaoyun (her cousin) and Hu Defa, who were married in 1977 and, like so many others, signed a contract in the early 1980s to farm land once controlled by the collective. The family became quite prosperous and before long Hu had an affair with a woman who worked as an accountant for the farm. Hu began to physically abuse his wife and arranged for the family's money to be managed by the accountant. According to her cousin, Yang could not bear the humiliations and hung herself in 1995. The state was required to step in at this point because a death had occurred. It was because of the suicide that Hu Defa was convicted of spousal abuse and sentenced to two years in prison.

A related case involving marital infidelity, a feeling of helplessness, and female suicide occurred in Hainan province. Fu Cexiong, a former chicken farmer in the suburbs of Haikou, became wealthy selling construction materials. In 1992 he initiated a relationship in Haikou with Zhang Wen, a successful businesswoman. Fu's wife, Xin Yifen, remained in the countryside. But in 1994 Xin moved to Haikou with their two children in order to keep an eye on her husband. Fu avoided his wife and children, and at a certain point he no longer bothered to conceal his extramarital affair. In fact, Fu made arrangements for his lover to live in the same apartment with his wife for two months. When Xin objected, her husband said, "Try to understand. If you can't, I'll divorce you!" Before long the husband demanded a divorce, but Xin refused to cooperate. Soon her husband stopped coming home and gave Xin little money. In winter 1995 Xin attempted suicide by inhaling gas but was saved by her neighbors. Her husband's own family, not the courts, became involved at that point. Fu was forced to drop the idea of divorce and to provide his wife with enough money to cover living expenses. Once again, asking for help from government organs or official women's groups was not seen as an option.[23]

## DOMESTIC VIOLENCE

Arranged marriages and broken marriages are topics of great concern among rural women, but references to domestic violence are so common in accounts of family disputes that violence itself deserves to be categorized as a central concern of rural women. Indeed, violence appears to be one of the most important means by which men maintain patriarchal authority. Fathers brutalize daughters and husbands brutalize wives. Women themselves engage in violence directed at other women. In some cases, women seeking revenge or engaging in self-defense commit extreme violence against men.

The concept of "domestic violence" is new in China. The official publication *Zhongguo funü* (Chinese Women) introduced the term in 1997 and began carrying a few articles on the subject. By contrast, the *Rural Women* group has been openly sympathetic to victims of domestic violence and has covered the topic in far greater detail, including the publication of firsthand accounts from the countryside. Once again the urban women complain that the law is vague and both informal and formal enforcement are erratic at best. As a consequence, victims do not know about their rights or where to turn for support. Many people believe there is nothing illegal about beating a wife or a child.

Conflict between parents and daughters over arranged marriages is a case in point. Young women are likely to see such conflict as a manifestation of a generation gap, but parents are more inclined to see resistance as a challenge to patriarchal authority. The cases that have been documented in *Rural Women* show that there are important differences between the reactions of mothers and fathers in instances of resistance to arranged marriage. According to the testimonies of victims themselves, it is usually the father who resorts to violence to enforce parental decisions. Mothers employ a softer approach that relies more on tears and persuasion. In some cases the mother herself has been a repeated victim of spousal violence, and her emotional pleas for cooperation and nonresistance are motivated by fear for the safety of her daughter.

In the case of the Sichuan primary schoolteacher, Cao Yishu, discussed briefly above, it was the threat of violence, not its actual use, that achieved the patriarch's goal. Cao's father had a long history of violent behavior, including frequent beatings of Cao's mother. When Cao was sixteen, her father beat her mother so severely he broke her arms. The mother was frequently bedridden and Cao was the person primarily responsible for her care. Unlike the father, who thought schooling for girls was a waste of time, Cao's mother had always been sympathetic toward her daughter's desire for education. The mother apologized to Cao when the mother's need for care and the family's financial difficulties prevented Cao from completing junior high.

Cao experienced her father's chilling threat to drive her out of the house as a form of violence as disturbing as "thunder on a clear day." As an elementary schoolteacher, Cao was economically self-sufficient. She had received several marriage proposals from men with nonfarming jobs. Thus Cao's decision to stop resisting was shaped more by the fear that her mother would have to go without care if Cao was driven from the home than by the prospect that she herself might be cut off from her natal family. These factors explain why it was possible for the older woman to convince the younger woman to sacrifice herself with the plea, "For your mother's sake, please agree to this marriage!"[24]

In Cao Yishu's case, practical concerns for her mother caused her to agree to her father's demands. In other cases, the issue was not so complicated. Violence was used as a means of beating back challenges to established decision-making practices. In the story of Liu Xiurong, discussed above, her father chased her boyfriend with a knife and threatened to expel both Liu and her mother from the house if Liu continued to see her boyfriend. Liu was shocked by her father's violent behavior because he had always seemed reasonable. This time he offered no explanation for his actions. Liu's mother had to tell her privately that the old man objected less to this particular boyfriend than to the challenge to his authority. Liu's elder brother and sister-in-law had worsened matters by criticizing the father for tolerating this serious challenge to his authority and to community marriage norms. They even threatened to take matters into their own hands if the patriarch failed to control Liu.[25]

In the conflict between Wang Xianxiu and her father discussed above, the issue was supposedly about the father's desire to get his daughter out of their remote mountain village by arranging a marriage. But once the father began beating Wang it became clear that the main issue was Wang's bold assertion that she had the right to decide her own future. When her father became enraged and threatened to kill both Wang and her boyfriend, Liu, she responded, "As long as I'm alive I belong to the Liu family, and I'll be a ghost in the Liu family after I die!" The old man's violent threat caused the couple to flee their beloved village after they obtained their marriage certificate.[26]

Compared with violence committed against daughters who resist arranged marriages, wife beating is a longer-term form of abuse. Accounts published in *Rural Women* suggest that men who beat their wives fall into two broad categories. One group consists of men who have always been poor and better-off men who have fallen on hard times. Given the relative shortage of potential marriage partners in many villages, these men constantly worry about losing their wives. Violence is a primary means of maintaining control of the wife, especially if she is suspected of adultery. Men in this group also beat their wives to vent their frustrations. A second, though smaller, group consists of men who have been successful economically. They batter their wives in order to get rid of them. As money, power, and sexuality have become increasingly intertwined under market socialism, these men often seek to replace the wives they married in times of hardship during the collective era with women who are more desirable by current standards.

The story told by Ping'er, a young woman from Dongkan village, Huaimao district, Gansu, is a good example of wife beating as a means of establishing male authority in arranged marriages, especially when the woman is sold to a poor man. In 1983 Ping'er's parents decided for financial reasons to marry her to a poor man hundreds of miles away. It was disheartening when Ping'er, who loved school as a youngster, discovered that her new husband, said to be a high school graduate, was actually illiterate.

Like many women sold into marriage, Ping'er believed she would not be trusted by her in-laws until she had a child. She was watched closely by her sister-in-law after the wedding. Living among strangers whose dialect she did not understand, Ping'er felt that each day was "as long as a year." On one occasion she attempted suicide by dashing in front of a car.

After recovering from her injuries, Ping'er began to feel sorry for her husband and his impoverished family. She realized that if she had died the family would have lost money and a bride. She resolved to work hard for the family, but her new attitude did not result in better treatment. When she was pregnant with her first child, she could not eat anything because of morning sickness. When she fell asleep at work one day her husband battered her, saying, "Animals eat and drink when they're about to have babies. I don't believe you can't eat or drink now that you're about to have a baby!" Ping'er was no longer suspected of wanting to run away after she gave birth to a daughter, but her husband never allowed her to touch any money. For the next seven years she was beaten by her husband whenever she tried to get him to spend money on improving their living conditions rather than on his excessive drinking and smoking. According to Ping'er, she tolerated the assaults for the sake of her daughter, but her husband understood this to mean that Ping'er was afraid of him.

In 1991 Ping'er and her daughter fled to her native village to live and work. When the Party secretary of her husband's village heard that Ping'er was gone, he told her husband to bring her back. This is one of the few cases under review in which a local official became involved in a marriage dispute. Clearly, urban women reformers suggest, the secretary was more interested in helping the husband keep his wife than in preventing Ping'er from being physically abused. Ping'er reported that her husband's behavior improved when his income increased.[27]

Wife beating is by no means limited to cases of couples involved in arranged marriages. Women are also battered within the framework of free-choice marriages. Liu Jianping, a resident of Baozicun village, Dali county, Shanxi, wrote to *Rural Women* about the collapse of her own free-choice marriage. She reported that she was attracted to a good-looking man with whom she worked in a restaurant. Liu distanced herself from her own parents and siblings because they objected to the marriage. Only after the marriage did she discover that her husband's family had a long history of domestic violence. Her father-in-law severely battered her mother-in-law whenever he suspected her of disloyalty and stood by passively when she committed suicide by swallowing poison. Liu's husband regarded his father as a virtual murderer. Liu personally witnessed numerous violent confrontations in which the two men fought with clubs and hatchets. Within a month's time the old man threw the young couple out of the house.

Liu suggested that they return to the restaurant to work, but her husband refused, accusing her of failing to support him when he had fought with his father about family property. Liu threatened to leave her husband in hopes that the threat would scare some sense into him. But her husband countered by saying, "If you try to divorce me, then the three of us will die!" Frightened for her safety, Liu put on a layer of "thick skin" and returned to her own family, whose earlier criticisms were still fresh in mind. But her husband pursued her, fought with her parents and siblings, and forced her back to his village. Liu attempted to flee several times, but on each occasion her husband dragged her back and inflicted a painful beating. Liu said that she realized her husband was angry about the death of his mother but feared that "the tragedy of the mother was about to be repeated" on her. Although Liu finally escaped, she insisted that horrible memories of terror had cast a shadow over her new life. "I worry every minute [about being found by him]," she wrote, "and often wonder whether I still have my sanity."[28]

In the cases of Ping'er and Liu Jianping, the woman's natal family was close enough to help out when violence erupted. Many women believe that it is extremely dangerous to end up with a family in a village far from one's own. Owing to travel and residential prohibitions, brides rarely moved to faraway provinces during the collective era. In post-Mao times, however, many men prefer buying a wife from a distant place because it is easier to get such women to submit to patriarchal authority.

Li Tao, a reporter from *Rural Women*, witnessed a case of this sort. In January 1997 Li traveled with Wang Dingbi, a young migrant worker residing in Beijing who was on her way to visit her sister, Wang Dingju, in Xi'an. The Wang sisters are from Xiangshui village in Liangping county, Sichuan. The reporter learned that Dingju had migrated to Xi'an in 1989 to work in a dairy factory. The following year she married a local man, Xi Fuxing, who labored as an electrician in suburban Xi'an. Dingju thought she would be happy now that she was out of rural Sichuan and living in the suburbs of a large city. A few months after the marriage, however, Xi lost his job. Xi remained unemployed and spent much of his time playing *majiang*. Since he did not farm enough land to support his dependents, the family often ran out of grain and other staples. The couple lived in one room that doubled as a kitchen and bedroom. Furnishings amounted to little more than a bed, a desk, and a cabinet, all of them in serious disrepair.

Short and thin, Xi claimed he had no energy to work but always had enough stamina to beat his wife. When he became upset, Xi used a switch, a metal rod, and even a wooden bench to thrash Dingju. Moreover, he warned Dingju that if she dared to return to Sichuan he would follow her and kill all her family members.

Wang Dingju's life was made even more unbearable by the fact that her in-laws looked down on her. Rural Chinese culture underscores the need for women who have given birth to remain in bed for a spell. But no one in her husband's family looked after Dingju. The day after she gave birth she was expected to cook for the family. She hemorrhaged and lost consciousness by the stove.

The reporter from *Rural Women* observed that there were more than twenty such female migrant workers from distant places married to men in Xi's village of Changjiawan. Local men apparently welcome this type of marriage precisely because the brides from afar have no local support networks. When Dingju's sister asked her to return to Sichuan and divorce her husband, Dingju lamented, "It's not that I never thought about divorce, but my two kids are still very young, and I can't handle leaving them behind. . . . And who's to say if life's going to be better back home?" In her native village Wang's case was frequently cited by local women as a prime example of the danger of marrying a man from a distant province.

When Xi was asked why he mistreated Dingju, he blushed and replied, "I have a bad temper." He assured the reporter that Dingju's sufferings were only temporary. Within four years he would be rich and live in a new house, he confidently predicted. "In our place," he asserted, "important matters are handled by the men. Dingju should just be content, stay at home, and take good care of the kids."[29]

If one can speak of gradations of physical abuse, the violence perpetrated on women suspected of marital infidelity often goes far beyond the levels mentioned in the Wang Dingju case. Xiao Lingxia, a resident of Tangying county, Henan, reports the story of a "fashionable" unnamed woman in her thirties who for a time lived in apparent harmony with her husband and two sons. But while her husband was out working as a migrant laborer, the woman began an affair with a "bare stick" poor man in his forties who lived near her house. She was said to be grateful because the man offered timely assistance whenever she had trouble with heavy farmwork.

The woman's in-laws heard rumors about the liaison and sent a telegram to her husband. The husband returned and promptly confirmed his own "green cap" status: he was a contemptible cuckold. After a series of savage beatings, the woman ran off with the "bare stick." This further humiliated her husband, who thrashed their thirteen-year-old son and evicted him from the house. Then he pummeled his eight-year-old son, crippling the lad in the process. Unfortunately for the runaway woman, her "bare stick" turned out to be even more violent than her husband. She left him too and remarried in another district far away from her children and her miserable past.[30] Among other things, this case points to the double standard that applies to rural men and rural women who have extra-marital affairs. Many men believe they have a right to beat an unfaithful wife.

On occasion *Rural Women* publishes letters or reports from a man on such subjects as spousal abuse. For instance, a man named Zhongqi from Zhangcun-zhen village in Lixing county, Anhui wrote to say his marriage was destroyed by his chronic wife beating. He recalled that the couple enjoyed a time of happiness when he made good money running a carpentry workshop at home. However, he was injured in a traffic accident and was unable to keep up the shop. His medical bills amounted to ¥2,000.

The marriage relationship worsened over time, and then there were rumors accusing the wife of spousal infidelity. By his own account, Zhongqi was insanely jealous and beat up his wife without giving her a chance to explain. He then forced the woman to promise to be obedient. On several occasions the woman tried to run away because, Zhongqi admitted, "my violent outbursts caused her too much pain." In 1995 she succeeded in escaping. Two years later he received a letter from her with no return address. "You shouldn't wait for me," she wrote. "I'll never live with you again."[31]

Husbands beat wives who engage in extramarital affairs, but they also resort to violence against wives during times when the husbands themselves are engag-ing in adulterous behavior. As already noted, rural men who become prosperous sometimes show off their new economic power by engaging in casual extramari-tal sexual activities, including liaisons with prostitutes. According to *Rural Women*, however, such men are not always satisfied with the sort of "secret" liai-sons that are tolerated by some rural wives. They want to replace their "yellow-faced old lady" (*huang lian po*) with a more "up-to-date" woman. It is at this stage that rural wives are likely to engage in stiff resistance. They feel that because they have shared so many hardships with their husbands and have sweated alongside them for so long to achieve financial success that they would rather die than agree to be removed from the family. Men understand only too well why rural women are reluctant to agree to a divorce. Some men reason, therefore, that the only way to get rid of an unwanted wife is to make life hell for her. It must be noted, however, that such cases are relatively rare. Most pros-perous men prefer to maintain the facade of the old marriage even as they carry on with other women.

Xiao Lingxia, the elementary schoolteacher from Tangyin county, Henan, who reported the story of the cuckold, also tells the tale of a local couple who had been married for twenty years. The man was said to be quite handsome, but the family was dirt poor. His father forced him to marry a woman who was regarded as unattractive, saying that the young man was lucky that any family was willing to give up their daughter to him. As a wife, the woman met all the customary standards of virtue: she was a filial daughter-in-law, she worked hard, and she gave birth to three sons. When her husband won a contract to run a brick kiln far from home, she farmed their land and raised the children by herself. But once her husband became prosperous, he became involved in extramarital affairs. She swallowed her pride and pretended not to know in order to save face for the family. It appears that the woman was prepared to continue living this way indefinitely as long as she was allowed to maintain the nominal status of wife.

Despite her toleration of his adultery, the husband demanded a divorce. It was rumored that her very existence in the family reminded him too much of the hard days of the past. She refused, stating flatly, "Not until I'm dead." Determined to get rid of her one way or another, the man turned to violence. As Xiao Lingxia put it, the husband served up verbal and physical abuse "like daily dishes" for his wife.[32]

Some women, brutalized by adulterous husbands, resort to murder. In 1997 a fifty-one-year-old woman named Wang who resides in Shuangyu village, Shuanggang township, Anhui, found three pieces of candy while making breakfast at home. Instead of eating it herself, she gave the candy to her five-year-old grandson, her four-year-old granddaughter, and the seven-year-old grandson of her cousin. Shortly after eating the candy, the children collapsed. They were taken to a hospital, but all three died. After a brief investigation the police apprehended a forty-five-year-old woman named Ju Youlian who admitted she was responsible for the poisoned candy.

Ju married a man named Bi in 1974. Their marriage seemed stable and they had a son and a daughter. In 1988 Bi was asked by the village leadership to come to the aid of the village Party secretary, who had cancer. His assignment was to accompany the Party secretary and his wife, the same woman mentioned above named Wang, when they went out to get medical care. Within a year, however, the Party secretary died of cancer. Bi became the village head and began an extramarital relationship with Wang, the widow of the Party secretary.

Ju Youlian sensed there was something wrong because her husband spent less and less time with her and seemed irritable whenever he was home. One day her husband told her he was going to a meeting, but she observed him sneaking into the widow's home. Her suspicions confirmed, she confronted her husband, but her teary appeals came to naught.

Worried about potential damage to his political career, the husband never asked for a divorce. Instead, he tortured Ju with escalating violence. On several occasions he beat her into unconsciousness. On cold winter nights he sometimes dragged her out of bed and locked her out in the snow. Another time Ju nearly drowned when her husband pushed her head into a nearby pond.

Ju thought about divorce but abandoned the idea when she thought about the humiliations the family would have to endure in the village. This may seem strange, but many rural women who have been married for years identify closely with their husband's family. Middle-aged daughters-in-law are not likely to leave the family on their own accord. They think of themselves as inseparable from the family and worry about its reputation.

For a time Ju worked outside the village. Before long, however, her brother-in-law persuaded her to return home. She reported her husband's behavior to the township and local security authorities in hopes of resolving the issue. An investigation was mounted, but with her husband still denying any wrongdoing, the inquiry went nowhere. Desperate, Ju went to see widow Wang. "If only he stopped beating me, I wouldn't care what you two do," she pleaded. "I'll treat you like my older sister."

Widow Wang ridiculed Ju. For her part, Ju hated Wang more and more because she felt that Wang incited her husband's abusive behavior. One day, after Wang failed to get some funds from her husband to buy fertilizer, the husband and wife had another explosive confrontation. It was at this point that Ju applied rat poison to three pieces of candy and placed them in Wang's kitchen.

The woman who reported this story, an official of the Women's Association in nearby Tongcheng, visited Ju in prison. She found it hard to believe that the frail and battered woman who sat before her had committed murder. Ju expressed sincere regret that the children were the victims of the poisoned candy. Remarkably, she had fallen to her knees and begged the local government to allow the parents of the dead children to have additional children. Ju was convicted of murder and sentenced to death. Her husband, on the other hand, was never charged with a crime but was removed as village head and expelled from the Party.[33]

## SEX CRIMES

Sex crimes against rural women are extremely hard to document. Our field research interviews shed almost no light on the subject. Readers of *Rural Women* are not at all likely to write in with information about their own experiences. Xie Lihua, the editor of *Rural Women*, publicly called on women to open up on this topic, promising that their names would not be disclosed. No one responded with a first-person account. There are secondhand accounts, however, which must be taken seriously. Some involve old patterns, the kinds of assaults that have long plagued China and every other part of the world. Other accounts suggest that some of these sexual crimes are better understood in the context of reform-era commercialization and labor migration.

Pointing to the broad dimensions of the problem, an official in the Party school located in Zhongmo county, Henan, wrote to *Rural Women* to identify fifty cases involving local women committed to a mental institution because of traumas associated with the loss of virginity. In nine cases the women had been raped. In the other forty-one cases the women had been seduced and then aban-

doned by men who failed to follow through with marriage plans. Sixty-eight percent of the victims were between the ages of sixteen and eighteen.

Researchers were startled to discover that many of these women had been vic-
timized by men to whom they were formally engaged. In almost every case the
engagement had been arranged by parents. The women themselves hardly knew
the men. In many parts of rural China, however, a woman is regarded as "belonging" to her fiancé once the arrangement has been finalized. Moreover, when she
is alone with the man she is very likely to be forced to satisfy his sexual desires,
even if she is not a consenting partner. Frightened young women are often
unwilling to report these sexual assaults. Victims feel a deep sense of shame.
Older women pressure younger women to say nothing out of concern for the
reputation of their family. In other words, those who make public accusations
run the risk of staining their own reputations. Victims of such sexual crimes are
also told to keep quiet because they are far more likely to be mistreated or even
persecuted by in-laws after the marriage if complaints are aired before the marriage. According to investigators, many women who remain silent about sexual
assaults eventually show symptoms of mental illness.[34]

Fang Wenzhong, a man currently residing in Zhongxiang, Hubei, wrote about
a rape that occurred in his own village, one that had nothing to do with an
arrangement in progress. This story is an excellent example of the reluctance of
rural women to report sexual crimes. The victim was a young woman named Liu,
a high school graduate who had tailoring skills. According to Fang, the young
woman was regarded as good-looking and many young men from surrounding
villages dreamed of marrying her.

One of Liu's frustrated suitors was a local hoodlum known as Li Er. One day,
when Liu was walking home alone, she was raped by Li Er. Distraught, Liu
reportedly gave some consideration to reporting the crime. But, fearing irrepara-
ble damage to her reputation, she remained silent. Once Li Er determined that
Liu was not going to say anything, he engaged in frequent stalking and harassment. Each time Liu resisted his advances, Li Er threatened to spread rumors
about their relationship. In order to discourage Li Er, Liu soon agreed to marry
a man from a nearby village. On the wedding day, however, Li Er demanded to
be included in the group selected to accompany Liu to her fiancé's home and
then hid out in the couple's bedroom. When Liu's husband was absent from the
room due to his participation in customary ritual activities later that night, Li
Er tried once again to rape Liu. This time Li was apprehended by the police.[35]

A newer type of sexual crime targets women who remain behind when their
husbands go out to do migrant labor. In 1996, at a training session run by *Rural
Women* for new reporters, a woman named Rao Meiqin from Jiangxi called attention to the epidemic of sexual harassment activities directed at "women who stay
behind" in the rural sector.[36] A typical secondhand account of this phenomenon
was offered by Sun Jinli of Yichuan county in Henan. The case involved a man

named Wang Guangda, a serial rapist who had a chronic scalp fungal infection that earned him the nickname Loathsome Wang (Wang Laizi).

Wang was brawny and was often hired by village women to help with farmwork when their husbands were away toiling as migrant laborers. One day Loathsome worked late into the day for a "woman who stayed behind" named Li. Out of politeness, the woman invited Loathsome to stay for dinner. After a few glasses of a local brew, however, Loathsome raped the woman. Apparently Li said nothing about the incident, so Loathsome became more daring and raped several other women in the village. His crimes were detected in 1996, when one of his victims was institutionalized for treatment of mental health problems.[37]

The great majority of rural victims of sexual assault suffer in silence rather than expose themselves to public ridicule. Some, however, have made an attempt to report these crimes. The difficulties they have encountered make it clear why most victims remain silent. Xie Lihua, the editor of *Rural Women*, tells the story of a woman who appeared in rags at her door in 1995. "I'm desperate, please help me!" the woman said as she produced a pile of documents.

Four years earlier the woman had been raped when her husband was not at home. The perpetrator was a man from the same village who got into the house by crawling through a window late one night. The woman reported the attack, but the man completely denied the accusation. The case instantly became a lively topic of conversation in the village. Many people said that Li was probably having an adulterous affair with the man. Thus, in this notorious case the rapist went unpunished, while the victim was subjected to repeated ridicule. Charged with making false accusations against the man, the woman was fined and detained for a time. Unable to endure these humiliations, the woman left home to become a "professional petitioner" *(shangfang zhuanye hu)*. She went to the official *Chinese Women's News* (Zhongguo funü bao) for help, but she told Xie she could not get anyone there to show an interest in the case.

Xie read the documents and asked the woman whether she had any hard evidence concerning the rape. All she had was a letter from her husband testifying that the local police had indeed come to the house to investigate. The woman insisted that she could win the case if Xie Lihua helped her. The fact was that the legal system would never recognize the woman as a victim if she could not bring forward convincing evidence. Xie consulted with a lawyer who confirmed that the case was hopeless.[38]

The editors of *Rural Women* consistently urge people who have been forced into marriages or abused by their spouses to take legal action. In cases involving sexual crimes, however, it is especially difficult for rural women to turn to the courts. It is hardly surprising, therefore, to learn that victims of sex crimes sometimes take the law into their own hands. A legal reporter based in Yangcheng, Jiangsu wrote to tell the story of Ji Renqin, a twenty-eight-year-old who lived in Zhonggang village outside Yangcheng. It seems that Ji and her husband, twenty-eight-year-old Xiao Darao, were admired, even envied, by many. Xiao was strong and diligent. Ji was gentle and said to be exceptionally beautiful. They also had a five-year-old son.

In winter 1996 Xiao left home to join a new wave of migrant workers. In his absence, Ji became the prey of forty-eight-year-old Tao Budao, a local tough who lived across from the couple's house. Nicknamed "the Rogue," Tao limped around on a bad leg. But he had once been a powerful figure in the village. Thus he and the band of hoodlums he controlled were well treated by village officials.

One day Tao entered Ji's home and proclaimed that he would be her companion while her husband was away. Ji cursed Tao and firmly rebuffed his advances. But Tao did not give up and continued to harass the young woman. Ji told Tao's wife about his behavior in hopes that she would intervene. But Tao's wife was terrified of her husband and did not ask him about Ji, who then went to the head of the Xiao lineage to ask for help.

Nothing worked and Tao continued to pursue Ji. "Watch out for your house and your kid if you refuse to be with me," he threatened. "If I give a wave of my hand, my toughs will come over to beat you and throw your kid into the river." "Nobody dares to bring charges against me and nobody dares to say bad things about me," Tao continued. "Even if you manage to get me convicted, I'm not afraid. I have a certificate of disability and can request to be let out on bail for medical treatment."

One night Tao raped Ji in her home. And he continued to rape her whenever he had the urge. According to the reporter, Ji did not have the strength to resist. Furthermore, Tao set down rules that would guarantee his long-term domination of Ji. "When Darao is not home, you can only be with me; you're forbidden to be with any other men," he said. "You can't refuse me when I come over." Tao even installed a new window in his house so he could kept a close eye on Ji.

Terrorized night and day, Ji wrote to her husband, who was working in Hefei. "Bad things have happened since you left," she said. "Tao Budao has harassed me so much that I can't stay at home any longer. Please come back and save me." At 2 A.M. on the morning of 2 January 1997 Xiao arrived at his house. Ji immediately told him what had happened and the two broke into tears. Tao happened to wake up at that time and noticed that the lights were on in Ji's house. He suspected that Ji was with another man and went over to see. "Open up! I heard a man in your house!" Tao bellowed. With Xiao by her side, she no longer feared Tao. Hoping to punish Tao, she told Xiao to hide behind the door. Tao barged in and began hurling obscenities at Ji as he searched the premises. Enraged, Ji grabbed a steel bar and struck Tao on the head. Once she started smashing Tao's head, she could not stop.

Xiao tried to wrestle the bar away from Ji, but Tao had already collapsed in a pool of blood. Full of rage, Ji stripped off Tao's pants, grabbed a hatchet and chopped off his penis. "Why did you do such evil things?" she screamed. It was only when Xiao, watching in horror, said, "You've made a big mistake!" that Ji realized she had killed Tao. She begged her husband to help her dispose of the corpse. They placed the body in a sack and threw it into the river. But the homicide was soon discovered and Ji was sentenced to life in prison for intentional manslaughter. Her husband, convicted of assisting in the manslaughter, was sentenced to two years.[39]

As hard as it is for rural women to come forward in such cases, they experience even more difficulty when it comes to marital rape. Only under unusual circumstances do details about this phenomenon surface. Sun Jinli, a resident of Yichuan county, Henan, wrote to *Rural Women* about a case that sent shock waves through the mountainous region of western Henan. Sun wrote, "I couldn't believe that a village woman who looked so timid and kind was capable of raising a hatchet to kill the husband with whom she shared bed and pillow for the last fifteen years."

According to Sun, the woman involved in this case was named Liu. She had been married to a man named Xie since 1982. In her confession to the police Liu said, "One can say that he was a good man. He was honest and worked diligently by day. He didn't fool around, gamble, smoke, or drink. Everyone in the village admired me because I was married to such a good man."

But, Liu continued, "he was like an inhuman monster at night. He forced me to have sex whenever he wanted it. If I was unwilling to do it, he bit me on the face and beat me. He didn't even give me a break when I had my period."

Liu was ashamed to tell anyone about the torture she endured. One day her younger sister discovered the bruises on her body and asked her what had happened. Liu smiled sadly and said, "You won't understand even if I tell you. It's too hard being a woman." When their daughter died suddenly in 1985, Liu was depressed and regarded Xie's sexual assaults with more disgust than ever. Still, Liu gave birth to son the following year.

Xie never considered whether Liu was willing to have sex with him and continued to force himself on her. Eventually Liu began to fight him off. When their neighbors complained about the noise at night, Liu was forced to stifle her desperate cries.

Two years later her son died. Liu's depression deepened. She became irritable and anemic, and she suffered frequent nightmares. Her hatred of her husband increased each time he forced her to have sex. "It was as if I was being taken by the devil," she said later.

One day in summer 1996 Liu worked all day in the fields and then returned home to cook, wash dishes, and feed the pigs. She was exhausted when she finally went to bed. But Xie wanted to have sex. As usual, Liu lay on the bed numb, allowing him to have his way. Two hours later Xie wanted more sex and again Liu submitted in hopes of being able to get some sleep afterward. But just as she fell asleep, Xie woke her up yet again. This time she lashed out frantically at him, hitting him, biting him, and pushing him off her body. "You beast, are you going to let me live?" she wailed. Xie was furious and responded by beating his wife. "You're my wife, so I can do whatever I want to you! I still want to have a son!" Xie screamed. In a rage, Liu pulled out a hatchet from under the bed and swung it at Xie in the darkness of the night, killing her husband. Shocked by her own actions, Liu turned herself in. She told the police she was very confused and regretted what she had done.[40]

Xie Lihua's decision to publish this particular account sheds light on the political and legislative agendas of *Rural Women*. In cases involving forced marriage, flagrant physical abuse, rape, and murder, *Rural China* is not lobbying for new legislation. It is asking for the enforcement of existing laws, even when they conflict with customary practices. In the case of marital rape, however, the group is raising a new legal question. A year after *Rural Women* published the details of the case mentioned above, the official journal *Chinese Women* (Zhongguo funü) responded, conceding that the current marriage law is vague and that it is difficult for a woman to legally rebuff her husband's demands for sex. In fact, the law indicates that marriage partners are obliged to consent to intercourse unless there is evidence of health problems. According to the author, 85 percent of husbands do not believe their wives have the right to reject demands for sex, while 90 percent of women are unaware that they may have rights in such matters. The author, a respected legal expert, agreed that the marriage law needed to be revised to provide women with more protections in this area. "There are very few legal cases that have dealt with the issue of rape within marriage," the author concluded, "but the number of such rapes cannot be small."[41]

## ANCIENT LEGACIES AND NEW AGE COMMERCIALIZATION

The unusual personal narratives discussed in this chapter show that rural women in contemporary China worry a great deal about marital tensions, coercion, and domestic violence. It is by no means the case, however, that all rural women experience the sort of terrors described in *Rural Women*. There is no way to show that even a majority of rural women have had personal encounters with such traumas. The cases discussed here may be the exception rather than the rule. Still, it is difficult to deny that there is a major problem or to doubt that victims and nonvictims alike spend time thinking about these disturbing issues.

Given the lack of similar late imperial, republican, and Mao-era sources, it is hard to say with confidence that domestic violence, female suicides, sexual harassment, and sexual crimes are more common in the post-Mao era than in the past. There is every reason to believe that problems of this sort abounded in the past, but we reject the notion that the difficulties of today are nothing more than the perpetuation of age-old patterns that were identified and criticized in the late nineteenth and early twentieth centuries. Neither do we believe that the violence of today is entirely new, a clear by-product of decollectivization and market reforms. The gripping testimonies of rural women themselves indicate that the problems of today involve a complex combination of the old and the new. It is clear, for example, the old practices—including forced marriage arrangements and domestic violence—denounced so passionately by May Fourth liberals and Maoist revolutionaries alike, were never eradicated. With the retreat of the state in some areas of rural life in the post-Mao period, and with the advent of relative political liberalization and the information revolution, these customary practices have become highly visible. At the same time, the rise of market socialism and the commercialization of rural society allowed old practices to take on new forms and allowed entirely new patterns of discrimination and gender inequality to surface.

The women who write to *Rural Women* seem to be saying that rural families were happy to rush out of the crippling collectives. In the Chinese case, however, the postcollective division of labor left women in the villages tending to farmwork, children, and the elderly. Rural men went out on the road into the brave new world of individual moneymaking. Commercial activity sometimes included marketing one's own daughter to generate cash. Some men who were successful making money initiated extramarital relationships, ignoring and even abandoning their collective-era spouses and families. Some successful men were not inclined to share much of their new prosperity with collective-era wives, preferring, instead, to start a new life and to enjoy new modes of consumption outside the old village environment.

The testimonies in *Rural Women* indicate that many women accept their tragic plight because of custom or because they have no realistic alternative. But increasing numbers of rural women have become aware of their rights, and they resist patterns of victimization associated with both the cultural legacies of the past and the commercial reforms of the present. A minority of those who protest win justice. Many others who speak out are subjected to beatings and other forms of abuse. Some are killed, some become killers themselves, and thousands of others are driven to suicide. "Women who stay behind" compose an entirely new category of somewhat older women who are sexually harassed by village men. Women are even sexually assaulted by their own husbands.

Village government and Party organizations have been cut back in the reform era. This has been good for the rural economy, but, it appears, not so good for rural women. With the market reforms that show new respect for the private sector, the new village leadership has not been inclined to intervene in "private" family matters. In any case, women, like many others in rural society who had experienced decades of unwelcome Party-state domination, remain suspicious of village power wielders, most of whom are males, and are reluctant to call on the local authorities to step in. Furthermore, the residual hold of Confucian norms prevents women from protesting in ways that might damage their own reputation or the standing of their husbands' families in the small village setting. To make matters worse, the fostering of independent local judicial systems, never a goal during the Mao era, remains a low priority today.

Rural Women understands the issues that confront village women. Xie Lihua and the other urban crusaders embrace and endorse the economic reform agenda, including commercialization and globalization, but they know that fruits of the economic miracle have not been distributed equally within family units. They see that the outrages of today involve a combination of customary and new practices. They recognize that the disruptions which have destabilized rural families since decollectivization will continue to pose serious problems for rural women, especially middle-aged and older women, for many years to come. They show that economic progress has not resulted in greater gender equality. Indeed, in some areas of family life the result has been greater gender inequality. Far from liberating rural women, the reforms have created new conditions that tend at once to perpetuate and transform earlier forms of patriarchal domination. Far from empowering rural women, the commercialization of the rural economy has resulted in the commodification of women, especially younger women. There may be a shortage of marriage-age women in rural China, but commodification means they are likely to be treated as property, not as newly independent social actors.

Rather than wait for the Party-state to address these issues, Rural Women has assumed an advocate's role. Its leaders seek to do much more than publicize the plight of rural women; they want to bring about two types of change. They are committed to mobilizing rural women (a role that sometimes causes them to preach down to rural women) and to forcing the state to make significant changes in the realms of law enforcement and legislation.

More than anything else, the magazine's message to rural women is that they must become more aware of their legal rights. The editors firmly believe that the letters and reports written by rural women make a difference. Urban women are shrewd practitioners of the politics of the new information revolution. Public awareness is beginning to increase, and the consciousness of a segment of rural women is starting to rise. Xie Lihua, the chief editor of Rural Women, claims that low self-esteem prevents women who are isolated in village homes from understanding and demanding their rights in the highly underdeveloped, but evolving, rural legal system.[47] She argues that the economic reforms have contributed to new forms of gender inequality and strengthened the rural patriarchy in a variety of unanticipated ways.

But there are ambiguities in the relationship between Rural Women and its audience. In some very important ways the urban women are in tune with the hopes and fears of rural women on issues like forced marriage, economic rights, and rape. In other respects, however, the urban women seek not just to reflect the agenda of the rural women themselves, but to set new agendas that are unfamiliar to most rural women. This includes the relatively new issues of sexual harassment, domestic violence, and sexual rights within the framework of marriage.

Xie's point is repeated time and again. She tells rural daughters that they can and should exercise the right to resist arranged marriages, economic injustices, and physical abuse. She tells rural wives that there is no acceptable alternative to going public and thus turning to the police and the courts when men refuse to share family resources, commit bigamy, and engage in domestic violence, including sexual assault. She tells women that they have a right to a fair divorce settlement if the sorts of problems mentioned here cannot be resolved. But the letters and reports written by rural women who have decided to step forward and speak for themselves demonstrate another, more sobering, reality: it is much eas-ier for well-intentioned urban intellectuals to advocate these courses of action than it is for rural women to pursue them.

## NOTES

The authors would like to thank Li Huai for her help in conducting interviews with rural women in summer 1995.

1. The names of villagers have been changed.

2. The first person to make this suggestion was Richard Madsen, and we thank him for his guidance.

3. The paragraph draws on information contained in a pamphlet entitled *Nongjia nü bai shi tong* (Beijing: n.d.).

4. See Gao Xiaoxian, "Nongcun funü yanjiu zongshu," *Funü yanjiu* 4 (1997): 59–64.

5. See Wang Jinling, "Fei nong hua yu nongcun funü jiating diwei bianqian de xing-bie kaocha," *Funü yanjiu* 2 (1997): 58–63; Jin Yihong, "Fei nong hua guocheng zhong de nongcun funü," *Shehuixue yanjiu* 5 (1998): 106–14.

6. Song Meiya, "Nongcun liu shou nü de mingyun," *Zhongguo funü* 7 (1998): 9.

7. This chapter does not deal with the black market in women because, until quite recently, *Rural Women* did not tackle the issue in a detailed way. See Elisabeth Rosenthal, "Harsh Chinese Reality Feeds a Black Market in Women," *New York Times*, 25 June 2001, A1.

8. Zhang Zhenlan, "Dinghun nei nian," *Nongjia nü bai shi tong* 9 (1996): 35. Hereafter this magazine will be referred to as *NJN*.

9. Liu Mei, "Xiaosan," *NJN* 12 (1996): 24.

10. Zhou Hongyun, "Honger, hai hao ma?" *NJN* 3 (1997): 50.

11. This information is based on interviews conducted in rural Jiangsu in 1995–1996. The names of villagers have been changed.

12. Pei Chunsu, "Zi li, shi women baituo hunjia zhong de kun huo," *NJN* 10 (1996): 26; Yan Cailing, "Mo rang beiju chong yan," *NJN* 10 (1996): 27.

13. Cao Yishu, "Nühai zhen di ren yi deng ma?" *NJN* 8 (1997): 23–26.

14. Shang Jianling, "Wo ying zenyang xuanze?" *NJN* 4 (1997): 39.

15. Liu Xiurong, "He ta xiang ai de rizi," *NJN* 7 (1997): 30–31.

16. Li Ping, "Xiuzi, ni zou xiang he fang?" *NJN* 3 (1997): 22–23.

17. Xu Jidong, " 'Si ben' fangfa bu ke qu," *NJN* 6 (1997): 53.

18. Lin Meihua, "Wo zhangfu zhe zhong qingkuang suan chonghun ma?" *NJN* 12 (1995): 36.

19. Sun Jinli, "Nongcun 'liu shou nü,' " *NJN* 9 (1997): 25–26.

20. Chen Jianping, " 'Nitan' zhong de dajie," *NJN* 8 (1997): 29.

21. Wang Lixia, "Ni zai shi shang huozhe, jing bu zhi wei ge sha," *NJN* 11 (1996): 39–40.

22. Wang Lixia, "Ni zai shi shang huozhe," 40.

23. Zheng Zhou, "Zhangfu fa ji zhi hou," *NJN* 8 (1997): 40–43.

24. Cao Yishu, "Nuhai zhen di ren," 23–26.

25. Liu Xiurong, "He ta xiang ai de rizi," 30–31.

26. Li Ping, "Xiuzi, ni zou xiang he fang?" 22–23.

27. Ping'er, "Zao chun de xue di," *NJN* 9 (1997): 21–22.

28. Liu Jianping, "Ai mu xu rong jie ku guo," *NJN* 5 (1997): 32–33.

29. Li Tao, "Hui jia," *NJN* 4 (1997): 7–8.

30. Xiao Lingxia, "Liangge nüren de gushi," *NJN* 7 (1997): 26–27.

31. Zhongqi, "Bei huan li he cong tou shuo," *NJN* 6 (1997): 43.

32. Xiao Lingxia, "Liangge nüren de gushi," 25.

33. "Yi chang bu gai fasheng de beiju," *NJN* 4 (1997): 54–55.

34. Guo Wubei, "Nongcun guniang fang shi shen," *NJN* 3 (1997): 56–57.

35. Fang Wenzhong, "Ruo nü qiqiu bao ming sheng qi liao xin hun zai zao ru," *NJN* 3 (1997): 62.

36. Guo Wubei, "Nongcun guniang fang shi shen," 57.

37. Sun Jinli, "Nongcun 'liu shou nü,' " 26.

38. Xie Lihua, "Rang falu gei ni yi ge hu shen fu," *NJN* 12 (1995): 4–5.

39. Song Changqin, "Yi ge shao fu de beiju," *NJN* 8 (1997): 50–52.

40. Sun Jinli, "Gushi zhi er," *NJN* 5 (1997): 52–53.

41. Gao Yaobing, "Funü hun nei xing chuanli xuyao falü baohu," *Zhongguo funü* 8 (1998): 50.

42. Elisabeth Rosenthal, "Women's Suicides Reveal Rural China's Bitter Roots," *New York Times*, 24 January 1999, A12.

# 4

## Shunkouliu: Popular Satirical Sayings and Popular Thought

*Perry Link and Kate Zhou*

With the possible exception of Chinese Central Television and Radio, no medium in China in the 1990s was as widespread as the oral network that carries the rhythmical satirical sayings known as *shunkouliu* (slippery jingles) or *minyao* (folk rhymes).[1] Western observers of China generally ignore these sayings, and Chinese scholars tend to discount them as marginal or lightweight material. But this is unfortunate because they reflect genuine popular ideas, values, and attitudes with extraordinary vividness. And unlike Central Television, they are utterly uncensored. Mild examples are published in official media in China. The government bans harder-hitting examples but at the same time collects them and circulates them in classified reports designed to let officials know what the people are really thinking.[2] *Shunkouliu* thus resemble what James Scott has called "hidden transcripts" of popular thought and sentiment.[3] Although officially hidden, they are very easy to discover through informal oral contact.[4] They also have been published uncensored in books and magazines outside the People's Republic.[5]

### DEVELOPMENT BEFORE AND DURING THE COMMUNIST PERIOD

The range of the terms *shunkouliu* and *minyao* overlap with a number of others: *yanyu* (proverbs), *suyu* (vulgarisms), *liyu* (slang), *chengyu* (set phrases), *yeyu* (wild language), and *duilian* (rhymed couplets). In each of these, essential truths about life are distilled into a pithy form that involves rhythm as well, sometimes as rhyme and/or parallelism. These formal features are important not only for esthetic reasons but because they facilitate memorization, which in turn has been important to the spread of sayings within illiterate populations or, in the modern world, literate societies that live under repression.

In the early part of the twentieth century, *minyao* and *shunkouliu* centered on a few topics that were closely related to the life of China's farmers, who invented them. The following five topics were common:

1. The weather, naturally a perennial concern to farmers:

> When the sky is red at the end of the day,
> Wind if not rain will be on the way.[6]

The frigid weather of north China produced the following example:

> Until you see a Duanwu\* boat,
> Don't give anyone your winter coat.

2. The rewards of hard work:

> If you put in your due, the earth will too.

3. The distinctive features of local geography or manmade products. A well-known example is:

> The scenery of Guilin beats any in the world.

For Northeast China we have:

> Three precious things lie east of the pass:
> Ginseng, mink fur, and *wula* grass.†

4. Commentary on human relations:

> When poor, you can walk in a crowd and never be seen;
> When rich, you can hide in the woods and be obvious to all.

Commentary on human relations could take the form of watchwords to help a person through the jungle of life:

---

\*A festival in May that features boat races.
†Used for keeping the feet warm.

The will to hurt people you must not have.
The will to defend yourself you must not lack.

5. Political satire. A well-known example from the Qing period during its decline complains about endemic corruption:

One term as a Qing official,
One hundred thousand lumps of silver.‡

Satiric *shunkouliu* appeared in the People's Republic as early as the Great Leap Forward in the late 1950s, and more examples appeared during the Cultural Revolution years of 1966–1976. The cataclysmic events of the Mao era produced widespread popular dissatisfaction, but through the same years repression was sufficiently strong, and penalties sufficiently severe, that a public or even semi-public *shunkouliu* subculture could not develop. Passing *shunkouliu* from person to person could be done only in tightly guarded contexts. By contrast, the relative openness of the reform era of the 1980s and 1990s produced conditions for the spread of satiric *shunkouliu* that were almost ideal: dissatisfaction with corruption and other social ills remained high while repression of daily life speech gradually relaxed. People everywhere began inventing *shunkouliu* as a way of illustrating what bothered them. Exchange typically occurred in relaxed social contexts—often over meals—in atmospheres that were jocular even though the complaints that *shunkouliu* expressed were genuine and sometimes strongly felt. A person was admired who commanded a large repertoire of *shunkouliu* and could apply them fittingly to daily life situations or weave them into jokes or stories.

Most of the examples of *shunkouliu* in this chapter are political or social satire, reflecting the nature of the material, not a choice of the authors. The overwhelming majority of contemporary *shunkouliu* are of this kind.[7] The humor in *shunkouliu* not only served to lighten people's spirits but could, in addition, have a certain protective effect because the sting of a criticism (and therefore the risk to the criticizer as well) was lessened by its presentation in joke form. Another and more important protection built into *shunkouliu* came from the fact that their oral transmission was not traceable. They left no written evidence of offense, and no sign of an author. Like jokes and proverbs in other societies, *shunkouliu* only rarely could be traced to a specific creator.

The tide of *shunkouliu* in the 1980s and 1990s originated in the countryside and spread to the cities. It reached all social groups, including intellectuals and officials. In these decades *shunkouliu* also achieved a new ability to spread rapidly nationwide. Well-known examples could be heard from Harbin to Hainan Island. In earlier times, except for well-established clichés, all *shunkouliu* were

‡All the *shunkouliu* translated for this essay can be found in their original Chinese in the glossary at the end of the book.

local *shunkouliu*. One cannot attribute this new pervasiveness to radio, television, or newspapers because the official media did not carry satiric *shunkouliu*. The spread was still primarily oral, and the added efficiency of the oral network seems to have come from increased use of telephone as well as increased mobility of the population (mobility rose sharply in the 1990s as residence permit requirements were widely ignored). For a privileged elite, e-mail also played a role.

There is another, more subtle reason why some satiric *shunkouliu* have elicited a prompt nationwide response: official propaganda, without meaning to, has paved the way for them. Especially in the Mao years, the reach of the central media was so exhaustive, and its content so unitary, that virtually everyone everywhere absorbed certain phrases and sentences word for word. A satiric *shunkouliu* that played on the same words therefore had the potential to resonate in every corner of China. For example, a line of Mao Zedong's poetry that was included in a nationally disseminated song during the Cultural Revolution reads:

One million male lions cross the mighty Yangzi.

Here "male lions" is a metaphor for fearless soldiers. The Red Army is crossing the Yangzi River to attack Chiang Kai-shek's troops at Nanjing in the late 1940s, and the point of the song is to show how the forces of socialism are overthrowing capitalism. In the early 1980s, when free agricultural markets ("capitalism" in another guise) gained political favor, Subei farmers responded by carrying chickens, ducks, and other fowl across the same Yangzi River for shipment by rail to Nanjing, Shanghai, Ningbo, and other urban centers in the Yangzi basin. The sharp irony of a situation in which the Yangzi is crossed first to oppose capitalism and then to practice it is the kind of thing that stimulates satiric *shunkouliu*, and this one eventually appeared:

One million roosters head down to Shanghai.

Although the poultry markets of the lower Yangzi were a local concern, this *shunkouliu* spread quickly to all of China, appearing even in newspapers and journalism textbooks. The Cultural Revolution song based on Mao's poem had paved the way for it.

Just as some *shunkouliu* play off phrases from the Mao period, others play off set phrases from earlier times. The phrase "repairing the east wall with bricks from the west wall," for example, has long been used to mean roughly the same as "robbing Peter to pay Paul." In the 1980s and 1990s, the same phrase has been used to satirize "reform" that does not really change anything.

In our analyses that follow, we assume that *shunkouliu* broadly reflect popular attitudes about public issues of the 1990s. Some of the concerns (e.g., about corruption) seem perennial, while others (e.g., inflation in the later 1980s) rise and fall abruptly. In most cases *shunkouliu* mirror popular concerns that are independently observable elsewhere, for example, in opinion surveys, wall posters, cartoons, jokes, and gossip from the oral network of "alleyway news" (*xiaodao xiaoxi*). But it is a mistake to expect *shunkouliu* to sketch a popular worldview that is perfectly consistent. "Folk wisdom" can be eloquent on both horns of a dilemma, as anyone who reflects on the English proverbs "Look before you leap" and "He who hesitates is lost" can easily see. Moreover, some *shunkouliu* tend to be popular only among certain social groups—farmers, workers, intellectuals, or officials, for example. Since the values and interests of these groups can diverge, so can the messages of their preferred *shunkouliu*.

## FORMAL FEATURES OF *SHUNKOULIU*

As our translations suggest, *shunkouliu* often involve rhyme. But not always. The only indispensable formal feature seems to be rhythm, and certain rhythms predominate. All of the examples quoted so far, for example, fall into patterns of either five syllables per line with a rhythm of 1-2, 1-2-3 or seven syllables per line with a rhythm of 1-2, 1-2, 1-2-3. Scholars of Chinese poetry will immediately recognize these patterns as belonging to the "regulated verse" (*lüshi*) that originated in the fifth century A.D. and flourished in the Tang period. But for centuries the same patterns have appeared not only in elite poetry but in folk songs and daily life sayings of many kinds. It is ironic that Mao Zedong sought to "tear down the four olds" (old ideas, old culture, old customs, and old habits), but he received throngs of Red Guards at Tiananmen and listened to them chant, "Women yao jian Mao Zhuxi!" (We want to see Chairman Mao!) in perfect 1-2, 1-2, 1-2-3 rhythm. Similarly today, when you cross a street in Beijing, a sign warns you to "first look, second go slowly, and third cross over" (*yi kan, er man, san tong guo*)—again a 1-2, 1-2, 1-2-3 pattern. The rhythm is everywhere. Basketball cheerleaders at Nankai University (and probably elsewhere) chant "jia you! jia you! duo yong li!" (literally "add fuel, add fuel, use more strength").

These five- and seven-syllable rhythms are so deeply ingrained in Chinese oral culture that most people who use them are not consciously aware of them, just sensing that they "feel right." We can be sure that this was the case for the Red Guards who chanted ancient rhythms to Mao at Tiananmen. Mao no doubt shared in the unexamined satisfaction. Even though (or maybe precisely because) the rhythms are taken for granted, we need to ask what import they have. As noted above, one function of rhyme and rhythm in *shunkouliu* is to make them more memorizable.[8] But there is more to it than that; rhythm can also affect the power of what is said. When a rhythmic phrase feels "right," it somehow seems more true, rather as if nature itself concurs in the thought expressed. Imagine, for example, the effect if Red Guards at Tiananmen had shouted an unrhythmical "Women lai kan weida de duoshou!" (We're here to see the Great Helmsman!). Their basic message would have been the same, and their reference to Mao just as laudatory, but without the "right" rhythm their demand would have seemed not only awkward but much less exalted.

This "exaltation effect," if we may call it that, increases when rhythmic lines are grammatically parallel. (Here too there is an obvious similarity to *lüshi*.) The *shunkouliu* that we have translated above as "The will to hurt people you must not have; the will to defend yourself you must not lack" (*hai ren zhi xin bu ke you, fang ren zhi xin bu ke wu*) exhibits this parallelism. It also shows (in yet another similarity to traditional verse) how corresponding syllables in parallel lines are sometimes semantically antithetical. *Hai* (harm), which begins the first line, is grammatically parallel to but semantically opposed to *fang* (defend), which begins the second line; similarly *you* (have) at the end of line 1 matches grammatically but inverts semantically *wu* (not have) at the end of line 2. Among elite poets such features can sometimes seem mere wordplay, but in popular forms like *shunkouliu*, their function is to create an aura of dignity and credibility about what is expressed. This effect is not limited to Chinese culture.[9] John Kennedy's inaugural address, to take but one example, made liberal use of grammatical parallelism and semantic inversion: "United there is little we cannot do, divided there is little we can do"; if a free society "cannot help the many who are poor, it cannot save the few who are rich"; and so on. For millions of American listeners, these features enhanced the dignity and credibility of Kennedy's message in a form quite similar to *shunkouliu*. Rhyme, rhythm, parallelism, and antitheticality all conspire to give *shunkouliu* the sense of "this is the real truth; I kid you not." The sense can be so strong as to say "it's written in nature." And this fact, in turn, is important for our study of the content of *shunkouliu*. Their artistic features underscore their claims to truth and importance.

In some *shunkouliu*, terseness of expression can convey the impression not only that "this is the truth" but "this is the highly distilled essence of truth." For example, a popular analysis of the structure of corruption—that you can buy an official's power by inviting him to dinner, that it is even better to have a durable personal connection with him that operates with or without such banqueting, and that the route to building this kind of durable connection is to arrange sex for him—is captured in eighteen syllables (three parallel lines, six syllables each) as

Zhangzi buru kuaizi, kuaizi buru mianzi, mianzi buru bianzi. (Chopsticks outweigh a chop, face outweighs chopsticks, pigtails outweigh face.)

Metonymy (as in terms like "chopsticks," "chop," and "pigtails" that stand for much more complex ideas) helps achieve the terseness that characterizes these examples.

A particular form of Chinese verbal parallelism popularly known as *duilian* (corresponding couplets) are composed of two lines of equal length, written vertically, and often a shorter "crosspiece," written horizontally and summing up the meaning of the two vertical lines. At New Year, Chinese families like to paste the vertical lines at the two sides of their doorways, and the crosspiece above it. New Year *duilian* normally bear auspicious messages about bounty in the coming year. But in the hands of *shunkouliu* artists, the form becomes satirical. For example, after inefficient government-run grain procurement stations mishandled farmers' harvests, allowing good grain to rot, this *duilian* appeared:

Store the good, sell the spoiled;
Sell the rotten, rot the good.
    crosspiece: out with the old, in with the new.

The saying in the crosspiece is ironic because normally it expresses a positive idea: get rid of old ways and bring in fresh ideas. Here, therefore, the crosspiece highlights the hypocrisy of officials who hide behind masks of progressivism while actually presiding over rot.

Several other formal features of *shunkouliu* are worth noting. In political *shunkouliu* irony is extremely common, as several examples both above and below illustrate. Punning is also common, not only for its humorous effect but as a way of referring to sensitive matters indirectly. A *shunkouliu* from Hubei in the early 1990s, for example, complained about the rapid growth of government corruption and commercial fraud, especially the marketing of phony commodities. By chance the provincial governor Jia Zhijie had the surname "Jia," a homonym for "fake," while the provincial Party secretary Guan Guanfu's surname "Guan" was a homonym for "official." The stage was thus set for:

Phony wine, phony medicine, and Governor "Phony";
Official commerce, official corruption, and a Party Secretary for the "officials."

Simile often appears in *shunkouliu* to describe kinds of people and their social behavior. The following example, which originated among farmers in the 1980s, likens local officials to various kinds of animals, who

Ioot their own horns like braying asses,
Fawn to superiors like Pekingese dogs,
Roar at underlings like wild tigers,
Devour public banquets like hungry wolves,
Snatch small advantages with the quickness of a rabbit,
Perform their duties in the manner of a monkey,
Face difficulties with the courage of an earthworm.

A discussion of the formal features of *shunkouliu* also needs to account for their mutability, which is a result of fluidity in their creation and transmission. Their anonymous authors are sometimes a single person and sometimes several, who might toss an example back and forth, improving it as they go. Once "finished" it is of course never finished, as every person who picks it up and repeats it is free to alter it, embellish it, or weave it into conversations, stories, or jokes. It is impossible to catalogue all the ways in which this happens, but we offer below just one example, an extended joke in which several *shunkouliu* appear[10]:

Some officials in a county government were drinking together when one of them proposed a contest. Each, in turn, would have to describe his work in a *shunkouliu* that used the terms "sharp," "round," "thousands," and "millions" in that order. Then he would have to submit to questioning by the others. If the others were satisfied that he had answered truthfully, his turn would be finished. But if the others determined that he was lying, then he would have to pay the dinner bill for the whole group. The county chief's chauffeur went first:

"My eyes are sharp, my steering wheel is round,
I've driven thousands of miles, and violated millions of rules."

Someone then asked him, "Have you ever been fined?" and he said, "No." Since everyone knew that the police would never dare to fine the county chief's car, the driver passed the test of truthfulness. Next to play was the chief of police, who said:

"My billy club's sharp, my big hat is round,
I've handled thousands of cases and arrested millions of people."

"Ever arrest anybody who was guilty?" he was asked, and the policeman said, "No." Everybody knew that this was the truth, so he passed. Next to play was the chief of the organization [i.e., personnel] department, who said:

"My mind is sharp, my official stamp is round,
I've appointed thousands of officials and investigated millions of them."

"Ever run across an official who was both competent and honest?" he was asked. The chief said no and passed the test. Next to play was the chief of propaganda, who said:

"My pen is sharp, my mouth is round,
I've written thousands of reports and made millions of speeches."

"Ever told the truth?" he was asked. "No," he said. This was the first time he ever told the truth, and he passed. Next was the county chief, who said:

"My chopsticks are sharp, my wine glass is round,
I've eaten thousands of delicacies and drunk millions of glasses of good wine."

"Ever paid?" His "no" answer was so obvious it hardly needed to be said, and he passed. Finally it was the turn of the Communist Party secretary of the county, who said:

"The high heels are sharp, the skirts are round,
"I've been to thousands of dances and embraced millions of girls."

"Ever slept with one?" he was asked. "No," he said and elicited a chorus of "liar! liar!" He smiled good-naturedly, reached into his pocket for his checkbook, and wrote a check on public funds for the whole banquet.

## THEMES OF *SHUNKOULIU* IN THE 1990s

Although it is safe to say that political and social criticism dominated the *shunkouliu* of the 1990s, categorization of subthemes is inevitably somewhat arbitrary. Below we choose and illustrate seven.

### A Society Driven by Money

Popular zest for making money grew in China in the 1980s and accelerated after Deng Xiaoping's "southern tour" in 1992, when Deng urged that people throw themselves into moneymaking "even more boldly" than before. In the 1980s rural areas led the way in converting to a market economy, and after 1992 large parts of the urban population also "jumped into the sea" of the free market. At the same time a number of problems arose: inequality, exploitation of labor, production of phony products, smuggling, and even such things as markets in young women for wives and male toddlers to continue family lines. A number of *shunkouliu* noted the marked difference between these patterns and those of earlier decades. This one is archly entitled "A Short History of Comradely Sentiment":

In the '50s we helped people;
In the '60s we criticized people;
In the '70s we fooled people;
In the '80s everybody hired everybody else;
In the '90s we "slaughter" whomever we see.

Here "slaughter" is our translation for *zai*, a piece of slang roughly equivalent in tone and sense to "rip off" (as a verb) in American English. In this example the object of attack is not moneymaking per se so much as the crass cynicism that results when other values are obliterated. Another example says:

Officials are addicted to money
While the people labor and sweat.
If something else counts, then it's funny
That no one's run into it yet.

## Corruption

We have already noted some examples of *shunkouliu* that take aim at corruption in officialdom. Not all accusations of corruption were aimed at officials, however. Some spoke of corruption among the common people, while excusing it as a necessary means for getting by in the world. When a little person seeks a favor, for example:

> A cigarette gets you
>    in the door,
> And with wine you're able
>    to hear the deal.
> But if you want
>    the problem solved
> It's gotta be
>    a great big meal.

Some examples actually cast corruption in a somewhat favorable light because, without it, there was no way to drag politically conservative officials "into the sea" where the nonstate economy could grow:

> No food and no drink?
> The economy will stink!

Corruption appears at its ugliest when people with political power are seen to divert public property for their own economic gain:

> He's got the finance system on his left,
> And the banking network to his right.
> He taxes all of industry
> With all his beastly might.
> He's the king of electric current
> And prince of the water pipe,
> But what's he care for kids at school?
> Not a strip of tripe!

Farmers' *shunkouliu* showed a preference that officials stay in the cities. When they did not,

> A horn sounds *beep! beep!* through the mists
> Here comes a carload of Communists.
> Chickens and geese fly up from the ground
> And soon—*clink-clink!*—wine glasses sound.

Another is terser:

They came out a bunch of sleepy clunks,
And went home a bunch of sodden drunks.


## The Disappearance of Socialist Values

Socialism in China, which had genuine popular appeal in the early years of the revolution, steadily lost its attractiveness from the 1960s through the 1980s because of the double body blow of Mao Zedong's huge and disastrous social experiments and Deng Xiaoping's emphasis that only moneymaking—and no talk of social or political ideals—was permissible in public discourse. Yet the language of socialism, still required by state machinery, lived on. Such idealistic-sounding phrases as "serve the people" were still used, but only as empty words, and the irony implicit in this condition became fruitful turf for inventors of *shunkouliu*. Once Party members were supposed to be selfless citizens, and it used to be hard to get into the Party. Now:

Joined the Party yet?
Pay a few bucks and you're set.
Except for the dues and the name,
Everything else is the same.

As he encouraged China's drive toward moneymaking in the 1980s, Deng Xiaoping also found it necessary to draw an ideological baseline in order to maintain political control. He devised the Four Basic Principles, also known popularly as the "Four Insists," that call on China to adhere to (1) the socialist road, (2) the dictatorship of the proletariat, (3) the leadership of the Communist Party, and (4) Marxism-Leninism-Mao-Zedong-Thought. These curious guidelines, in one sense far removed from daily life but in another sense deadly serious, inspired a number of *shunkouliu*. According to one, the "basic principles" of a Party member indeed numbered four:

My salary? Basically stored.
Liquor? I basically hoard.
My wife? Is basically bored. [Because I use other women.]
My job? Basically ignored.

Reformers in the 1990s hoped that a new generation of Party leaders, referred to as the "third echelon," would outshine their two elder generations who had, respectively, either been stunted by narrow, Soviet-style educations in the 1950s and early 1960s, or missed out on full educations because schools were closed during the Cultural Revolution years (1966–1976). But the third-echelon leaders did not do too well in *shunkouliu*. These young men:

Dance all night until the dawn,
Throw back booze and don't feel gone,
Bed eight girls and still feel brawn,
Never touch what they're working on.
—Turns out they're the "third echelon"!

For elderly citizens who had embraced the revolution in good faith in the 1950s, the collapse of socialist ideals was not just material for sarcasm but an actual blow to their economic well-being. The following *shunkouliu* adopts the viewpoint of a retired worker in an urban state enterprise:

I worked my whole life for the Party,
And had nothing at the time I retired;
Now they tell me to live off my kids,
But my kids one by one have been fired.

The twists and turns—and some complete reversals—of Party policy over the years provided people of middle age and older with another source of *shunkouliu* material, which we treat next.

### Retrospection on the Course of the Revolution

Each paramount leader of the People's Republic, according to one 1990s *shunkouliu*, had asked the people to "take a plunge" of one kind or another:

Chairman Mao led us to plunge into the countryside;
Deng Xiaoping led us to plunge into the sea [of moneymaking]
Jiang Zemin led us to plunge into unemployment.

After some time had separated them from the pain that Mao Zedong had caused, people were able to look back at Mao with varying shades of nostalgia.[11] At least the old man had stuck with certain principles:

Chairman Mao is like the sun:
The earth is bright where it casts its rays.[12]
Deng Xiaoping is like the moon:
It changes every fourteen days.

The perception that, after four decades, society had descended to a state just as bad as, or worse than, the chaos of the late 1940s led older people to a sense of having come full circle. The revolution had aimed at eliminating corruption, fraud, disease, exploitation, large gaps between rich and poor, and so on; for a time this enterprise went well, but later it collapsed, and now the country seemed back to square one:

For forty-some years, ever more perspiration,
And we just circle back to before Liberation;
And speaking again of that big revolution,
Who, after all, was it for?

The explosive last line of this piece suggests that the working classes—the supposed beneficiaries of the revolution—had been duped by the Party elite, who told the workers it was their revolution but in fact took the fruits for themselves. This kind of barbed political challenge appeared in other 1990s examples.

## Political Challenge

In the 1990s *shunkouliu* began explicitly to name the Communist Party and its high officials in connection with corruption and other ills. One example, which must be translated awkwardly because its true cleverness lies in its punning on the names of leaders, says:

> Embezzlement and corruption have become systemic [where *cheng xitong*, "have become systemic," is a pun on the name of Beijing mayor Chen Xitong];
> Anticorruption campaigns get nowhere [where *wei jian xing*, "get nowhere," is a pun on the name of the minister of supervision, Wei Jianxing];
> Private and public affairs are hard to separate out [where *li nan qing*, "hard to separate out," is a pun on the name of the first deputy premier, Li Lanqing];
> In the whole dynasty top to bottom no official is upright [where *wu guan zheng*, "no official is upright," is a pun on the name of Wu Guanzheng, governor of Shandong];
> The El-Nino river inundates the people[13] [where *jiang ze min*, "river inundates the people," is a pun on the name of President Jiang Zemin];
> Is it easy for the people to put up with this? [where *rongyi ren*, "easy to put up with," is a pun on the name of communist China's leading Party-approved capitalist, Rong Yiren].

The following summary view of corruption seems to have been created by Beijing taxi drivers following the embezzlement trial of Beijing Mayor Chen Xitong in 1998.

> If we don't root out corruption, the country will perish.
> If we do root out corruption, the Party will perish.

In this example the ambiguity—whether the possibility that the Party might perish is a good or bad thing—harbors a powerful barb. The sense that corruption is overwhelming, and the desperate extremes to which that sense can lead people in framing their thoughts, is captured in the following 1990s saying:

> If you line up all the officials and shoot the whole line, a few innocent ones are going to get killed; but if you line them up and shoot only every other one, an even larger number of the guilty will get away.

Although the great majority of 1990s *shunkouliu* are related to politics, traditional themes such as regional differences continued to appear, and some contemporary twists to the old theme of sex roles have emerged as well.

### Regional Differences

We have noted above how the distinctive geography and local products of different parts of China have been traditional themes for *shunkouliu*. In examples from the last two decades, these regional differences take on contemporary colors. In the following example, Cantonese are said to be hung up with their cuisine and Shanghainese with their dress; Beijing people take politics too seriously and are always complaining and criticizing, while farmers, who are more practical, are the first to grab the chance to make money:

> Cantonese will eat anything;
> Shanghainese will wear anything;
> Beijingers will denigrate anything;
> Rural people will sell anything.

Another example is set against a background in which layoffs in state factories in northeast China had led to some brazen robberies by disgruntled workers. By contrast, Beijing, as usual, was packed with big officials and Guangdong was making money hand over fist, while Hainan was so full of prostitutes that customers got worn out:

> The smallness of your daring is apparent in the northeast;
> The smallness of your prestige shows up in Beijing;
> The smallness of your wallet is clear in Guangdong;
> And the smallness of your sex drive is obvious in Hainan.

### Sex and the Social Role of Women

When Western social scientists began to do fieldwork in China in the early 1980s, they produced a number of books and articles that, in general, expressed disappointment that the "liberation of women," which was supposed to have been an important part of the communist revolution, in fact had not gone as far as they had hoped and supposed.[14] Women still tended to defer to the men in their life, and their social status still tended to depend on their success in producing male heirs for the families into which they married. To be single past thirty or childless past forty was truly frightening. But to judge from the *shunkouliu* of the 1990s, it may be that the rough-and-tumble of China's new market economy has loosened certain fetters that Communist rhetoric could not. One that arose in urban areas in the mid-1980s says:

Marriage is just a big mess-up;
Children result from a mix-up;
Divorce is the beginning of wake-up;
Staying single is the ultimate wise-up;
And taking no lovers is just plain dumb.

Some *shunkouliu* take aim at traditional taboos against women's involvement in extramarital sex. This purpose, combined with the moneymaking ethos of the 1990s, produced the following:

When men get money they turn bad.
When women turn bad they get money.

In this example "bad" might be thought of in quotation marks because the main thrust is that there is really nothing wrong with women seeking their own income, taboos notwithstanding. Some *shunkouliu* display a benign attitude toward prostitution and even sympathy for the prostitute's point of view. A 1980s example called "A Three-Accompaniment Girl Tells Her Own Story"[15] goes this way:

First, I don't pilfer,
Second, I don't rob;
I just embrace Communists;
That's my job!

The notion that women who work in the entertainment trade do have moral standards (don't pilfer, rob) may have been part of a modest improvement in their social status. Many local governments in the 1990s began to ask "three-accompaniment girls" to begin paying income taxes—although one can argue over how much this represented a rise in the social status of these women and how much a fall in the standards of local governments.

## *SHUNKOULIU* FOR CERTAIN GROUPS

Although *shunkouliu* have spread to all areas of China and through nearly all social strata, some of them tend to articulate the viewpoints of certain groups. We have already seen how they sometimes speak sympathetically from the viewpoint of a retired worker, a three-accompaniment girl, or other person of specific station. The only groups that tend not to invent and use *shunkouliu* are those that do very well, for example, high officials or the successful new bourgeoisie. This is natural, given that the essence of *shunkouliu* is to complain. Without attempting a full taxonomy, we consider four groups that, at least to some extent, have "their own" *shunkouliu*. Note that group-specific *shunkouliu* tend to thrive on one group's making fun of another.

## Farmers

Farmers originated *shunkouliu* centuries ago, and in the late 1970s they led the way in dismantling the commune system and replacing it with a "responsibility system" that let families work on, and take the harvests from, their own pieces of land. The following *shunkouliu* claims that this system gets the incentives right:

> It energizes all the hard workers
> And cures all the slippery shirkers.

Another rejoices that the new system gets commune officials off farmers' backs:

> The grain now comes to us;
> Who gives a XX about them?

Following their success with the responsibility system, farmers began in the 1980s to set up small-scale "sideline industries" that produced things like noodles, soy sauce, shirts, and toys. This activity received enthusiastic reviews in *shunkouliu*. The one that follows claims that in a sideline industry one can earn even more money than officials do:

> Set up your crate,
> And beat the magistrate.
> Open a workshop door,
> And beat the governor.
> Gather your family by threes and twos,
> And the big Party secretary's gonna lose.

By the end of the 1980s the rural economy had slowed down and in some places had begun to decline. This happened because the one-time gains that resulted from dismantling the communes had run their course, and meanwhile rural officials had learned that simply taxing farmers could replace the commune system as a way of extracting their wealth. Ad hoc "fees" of many kinds sapped farmers and led to corruption in officialdom. Hence farmers' *shunkouliu* in the 1990s were notably less optimistic than they were in the 1980s. A negative example is:

> Farmwork is tough: the sun is hot, the earth rough.
> Farm life is tense: fees are unending, taxes immense.
> Farm homes are dejected: no tuition, kids rejected.

## Workers

While China's rural economy was shifting to a market system in the 1980s, the large state industries located primarily in the cities remained intact. But increasingly they lost money as the more efficient free market sector of the urban economy grew up around them. Fearing political instability, government leaders poured large subsidies and loans into the outmoded state enterprises. Yet, especially in the 1990s, many of those enterprises had to delay payments to workers, pay them in IOUs, or lay them off. To a group who once saw themselves as the "vanguard of the revolution," such treatment came as a shock—and provided, naturally, food for *shunkouliu*. Workers' *shunkouliu* often took aim at the officials and managers in their own workplaces, who were the most proximate symbols of what they saw as their unfair treatment:

Our salaries get stopped for a month or two,
But our leader still rides his VW.
Our pay and our benefits keep going down,
But our leader rides high in his Toyota Crown.
Who can now say where all of this ends?
—Except that our leader will still have his Benz.[16]

Workers in Wuhan in 1998 carried signs that read "Sell off the luxury cars to pay workers' wages."[17] A *shunkouliu* from urban workers in north China seeks to explain how it is that factory managers can embezzle so easily:

Workers are poor? Managers rich?
There's no one to watch the sons of a bitch!

## Intellectuals

During the Cultural Revolution Mao Zedong stigmatized intellectuals as "the stinking ninth" (i.e., lowest) social category. Workers were in theory number one, and farmers number two. After the Cultural Revolution, a Communist Party "policy on intellectuals" was supposed to upgrade their position, but many intellectuals felt that the upgrade was symbolic only, as they continued to be underpaid and poorly housed. An early 1980s *shunkouliu* expresses their ironic view of the social ladder:

The first elder brothers [workers] are stepping down;
The second elder brothers [farmers] are making money;
The ninth brothers [intellectuals] are parading bare-assed in fancy sedan chairs.[18]

Intellectuals' complaints that the value of their contributions to society remained largely unappreciated was expressed in these widespread examples:

The one who operates on the brain makes less than the one who shaves the scalp.
The one who plays the piano gets less than the one who moves it.
The missile researcher makes less than the egg seller.

(The third line depends on a pun on *dan*, which can be heard as either "missile" or "egg.") By the 1990s many intellectuals had figured out that the only way to get more money was to "plunge into the sea" and take such moonlighting jobs as teaching English, setting up computer systems for businesses, and so on. But others, whether from honesty or dull-wittedness, remained in their original jobs and continued to live on their small, fixed salaries. One *shunkouliu* speaks for underpaid schoolteachers:

Teachers are like salt,
Nothing to exalt.
You need them but it's funny,
They just aren't worth your money.

## Officials

Although frequently the butt of everyone else's *shunkouliu*, middle- and low-level officials did invent and circulate some examples of their own. These tended to complain about how reform was goring their ox. Opposition to the dismantling of the communes in the late 1970s was expressed this way:

We struggle for years, through best and worst,
And then overnight, it's all reversed.

In the 1980s Deng Xiaoping pursued a policy of replacing officials whose expertise was essentially political with officials who had some technical skills. Naturally this generated jealousies. The point of view of the technical officials, in criticism of the purely political officials, is expressed in this *shunkouliu*:

Technical officials are like pumpkins: the older the sweeter.
Political officials are like towel gourds: the older the hollower.

## THE PLACE OF *SHUNKOULIU* IN THE LARGER SCENE

The evidence for the popularity of *shunkouliu* is overwhelming. There can be little doubt that they are genuine, indigenous, and widespread. The biggest puzzle in their interpretation might be how to understand their inveterate negativity. Can it be that the thinking of the Chinese populace really is as out-and-out negative as what they present? How could daily life get done if people were as sarcastic in all their thinking as they are in these sayings? One might argue that *shunkouliu* are mere jokes, marginal to daily life and not worth studying as indicators of serious opinion. This, we feel, would be a mistake. *Shunkouliu* address issues at the heart of daily life and address them with passion; they are hardly marginal. The puzzle of their negativity thus becomes a question of how to place them within larger patterns in a person's thinking. How does the niche that these acerbic barbs occupy fit into the rest of daily life?

Some aspects of the answer to this question are probably universal, and parallels might be found elsewhere. In a rough sense, for example, the place of *shunkouliu* in Chinese thinking bears some similarities to political humor in the United States. When Jay Leno tells stories about Bill Clinton and Monica Lewinsky, he can go a whole year without a single positive comment. His audience craves this negativity and would complain if he watered it down. But it does not follow that all of the audience's thinking is wholly negative. The jokes play certain roles within a larger constellation of ideas and values.

There is a sense, moreover, in which any complaint must rest on a positive value. A factory worker does not complain about a manager unless he or she has in mind a better model for how a manager should behave. The concept of political corruption depends on an implicit standard for clean government. Hence the widespread sarcasm in *shunkouliu* can actually be read as strong expression in favor of ideals. A related—and again probably universal—function of sarcasm is to buoy its user; when A denigrates B, A implicitly claims a higher position than B. When B in this formula is the high and mighty of society (as is often the case with *shunkouliu*), a satisfying feeling of social leveling can emerge. In joking about Jiang Zemin, Bill Clinton, and others, tellers and hearers of jokes are temporarily transported in their imaginations to parity with (or, morally, superiority to) these august persons. The same "leveling" can work in sarcasm about an officious boss, provided only that there is a certain resemblance between the boss in the joke and one's own boss. Finally, there is also a positive value of camaraderie in the sharing of *shunkouliu* or jokes. Knowing that others share one's complaints reinforces confidence that the complaints are justified. For all these reasons—and probably others—"negative" jokes can be complexly intertwined with positive values.

But these universal aspects of sarcastic humor are only part of the social importance of *shunkouliu* in China. As in other societies that control public complaint, the role of private complaint becomes magnified. When the *People's Daily* and other media limit themselves to officially approved views, they generate pressure for the expression of unapproved commentary, and this pressure generates the whole informal network of "alleyway news," including *shunkouliu*, jokes, and rumor. In this sense *shunkouliu* might be viewed as a sort of countermedium to the official media. On politically sensitive issues, the *People's Daily* reports the bright side and *shunkouliu* tell the other side. Although neither medium is very "objective," the rhetorical functions of the two are in some ways importantly different. The aim of the *People's Daily* is to engineer readers' thoughts—to get them to believe what the leadership wants them to believe. But *shunkouliu* are not trying to tell others what to think; their role is to facilitate the expression of feelings that people already have. This simple function—of bringing out feelings that are already there—is much more exhilarating when done in contexts of repression. Writing of the Soviet Union, Victor Erlich has observed that "the simple act of calling a spade a spade, of naming the unspeakable, becomes an epiphany."[19]

What does "speaking out" via *shunkouliu* achieve? It allows individuals to release their feelings and might therefore promote mental health. From the viewpoint of society as a whole, the same function can be viewed as a safety valve. If corruption is endemic, hard to uproot, and widely detested, the danger of social unrest increases. In such a context the expression of indignation through *shunkouliu* might not change social reality but at least relieves tension. From this point of view the Communist Party of China, whose leaders were very concerned for "stability" during the 1980s and 1990s, might have welcomed a certain level of satiric *shunkouliu*. They did not, however. In November 1982 the *People's Daily* carried an article called "Don't Make Up Irresponsible *Shunkouliu*"[20] and since then has allowed only the most innocuous examples to appear in the open press. It is questionable whether Party leaders ever felt secure enough in their power to recognize the "safety valve" function of *shunkouliu*. But assuming that they were, and that they decided to oppose *shunkouliu* anyway, they may have been concerned about the longer-term effects of sarcasm. To let citizens blow off steam about corruption today might make them feel better tomorrow, and this could be socially ameliorative. But to allow them to fall into persistent habits of harping on entrenched corruption could undermine public faith in society and its leaders. In this longer-term sense *shunkouliu* probably had a corrosive effect on the legitimacy of the Communist Party and Chinese state institutions.

## NOTES

1. *Minyao* (folksong) has generally referred to singable verse, but since the 1980s the term has also referred widely to rhymes or sayings that are not sung.
2. Reported by a reliable source who wishes to remain anonymous in the State Administration of Radio, Film, and Television.
3. James Scott, *Domination and the Arts of Resistance: Hidden Transcripts* (New Haven: Yale University Press, 1990).
4. We are grateful to Ji Hong, editor of *Zhongguo hangkong bao* (Chinese aviation news), for sharing his personal collection with us.
5. Three of the larger recent collections are Lu Feilang, ed., *Zhongguo dangdai minyao* (Contemporary Chinese *shunkouliu*) (Brampton, Ont.: Mingjing chubanshe, 1998); Li

Jie, ed., *Laobaixing de zhihui: Dalu dangdai* shunkouliu *shangxi* (The wisdom of the common people: An analysis and appreciation of contemporary mainland *shunkouliu*) (Monterey Park, Calif.: Evergreen, 1997); and Gan Tang, ed., *Zhongguo dalu* shunkouliu (Mainland Chinese *shunkouliu*), vols. 1–2 (Taibei: Zhongguo dalu wenti yanjiusuo, 1988–1989). A collection published in China is Lu Wen, ed., *Baixing huati: Dangdai* shunkouliu (On the tongues of the people: Contemporary *shunkouliu*) (Beijing: Zhongguo dang'an chubanshe, 1998).

6. The original texts of the *shunkouliu* that appear in this chapter are listed in the glossary on pp. 301–4. Our translations of *shunkouliu* sometimes bend denotative meaning in order to capture rhythm or rhyme. We believe this practice is more faithful to the originals than the alternative of closer denotative approximation that is achieved at the cost of rhythm and rhyme.

7. Our claim here is based on our participant-observer experience in China as well as on all available published sources, including the books noted in note 5.

8. The importance of rhythm in verbal memorization is more than one usually realizes. Try, for example, to say your ten-digit home telephone number aloud. It was probably easy, and you probably said it in 1-2-3, 1-2-3, 1-2-3-4 form. Now try to say it aloud in any other form, for example 1-2, 1-2-3-4, 1-2-3, 1. In order to do this, you will probably have to write the number down and then read it off. If this happens, then it is true that you "remember" your phone number only in a certain rhythm.

9. The question of whether Chinese language and culture use rhythm more extensively than others do is interesting. We suspect yes. On Beijing buses, for example, ticket sellers say, "Xia yi zhan, Wangfujing, mei piao mai piao!" (The next stop is Wangfujing, get a ticket if you don't have one!) It is spoken in a lilting 1-2-3, 1-2-3, 1-2, 1-2 pattern that a conductor on the Long Island Railroad would not dream of using. On the complex topic of prosody in daily life Chinese, see Feng Shengli, *Hanyu de yunlü, cifa yu jufa* (Interactions between morphology, syntax, and prosody in Chinese) (Beijing: Beijing daxue chubanshe, 1997).

10. Due to its length, we have omitted this example from the glossary.

11. See Geremie R. Barmé, *Shades of Mao* (Armonk, N.Y.: Sharpe, 1996).

12. This is a line from the Cultural Revolution anthem "The East Is Red."

13. Referring to the record-setting Yangzi River floods of summer 1998.

14. For example, Kay Ann Johnson, *Women, the Family, and Peasant Revolution in China* (Chicago: University of Chicago Press, 1983); and Margery Wolf, *Revolution Postponed: Women in Contemporary China* (Stanford: Stanford University Press, 1985).

15. A "three-accompaniment girl" *(sanpei xiaojie)* sells her company in eating, drinking, and song (and/or more).

16. We have taken greater liberties in translating this *shunkouliu* than others; we feel the result is loyal to the spirit of the original, and without the liberties an adequate reflection of the structure and rhyme would have been impossible.

17. Personal observation of Kate Zhou.

18. That is, as emperors without new clothes.

19. Victor Erlich, "Post-Stalin Trends in Russian Literature," *Slavic Review*, September 1964, 418.

20. "Buyao luan bian shunkouliu," *Renmin ribao* (People's Daily), 25 November 1982.

# 5

# The Rich, the Laid-off, and the Criminal in Tabloid Tales: Read All about It!

*Yuezhi Zhao*

Though the term "tabloid" invokes images of such feisty British dailies as the *Sun* or such sensational American supermarket weeklies as the *National Enquirer*, postsocialist China may well be the world capital of tabloids. Coming from all corners of the country, tabloids, considered a politically suspicious and morally decadent bourgeois cultural genre that was banned during much of the Maoist period, have returned with a vengeance as part of the unfolding "dialectic of the Chinese Revolution"[1] in the reform era. They are ubiquitous on urban newsstands. Their sensationalistic excess contrasts sharply with stale official organs, and the sheer number of available titles creates the appearance of diversity. I counted more than fifty different titles on one newsstand alone at a Beijing subway station in summer 1998.

There are different views on these tabloids. Some emphasize their transgression of Party propaganda codes and characterize them as part of China's "alternative media, which the Party has found to be disturbing, but impossible to curb."[2] Others dismiss their political relevance, frown on their vulgarity, or view them as "the new opium" that distracts the masses from harsh realities and from challenging the Party's power monopoly.[3] Jianying Zha, on the other hand, noted that China's post-1989 media elite generally believe that although tabloids are not practicing "real journalism," they help liberalize society and loosen up the official press.[4]

Few have taken a detailed look at the tabloids. We all know their manifest fare—crime, sex, money, corpses, lovers, corrupt officials, show stars, and other lowest-common-denominator and man-bites-dog stories; but we know little

111

about the universe of meanings they construct for readers. Moreover, circulation figures are difficult to come by, and given this genre's low cultural status, few elaborate on their reading experiences with enthusiasm or frankness. Although readers are not entirely free in interpreting a text, they do have discretionary powers. Ian Connell's cautionary note about trying to understand British popular thought through the tabloids is highly relevant:

> There has been no survey and analysis of the ways in which tabloid papers are read by anyone other than myself. I am unable to say whether the articles which caught my attention would have caught anyone else's; whether others would have chosen to read them as closely and fully as I did, nor anything about the sense they would make of them. . . . I do not think that we can *presume* that tabloid storytelling has its roots in, expresses, or even constructs thoughts and sentiments that are popular, that is, widely shared across a given population.[5]

Nevertheless, few can ignore the tabloid press as an important dimension of the postsocialist experience in China, not least its impact on mainstream journalism, which is captured by the phrase "big papers copy small papers" (for marketability), a reversal of the Cultural Revolution–era phenomenon of "small papers copy big papers" (for political correctness). Tabloids, however trivial, bluntly market-driven, and easily digestible as "cultural fast food," are not "mere" entertainment or "innocent" texts. Although political persuasion is not their primary objective, they are socially embedded. Behind the bizarre and apparent deviations from the norm are consensual views about the social world and taken-for-granted assumptions about what these norms are or ought to be. Though this is not necessarily a direct expression of popular thought, as Connell goes on to note, the tellers of tabloid stories must assume a common ground on which to establish a reciprocity of perspective with readers. They must find ways to keep readers on their chosen ground and make assumptions about them. Thus, "while it is not possible to comment upon how well the tellers have judged their readers' interests, attitudes, prior knowledge and expectations of a good story, it is at least possible to reconstruct their judgments from the stories themselves."[6] In China, of course, such judgments were made with constant references to permissible political boundaries set by the Party.

This chapter presents a twofold analysis of China's tabloid press as a means of social communication and as a potential forum for popular expression. First, to locate the tabloids within the structure of the Chinese press, I provide an overview of a range of popular press genres and look at the evolution of the popular press as an index to social stratification in postsocialist China. Second, I analyze the content of a particular segment of the popular press, namely, the street tabloids, by looking at their portrayal of four social groups—the rich, laid-off workers, migrant workers, and peasants—and the ways in which these papers make sense of social divisions for readers. Because personalization and characterization are key discursive features in tabloids, the portrayal of various social groups provides a fruitful point of entry into their universe of meanings.

Inevitably, I have to limit my choice of "tabloid characters." I do not single out corrupt officials and women as distinctive analytical categories, although both are prominent tabloid characters. Publicly exposed corrupt officials are the subjects of much indignation in tabloid stories. Given popular resentment against corruption and official anticorruption campaigns in the late 1990s, it is not surprising that tabloids capitalize on a populist "people versus corrupt officials" theme. Their anticorruption discourse shares similar characteristics and limitations with those of quasi-legal magazines discussed by Richard Levy in this volume. Though women are featured frequently and the term "female" *(nü)* is arguably one of the main attractions in sensationalistic and often sexist tabloid headlines, I discuss the gender dimension in relation to women's economic roles. Finally, following the tabloids, the category "the rich" encompasses both entrepreneurs and the managerial and professional elite.[7] I do not have the opposite category, "the poor," because it is virtually nonexistent in tabloids. My analysis is based on more than two hundred newsstand papers from the post-1992 period.[8]

## THE NEWSSTAND AS AN INDEX TO SOCIAL STRATIFICATION IN POSTSOCIALIST CHINA

The Chinese press is sharply divided between official organs that depend on office subscriptions and popular papers sold at newsstands to individual consumers. The common term for the popular press is "small papers" *(xiaobao)*—or tabloids—in contrast to "big papers" *(dabao)*—or official organs. Technically, a tabloid is a newspaper that is half the size (a quarto, i.e., a sheet folded into quarters) of a regular paper (a broadsheet or folio, i.e., folded once). The term also connotes a sensationalist, personalized, and storytelling rather than an analytical approach to journalism because the first papers in the West to adopt this format tended to emphasize crime, gossip, and entertainment. Instead of focusing on macrolevel political and economic issues, tabloids "make immediate individual experience as the prime source of evidence and value."[9] In mainstream Chinese culture, the term "street tabloids" *(jietou xiaobao)* is almost a synonym for sensationalism, fabrication, and vulgarity.

Although most newsstand papers are technically in the tabloid format, not all of them are considered "tabloids" in the derogatory sense. There are different genres and there is a "hierarchy of respectability" among them.[10] The most common genres are evening papers published by local Party committees or Party organs and weekly radio and television guides published by broadcasting authorities. These papers appeal to the average urban family and are core newsstand sales. Evening papers have a human interest, lifestyle, and entertainment orientation, but they contain at least some news on macrolevel political and economic issues and operate well within the Party's propaganda guidelines and standards of decency. The second category consists of various weekly news digests—usually subsidiaries of major papers that mix analytical short essays on substantive issues with all sorts of tidbits. The third category consists of "law-and-order" papers published by law enforcement agencies and related institutions. These papers are packed with detailed crime tales. The fourth category, the largest in number and broadest in range, is what is generally referred to as "weekend editions" (*zhoumo ban*)—general interest "weekend," "midmonth," "end of month," "society," "metro," "leisure," or "special" supplements to Party organs and trade papers. Although "weekend editions" share a common content orientation in social, lifestyle, and law-and-order issues, they are not created equal. At the top of the respectability hierarchy is *Nanfang Weekend* (Nanfang zhoumo), published by the Guangdong provincial Party organ, *Nanfang Daily*. It is among the few weekend papers that have independent license numbers and thus legal status as distinct newspapers. Selling at ¥1.50 a copy in 1998, the paper attracts urban intellectuals with its liberal views, exposure of corruption and social problems, and expression of middle-class sensibilities. The numerous crime- and sex-filled "weekend editions" of the local and bureaucratic press, on the other hand, are sold at a much lower price (usually 60 fen [cents]) and read by the lower classes: blue-collar workers, office clerks, less educated urban youth, and occasionally the "floating population." The majority of these papers do not have independent licenses, and some are on the borderline between legal and illegal publications. Finally, there are business and lifestyle papers specializing in stock markets, shopping, sports, theater, popular music, and other subjects.

The evolution of these newsstand genres both reflects and helps constitute the social stratification of urban China in the reform era. The urban newsstands began as distributors of family-oriented evening papers and television guides in the early 1980s. Gradually, lifestyle papers, news digests, and crime tabloids from faraway places arrived for the individual consumer, with the development of an alternative national distribution network outside the postal system. This created the first wave of tabloids in the mid-1980s. "Weekend editions" began to flourish in 1992, as the official press found a way to go commercial in response to Deng Xiaoping's call for further marketization and the state's withdrawal of press subsidies.[11]

The post-1992 period has witnessed an intensified pursuit of national mass readership through lowest common denominator content by crime tabloids, news digests, and "weekend editions" on the one hand, and an upward mobility of newsstand papers for the rising urban middle class and emerging subculture groups on the other. In 1993 *Culture Weekend* (Wenhua zhoumo), notorious for its stories on nudity, and *Youth Weekend* (Qingnian zhoumo), with its trendy topics and bold social critiques,[12] were the "coolest" tabloids on Beijing streets. In the mid-1990s, one of the hottest-selling Beijing tabloids was *Shopping Guide* (Gouwu daobao), started in late 1992 as a quasi-private subsidiary of *China Light*

*Industry Herald* (Zhongguo qinggong daobao) for the mass consumer and devoted exclusively to the art of consumption. By the late 1990s, however, its street sales had been surpassed by *Fine Goods Shopping Guide* (Jingpin gouwu zhinan), a more upscale competitor catering to the urban professional and managerial elite. As the "bible of China's shopping class,"[13] these papers provide the primary frame of reference for the Western lifestyle. Stylish features and consumer testimonies celebrate the pleasures of consumption, fetishize the transformative powers of such items as a ¥580 Pierre Cardin wallet, and advise readers to use the latest Western designer fashion to conceal, according to a front-page article in the 23 April 1999 issue of *Fashion Times* (Fuzhuang shibao), "the unsatisfactory features of our Asian bodies." These papers help construct the identities of the urban managerial and professional elite and integrate them horizontally with the global consumer culture. They make little reference to social groups beyond their targeted readerships. More recently, such titles as *Net Culture Weekly* (Wangluo wenhua zhoukan) and *Auto Fan* (Che mi) have emerged to serve the net-surfing and car-owning market niches.

Proximity to the mainstream journalism style of hard news reportage and analytical writing and the social status of readerships are two useful indicators of the "respectability" of various popular genres. However, the fragmented and multi-layered structure of the popular press means that it is impossible to draw a clear demarcation between tabloids in the technical sense and street tabloids in the connotative sense. In general, the evening papers, radio and television weeklies, and business and consumer papers catering to the urban middle class, as well as *Nanfang Weekend*, are at the higher end of the respectability continuum. News digests, crime tabloids, and most "weekend editions" are considered street tabloids. They are the focus of my textual analysis.

Periodical government crackdowns, market failures, and other operational constraints contribute to an unstable and irregular institutional existence for many street tabloids. Intense market competition among undistinguished titles drives these papers toward excessive commercialism. Commercialism is further intensified by the nature of content production in this sector. Instead of relying on staff reporters, many papers depend heavily on unsolicited submissions by freelance writers. As cultural entrepreneurs aiming to make a primary or secondary income, tabloid contributors consider marketability as their foremost criterion. Though some individuals may take the journalistic convention of factuality seriously, many engage in overt fabrications and draw liberally from rumors and unconfirmed street sources *(daoting tushuo)*.[14] Some street tabloids contain nothing but a random collection of sex and crime tales and advertising features for doctors and clinics offering cures for cancer, infertility, and venereal diseases, formulas for breast enlargements, and other beautification treatments. To prolong their shelf life on the newsstand, some tabloids either hide their publication dates at inside corners or do not carry a specific date.

Although such popular genres as the evening papers have been well integrated into the official journalistic culture, most street tabloids fall short of the Party's pronounced propaganda standards. Consequently, the Party has tried to coopt, discourage, and suppress them. Soon after the proliferation of "weekend editions" in the immediate post-1992 period, for example, the Party issued a set of guidelines that incorporated this genre as "an important front for the promotion of socialist spiritual civilization" and required it to "aggressively promote patriotism, collectivism, and socialist ideas."[15] Still, many "weekend editions" have remained "dark, yellow, and false" and have continued to violate the Party's press codes. In general, the Party, perhaps by the sheer inability to enforce its guidelines, limits its controlling role to the announcement of rules, periodic clampdown campaigns, and occasional closures. Its policy of differentiated press control (tight at the center, loose at the peripheries; tight on political issues, loose on soft news; tight with Party organs, loose with other papers) means that tabloids have considerable freedom in nonexplicit political subjects. Whereas a labor activist who published an independent newsletter advocating for workers' rights received a ten-year prison sentence,[16] reprimands and removal from posts are more likely punishments for tabloid editors and publishers. What view of the social world do street tabloids portray? How do they portray various social groups? In whose voice do they speak?

## The Rich

Private jets and yachts are entering the lives of some families. "Big shots" buy mansions and villas equipped with everything from swimming pools, to exercise rooms, to tennis courts, in Beijing, Shenzhen, Qingdao, Dalian, Hangzhou . . . even in the United States, Switzerland, France, and Australia. They don't even blink when they gamble away tens of thousands overnight. They win a smile from their brides at weddings by throwing piles of money at guests. They toss money as a competitive sport on the streets. They fly to several cities to meet lovers and travel abroad frequently to meet foreign sweethearts. They hunt in Australia, ski in Switzerland, and surf in Hawaii. They purchase jewelry worth millions of yuan for their wives and lovers. Their wives spend several thousand yuan on their hairdos, and the puppies in their arms cost tens of thousands of yuan.

So begins an item in an apparently unregistered tabloid sold to me by a woman at a bus depot in Hangzhou on a winter day in 1998. It then goes on to reveal the legal and illegal means by which these people get rich, without any critical reflection. A commentary interprets the current economic system as an implementation of the proverb "people die for wealth, birds die for food," and it promotes the publication as a means for arousing people's ambitions to become rich.

If this is extreme in its depiction of the lifestyle of the rich and in its expression of a "getting rich by all means" mentality, there are also matter-of-fact announcements about the emergence of a rich "stratum" *(jieceng)* in China. The "Lifestyle Edition" of *Jilin Science and Technology News* (Jilin keji bao), for example, printed three articles under the banner "A Rich Stratum Has Emerged in China." One article describes an income gap that grows at an "astonishing rate." Rather than use a more sensationalist headline to highlight the division itself or the extent of this division (wider than that in the United States, according to the article), the headline announces the emergence of the rich in a straightforward manner. The other two articles explain the composition of the rich and the ways in which they have acquired their fortunes, including illegal means whereby some people "extort and expropriate other social groups." The 26 July 1998 "Society Weekly" of *China Business News* (Zhongguo shangbao) described in favorable terms how managers and board members of state enterprises have turned themselves from "wage earners" into millionaires and owners of stocks. It claims that this transformation reflects society's new value orientations and its rewards to these deserving people.

Among other things, the rich flaunt their wealth with purchases of European "superfamous brands" at the Wangfu Hotel shopping gallery in Beijing. A front page story in the 30 July 1998 weekend edition of *Beijing Economic Times* (Beijing jingji bao) provided a vivid depiction of Wangfu's exclusive boutiques and their patrons in a front page feature entitled, "Who's Afraid of the Astronomical Prices of 'Superfamous Brands'?" As Chinese tourists roamed European capitals in the early 1990s and stunned local merchants with their lavish spending, European "superfamous brands" flocked to China and found earnest consumers. Here, a suitcase costs ¥60,000, a winter coat ¥30,000, an umbrella more than ¥3,000, and a towel more than ¥2,000 (the 1999 official poverty line for urban residents in most major cities was less than ¥200 per month).[17] Moreover, China's nouveau riche is gaining the cultural capital for appreciating the profound esthetic values embodied in the most exquisite European designs. The article distinguishes between the respectable and deserving rich (white-collar professionals and real entrepreneurs) and the undeserving and disreputable ones (young women who prey on rich men and people who "are fond of spending public money"). It even offers a tip for distinguishing real purchasers from window shoppers: "Real purchasers have a unique disposition that puts them above the prices of the commodities. This is something that nobody else can imitate."

Also admirable among the rich are the Confucian entrepreneurs (*ru shang*)—a new identity that embodies the fusion of a redeemed Confucianism, which traditionally looks down on the merchant, and capitalism. These are the intellectually cultivated and politically savvy who neither forget their social responsibilities nor lose their common touch. "The Richest Man in China Spends More Than Half of His Time Studying Politics," claimed a front page story in the October 1997 issue of *Special Zone Digest* (Tequ wenzhai). The article idolizes Luo Fuzhong, *Fortune* magazine's richest man in mainland China, celebrating his business acumen and his dictum that the successful Chinese entrepreneur must be first and foremost a scholar of politics. For Luo, mastering politics means riding successfully on the unpredictable waves of policy changes and cultivating relationships with political patrons, and "political economy" means using knowledge about politics to make money. Unlike connoisseurs of European "superfamous brands" and conspicuous consumers who still need to display wealth to assert their social status, Luo is frugal, devoted to entrepreneurial endeavor, and reputed for his ascetic taste and lifestyle. He is confident about himself and his pursuits: "As I earned more money, I became less interested in material things. Although costs and profits are still my strategic considerations, profits are no longer my ultimate pursuits. I aspire to continuously outperform myself and generate more wealth for society." Luo thus embodies the idea that accumulating wealth by deploying political capital is at once a form of altruism, a means of individual self-perfection, and an exercise in social responsibility.

The rich also provide a symbolic resource for fantasies about the ultimate affluent nation. The "Society Weekly" of the 3 May 1999 issue of *Modern Women's News* (Xiandai nü bao), a hot-selling paper published by the Dalian Women's Federation, for example, carried a full-page feature about China's tiny minority of "flying brothers." They are the country's forty-one individuals who have permits to fly private airplanes and the many more whose only obstacle to enjoying this freedom is the government's licensing restrictions. The article noted that ownership of private airplanes is a "commonplace phenomenon" and that there are as many private jets as dragonflies in developed countries. It predicted that learning to fly will be China's next fad, and once the government deregulates civil aviation and increases radar services, "private planes will fly all over our sky like dragonflies." By referring to members of this exclusive group as "brothers" and by implicitly invoking the "catch up with the developed countries" theme, the article constructs a nationalistic frame and invites its female readers to identify with rich males as heroes of national development and to fantasize about the ultimate rich life with them.

Not every story relates to the rich with European cultural sophistication, Confucian civility and cultivation, nationhood, and brotherhood, of course. Nor are the rich always the subjects of admiration. Stories on the controversy over Mou Qizhong, who was also once on the *Fortune* list but was later charged with fraud, raised issues about means and ends. They demonstrated that the boundaries between the "richest man" and the "biggest swindler," between the *ru shang* and the money-worshiping lunatic who plundered public funds, were unclear. The counterhero of the *ru shang* is the arrogant, ignorant, decadent, and often lawbreaking "big shot" *(dakuan)*. These big shots are condemned in highly moralistic tales about how money does not bring happiness and how the single-minded pursuit of wealth leads to a dead end. Sensational headlines underscore this theme: "Greedy, the Gravedigger," "A Broken Money Dream," "A Female Big Shot's Road to Self-destruction," "A Female Big Shot's 200,000 Yuan Could Not Buy Passion and Love," and "A Fanatical Female Big Shot's Road to Death Was Paved with 360 Million Yuan." Whereas wealth is the source of happiness and status in lifestyle papers for the rich, money is related to misery and criminality in these tales.

The sexist image of the decadent rich female contributes to a further sense of wickedness. Since the term "big shot" is precoded as being male (the term "male big shot" sounds awkward), any connection between the female and the rich is sensational and usually negative, making it the perfect tabloid subject. They got rich by all means. Liao Zheng, a young factory worker, seduced the factory director and used her body as a form of currency to exchange for the director's power and then exchanged that power for money. Rather than a victim, Liao is a coconspirator in this sex-power-money three-way transaction as reported in the 29 June 1998 issue of *Land Bridge News* (Dalu qiao bao). Han Yuji, a Jilin woman who is the main character of a lengthy tale in an undated special issue of *Rural Medicine News* (Nongcun jiyaobao), made her way up from a street vendor to a successful businesswoman. But her money dream went out of control. Originally intending to borrow money to finance her manufacturing operation, Han ended up running a massive illegal fund-raising scam and turned herself into a "super-rich woman" (*chaoji fupo*) almost overnight. (In this context, *po* connotes unattractiveness as a woman rather than old age.) "Once rationality is corrupted by money, the originally industrious and virtuous Han Yuji ceased to exist. In its place was only madness. Han had been inflicted with 'the money disease,' " the article said. To conceal her fraud scheme, Han transformed her original corner store into a "memorial hall," a monument to her entrepreneurial spirit. Moreover, she secured a number of political titles, including "model female entrepreneur" and directorships of the Jilin Association of Private Entrepreneurs and Jilin Women's Federation. Han believed in the magical power of money even when she was under investigation. She was sentenced to death.

Even if rich female characters avoid self-destruction, other factors will ruin their lives—drugs, gambling, and other women are common perils. Pan Ruolan, a stunningly beautiful young pop star, managed to resist monetary temptations and male power against all odds. She won wide respect among her audiences by standing up against an insulting male big shot who ordered her to sing a song for ¥60,000 against her will. But a fellow female singer, a drug addict with an eye on Pan's swelling purse, hooked her on drugs. Moreover, Pan was ruined twice. She was rehabilitated in the first round, and this enhanced her popularity when she reappeared at the hotel bar. To make more money out of her, the hotel's female boss first swore sisterhood with her and then enticed her to smoke again and became her drug supplier. Pan went broke and finally sold the virginity she had safeguarded so strenuously for two packets of white powder. More tragically for her, the man who sold her the drug and had "the right to her first night" turned out to be the police officer who had initially arrested her for drug smoking. "When he stripped off Ruolan's last piece of clothing with a lewd grin, he swiftly pulled out his pistol, which was wrapped in red silk, and stuck it under the pillow," or so goes the narrative. When the female boss could no longer extract money out of the withering Pan, she sold her to an underground brothel. So much for sisterhood.

Zheng Huifang, the main character of a 14 May 1998 *Jianxin Business News* (Jianxi shangbao) story, faced a different set of problems. Zheng was a rural Anhui woman who got rich though a business operation in northeast China. Just as Zheng and her husband, Tian Fugui, returned to their hometown during the Spring Festival and were about to build their dream house, Tian began to gamble. When Zheng tried to intervene, Tian's cohorts provoked him to act like a real big shot and stand up as a true man. Tian beat her up and declared, "I have money now, and I can do whatever I please!" Seeing money as the source of her misery, Zheng burned all the money they had saved for the house. Afterward, the couple went to Guangzhou and earned even more money. When yet another Spring Festival arrived, Zheng sent Tian back to build the house again. When Zheng knocked at the door of her grand new house upon returning from Guangzhou, however, she was greeted by a snarling woman who had just slept with her husband. In madness, Zheng smashed all the household items in sight and torched the house.

While personalized tales of money dreams that went sour dominate the tabloids, a front page item in the 30 August 1998 issue of *Press Digest* (Baokan wenzhai) mocks the "aristocratic being" of the rich and articulates a populist critique of ostentation and privilege:

> Ladies in television commercials tell children to drink "prince milk." Real estate developers promise "noble district, imperial style" in newspaper advertising. One must drink "dynasty" *(haomen)* brand beer, wear "boss" brand suits. "Princelings" are nurtured in "aristocratic" schools; shopping is done at "fine goods boutiques." Don't boast your "milk bath" yet: I have a golden bed worthy of millions.

The article uses a popular joke to underscore the vulgarity of this "aristocratic being": the son of a "big shot" asks his father about their "nationality" *(minzu)*. The father replies sincerely, "aristocracy" *(guizu)*.

Two articles express the equality principle by questioning the elite's proposal to raise the salaries of government officials to curb corruption. Such a proposal, argues a front page article in the 28 February 1998 supplement to the Xi'an-based *Health Herald*,

> is out of step with reality, with our national conditions, and with the masses. It ignores the fact that we are still a developing country and at the primary stage of socialism. It ignores the fact that there are still more than sixty million people living in poverty, millions who have unpaid salaries, tens of millions of unemployed and laid-off workers, and tens of thousands of children who cannot afford school. Under such circumstances, a policy to promote official integrity through high salaries will have grave consequences for the Party and the state.

Although existing inequalities are identified, in the end it is not the principle of equality itself that is paramount. It is the interest of the Party and the state.[18]

## Laid-off Workers

Concurrent with the emergence of a "rich stratum" and the transformation of state enterprise managers into millionaires is the economic and social dislocation of tens of millions of workers.[19] This is one of the most explosive issues in China and is a highly contentious subject ideologically. How is it that the Communist Party, the self-proclaimed vanguard of the working class, pursues an economic program that displaces workers on such a massive scale? Managing media discourse on this issue is the Party's top propaganda priority. Official propaganda guidelines emphasize the need to acknowledge the problem, to promote nonsensational and constructive reporting, and to supply the media with information about government reemployment efforts.[20] The tabloids' treatment of layoffs is uncharacteristically restrained. Either by pressure from above or by a collusion of interests and perspectives between the ruling elite and tabloid editors and writers, the tabloid discourse on laid-off workers tells much about its pro-establishment character and reflects a neoliberal perspective in many ways.

Although the reasons for getting rich are explained, neither the macropolitical economy nor the micropolitics of layoffs is explained in any detail. In the words of an article in the 1 August 1998 supplement to *Shopping Guide*, "Layoffs are a given fact. . . . a sharp sword hanging over the head of Chinese workers by God in the 1990s." Elsewhere, the paper invokes another metaphor: "waking up from a forty-year dream, we suddenly encountered the uninvited guest of unemployment at the doorsteps of our socialist China." Though most articles view layoffs as beyond the control of workers, this article invokes the socialist memory and constructs a narrative about a socialist dream gone astray because of the deteriorating work ethic of the working class:

> We still remember the famous model workers and the masters of socialism of an earlier period. Under their influence, workers in all trades took hard work as their dictum and within a short period, the new China, just coming out of a hundred years of destruction by wars, witnessed tremendous changes. In just a few decades, however, the factories where enthusiastic workers once worked have been transformed into something totally different: fully one hour after the work bell, workers are still coming in; inside the workshops, groups are playing cards and chess, and knitting sweaters. . . . Our masters have degenerated! Our masters have smashed their own rice bowl.

An even darker vision sees unemployment as essential to social progress. In an essay entitled "China Needs the Catfish Effect," the above-mentioned August 1998 supplement to *Shopping Guide* invokes a folktale to explain the virtue of naked market competition and unemployment. The tale tells of a clever fisherman who keeps his sardines alive by putting a catfish in the tank. Fearing that the catfish will gobble them up, the sardines arouse their survival instincts and stay alive all the way to the market, getting the fisherman a good price. The article then reasons:

> The process of reform requires some enterprises to go bankrupt, to make others feel the pressure of survival. [It] also needs to lay off some people, which will pose a threat to those remaining on the job and motivate them to work harder. [It] also requires some to get rich first, to let the poor have a goal in mind. Competition knows no passion. It is bloody. Either you die or I die. (emphasis original)

No other words describe the logic and virtue of competitive capitalism better. The laid-off workers, as the "reserve army" of laborers, are necessary for the effective functioning of a market economy. The word "capitalism" and related Marxist terminology, of course, are not to be invoked. This is the biggest taboo in postsocialist China. If the emergence of a capitalist class is celebrated in positive portrayals of the deserving rich, here the logic of competitive capitalism itself is implicitly affirmed as a law of nature.

Nevertheless, laid-off workers need to be reintegrated into the new social order, and street tabloids are doing their share. Notwithstanding their characteristic negative content orientation, positive stories dominate this topic. Government meetings and institutional announcements, the most unlikely tabloid content, are commonly found in headlines. State authorities and all walks of society are taking care of the laid-off workers, announcing preferential policies, and providing supports. Best of all, two headlines claimed: "Laid off Domestically, Get a Job Abroad," and "An American Job Expert Says: Unemployment Is No Big Deal, It's Part of a Global Trend."

Reporting on positive role models, a key mainstream journalism feature, is rare in street tabloids. The usual cast of characters is headed by social deviants, and a common theme is the condemnation of social decay and moral bankruptcy. But laid-off workers are exceptions. There are several lengthy tales, including first-person narratives (though in two cases clearly not written by the workers themselves), about how laid-off workers, after all kinds of setbacks, were able to "discover and mobilize their enterprising selves"[21] and establish themselves as successful entrepreneurs. Since the majority of laid-off workers are middle-aged women, they were the main protagonists. Modern Women's News, for example, ran a regular full-page feature column on "laid-off households" in summer 1998. Such inspiring titles as "Taking Charge of My Own Future, I Am No Longer Afraid" and "Endeavoring to Find Opportunities, I Am Fully Confident in the Future" told stories of successful self-transformation. In contrast with the self-indulgent rich female, these are virtuous, realistic, and resilient women who took control of their own destinies and made the best out of their circumstances.

Jiang Fengrong, the protagonist in a Modern Women's News story on 24 July

1998, is one such example. She was laid off in 1995. Her husband, who was also laid off, lost the family's entire savings on the stock market. So Jiang shouldered the responsibility of sustaining the household. She first found a job cleaning washrooms in a hotel and earned all A's in her daily job evaluations. Her husband, in contrast, looked down on her job and attempted to make easy and quick money by selling pornographic material. He was caught and received a three-year prison sentence. Jiang lost her job at the hotel and subsequently took a job attending a sick old woman—a job many others had rejected for being too dirty. When the old woman died, Jiang went to the countryside to work in her brother's greenhouses. As a former worker who possessed more advanced consciousness and knew that "knowledge means efficiency, and science means money," she began to use scientific knowledge to cultivate new fruit crops and outperformed her conservative peasant brother. She was fully redeemed as an entrepreneur. When she reappeared in the hotel where she once worked as a cleaning lady, she was talking with its vice president over a fruit supply contract.

Though details vary, the moral of these tales is consistent and simple: There is nothing to fear. Being laid off is painful, but it is also an opportunity. Chinese workers have nothing to lose but their undesirable jobs at state enterprises. They have fortune and fame to gain in the market.[22]

If there are any character weaknesses on the part of laid-off workers, it is their sense of dependence and their archaic notions of job security, welfare entitlements, and social status. Consequently, they are called on to make psychological adjustments, lower their expectations, accept low-paying and low-status jobs, and settle in their places in the new division of labor in the "socialist market economy." If the rich are the subjects of hedonistic admiration and populist mockery, laid-off workers are the targets of psychological counseling and thought engineering. In this way, the tabloids perform an important ideological role in greasing the wheels of the painful process of economic polarization for people at the bottom of society and in turning social stratification into a matter of personal psychology. Shanghai's laid-off female workers have liberated their thought and driven thousands of migrant rural women out of the domestic servant job market. Why is it that their Beijing counterparts cannot change their mind-sets, lower their sense of social status, and become domestic servants as well, asks a front page article in the 4 April 1998 "Chinese Family" edition of *China Society Journal*. A widely circulated story, entitled "[Party] Secretary Polishes my Shoes!" in the volume 24 (1998) issue of *Press Digest Herald* best symbolizes this line of persuasion. It tells how Hu Fuguo, Shanxi provincial Party secretary, after visiting a shoe-polishing team consisting of laid-off workers and having his shoes polished, performed a reciprocal service and extolled the virtue of labor.

Just as there is no reporting of protests by laid-off workers, there is little reporting of their plight, their frustrations, and their anger. The story about the suicide of a laid-off female worker is the only exception in the forty-one stories on layoffs. It is the leading article in the "Layoff Special Page" of the above-mentioned supplement to *Shopping Guide*. The treatment of the story underscores the paper's concern for social stability and its commitment to the ideology of market liberalism. "Female Laid-off Worker Commits Suicide" would be a perfect tabloid headline, given the tabloids' inclination to exploit the female and the corpse. But layoffs are not a topic to be sensationalized. Indeed, the death of a laid-off worker, an apparent victim of the economic reforms, is not to be made explicit even in a tabloid headline. Nor is her gender. "Chose Death" is the title. Mixing narrative with analysis, the article tells the fate of Zhang Min, who hanged herself on New Year's Eve. The analysis describes how the institutions and individuals in her life failed her one after another. Her original employer, as a bad apple in a country that has "a relatively good welfare system," sacked her without any compensation. Coworkers at her second job accused her of stealing simply because she was once a laid-off worker. Her third employer—a household in which she worked as a domestic helper—happened to have a son who attended the same school as her son. Being bullied and humiliated by his more privileged classmate, Zhang's son begged his mother to quit. Meanwhile, Zhang's husband had an affair with another woman and divorced her. All these contributed to Zhang's death, according to the article. But in the end, the article blames Zhang's own character weakness and calls for "a correct mind-set" on the part of millions of laid-off workers. The will to survive is their only hope. "Although sympathy and support from society are important, people must survive without these. To survive, one must rely on oneself! Zhang Min died. Hopefully, those of us who are still dragging on in hardship will learn a lesson." Karl Marx comes to the rescue of would-be Zhang Mins. His notion of organized struggle as the way to the salvation of the working class, of course, is irrelevant. Instead, the paper printed the following quotation from Marx to inspire Chinese workers and to set the ideological frame for its "Layoff Special Page:" "Life is an ocean. Only those who have a strong will can reach the other side." In postsocialist China, only the neoliberal mind finds Marx inspirational.

## Peasants, Migrant Workers, and Criminals

Though I was able to find forty-one stories related to laid-off workers, there are very few items about peasants and migrant workers as collective social groups. At a time when an urban bias is increasingly apparent in the mainstream media, the marginal role of the peasantry in street tabloids of the 1990s is not surprising. Peasants appeared as victims of corrupt local officials and as legitimate social actors defending their own interests in a few short news excerpts. In a case reported on the front page of the 22 May 1998 issue of *Qiantang Weekend* (Qiantang zhoumo), a group of peasants took a township government to court for arbitrary taxation. The story presented the case as the triumph of the rule of law and as evidence of the peasantry's increasing awareness of its legal rights and its political maturity as a law-abiding citizenry. In a rare case reported in the 30 July

1998 issue of *Legal News Digest* (Fazhi wencui bao), peasants organized to resist local authorities over tax collection. But since the group acted outside the existing political institutions by creating an illegal organization and holding illegal rallies, it was "an evil feudal force" with no legitimate claim against the state. The story begins with the arrest of seventeen peasant organizers.

There are more stories about migrant workers as a group. In a page devoted to *dagongzhe* (a popular term that refers to the wage laborer but does not carry the political baggage associated with either "worker" or "laborer"), the 15 May 1989 special edition of *Huanjiang Business News* (Huanjiang shang bao) printed a first-person narrative by a young migrant worker. But it is a highly abstract and idealized description of the migrant experience, written, probably, by a college freshman with a rural origin. The writer displays the perfect "mobile personality," a key character identified by modernization theorist Daniel Lerner as necessary for the peasantry to overcome backwardness and enter modernity.[23] Although the author wishes to become an urban resident, he also desires to develop his hometown. The purpose of his migration is to "liberate my thought . . . expand my horizon, and learn advanced technology," and he intends to return home to "build factories, cultivate orchards, and raise fish and shrimp." The idealized role of migrant laborer as an agent of rural development is fully embodied. A second story, entitled "A New Notion among Migrant Workers: Better to Acquire Skills Than to Earn Money," provides a group portrait of migrant workers busy attending night schools and spending lavishly on technical education in the cities.

A story in an undated special issue of *Popular Health News* tells a fairy tale about an oppressed rural woman's road to liberation and the overcoming of the rural–urban divide. Du Juan, a sixteen-year-old girl, ran away from her village in the south to escape an arranged marriage. At a bus depot in the north, she was cheated and sold to an old man as his wife. She escaped and ran into Wang Qing, a female army officer and a selfless savior. Wang found her a babysitting job, and when the job was no longer available, took Du home and paid her ¥100 a month for light household work. More importantly, Wang revealed to Du the road to salvation: "If a woman wants to stand on her own feet in society, she must have skills." Du subsequently learned multiple skills under Wang's guidance and completely transformed herself. Her stunningly urbane speech and demeanor landed her a public relations managerial job, although her dream was to eventually become a boss *(laoban)* herself.

Other stories, however, reveal a more threatening image of rural migrants. In one case, peasant construction workers appeared as thugs hired by developers in a conflict with urban residents over a housing project. They were seen as mobs threatening the life and property of urban residents. In other cases, they are presented as a destabilizing force destroying the fabric of urban social life and family, as in stories in which the young migrant babysitter/domestic worker seduces the urban family man.

Occasionally the tabloids speak on behalf of this group and crusade for its welfare. There are sympathetic articles about migrants' poor living conditions, their miserable social and cultural life, and their lack of resident status (*hukou*) in urban China. An article in the 14 August 1998 issue of *Eastern Weekend* (Dongfang zhoumo) tells several stories about young rural migrant women's experiences of love and marriage, especially their sexual exploitation by urban men, who see them as sexually attractive but from a socially inferior class. Qian Dongdong was such a victim. She went to the city to escape the traditional rural marriage pattern but ended up in an abusive relationship with an urban worker. Worse, she was trapped in the alienating urban setting and found no social support. When she complained to her husband's factory director about his adulterous relationships with other women, he replied, "No big deal. Nine out of ten men here are greedy for women." When she sought divorce, local authorities refused to take up her case because she did not have an urban resident permit.

Even the occasional lucky one who "made it" and found unconditional love with an urban man found life difficult. Zhao Yong boarded the train to Beijing with two sacks of rice when she failed the college entrance exam in 1984. All she had dreamed of was the life of an ordinary urban woman. She worked hard as a domestic worker, managed to get a college degree, and became a temporary worker at a cultural institution. There, her quiet personality and extraordinary migration experience attracted Zhang Bin, a college graduate with an elite Beijing intellectual family background. Knowing that she was no match for Zhang, Zhao escaped from her love. She quit her job in Beijing and became a saleswoman in the south. Zhang continued to pursue her, and eventually they were married. In 1995 Zhao got an urban *hukou* in the south through her company, but not in Beijing. By 1998 Zhao had led a floating life in urban China for fourteen years. She cried, "Fourteen years! Fourteen years! What's a *hukou*? Invisible, intangible, who can tell me what a *hukou* is?"

Peasants and rural migrants received the most attention not as social groups with collective social interests and problems, but as individuals in morality tales and, more often, in crime stories. This reflects their role as backward, narrow-minded, inhumane, irrational, greedy, and law-blind individuals who commit all kinds of atrocities against family members and others. From "Beastly Husband Cuts Off Tip of Wife's Nose and Cheeks to Go with Wine" to "Female, Committed Rape," distorted human relationships—the suffering, the blood, and the revenge—not revealed in mainstream papers receive extensive treatment. An elementary school teacher routinely raped girl pupils in the classroom, a husband solicited clients for his prostitute wife, a mother assisted her prostitute daughter in robbing her clients, and a wife treated her husband to a virgin to sustain their marriage. Worse, the victims do not even know the source of their misery. Residents in the tiny Henan village of Gelou are a hopeless crowd in an extended story in the 3 July 1998 supplement to *Hebei Business News* (Hebei shangbao). Five six-year-old children died mysteriously between 1997 and 1998. Nobody reported the deaths to the police. Villagers believed that heaven was recalling six-year-olds. When an outsider called in the police to investigate, they refused to cooperate and continued to appeal to the gods for mercy. It turned out that the children had been murdered by a village woman as an act of revenge against their families. Rural and transitional society in its "natural" state of affairs is the realm of ignorance, crime, and darkness in these tales.

Sex and property crimes constitute the bulk of stories about underclasses. One typical plot involves a shameless migrant woman who exchanges sex for money and then resorts to robbery or murder, or is herself the murder victim. Rather than work hard to make some honest money and then "return home, get married, and set up a happy family," as the volume 33 (1998) supplement to *Safety Herald* (Anquan daobao) suggests, they resent hard work and gamble on their youth and beauty. Another typical plot centers on the young rural male, individually or in an organized property crime group. The characteristics are always greed, moral bankruptcy, and a "get-rich-by-all-means" mentality. The narrative is often couched in a "good versus evil" frame, with earnest calls for the restoration of morality and the maintenance of law and order. After analyzing the crime trajectory of a peasant highway robbery gang and their psychological profiles, an article in the 16 May 1998 supplement to *Tibetan Youth News* concluded:

> The collapse of personal value systems is the main cause for the actions of these death row criminals. In their eyes, enrichment policies are not enough. Robbery is a heaven-mandated means to get rich quick. . . . A distorted personal philosophy leads to the violation of laws and the degradation of morality. However, an evil person one should not be; a devilish action one should not take; and a gangster philosophy one should not have. These robbers' fates offer the best warning for the rest of us.

The lack of economic opportunities for the rural poor, the shortage of jobs for migrant workers, their harsh working conditions and meager incomes in the urban areas, and the lack of effective supporting social structures in rural and migrant communities are seldom considered as possible macrostructural reasons for crime. In some stories, property criminals and prostitutes were explicitly blamed for deviating from the norm: "the getting-rich-through-hard-work road, a gold-plated avenue full of hopes," as the story in the *Tibetan Youth News* put it.

These crime tales contrast sharply with the following account about prostitution by "eastern European sisters" in the 23 April 1999 issue of *Youth Reference* (Qingnian cankao), which begins:

> Since the change of governments in eastern Europe, the economy faces a painful transformation, and the society is severely polarized. Those unable to get out of poverty through normal means turn their eyes abroad, especially to neighboring western Europe. Although it is possible for men to find jobs, there is little chance for women to find normal jobs. Cheated by human traffickers, many young women end up becoming prostitutes.

This piece explains, contextualizes, and encourages the reader to reflect on social structures, whereas tales about peasants and migrant deviants personalize, sensationalize, and normalize. My point is not to deny that crime is a legitimate concern. Nor am I taking issue with the "overrepresentation" of peasants and migrant workers as criminals. However, these particular types of crime tales transform issues of social divisions into those of character, morality, and law and order. These stories are thus profoundly conservative in their political and social implications.

Crime stories, especially those published in "law-and-order" papers sponsored by law enforcement agencies, typically fuse sensationalism with the celebration of the bravery and efficiency of law enforcement apparatuses. Although the Party's anticorruption campaign in the law enforcement agencies has led to increased exposure of power abuses by the police and the court system since 1997, the basic structure of the crime story remains the same. Rather than crusade for justice on behalf of victims, crimes are typically reported after the cases have been closed and it can be shown that justice has been done.[24] The typical narrative either starts or ends with the capturing of the criminals and their punishments. Moreover, neither the self-contained narrative form nor the personalized plot and the condemnatory language "encourage reflection on the social and political structure."[25] Crime stories create fear and anxiety, and they call for harsh punishments. They reinforce the "hard strike" (*yanda*) law-and-order campaigns the authorities have waged since the mid-1990s and could potentially contribute to the construction of an "authoritarian consensus."[26] Populist authoritarianism is a common mode of market-driven tabloid journalism in many media systems.[27] Chinese tabloids are no exception.

## SO, WHAT ARE THE TABLOIDS SAYING? CLASS, IDEOLOGY, AND MORALITY IN POSTSOCIALIST CHINA

The popular press in postsocialist China caters to a highly stratified readership. Among the readers are the beneficiaries of the economic reforms, the professional and managerial elite, and the urban middle-class consumers, who are invited to indulge themselves in the pleasure of consumption and relate themselves horizontally to middle-class lifestyles in the West. More and more newsstand publications have emerged to serve this readership since 1992. This is an important development in the Chinese popular press. Consumerism is a key popular experience at the urban newsstand. "We've been exposed to the Western lifestyle now, and we want to enjoy it too."[28] This statement, made by an avid reader of *Fine Goods Shopping Guide*, articulates a powerful impulse. Although high heels and blue jeans were once truly popular as symbols of opposition to the official culture of state socialism, in the context of state-mandated consumerism in postsocialist China, a reader's experience with a ¥580 Pierre Cardin wallet tells a story of status and class privileges. It embodies the ideology of commodity fetishism.[29] This broader ideology, as Richard Ohmann argues, is more conse-quential and a stronger integrative force than ideology in the narrow sense—a particular set of ideas found between lines and behind narrative frames.[30]

If consumer and lifestyle papers help construct the urban middle-class identity and provide a forum for affluent consumers to speak about their consumption experiences and celebrate their status and class privileges, the thematic orienta-tions of low-brow street tabloids are more complicated. There is no single sys-tematic, calculated, and coherent voice in the tabloid tales. A range of voices, by no means equal in volume, and different layers of meanings are present. They are ambiguous and contradictory, and they resonate with official myths and pop-ular practical consciousness in different ways, with different political implications.

At one level, it is possible to argue that tabloid tales make sense of the social world in highly ideological ways—ideological in the sense that the meanings embodied in them serve to establish and sustain relations of domination.[31] Though corrupt officials as individuals are condemned, the economically privi-leged as a social group are celebrated and their lifestyles are admired. Not only is the term "class" taboo, the rich as an economic and social category is coded in highly nationalistic and cultural terms: "socialist" China now celebrates its own wealthy champions and national capitalists ranked by *Fortune* magazine.

There are populist sentiments against economic privilege, ostentation, vulgar-ity, and even a reference to expropriation by the illegally enriched. But there is little critical reflection on class formations in society. Marxism as an analytical framework is virtually absent: it is perhaps at once too official and too discredited to be invoked (after all, even the mainstream press has ignored it) and too sub-versive to be allowed to apply to postsocialist Chinese realities.[32] The vocabulary for social analysis goes back to the pre-Marx age. The economic system is made sense of through a proverb that reduces human beings to wealth-pursuing crea-tures; the virtue of a competitive market system is introduced through a cruel folktale whose truth is self-evident. Layoffs are God's will, and the making of the working class itself is an international trend and a means to prosperity. Though the benign state, various social institutions, and exceptional individuals are doing their best to help, the only road to salvation for the economically and socially displaced is the personal will to survive, and those who overcome their own psychological barriers have fame and fortune to gain. In this postsocialist order, the pursuit of wealth by exploiting policy loopholes and cultivating politi-cal patrons is a social virtue. Defending personal economic interests through the courts is positive news, while any organized opposition to collectively redress economic injustices is by definition evil. Though rural migrants receive some sympathetic treatment, people really fear them, imagining them as potential members of a street mob. The implicit hierarchy of social interests is revealed in the positive statement about how Shanghai's laid-off workers have driven away rural migrants in the job market, as well as in frequently expressed expectations that these people will return to their villages.

The predominant role of peasants and migrant workers is that of the criminal—the target of discipline and punishment. With few exceptions, stories about laid-off workers and migrant laborers do not critically reflect on their state of being and their current social trappings. Instead, they are about the transcendence of their social existence at the individual level. Former laid-off workers told of their successful transformation into business owners, the migrant peasant dreamed of becoming one upon returning to his or her native village, and the runaway rural young-woman-turned-public-relations-manager saw it as her ultimate career goal. The business entrepreneur is the undisputed cultural hero (an early 2000 survey reported that 84.4 percent of urban residents between the age of fifteen and fifty-four want to be a business owner, or *laoban*).[33] The notion of personal and social development through the market, along with a nationalistic ideology of catching up with the West, an Enlightenment belief in the instrumental use of knowledge, and an authoritarian emphasis on law and order, is deeply embedded in many tabloid tales.

The tabloid format is by definition less analytical and more personalized. Perhaps the tabloids cannot be expected to make the connection that the same "gold-plated avenue" that leads some to wealth and turns state enterprise managers into millionaires is the same path that leads workers into unemployment and some into crime.[34] But this would not explain why staggering social polarization and the suicide of a laid-off worker are not sensationalized in the headlines. Nor does it explain why the idea of equality is couched in the interest of the Party-state. The pro-establishment coverage of layoffs, the differentiated treatments of two types of peasant collective actions, as well as the way in which the story on prostitution by eastern European women was written, suggest that street tabloids reflect the hegemonic views of the dominant elite in many ways. They have a stronger official character than is commonly assumed. Though they may break the Party's propaganda codes in some ways, they more often extend official press discourses and reinforce the Party's ideological hegemony in other ways. What the Party finds disturbing is not necessarily subversive. Crime stories, which the authorities dislike for their exposure of the dark side of society and their potential to incite criminal acts, for example, may serve a functional means for a deeply strained society to come to terms with its pathological symptoms. Moreover, they may be seen as pro-establishment not only in their law-and-order orientation but also in their moralistic condemnations. Since norms "do not appear to be imposed by one class upon another, but present themselves as common sense that applies equally to all," moralizing crime tales about under classes help conceal unequal political and economic power relations.[35]

Moreover, precisely because writers and editors of tabloid tales are driven by commercial imperatives and are acutely aware of their fragile institutional bases, they tend to focus on safe and convenient subjects, such as readily available crime tales about the lower classes from police sources. Crime stories and their pro-establishment orientation, therefore, are as much a result of the tabloid market structure as the explicit ideological intentions of tabloid writers and editors. It is also possible that writers may invoke an official myth not as a matter of conviction but as a defensive rhetorical strategy to wrap an engaging narrative, which is the main selling point. Similarly, a writer may accept the supremacy of the Party-state (in the case of couching the idea of equality in the interest of the state) as a means to reaffirm a residual state socialist ideal that has lost official favor.

Finally, although the marginal existence of street tabloids affords them greater opportunities to print crime and human interest stories, this relative freedom also allows writers and editors of an elitist and market-authoritarian bent to vent their own fears and prejudices against the lower classes or express the perspectives of the beneficiaries of the market reforms more freely. If *People's Daily* is still obligated to pay lip service to residual state socialist categories such as "the working class" and "the people," street tabloids can easily ignore such hypocritical rhetoric. Their writers and editors can blame the working class for their own plight more openly and celebrate the virtue of layoffs more freely. Tabloid voices thus include the voice of the emergent neoliberal elite presented as the universalizing and naturalizing "laws" of the market economy. Although street tabloids are intended for the lower classes, they are published by cultural entrepreneurs affiliated, however loosely, with the Party and business press. Though a few writers may have grassroots connections, it is unlikely that many of them have close associations with the lower classes or coherent political commitments to improve their lot. Judged from their tales, it is clear that street tabloids do not adequately reflect the perspectives of disenfranchised social groups, especially the angers, frustrations, and political consciousness of those who have rebelled openly.[36] Given the dominant elite's embrace of market authoritarianism and the Party's all-out effort to prevent progressive intellectuals from building alliances with discontented workers and peasants,[37] it is not surprising that street tabloids, under the dual compulsion of political control and market constraints, are not forums for critical political consciousness.

However, in some other ways (though a much lesser extent), some tabloid tales do reflect popular concerns and incorporate fragments of popular consciousness. Although celebrating the rich and emphasizing the transcendence of existing social status for laid-off workers and rural migrants fit into official myths, they may also articulate the aspirations of many in these groups. The other side of the story about the rich—the prominent theme that money does not bring happiness—may also have resonance in popular consciousness, and a reader can potentially take these stories and "run" with them in different directions. It could be seen as expressing a sense of resignation that encourages those at the bottom of the society to be content with their present trappings. At the same time, these stories offer the voyeuristic pleasure of seeing the self-destruction of the economically privileged and articulate a populist and moralistic critique against the prevalent money-worship ethic and an economic reform program that is socially and morally bankrupt. It may well be that both the "getting rich" utopia (as an implicit broad narrative framework) and its dystopia (at the level of individual narratives) have popular underpinnings, although they are by no means articulated with equal unequivocalness.

Similar contradictions apply to the gender dimension. The tabloids make sense of social stratification in highly gendered ways, and they reflect both sexist and gender equality themes. Moreover, these contradictory themes have different articulations with popular sentiments, official lines, and an emergent neoliberal perspective. Though one can blame the tabloids for sexist headlines about rich females, terms such as *nü dakuan* and *fupo* are popular idioms. Similarly, dramatizations around Pan Roulan's beauty and virginity (therefore all the more tragic when ruined) reflect a deep-rooted patriarchal perspective in Chinese society. Though the story about Zheng Huifang seems to implicate patriarchy as a source of her plight, stories about shameless migrant women seducing (urban) men for economic gains may resonate with both urban men and women. Such narratives serve as self-rationalization for men, and for women, as a convenient way of scapegoating others for their husbands' real and feared betrayals. Rather than point to patriarchy and rural–urban disparities as potential reasons for the flourishing sex trade, popular discourses end up demonizing migrant women sex workers and blaming their moral bankruptcy. On the other hand, the call for rural migrants' urban resident status is advanced on the basis of migrant women's problems in marrying "up" to urban men (the migrant men have little chance to marry urban women, and so the problem does not arise from them). The gender subtext in the notion of the urban laid-off worker's need to rely on her personal will to reestablish herself, however, has a different twist. Here the official gender equality discourse about women's need for self-empowerment (*ziqiang*) and self-reliance (*zili*) is entangled with an emergent market liberal discourse about the (supposedly gender neutral) individual as the self-initiated economic agent.

 The heavy emphasis on morality is also a complicated phenomenon. As I argued earlier, crime tales have a commercial imperative and express political authoritarianism. But the appeal to morality has its own cultural logic as well. As Ci Jiwei has argued, part of the excess of the Maoist era was the subordination and even the reduction of the moral to the political. "The political project was everything; its collapse naturally caused everything, including morality, to collapse with it."[38] Within this context, morality tales and the call for the restoration of morality in society have a popular appeal. It cuts across stories about various social groups and is a popular response to the current social malaise and moral paralysis.

Tabloids are not carriers of oppositional political consciousness. Nor are they packets of "new opium" handed down by the Party's propaganda department. Rather, they contain a mixed and uneven bag of "residual," "dominant," and "emergent" (to use Raymond Williams's categories) forms of consciousness specific to the ideological landscape in postsocialist China. As the cultural products of a complicated and contradictory process of social transformation, they can be simultaneously functional to the dominant social order and expressive of people's genuine desires and needs, as well as their lived experience of this historical life process.

## NOTES

I would like to thank Richard Madsen, Perry Link, and Paul Pickowicz for their editorial guidance and invaluable comments at different stages of this project. Participants in the 1999 Princeton University symposium on popular culture and thought in postsocialist China offered many constructive criticisms on an early draft, and I am very grateful to all. Richard Levy deserves special thanks for his close reading of two earlier drafts and very useful comments. Finally, I want to thank Wang Xiaoying, Zhao Weichun, and Daniel Say for collecting some of the tabloids.

1. Jiwei Ci, *Dialectic of the Chinese Revolution: From Utopianism to Hedonism* (Stanford, Calif.: Stanford University Press, 1994).

2. Leonard L. Chu, "Continuity and Change in China's Media Reform," *Journal of Communication*, Summer 1994, 9.

3. The charge of vulgarity is common in Chinese publications. See Shi Tongyu, "The Perplexed and Flustered Situation of Societal News in China" (Zhongguo shehui xinwen mihuo yu kunjing), *Journal of Beijing Broadcasting Institute*, January 1994, 15. A Beijing media scholar articulated the more political "new opium" view in an interview.

4. Jianying Zha, *China Pop: How Soap Opera, Tabloids, and Bestsellers Are Transforming a Culture* (New York: New Press, 1995), 108.

5. Ian Connell, "Personalities in the Popular Media," in *Journalism and Popular Culture*, ed. Peter Dahlgren and Colin Sparks (London: Sage, 1992), 66; emphasis in original.

6. Connell, "Personalities in the Popular Media," 68.

7. This usage is in line with the broad definition of the "new rich" used by Richard Robison and David Goodman in their book, *The New Rich in Asia: Mobile Phones, McDonald's, and Middle-class Revolution* (London: Routledge, 1996). There is no question that there are conflicts and differences among the "new rich," but this is not a tabloid theme.

8. The first batch consists of fifty-four editions of twenty-nine different titles gathered from Beijing, Shanghai, and Hangzhou between 1994 and 1995. The second batch consists of 134 editions of 86 different titles collected in Guangzhou, Hangzhou, Guizhou, Dalian, and Beijing between 1998 and 1999. Although the irregular nature of the tabloids makes it impossible to collect a statistically representative sample, attempts were made to collect as wide a sample as possible. In Beijing, for example, I tried to buy samples from different neighborhoods. The national distribution of the tabloids also helps to ensure that the sample provides a comprehensive snapshot of available titles. Although there is more coverage of laid-off workers and more stories on corruption in the 1998–1999 sample (by this time, the Party had explicitly encouraged media exposure of corruption), thematic orientations between the 1994–1995 and 1998–1999 samples are rather consistent in other areas. Consequently, I focus on the 1998–1999 sample for the detailed textual

analysis. All articles about the four social groups are identified and thematically analyzed. Attention is paid both to explicit meanings and to implicit assumptions and frames.

9. Colin Sparks, "Introduction," *The Public* 5, no. 3 (1998): 7. Although the distinction between serious and tabloid journalism is not as watertight as people tend to think, the process of tabloidization has accelerated in the past two decades across media systems. Dahlgren and Sparks, *Journalism and Popular Culture*; and *The Public* 5, no. 3 (1998).

10. Peter Dahlgren, introduction to *Journalism and Popular Culture*, 8.

11. Yuezhi Zhao, *Media, Market, and Democracy in China: Between the Party Line and the Bottom Line* (Urbana: University of Illinois Press, 1998), 135–38.

12. Yuezhi Zhao, "Toward a Propaganda/Commercial Model of Journalism in China? The Case of the *Beijing Youth News*," *Gazette* 58, no. 3 (1996): 143–57.

13. Erik Eckholm, "Detectable Materialism Catching On in China," *New York Times*, 10 January 1998, A4.

14. Cao Peng and Zhang Lixian, *Zenyang dang ziyou zhuangao zhe* (How to be a freelance writer) (Beijing: Guangming ribao chubanshe, 1997).

15. Central Propaganda Department, State Press and Publications Administration, "Opinions on Strengthening the Management and Improving the Operations of Weekend Editions," in *Xinwen chuban fagui jianming shiyong shouce (1949–1994)* (A concise and practical handbook to press regulations), ed. State Press and Publications Administration (Beijing: Zhongguo shuji chubanshe, 1994), 152–53.

16. Han Dongfang, "Appeal to Delegates of the TUC Conference," www.china-labour.org.hk/2001e/detainees_lao_yue.htm. Accessed August 1999.

17. "China Sets Up Security Net for the Urban Poor," *Qiao bao*, 4 April 2000, A2.

18. Ironically, the state raised the salaries of its employees by 35 percent to 50 percent in June 1999.

19. The standard Chinese term for layoff, *xiagang*, used by official organs and tabloids alike, has an Orwellian newspeak quality. It literally means to "to step down from one's post," as if workers themselves are the agents who willingly "step down." The verb *xia*, the antonym of *shang* (to get on), also creates the illusion of mobility.

20. See, for example, "Municipal Party Committee Held a Seminar on Guiding Public Opinion on Reemployment," *Hangzhou Daily*, 22 May 1998, 1.

21. Jing Wang, "The State Question in Chinese Popular Cultural Studies" (manuscript, 2000), 22.

22. For a scholarly analysis of the political economy of layoffs and the survival of laid-off workers, see Dorothy J. Solinger, "Sudden Sackings and the Mirage of the Market: Unemployment, Reemployment, and Survival in Wuhan, Summer 1999" (paper presented at the annual meeting of the Association for Asian Studies, San Diego, 9–12 March 2000).

23. Daniel Lerner, *The Passing of Traditional Society: Modernizing the Middle East* (New York: Free Press, 1958).

24. Zhao, *Media, Market, and Democracy in China*, 160.

25. Colin Sparks, "Popular Journalism: Theories and Practices," in *Journalism and Popular Culture*, 41.

26. Stuart Hall, Chas Critcher, Tony Jefferson, John Clarke, and Brian Roberts, *Policing the Crisis: Mugging, the State, and Law and Order* (London: Macmillan, 1978); see also George Gerbner, "Television Violence: The Power and the Peril," in *Gender, Race, and*

*Class in Media: A Critical Text Reader*, ed. Gail Dines and Jean M. Humez (London: Sage, 1995), 547–57.

27. Sparks, "Popular Journalism"; see also Dan Hallin, "*La Nota Roja*: Popular Journalism and the Transition to Democracy in Mexico," in *Tabloid Tales*, ed. Colin Sparks and John Tulloch (Lanham, Md.: Rowman & Littlefield, 2000).

28. Eckholm, "Delectable Materialism Catching on China," A1.

29. The term "ideology" has a whole range of useful meanings, and I employ different definitions in my analysis. For analyses of this particular definition and other related ones, see Terry Eagleton, *Ideology: An Introduction* (London: Verso, 1991); and John B. Thompson, *Ideology in Modern Culture: Critical Social Theory in the Era of Mass Communication* (Stanford, Calif.: Stanford University Press, 1990).

30. Richard Ohmann, *Selling Culture: Magazines, Markets, and Class at the Turn of the Century* (London: Verso, 1996), 348–49.

31. See Thompson, *Ideology in Modern Culture*, for this notion of ideology.

32. Class analysis has largely been driven underground and employed by fringe Maoists and some protesting peasants and workers. For a substantial Maoist critique of the economic reforms by a mainland Chinese author, see Mei Yan, *Qingsuan gaige kaifang ershi nian* (Settling accounts with twenty years of reform and openness) (Hong Kong: Xiafei'er guoji chubangongsi, 1999). For an analysis of the use of class vocabulary by protesters, see Elizabeth J. Perry, "Crime, Corruption, and Contention," in *The Paradox of China's Post-Mao Reforms*, ed. Merle Goldman and Roderick MacFarquhar (Cambridge: Harvard University Press, 1999), 308–29.

33. "A Majority of Urban Residents Want to Be *Laoban*." *Qiaobao* (The China Press), 2 February 2000, A7.

34. I borrow this from Stuart Hall et al.: "The problem is that the 'present conditions,' which make the poor poor (or the criminal take to crime) are precisely the *same* conditions which make the rich rich (or allow the law-abiding to imagine that the social causes of crime will disappear if you punish individual criminals hard enough)." *Policing the Crisis*, emphasis in the original.

35. Fiske, "Popularity and the Politics of Information," 50.

36. "All power and wealth belong to the people!" "Down with political and economic exploitation and oppression!" "To hell with a socialist market economy, this is exploitation with Chinese characteristics!" These were the cries of protesting workers in northeast China. Yue Shan, "The Uprising of 100,000 Workers in Four Cities," *Zheng ming*, January 1998, 18–19. See also Perry, "Crime, Corruption, and Contention," 315–21.

37. Merle Goldman, "Politically Engaged Intellectuals in the 1990s," *China Quarterly* 159 (1999): 709.

38. Ci, *Dialectic of the Chinese Revolution*, 115.

# 6

# The New Chinese Woman and Lifestyle Magazines in the Late 1990s

*Julia F. Andrews and Kuiyi Shen*

Dong Xiaoyan, whose photograph is set against a bright blue background, is evidently a self-confident young woman (photo 6.1). She gazes at us with a friendly, open expression. Very up-to-date, her casual garb is a pleasing mixture of Chinese and foreign trends. With her delicate gold earrings and yellow gold bracelet, she wears a white v-neck sweater in a stylish ribbed knit. Although her jewelry and clothing appear to be of Chinese manufacture, her hair is swept up in a tousled coiffure of a kind popular in Japan, and her subtly shaded makeup is perfectly applied. Her eyebrows have been plucked to form a fashionably thin, very slightly bowed line. She is clearly a successful working girl, but her blue jeans tell us that she is relaxing on her day off, enjoying the leisure that her income affords her. In her casual prosperity she represents a new reality—one that many urban young people expect to become their own. This magazine cover, from the July 1999 issue of *Qingnian yidai* (The young generation), typifies the contemporary ideal of Chinese womanhood, just as the contents of the magazines on which the faces of this woman and her countless sisters appear describe the new world in which they live.

Visual images are critical components of a person's mental life. They can illustrate aspirations, recollections, and even desired identities. Our dreams of the future sometimes take visual forms, and pictures—be they photographs, posters, films, paintings, or our own mental snapshots—make up, at least in part, our memories, our assumptions, and our visions of what is to come. The sources and nature of these images of course differ from person to person and from place to place, but very few people in urban societies today can escape some input from

Photo 6.1  Cover of Young Generation *(Qingnian yidai)*, July 1999. Published by Shanghai People's Publishing House. Price $3.60. r.m.b.

the mass media. With urban China's extraordinarily rapid modernization in the 1990s, the constant appearance of dazzling new careers, extraordinary social trends, and previously unimagined consumer products may make the media's influence even stronger than in our own comparatively stable culture, with its somewhat slower-paced social change.

The media's power to expand our imaginary universe is as remarkable as its potential to direct or control the worlds to which we have access. We tend, on the whole, to absorb its messages, whether eagerly or absent-mindedly. In daily life our powers of vigilance against such unthreatening parts of our environment are inevitably limited, and the images that we absorb naturally become part of our reality.


## THE PICTORIAL MAGAZINE IN MODERN CHINA

Since the end of the nineteenth century, a significant source of mental images for Chinese city dwellers, both in coastal cities and far inland, has been the pictorial magazine. Although television may be more powerful today, the portability and privacy of the magazine format continues to ensure it an audience. This genre, originally imported from the West, has played a particularly important role in changing the image of the proper role of the Chinese woman in the family and society. An early women's magazine, *Funü zazhi* (The ladies journal), featured colored lithographs of the new woman at study and play on its first covers (photo 6.2). Even today the domestic comfort and tranquility of those images remain potent, despite their quaintness. They were, however, partially superceded in the 1920s and 1930s by images of more glamorous ladies. The most popular pictorials of those years, such as *Meishu shenghuo* (Arts and life) or *Liangyou* (Young companion) frequently attracted consumers by their cover images of beauties (photo 6.3). Carolyn Waara has argued that these images appealed to women—as models, friends, and in other ways—at least as much as to men.[1] *Young Companion*, as part of its "friendship" editorial scheme, ran covers that featured attractive female subjects who were not necessarily celebrities or professional models. They might be movie stars, but they might also be college students, daughters or nieces of famous officials, or society women. That they were real people made their allure more compelling—their glamour and way of life seemed true and could be emulated, at least on a small scale.

After the revolution in 1949, the Maoist emphasis on establishing models for proper behavior dovetailed nicely with the marketing strategy of the pre-1949 publishing industry. While the dreams being marketed were radically different during the period of high Maoism, on the whole they were absorbed in similar ways. China's generation of Red Guards, who today are middle-aged and represent a population bulge rather like America's baby boomers, spent their formative years gazing not only at the ubiquitous images of Chairman Mao but also at the model citizens with whom Mao shared the pages of pictorial magazines.

The variety and content of available publications was radically reduced during the Cultural Revolution years (1966–1976), but brightly colored propaganda magazines and posters were printed in countless numbers (photo 6.4). There was little else in the way of art or decoration to see, and such printed matter, particularly posters and pictorial magazines, was an integral part of the lives of children in the late 1960s and the 1970s. Xiaomei Chen, describing her youth in an essay about Cultural Revolution posters, claims to have been touched, intrigued, and even *constructed by* what she saw in these printed images. The pictures she stud-

Photo 6.2    *Cover of* The Ladies' Journal *(Funü zazhi), January 1915, with illustration by Xu Yongqing.*

ied at school or on her bedroom wall confirmed what she believed were her parents' aspirations: that she help to build "an ideal society in which men and women—rich and poor, educated and uneducated—could, through their collective efforts, share equally in wealth and happiness."[2]

Magazines of the period, such as *China Reconstructs* and *China Pictorial,* told the same story. We meet comrade Wu Xuezhen of Jilin province on the cover of the September 1969 issue of *China Pictorial* (photo 6.4). Her slightly fuzzy image (a real picture of a real person, no doubt) shows us a rosy-faced young woman with her face crinkled in a happy smile. Her hair, despite its tightly braided pig-

*Photo 6.3    Cover of* Arts and Life *(Meishu shenghuo), July 1937.*

tails, is windblown. She wears a faded blue cotton jacket that is formless because it was cut for a man. The jacket is ornamented only by a Mao badge that is pinned over her heart and is crossed diagonally, as though she were a soldier, by the olive green strap of her bag. The jacket completely obscures her figure.

Most Chinese viewers at the time would immediately recognize her as a rusticated urban youth (*zhishi qingnian*), and the magazine's text tells us that she is

Photo 6.4    Cover of China Pictorial (Renmin huabao, English ed.), September 1969.

teacher of the part-farming, part-study primary school of the Sanjiawobao bri-
gade, Liujiaguan commune, Lishu county, Jilin province. "She serves the poor
and lower-middle peasants whole-heartedly."[3] From her appearance we know
that she lives the life of the farmers she serves and is dedicated and happy in her
work. Her lack of adornment shows that vanity is absent from her mind. Her
plain, androgynous dress indicates a sacrifice of her individuality, including her
sexuality, and her rural setting suggests her temporary sacrifice of ties to family
and friends. For the model woman of the Cultural Revolution generation, renun-

ciation of privilege and service to the masses were ideals. Happiness, when it was achieved, was a collective feeling.

Such images were displayed over and over in the 1970s. In 1974 we find nearly the same rusticated urban girl working happily with a group of fellow farmers in Xishuangbanna in China's far southwest (photo 6.5). By contrast, the cover girls of the 1990s and today, like their American counterparts, are usually alone—or, if one appears in a group, she is not busy with its activities but posed so that her only companion at the instant of the photograph is the reader.

Although often alone on the bright rectangle of a cover (photo 6.6), today's cover girls form part of a visual crowd that competes for readers' attention. Thirty years ago magazines were usually sheltered in work-unit reading rooms, offices, factory dormitories, or homes, but today they have carried their dazzling array of color and image out onto the streets. They are displayed and sold in almost every public place. Telephone kiosks, from which the many urban Chinese who lack home or cellular telephones make their calls, often double as newsstands. As people stand at the counter or window to talk on the telephone, their eyes can hardly avoid the displays of the brightly colored covers that adorn the latest issues. Which magazines are on view varies from city to city (the public phone kiosks in Urumchi and Turfan, for example, display magazines in both Chinese and Uighur) but everywhere, the smiling young working woman, or a slight variation of her image, is never absent. Urban bus riders inevitably find kiosks, pushcarts, or sidewalk vendors peddling a great variety of visually appealing reading matter, including translated Japanese comics *(manga)*, sports, business, political gossip, and lifestyle magazines, to mention only a few. From the covers of almost all the magazines, the pretty models who sparkle at passersby often seem as vivid as the real people who bustle past.

## THE LEADING LIFESTYLE MAGAZINES AT THE TURN OF THE MILLENNIUM

Perhaps the most important example of a magazine that negotiated the transition from Maoist politics to the market-driven society of the 1990s is *Gushihui* (Story collections), which began publication in Shanghai in 1963 as *Geming gushihui* (Revolutionary story collections). In 1979, when its circulation stood at 100,000, its editors dropped the word "revolutionary" from the title and, although still focusing on socially engaged topics, began to target a broader readership. By 1985 circulation had grown to 7.6 million. Subsequently, under increasing commercial competition (including competition with hundreds of counterfeit issues of itself), circulation declined to about 4 million by the end of the 1990s. But its attractively low price of only ¥2.5 per copy has helped to keep it first or second in circulation for Chinese magazines and, its editors believe,

*Photo 6.5    Cover of* China Pictorial *(Renmin huabao), published by Renmin huabao she, Beijing, March 1974. Price $1 r.m.b.*

perhaps sixth in the world.[4] Themes have evolved away from social engagement and more toward psychological escape and vicarious exploration of distant lands. In spirit it is in tune with the lifestyle magazines, but because it relies on fiction and has very few illustrations, it is not a prime example of them.

The *Young Generation,* which displayed the cover image of Dong Xiaoyan (photo 6.1), used more pictures than *Story Collections* but not as many as the

Photo 6.6    Cover of Nüxing yuekan (Women's monthly) 6 (1999). Published by the Beijing Municipal Women's League. Price $8 r.m.b.

more expensive pictorials (e.g., *Elle*, *How*, and *Cosmopolitan*; see below) that were to come later. Founded in 1979 for "young" people (although the magazine's surveys revealed that some readers were as old as fifty), the *Young Generation* sought to satisfy the curiosity and intellectual demands of a generation eager to understand the world from which China had been cut off during the Maoist years. In the 1980s it earned a reputation for progressive, cosmopolitan reporting on social and emotional issues that faced young people while continuing to report on foreign literature, film, music, and society. Perhaps most important for a society in which opportunities were beginning to open up while most people were still poor, its descriptions of foreign countries and college life fueled dreams and aspirations that seemed, in their novelty, perhaps equally attainable by all.

By providing information that people needed in order to build new social and professional roles, the *Young Generation* probably contributed to the social fragmentation of the 1990s (compared with the Mao years) and, ironically, to the dissolution of the demographic basis of its own market. Its circulation peaked at about 5.5 million in the mid-1980s; at the turn of the century, amid dozens of competitors, its circulation is less than one-tenth that number but still higher than any of the other lifestyle magazines for youth.

The glossy lifestyle magazine (represented by *Elle*, *Cosmopolitan*, *How*, *Metropolis*, and others) was the major innovation in Chinese magazine publishing in the 1990s. It offered readers many more pictures (and correspondingly less text) than the *Young Generation* (¥3.60) and cost four to eight times as much. *Elle* (called *Shijie fuzhuang zhi yuan* in Chinese) was the earliest and most successful example (photo 6.7). Copublished by Shanghai Translation Publishing House and Hachette Filipacchi Press, *Elle* has maintained its orientation toward Paris but is not just a translation of the French version of the magazine. Like its counterpart offshoot in America, the Chinese *Elle* tailors some of its features to local audiences by covering Chinese celebrities as well as Chinese music, books, and films. *Elle*'s target audience has been the mature, wealthy, and educated woman—the cream of the rising professional class.

*Cosmopolitan* (Shishang), which is currently third in circulation behind the *Young Generation* and *Elle*, was founded in Beijing in 1993. In 1998 its Chinese publisher bought rights from the Hearst Corporation to republish and adapt text and photos from the American version of *Cosmopolitan*.[5] It has carried articles very similar to ones that appeared in the U.S. version but has issued them under Chinese bylines. Articles have ranged from workplace politics and boss–employee relations to relationships between the sexes, both private and professional; it had focused on sex to a greater degree than the other top magazines. Like *Elle*, but even more so, it has preferred Caucasian female models to Chinese. Its Western women have seemed overtly sexual, even predatory, whereas photo spreads featuring Chinese models have usually had them fully clothed, more modestly posed, and projecting a more subtle and delicate sexuality. Chinese *Cosmopolitan* seems to stand out for this juxtaposition of the exaggerated sexuality of white women and the more tasteful behavior of Chinese models.

A pictorial called *Hao* ("good," but romanized as *How* on the cover) was founded in 1994 as an offshoot of *Wenhua yu shenghuo* (Culture and life), which had first appeared in the late 1970s. *How* was originally priced at ¥28—the same high price that *Elle* demanded—and was conceived as a more Asian-flavored competitor to *Elle*. It was the first completely Chinese-owned full-color lifestyle magazine and, like *Elle*, has relied mainly on pictures and brief text. Most of the stars or models on the covers have been Chinese or, interestingly, Japanese. Japanese names have also appeared on the editorial roster as graphic designer, assistant to the editor, and foreign consultant; Tokyo firms have received photo and

*Photo 6.7    Cover of* Elle *(Shijie shizhuang zhiyuan) 4 (1999). Price $16 r.m.b.*

text credits. For a half century no publication in China has been as warmly open to Japan.

*How* has targeted young female office workers. If the college student was the apogee of social success in the 1980s, the young professional became the zenith in the 1990s. *How* has presented a range of topics in fashion and culture, but has distinguished itself from *Elle* by including some practical how-to features and by picturing fashions that are practical and attractive to fairly ordinary urban Chinese consumers. The garments displayed on its pages are often quite similar to those seen everywhere on the streets of Shanghai. It lowered its price from ¥28 to ¥20 in 1996. This practical bent has allowed *How* to build a circulation that, according to its editors, reached 150,000 in the late 1990s.

*Dadushi* (Metropolis), which appeared in 1998, is the ultimate copycat in the sense that it has no distinctive characteristics other than what it developed from the best of its predecessors' ideas. It even chose a Chinese title, *Dadushi*, that could be confused with the translated title of *Cosmopolitan* (Daduhui). But consumers have not objected. Street vendors told us that *Metropolis* was their best-seller because the features were practical and, at ¥10 the price was right. For many customers on the street, *Elle* and *How* were too expensive. It did not matter that they were better designed or that the Caucasian girls on the covers of *Metropolis* were not pretty (photo 6.8).[6]

The 1990s efflorescence of flashy lifestyle magazines stimulated some of the government-sponsored Women's Federation publications to repackage themselves as niche publications. *Women's Monthly* (Nüxing yuekan, photo 6.6), a publication of the Women's Federation in Beijing, in the late 1990s adopted the

*Photo 6.8   Cover of Dadushi (Metropolis), series 5, 1 (1999). Published by Oriental Publishing Center, Shanghai. Price $10 r.m.b.*

subtitle *Professional Woman* and the slogan "Female, Cultural, Trendy." There are many other new magazines on the Chinese market; we have here introduced only a leading few. One editor in Shanghai estimates that the number of nationally distributed magazines has expanded from approximately seven hundred in the early 1980s to more than nine thousand at the end of the 1990s.

Who were the magazine readers at the turn of the millennium? Editors and magazine vendors in Beijing and Shanghai told us that most of their buyers seemed to be young women who worked in private enterprises. Although the beauties pictured on the covers of magazines were presumably as attractive to men as to women, their posture, expression, and direct gaze were those of a savvy friend, big sister, or mentor. Newsstand proprietors wrapped the more expensive magazines like *Elle* in plastic to keep them clean, while cheaper ones like *Metropolis* were usually available for browsing by people who might not buy them. Vendors sometimes spoke contemptuously of state enterprise workers who came only to browse, not buy. While prosperity had brought greater buying power to readers, the established social practices of sharing publications with coworkers, friends, and family did not appear to have declined substantially. Thus images of our model women and their optimally managed lives probably extended to an audience beyond what circulation figures might indicate.

Although editors work hard to distinguish their products from those of the competition, it is striking that the overlap among them is greater than any differences. New interests, if pioneered in one or another magazine, are quickly emulated by the competition. In the end, subtle editorial distinctions have been almost insignificant in determining where the consumer has spent her money, while magazine editors have ridden the tide of much larger popular forces. In the magazines collectively there has been essentially only one ideal woman, one way to dress her, and one general approach to decorating her home. She is, however, not fixed but evolves from one time to another along with social, cultural, and business trends.

## IDEAL OF THE NEW WOMAN

The model new woman found in magazines of the 1990s has an attractive, regular face, a pleasant smile, and sparkling eyes—like Dong Xiaoyan, the cover girl for the July issue of the *Young Generation* (photo 6.1). She wears beautifully applied makeup that emphasizes her prettiest features and is garbed with grace in the season's fashion. The June 1999 cover of *Women's Monthly* is adorned with a young woman dressed in a miniskirt, gray sweater-vest set, and black boots (photo 6.6). She wears, with great charm, the same stylish clothing seen in the windows and on the display racks of the most elegant Shanghai and Beijing boutiques. The home of the typical new woman is tastefully decorated and has built-in furniture that makes clever use of the space available in new high-rise urban apartments. Elegant bathrooms, well-designed kitchens, and cozy computer nooks are essential. Modernist chairs and tables accent the space, which is also well stocked with books and music. Leisure hours are passed in quiet comfort. The new woman takes an interest in art museums and the new galleries in Shanghai and Beijing. She is plugged in to the Internet, popular music, and film. She knows where to shop and how to shop, and the lifestyle magazines help other young women see how to catch up with her.

An issue of *How*, for example, highlights stylish coats and hats from Tokyo and a seemingly endless array of delightful consumables: business suits, shoes, purses, jewelry, hats, sunglasses, scarves, skirts, blouses, watches, lipstick, perfume, eyebrow pencil, eyeshadow, pants, hairstyles, cameras, mineral water, and more.[7] At the end of the issue a cute working girl with a new haircut and wardrobe is shown in four moments of her day: at work, at leisure (shopping), ready for a date, and dressed for a formal dinner (photo 6.9). The presentation seems to summarize how the cornucopia of goodies on the preceding pages of the magazine can be put to practical use—for this girl actually and for countless readers vicariously.

In the same issue television hostess Yang Lan advises readers about designer clothing. "Because they are high quality," they "can actually save money because they last longer. For a white collar worker, it's better to buy one expensive outfit than several sets of cheaper clothes. It is not important how many you have, only how good they are."[8] A piece in *Metropolis* entitled "Clean and Harmonious Is Always Right for the Office" emphasizes that for the businesswoman good dress

*Photo 6.9   How (New life collection) 1 (1999): 130–31. Published by Shanghai Cultural Publishing House, a division of Shanghai Literature and Arts Publishing House. Price $20 r.m.b.*

is a necessity, not just a pleasure.[9] "Try to fit your fashion with the image of your company," the article advises. "Don't let your dress make your boss or colleagues feel uncomfortable. But also match your clothes to your own character and try to keep your own style." Another piece tells how Miss Wang, who works in an Italian company, always wears dark suits but adds a bright-colored scarf so that, in an office full of dark brown and black, her flair gives people a fresh, bright feeling. She thereby "established her own style."[10]

In one story a businessman grants a contract to one company rather than another based on the uniforms of the company drivers. In one case the uniforms were wrinkled and dirty, in the other fresh and well-pressed. If the driver knows how to keep clean, the man reasoned, the company must be well managed. Next the article quotes the advice of an Italian businesswoman: "No matter how chaotic your morning, you must never forget your make-up. Your shoes must be shined and your lipstick must match your clothes. Your perfume should be suited to the occasion; when meeting with customers, it should be natural and light. Never wear sleeveless blouses or sandals to work, and always keep an extra pair of stockings in reserve."[11]

The model new woman can afford what she desires, and this is because she earns plenty of money at an upscale white-collar job. Readers who are not yet modern office workers may strive to achieve this elegant position, while those already in the ranks may hope to move from secretary to manager. The stories of how this is done unfold in texts that accompany the glamorous pictures.

*Metropolis*, for example, ran a special feature on women of talent in its November 1999 issue. One illustration shows a confident woman pointing to the screen of her laptop computer while a male colleague with furrowed brow struggles to comprehend what he sees. An article entitled "Thirty Traits of the Talented Woman" lists her characteristics.[12] She is intelligent, sharp-witted, well-informed, knowledgeable, well-spoken, and has good taste; she is independent, self-respecting, and conscious of women's equality; she is principled but gentle, with a good sense of humor, and easy to get along with. She is understanding, generous, and sensitive to the feelings of others, but not suspicious. She is a doer—straightforward, efficient, and self-controlled. She is a bit of a rebel but not confrontational. While she may be attractive to men, her attraction is based on personality, not beauty. Her life is well-balanced; love is never her only concern.

But such descriptions are abstractions. How does the new woman get to be this way? What does she actually do in daily life? Lifestyle magazines frequently ran stories about successful women who exemplify practically all of the "thirty traits."

We meet, for example, thirty-six-year-old Liu Xiaohong, head of the legal department for the Greater China Region of the Asia-Pacific Division of Motorola (photo 6.10).[13] Somewhat older than a cover girl, she is a model of mature success. Her photograph shows her position. The dark wooden cabinets of her

刘晓红：
把律师当艺术家来做

*Photo 6.10    Shishang—yiren (Cosmopolitan), November 1999. Published by
China Tourism News (Beijing).*

well-appointed office, with the scales of justice in the foreground, signify her
legal degree. The way she holds a Mont Blanc pen to her face suggests thoughtfulness, an appropriate trait for a person of power whose signature on the documents she has approved will mean much. Her low-cut knit blouse, which exposes
her necklace and her lower neck, is covered by a white jacket, giving her a modern feel without compromising her professionalism. She is not particularly beautiful but is well-dressed and confident. Her story confirms what we see.

A 1984 graduate of the Chinese University of Political Science and Law, she
worked for two years as a reporter for a law enforcement magazine before going
to America to study English. Her experience in the United States was not easy.

She found that everything was different in a free society and that she had no idea how to make her own arrangements. She had to choose a graduate school by herself, as well as fill out applications, find out about fellowship competitions, rent a place to live, buy a used car, find a job, and convince complete strangers of her abilities. Her first big setback occurred after six months in the United States, when she scored a substandard 300 on the Test of English as a Foreign Language (TOEFL) examination that is required for admission to graduate school. But she resolved to do her best to achieve the goal she had set for herself. Three years later she earned a law degree and was hired by an American law firm. She passed the bar and worked in the United States for seven years before Motorola recruited her back to China to run its Beijing office. Her biggest challenges in this position were how to balance the different cultures of the Chinese and American employees in her division and how to guide an American company in dealing with Chinese customers. Her advice to aspiring businesswomen, which she claims to have learned from an old lady in the United States, is to be generous to people around you and keep your heart free from hate. If an unhappy situation develops, do not try to change other people, but adjust your own attitude so that you can face the problem. At worst, do what you have to do and simply avoid the person who is causing problems. Do not try to cast blame on other people or try to cover up your own mistakes. When she encountered prejudice against mainlanders in the company's Hong Kong office, she found that open communication, staff involvement in problem solving, and solicitation of suggestions for improving her own performance were good antidotes. As a lawyer, she believes that business must be treated as an art, not an opportunity to act tough. She concludes that success in itself is not important because hard work and new experience are rewards in themselves.

Intelligence and determination were also keys for Li Yifei, deputy general manager of Viacom in China.[14] She advocates independence, hard work, and a balance between personal and professional life. The same age as Liu Xiaohong, she was China's youth martial arts champion in 1977. Later she earned a bachelor's degree in international law in Beijing and a master's in international business in the United States. After working for two years for the United Nations, she moved to a New York law firm that lobbies for most favored nation trade status. She then married a Hong Kong banker and returned to Beijing, where she joined a prominent public relations firm. Although she admits to leaving her New York job for her husband's sake, she maintains her own career and her independence. She attributes her self-discipline and her ability to do several things at once to her childhood training in martial arts, which required two practice sessions per day in addition to a normal school schedule. Her advice is never to give up until you reach your goal.

Persistence and hard work are identified repeatedly as essentials for the successful woman. Zhao Yan is the customer service manager for a major advertising agency.[15] She joined the company as a secretary in 1992 and became a manager only five years later. She counts persistence in her chosen career and meticulous work habits as keys to her success. A customer once told her that solutions are always more plentiful than difficulties; she took this as her personal motto and has used it to overcome many difficulties. For her, honesty is the foundation of understanding; only with honesty can you work successfully with your colleagues, clients, customers, and boss.

Television hostess Yang Lan, whose advice on clothing we have noted above, speaks of the unity of character and beauty.[16] A graduate of the Beijing Foreign Languages Institute, she studied in the United States and now hosts the *Zhengda Variety Show* in Hong Kong. When asked how she built her image as a beautiful professional woman, she responds, "Am I a beautiful woman? There are plenty of women more beautiful than I on the streets of Shanghai and Beijing. I am just a B+. I've never thought about how to build my image, but I really want to build my character. You don't need to design your image; fifteen-year-old girls, no matter what they look like, will always outdo you with the beauty of youth. When I was abroad, I saw many old women who were wrinkled but knew how to dress in ways that suited them perfectly, so they gave people a beautiful impression. I think, as a woman, no matter how old you are, elegance is most important, but elegance is not very easy to attain. I'd rather be an elegant woman than a beautiful woman."

Not every model of the new woman studies overseas or is a media star. Lifestyle magazines of the 1990s also introduced the successful "female boss" (*nü laoban*), who presented, for most Chinese, a more attainable role model. Liu Lei runs her own design business, the Hundred Wing Studio.[17] After graduating with an art degree, she worked first as a teacher and then in an office. In 1996 she borrowed ¥30,000 to establish her own business and three years later was a millionaire. Her business principle is to be reliable and trustworthy: if she says she will do something, she does it. She considers understanding and communication extremely important in dealings with both her varied clientele and her employees. She finds it particularly important for a female boss to avoid misunderstandings with female employees.

She is sensitive to the social pressure she has suffered as a female in business. Clients tend to look down on her both because she is a woman and because she is young. A businesswoman must learn to accept this social pressure, she feels, but also must bear in mind that success depends ultimately on one's talent and hard work.

## PROBLEMS AND COMPROMISES

Some articles detailed not only the successes of the new woman but the difficulties they encounter and the compromises or self-control that they find necessary.

Their struggles can be much more complex and problematic than the idealized images on magazine covers suggest.

Problems with men are common. Business success barely compensates for the personal problems of an unnamed female entrepreneur in southwest China. After graduating from college, she worked in a company where she met and fell in love with a man who seemed kind. But her family learned that the man had a reputation for a terrible temper and asked her to break off with him. When she tried to do so, her suitor wept and pretended to faint, and she felt such pity that she was unable to carry through on her resolution. Later he sent people to threaten her parents for their meddling. Despite this bad sign, she married him anyway. Soon thereafter he turned violent. He did nothing for her when she fell seriously ill. She came to realize that his interest in her was to show that he had a college graduate for a wife.

She left him and went to Kunming for a job that better suited her education and interests, and soon she became extremely successful. When her husband learned of her prosperity, he followed her to Kunming to beg for reconciliation. She unwisely agreed, and he started to beat her again. This time she sued for divorce, but he asked for a huge financial settlement and child support. She could not meet his financial demands but borrowed money in order to be rid of him. She then found herself penniless, in debt, and unemployed, and took various odd jobs in sales in order to make a new start. She managed to set up her own distribution business for leather shoes and coats. Within a year her enterprise made a profit, and she now makes more than ¥10,000 per month and hopes to send her daughter to Oxford or Harvard someday. But she feels that her business success cannot compensate for the failure of her family or the loneliness of her life.

Her business principles, according to the article, reflect the rough-and-tumble of her southwestern environment, and yet she prides herself on staying clean: she does not use or sell drugs and does not rely on sex to do business. Her success came from hard work and intelligence. We might read the failures in her personal life as a warning against domestic violence, particularly the naïveté, stubbornness, and inadequate self-respect that led to her mistakes. But her story does show that a woman with money and talent can escape a terrible domestic situation.

Showcasing the difficulties as well as the successes of the new woman makes the lifestyle magazines more useful to ordinary readers. Not everyone can succeed instantly, of course, so the magazines' attention to problems—to the hurdles that separate the ordinary reader from the shining ideal—helps readers identify with the pursuit of optimistic goals. One article, for example, offered straightforward and upbeat suggestions about how to find a job:

1. Set your goals high and be brave, but also improve your own skills; 2. Read advertisements carefully; 3. Don't pass up any opportunity; 4. Use any possible way to sell

yourself; 5. Try to overcome your lack of self-confidence; 6. If it's time to quit your job, don't hesitate; 7. Don't be too picky about the starting salary, because your career is more important.[18]

Other articles discussed ways of handling a male boss. Many stressed self-defense but advanced more aggressive strategies. A special feature in *Metropolis* on office skills carried an article on "Appropriate Femininity in the Office."[19] The author offers advice in four categories:

1. *Feminine Eyes*. My friend's wife is a television media worker. She has big expressive eyes. Every time she talks to a man she makes him feel she is really concentrating on him, and that she is sincere. Such eyes will not arouse a man's sexual imagination, but another kind of eyes, full of flirtation, can cause men to have unreasonable expectations. Such eyes can easily lead to office affairs. A smart woman knows how to use the eyes. Eyes should be warm but not hot, soft but not flirtatious.

2. *Body Language*. Don't be too slow and relaxed when you walk, because this shows that you lack elegance or are weak. It also makes people think you are out of date. But if you walk too fast or in too masculine a way, you will lose the gentle beauty of a woman. People will think you are elegant if, at a banquet, you can show beautifully manicured fingernails or, at a party, can dance in a romantic but self-controlled way. If you unbutton your top button and show a little of your chest you will give people a modern feeling.

3. *Feminine Speech*. Don't talk too much because it will annoy people. On the other hand if you respond too slowly or don't make a point, you also will lose your attraction. You should know how to listen to other people and how to express your ideas appropriately. If a woman knows how to listen and how to speak, she will usually be quite attractive.

4. *Office Girl Voice*. When you answer the telephone, if you use a breathy voice it will make people feel that you are excessively friendly and can give men a romantic fantasy. On the other hand if the telephone next to his bed rings and he picks up to hear a loud and unfriendly tone, he will be in a bad mood all day.

More serious than this kind of general advice about work-a-day behavior is the issue of how to handle the boss's specific quirks and foibles. A 1999 article called "How Do You Deal with a Male Boss?" offered nine tips:

1. *It Can Be Smart to Pretend You Are a Bit Dumb*. Whenever a certain office worker, whom we will call May, finished a project, she always listed her boss as the first author even if he wasn't involved in the project. Her colleagues made fun of her and said she was just trying to curry favor. They also said the boss was shameless, but May ignored them. A year later she was summoned to company headquarters in the United States. It turned out that her boss was the nephew of the company president, who gave her a job in the Asia-Pacific division at United States headquarters.

2. *Don't Display Your Shortcomings*. Zhu Ling had just gone to work as a news editor at a TV station. She was supposed to learn to work independently within

three months, but she didn't know how to do the job. Her advisor, an old editor, could produce ten minutes of news copy in only thirty minutes of editing. Zhu Ling asked him many times how he did it, but he never really told her and constantly criticized her. So she changed her strategy and stopped asking questions. She just watched how the old editor worked. After a while, when he saw that her work had improved, he began actively teaching her, and by the third month she was certified to work independently. When you meet an impatient male boss, hide your weaknesses and don't ask too many questions. Just watch, quietly practice by yourself, and give this kind of boss a surprise.

3. *Sometimes You Have to Be Tough.* Ling Yu's male boss is very smart and creative. Every two or three months he has a new project or new plan that he asks his staff to carry out. Once he asked Ling Yu to deal with a difficult client and allowed her only a week in which to solve his problem. Until then Ling Yu had been very compliant. No matter how unrealistic or stupid an assignment was, she did it. But this time Ling Yu decided to complain, and her male boss was shocked. He started to question himself and to realize that his subordinates also had their difficulties. From then on the relationship between Ling Yu and her boss was much smoother. So do not be too modest. Not every male boss is so bad—you do not always have to swallow insults.

4. *Use Softness to Overcome Hardness.* A certain new office boss, on his first day, asked everyone to remove everything personal—cartoon dolls, family photographs, etc.—from their desktops. All the young women felt depressed at the loss of the warm and friendly feeling in the office. They tried without success to negotiate with the new boss. Later, on the boss's birthday, they decided to decorate his office with a birthday cake and flowers, and they put the cake on his desk. He was happy and, indeed, quite moved, whereupon the young women took the opportunity to tell him how important a friendly environment is to their own productivity. The boss relented and let them arrange their desks as they pleased. So if a boss is overconfident or stubborn, it may be best not to confront him directly. You can reach your goal by detour.

5. *Understand the Boss's Shortcomings.* A boss who lacks self-confidence will be high-handed and will expect you always to follow his ideas even when they are unreasonable. In dealing with this kind of boss you have to be patient and should prepare several options for him to choose among. If you give him only one option you will have to argue with him if he doesn't like it. Because he lacks self-confidence, you should help him build it up.

6. *Dealing with an Overconfident Boss.* This kind of boss presumes to know everything and does not give you the chance to express yourself or to show your ability. To deal with him, you must ask his help and let him think his ideas are useful and helpful to you. Look at the bright side—with such a boss you don't have to pay tuition to learn how he deals with problems. You should treat him as a teacher and never show any disrespect in front of him.

7. *Dealing with a Suspicious Boss.* This kind of boss is usually afraid of losing his position because it was not very easy for him to get it. Hence he is very self-centered. He will want you to be open with him in everything and tell him every detail. So do tell him every detail and be careful not to give him the impression that you don't respect him or that you are trying to hide anything from him.

8. *Dealing with a Foreign Boss.* The foreign boss usually doesn't know much about Chinese culture and believes that things work the way he thinks they should work. Complicated matters can seem simple to him. He may not understand even after you explain all the details to him. You have to introduce this boss to Chinese customs. Tell him all the potential results of a proposed action. When he gradually understands the reality of China he will eventually change his foreign way of thinking.

9. *Dealing with an Unreasonable Boss.* This boss never pays attention to the opinions of subordinates. It is best to avoid him and leave him alone. Do not confront him directly. If you find something is wrong, just avoid discussing it with him.[20]

An issue of the *Young Generation* raised the problem of sexual harassment in the workplace and recounted stories and complaints of both male and female contributors.[21] Xu Cheng, a male, tells a story from the private company where he worked for several years. His boss had a wife and two children, as well as another child by a former mistress. He always kept a mistress, and whenever the company searched for a new secretary or public relations coordinator, everyone knew that in fact he was looking for a new girlfriend. One year he hired a new secretary who said she was single. The boss took her everywhere with him. But suddenly one day the boss called to say he had fired this secretary. When the secretary came back to the company to process her paperwork, she told everyone that her boss did private business on company time and abused his power by retaliating against people for nonbusiness reasons. She lost her job but kept her self-respect.

Another male reader, Huang Zhonghan, writes that some bosses summon beautiful girls to their offices to "discuss business" and then sit next to them and make promises about salary, promotion, or housing. When the woman expresses gratitude the boss's hands wander to her hip, shoulder, waist, or elsewhere. She is put in an unbearable dilemma: she can't say no because a conflict with the boss would be costly, but if she says nothing the boss will persist. He may ask to meet her in a bar, or even worse. "In such a case," the writer advises, "the woman should find an excuse to leave the office."

Si Xiaohong, hostess of a radio talk show on psychology, says China really needs a law on sexual harassment.[22] She knows of a telephone operator who worked alone at night and was driven to attempt suicide because of continual harassment by her male boss. She writes:

What I can't understand is why her parents, boyfriend, and co-workers don't sympathize. Instead they blame her for behaving frivolously. "Otherwise," they say, "Why would he harass you instead of somebody else?" This kind of thing happens often. People who have been sexually harassed don't know how to deal with it and don't want to tell anyone else what has happened. A college student riding a crowded bus in the summer was alarmed to discover that someone was touching her. She was frightened to death and afraid to say anything until finally the ticket seller stopped the hoodlum. If women encounter this kind of sexual harassment they should speak out. They should report it to the Women's Federation or another organization.

Among the stories about male harassers were some about aggressively flirtatious females. Zhang Lingchuan, a company president, confides a problem he had with a female employee who was a distant relative of his wife:

> She's a college graduate and a relative, so I never checked her identification. She appears to be in her thirties, much younger than my wife, and she acts seductively. When she walks she always wiggles, and her voice is always soft and flirtatious. She is especially "nice" to me—even blows on my tea to cool it down. When she makes reports she stands very close to me, even touching me with her body. Sometimes she says it's too hot and pulls on her shirt to bare part of her chest. I am a man. I am also quite well-educated, but I find it very difficult to deal with this situation. I have watched her and have observed that she doesn't flirt with just anyone—only with people who have money or power. I'd like to fire her but am afraid that if I do my wife will be unhappy—or may be suspicious that something happened between us. I can't say that her flirting completely disgusts me, but does it count as sexual harassment? I've talked about this with other company executives and they all say they have had similar experiences.

## CONCLUSION

The aspirations the new lifestyle magazines stimulate may have been well beyond the reach of most Chinese—urban and rural alike—in the 1990s, but this hardly diminished their role in the mental life of their readers. In Beijing, Shanghai, and other modernized places, successful women *did* wear imported scarves, gold jewelry, matching lipstick, and designer suits. Young women on the streets of Shanghai sometimes looked exactly like their counterparts in the pages of *How*. Yet even for them—to say nothing of their sisters in far less glamorous places— the world of the lifestyle magazine was recognized and admired. Readers seemed to use the magazines to help themselves bridge the gap between where they were and where they wanted to be. When the magazines described difficulties and offered advice on how to handle difficulties, they performed key functions. A Shanghai reader of *How* suggested in a January 1999 letter to the editor that more of the magazine's articles introduce fashions and entertainment suitable for ordinary people.[23]

The gap between the ideal new woman and the reality of most women's lives in China was very wide indeed. Did the lifestyle magazines that burgeoned in the late 1990s widen the cultural gulf between metropolis and village or narrow it? They certainly widened the spectrum of lifestyle alternatives, but they also spread—even to the countryside—at least an imaginary participation in a fairly unitary vision of the modern woman. They also may have attracted migration to the modern cities. Even if becoming a manager at Motorola was unimaginable, there may have been some modest job to be had in those elegant high-rise buildings.

In coming years, will these visions intensify economic resentment and potential social strife, or will they have the sedative effect of providing dreamers with vicarious escape? It is too early to predict such matters, but it is at least clear that people will face the future with a fairly consistent image of the new modern woman. This strong yet elegant educated lady dominates the popular imagination just as the cheerful, muscular farm girl of Mao's utopian China did a quarter century ago. Will such an image lead to social progress for women? Not by itself, of course, but on the whole it probably will do some good.

## NOTES

1. Waara looked especially closely at *Art and Life*, one of the most important pictorials of the time. Carol Lynne Waara, "Arts and Life: Public and Private Culture in Chinese Art Periodicals, 1912–1937" (Ph.D. diss. University of Michigan, 1994), 198–203, 248–59.

2. Xiaomei Chen, "Growing Up with Posters in the Mao Era," in *Picturing Power in the People's Republic of China: Posters of the Cultural Revolution*, ed. Harriet Evans and Stephanie Donald (Lanhan, Md.: Rowman & Littlefield, 1999), 104–5.

3. *China Pictorial*, September 1969, 44.

4. Behind *Reader's Digest* (first) and *National Geographic* (third), among others. Interview, June 11, 1999, Shanghai.

5. Unlike *Elle*, the Chinese *Cosmopolitan* is not registered as a collaborative venture and no foreign names appear on the editorial or administrative staff.

6. This phenomenon may be related to one observed by Daniel C. K. Chow. In the following passage, Chow describes his observations of Chinese consumers who knowingly purchase counterfeit goods because of their low price: "Some counterfeit products are of average and serviceable quality although inferior to the quality of the premium brands that are imitated. Counterfeit goods have also increased in both the quality of the packaging and the product itself as counterfeiters have gained experience in their trade. This has led to what appears to be a strong appetite for counterfeit products by a significant segment of the less affluent and less educated population. Not only will these consumers intentionally purchase counterfeit shoes and apparel, but they will also knowingly purchase such counterfeit daily use such products as shampoo, soap, and detergent. A common explanation is that less affluent consumers cannot afford to purchase premium goods and that counterfeits of premium goods . . . are of the same quality as that of local brands that sell for the same price as counterfeits of premium brands." Daniel C. K. Chow, "Counterfeiting in the People's Republic of China" (paper presented in Modern Chinese Studies OSU Lecture Series, Columbus, Ohio, 14 January 2000), 13.

7. *How*, January 1999.

8. *How*, January 1999, 120–21.

9. *Dadushi* (Metropolis) 5 (1999): 94–95.

10. *Dadushi* (Metropolis) 5 (1999): 95.
11. *Dadushi* (Metropolis) 5 (1999): 94.
12. *Dadushi* (Metropolis) 14 (November 1999): 102–3.
13. *Shishang* (Cosmopolitan), November 1999, 64–67.
14. *Shishang* (Cosmopolitan), June 1999, 62.
15. *Shishang* (Cosmopolitan), June 1999, 54.
16. *How*, January 1999, 121–22.
17. *Nüxing yuekan, zhiye nüxing* (Women's monthly) 6 (1999): 14–15.
18. "How to Get a Job," *Dadushi* (Metropolis) 1, no. 5 (1999): 100–1.
19. *Dadushi* (Metropolis) 1, no. 5 (1999): 96–97.
20. *Dadushi* (Metropolis) 14 (November 1999): 128–29.
21. "Sexual Harassment from Male and Female Viewpoints," *Qingnian yidai* (The young generation), 44.
22. "Sexual Harassment."
23. *How*, January 1999, 138.

# 7

# The Culture of Survival: Lives of Migrant Workers through the Prism of Private Letters

*Anita Chan*

In 1993 a fire in the south China city of Shenzhen, in Guangdong province, took eighty-seven lives and left forty-six injured. All were young female migrant workers from poor provinces. The management of Zhili Toy Company,[1] a Hong Kong–managed factory, had violated regulations by bribing local authorities and safety inspectors, bolting all exits, barring all windows, and blocking passageways with stock. When the fire broke out, the workers were trapped by the inferno.[2] The accident aroused unprecedented public outrage in China.

Soon after the fire, a Chinese researcher who was visiting the factory retrieved a few hundred personal letters that the victims had received from friends and relatives and were piled up to be discarded. He kindly passed on to me the letters that contain information about factory life. These seventy-seven letters, plus two resignation requests and a few hand-copied songs and ditties popular among migrant workers, form the basis of this chapter. They give a very different perspective from that produced by previous research about China's migrant factory workers.

Chinese migrant workers have been studied extensively, with almost all of the research being focused on female workers. Some of these studies discuss the women workers' places of origin and the conflicts that arise among groups of workers from different localities.[3] Other writings explicitly focus on gender, with the assumption that female workers suffer more than males.[4] Yet other authors explore the workers' self-images of inferiority that have been instilled by management,[5] or they examine the workers' efforts to get jobs and their status vis-à-vis the state,[6] their exploitation in the factories of investors from other Asian countries,[7] their social characteristics and role in the labor market,[8] or their social and family networks.[9] The writer who has come closest to penetrating the inner mental state, anxieties, and suppressed fears of the worker is Pun Ngai, who worked in a factory and lived in the workers' dormitory for more than six months.[10]

All this research adds significantly to our knowledge of the migrant workforce. But important aspects of the workers' situations and feelings are kept private and are revealed only in the intimacy of their letters to relatives and close friends. These letters cast light on a hidden part of their lives.

Of the seventy-seven letters, seventy-three were written by friends and relatives to the victims of the Zhili fire; only four were written by Zhili workers and had not been posted before the fire. Most of the letters were about a page long. Only sixteen letters were written by men (fathers, brothers, and husbands), and of these, just five were by migrant workers and described working conditions. Most of the letters were written by relatives, close friends, or fellow villagers of the Zhili workers. Eight letters were from relatives in the workers' home village or town, and the contents mainly concerned family matters. Sixty-five were from friends or relatives who were no longer in their own villages. Most were factory workers (among the men, a few were construction workers) who were working in Guangdong province.[11] These letters were channels through which the Zhili workers exchanged information on factory conditions with their friends and relatives. Because all parties were going through a shared experience, their descriptions of their work situations, living conditions, health, and feelings toward the factories were candid and intimate. These sixty-five letters provide the bulk of the information for this chapter.[12]

Obviously this collection of letters is not a random sample in the normal statistical sense. But it is a random sample of a "natural" kind, written by workers scattered across Guangdong province who can be taken as representative of a larger population of migrant workers in the province.[13] In analyzing these letters, I used a rule-of-thumb method. During a first reading of the letters I jotted down the topics or issues that the workers wrote about and came up with forty-three. Care was taken to keep the topics as disaggregated as possible in order to capture details. For example, over the issue of wages and money, subcategories include "amount of wages," "wages too low and therefore no savings," "wages too low, so cannot send money home," "amount of overtime pay," and so on. In a second reading of the letters, any references to each of these forty-three issues were recorded. The results are given in table 7.1, which lists the issues mentioned in order of frequency.

Several issues were mentioned more frequently than others. There were 107 references to wages,[14] 84 to finding another job,[15] 57 to work hours and overtime,[16] 50 to physical existence,[17] and 30 to loneliness and isolation.[18] (As this

**Table 7.1   Issues Appearing in Workers' Letters (in Order of Frequency)**

| Item | Number of Mentions | Issues |
|------|------|------|
| 1 | 38 | Trying to find work at another factory |
| 2 | 26 | Looking for and introducing someone to a job |
| 3 | 24 | Amount of wages |
| 4 | 24 | Amount of overtime work each day |
| 5 | 22 | Length of work hours |
| 6 | 18 | Relationship with the opposite sex |
| 7 | 17 | Ailments |
| 8 | 15 | Any reference to food and meals |
| 9 | 15 | Wages too low and therefore no savings |
| 10 | 14 | Longing to see friends and relatives |
| 11 | 13 | Workers do not have enough work, with adverse effects on their wages |
| 12 | 13 | Sending money home |
| 13 | 12 | Borrowing and lending money |
| 14 | 11 | Irregular pay |
| 15 | 10 | Someone not able to find a job |
| 16 | 10 | Any discussion about residential status and the need for work permits, identity cards, or unmarried-status certificates |
| 17 | 7 | Desire to remain at a factory; not looking for another one |
| 18 | 6 | Amount of overtime pay |
| 19 | 6 | Any reference to paying deposits *(yajin)* |
| 20 | 6 | Loneliness |
| 21 | 6 | Crying over hard life and loneliness |
| 22 | 5 | Overnight work or work until the wee hours of the morning |
| 23 | 5 | Exhaustion from long hours of work |
| 24 | 5 | Indication that the worker would go home in the next couple of years to settle down |
| 25 | 5 | Factory's business not doing well |
| 26 | 5 | Wages too low to send money home |
| 27 | 4 | Harsh discipline |
| 28 | 4 | ID card or other papers taken away by management |
| 29 | 4 | Longing for letters |
| 30 | 4 | Regrets about having left home |
| 31 | 3 | Factory owing wages to workers |
| 32 | 3 | Any reference to the factory keeping a portion of pay |
| 33 | 3 | Taking any kind of medication |
| 34 | 3 | Lack of sleep |
| 35 | 3 | Plans for New Year holiday |
| 36 | 2 | Occupational health and safety problems |
| 37 | 2 | Inability to move to another factory because the present factory will not let them go or because the factory owes them money |
| 38 | 2 | Marriage |
| 39 | 1 | Wages cut recently |
| 40 | 1 | Any reference to slowdowns, labor disputes, collective protest actions, strikes, etc. |
| 41 | 1 | Weight loss |
| 42 | 1 | No desire to return home, no matter how bad life is in the factory |
| 43 | 1 | Life is satisfactory in the factory |

chapter later discusses, a number of issues we normally would expect to appear in such letters did not surface.)[19] This chapter looks at wages, work conditions, and problems related to physical well-being and examines how factory conditions affected the workers' social situation and mental state by entrapping them in a "culture of survival."

## WAGES (PAID AND UNPAID) AND WORK HOURS

Among the workers' many concerns, issues related to wages topped the list. To gain a full grasp of the anxiety felt by these workers it is necessary to compare their wages against the minimum wage standards set by the city and district governments. These benchmark standards are established locally, based on a formula provided by the central government and pegged to the cost of living in an area.[20] The minimum wage excludes subsidies and payments in kind, and it is revised annually.[21] Paying below the minimum wage set for an eight-hour workday is illegal. The minimum legal wage set for Shenzhen in 1993 was ¥280 a month, and for other industrial cities and economic zones in Guangdong province, it was twenty to thirty yuan lower (except for Zhuhai, just east of Shenzhen).[22]

How did the wages cited in the letters fare against the legal minimum wage for Shenzhen? Of the letters that specified the writer's wage, only six mentioned a payment at or above minimum wage—¥280 a month. Of these six, two had been promoted to posts beyond the production line (the only two non–production line workers in the entire collection of letters), so only four workers earned the legal minimum, meaning that nineteen out of twenty-three production line workers received less than the minimum wage. Of these nineteen, two received ¥200–280, and the remaining seventeen were paid less than ¥200, with one making as little as ¥60.[23] Not reflected in these figures was the fact that the average normal workday was twelve hours instead of the officially sanctioned eight hours.[24] In other words, of the twenty-five letters that contained specific information on wages, almost all indicated that the workers were paid at rates much lower than the legal minimum wage.

Of the four workers who received at least the minimum wage, only one stated that she was working an eight-hour day. However, she was only earning ¥280 a month, exactly the Shenzhen minimum wage. She was the only one out of the twenty-three production line workers whose work conditions did not violate the legal limits for wages and work hours.[25] What is more, among these twenty-three workers, three wrote that the factory withheld a portion of their monthly pay, five wrote that wages were paid irregularly, and three reported that there was not enough work on the production line and so the opportunity to earn wages had been sporadic. That is, eleven out of the twenty-three workers faced serious problems in obtaining their wages, which were less than the legal minimum.

Although other letters did not mention specific wage amounts, similar problems over wages surfaced. Of these letters, eleven reported that the amount of work was irregular and the income was unsteady, nine reported that the wages were so low they had no savings, five reported that the factory paid them irregularly, and two reported that the factory owed them wages (one for two months and the other for three months).

Thus, in addition to the nineteen production line workers who gave specific information on their wages and were paid below the legal minimum wage, another twenty-seven workers received wages that were very irregular, unpaid, withheld, or extremely low. Of the workers who mentioned their wages in one way or another, forty-six had serious problems with their wages, whereas only four workers indicated they were at or above the legal minimum Shenzhen wage of ¥280.

The highest wage cited was ¥760 a month, earned by a woman who worked in the only factory mentioned in all the letters to have raised wages. However, the worker's health was deteriorating due to the very long work hours: "How could I have time to write home? I'm so exhausted that I'm now down to ninety pounds. But don't worry, dear sister, I'm still okay. Nothing has gone wrong yet. I bought three boxes of health supplements. But it hasn't helped."[26]

As is now obvious, illegally low wages and very long work hours were the norm in the factories that hired these migrant workers. The pay was so sporadic that the workers commonly asked one another, "Have you been paid yet?" The usual answer was, "Not yet." The norm was being owed wages instead of being paid. Consider this example: We have [finally] gotten our wages. Got December's pay on March 15. Got 140 yuan. I've sent 100 yuan home."[27]

After three months' work, the workers had been paid a pitiful ¥140, an average of ¥40-some a month. Elsewhere in the letter the writer indicated that she had little idea of how much she was supposed to be earning a month. There was no mention of the workers querying management about why they received so little or whether more wages would be forthcoming. It seems that even if there had been some sort of an established pay rate, it barely mattered to her. She was relieved finally to have some cash in hand.

It was common for the workers not to know how much they were supposed to be paid. One male letter writer observed:

Now the conditions in the factory are too bad, but there is no way out. To make money, to make a living, for myself and for the whole family, for father and for mother, for the whole family to be able to eat, I have to continue to work. I asked the workers who have been here a longer time and was told wages are *probably* nine to ten yuan a day. Eight hours of work during the day plus seven hours of overtime are counted as one workday. Every month thirty-six yuan is deducted for food and board, and twenty-five yuan for a security deposit that can be gotten back when we leave [emphasis added].[28]

It is clear that this male worker had begun working in the factory without being told the wage rates. He could only find out from fellow workers roughly how much he might be making. It is no wonder that when I was conducting field research in Fujian province, a typical response from migrant workers to a question on wages was a hesitant "I don't know." At first I thought they were reluctant to disclose their wages to a foreigner. I gradually became convinced that they genuinely did not know.[29]

A very similar situation exists with overtime work. Some workers understood "overtime" in the Western sense and as defined by the Chinese labor law—work days beyond eight hours. But to some workers, overtime did not begin after eight hours. Take these two letters as examples:

> Now I'm working in another factory. It's better than the Japanese umbrella factory. It's twelve hours' work a day. If my factory needs people, I'll tell you.[30]

> Here the work hours are like this: 7:30 to 11:30 A.M., 1:30 to 5:30 P.M., 6:30 to 10:30 at night [i.e., twelve hours' work]. Sometimes we also have to do overtime work. After 10:30 we get a fifty fen [cent] subsidy. There is a lot of work in this factory.[31]

In both letters, twelve hours was considered a normal workday. In the first letter overtime pay did not exist as a concept. In the second letter, only after having worked for twelve hours did the worker (and management as well) consider the work overtime. Under such circumstances, it is understandable why overtime rates were barely mentioned in the letters. Of the twenty-one letters that contained information on work hours, only five had references to overtime rates. But as the second letter quoted above indicates, the way workers were paid for their overtime was also unconventional by Western standards. What exactly did she mean by getting a fifty fen subsidy after 10:30 P.M.? There are two possibilities. It may be that no matter how long she worked after 10:30 P.M., all she received was an extra fifty fen. A more encouraging scenario would be that she received fifty fen for every hour of work after 10:30 P.M. The labor law defines the overtime rate as an added percentage of the regular hourly rate. But in all the letters cited above, because hourly rates were nonexistent, at least as understood by the workers, overtime rates were also nonexistent. Wages were merely management's arbitrary manipulation of figures. Irregular small sums of money called wages were doled out now and then to the workers. The function was not to provide a predetermined, calculable award for the workers' labor but to ensure that the workers stayed alive but did not become desperate enough to stage protests or run away.

It can also be seen from the above examples that being able to work for twelve hours a day was regarded as a blessing. The frightening alternative was suspension of production due to a lack of orders. There were thirty-four entries related to not having enough work and/or unemployment. In the following quotation a worker reports to her family back home on the situation of her younger sister working in another factory:

> She hasn't made that much money. She has little money to buy clothes. Since I've been here, their team has only worked for some ten days or so. They haven't gotten their January pay yet [the letter was written in March]. They don't even have money to buy breakfast or dinner.[32]

## THE BARE NECESSITIES OF LIFE: MEALS AND ACCOMMODATIONS

The normal practice of factories in Guangdong is to provide migrant workers with meals and subsidized lodging, which is usually a bed in a two-level or even three-level bunk. About ¥35–70 is then deducted from their wages to cover these amenities. This arrangement could superficially be characterized as Confucian paternalism; however, it is economically driven. Providing lodging and meals to workers makes controlling the workers' time much easier and puts them on call around the clock. It ensures that workers do not expend unnecessary time and energy in buying and cooking food or use up time going in and out of the factory compound. By the time the workers finish their twelve-hour workdays, there is little time left for leisure and commuting activities anyway.

The uneven nature of production requires that factories hoard labor. Most factories continue to let the workers stay and eat in the dormitories even when production is suspended. After all, it costs management relatively little to provide meals, and the beds are there anyway. Spending an additional small amount on food gives management the great advantage of having labor ready to restart the production lines the moment new orders arrive.

From management's perspective, the workers' "basic needs" are satisfied through a bed and food. But having visited some workers' dormitories in the Shenzhen area, I can only label them as unfit for human habitation. If they are lucky, eight people share a tiny room lined with bunk beds; if unlucky, up to a hundred workers share a single hall in a warehouse. In Chinese newspapers there has been no lack of anecdotal reports on unsanitary and dilapidated living conditions.[33] Yet of the sixty-odd letters from factory workers, not one complained of poor living conditions. They took the discomfort of the accommodation for granted. As long as there was a bed, the workers did not think to complain in their letters. Perhaps the living conditions back home left even more to be desired. Whatever the reason, the workers quietly tolerated the lack of privacy, the filth, and the noise.

Food is more important than lodging to physical survival. The letters included fifteen entries related to food, many urging the recipient to eat properly. Here are three examples. The first is a letter from a husband comforting a Zhili worker not to worry because she was unable to send any money home:

> But you should eat well. Don't be too miserly. If your health suffers it's not like being at home. Health is capital for revolution. Without health you can't make money.[34]

> Little sister, you should go to see the doctor. Don't take money too seriously. To have a body in good health is to have everything. Don't be stingy. Make sure you eat both breakfast and dinner.[35]

> In your factory do you have two meals or three meals? I hope you're not excessively frugal. If you're hungry, go buy something to eat.[36]

Chinese culture places a great emphasis on food. But the concern for adequate food and eating properly, as expressed in these letters, is a reflection of a culture of marginal existence. This explains why all information on food was on the number of meals and the quantities served rather than on quality. The supply of food varied from factory to factory, as did the charges. The amount of food seemed adequate and most people seemed satisfied at being given three meals a day. But for people coming out of a culture of marginal existence in a rural setting, the question of whether they were being fed enough continued to be a topic for discussion.

> Here we have to pay for our food: fifty fen for breakfast, one yuan each for lunch and dinner—two dishes with meat, and one entirely of vegetables.[37]

> Each day there are three meals: breakfast, dinner, and lunch. In the afternoon there are three dishes. Living is okay.[38]

> As for me, two meals a day means I get very hungry before the morning meal. But I guess once I get used to it, it will be okay.[39]

## IMPAIRED AND DISPOSABLE BODIES

Having enough to eat is not, in and of itself, enough to sustain a healthy body. Very long work hours, repetitive work, and less-than-pleasant work environments, not to speak of occupational safety and health problems, take their toll. There were seventeen entries in the letters discussing ailments, one entry on weight loss, and eight others discussing exhaustion and lack of sleep. The most frequent ailments were headaches, fever, and leg pain. It cannot be established from these letters whether these were symptoms of occupational diseases. But according to one study carried out in Shenzhen city in 1994, slightly more than half of the 10,942 factories could be classed as hazardous in terms of occupational health and safety (OHS) standards. Of these hazardous factories, 4,000 were foreign-funded enterprises (FFEs) employing approximately 250,000 workers. It was discovered that 3,108 of these FFEs had not installed any OHS preventive facilities.[40] Considering the high proportion of hazardous workplaces, the workers who complained of health problems in these letters had a high chance of having contracted chronic OHS diseases. The following descriptions of sickness could well be symptoms:

> Now I'm in great misery. I have a fever every day. It's so hot that it is killing me. The pain is unbearable. I also have anemia. Can't eat even a mouthful of rice.[41]

> When I was at Decheng factory, the smell of the umbrella material gave me headaches. I couldn't bear to work there any longer. Got two months of pay for three months of work.[42]

> I heard from third older sister that she has lost quite a bit of weight. She always has headaches. I hope you can write to her more often to comfort her spirits.[43]

> At the time I got your letter my leg was so painful. I couldn't even walk. I was not in the mood to write back. Sorry.[44]

Despite the serious nature of the symptoms, only one worker mentioned that she had taken a few days off. All the others seem to have continued working. At the most, they took some "health supplements." None mentioned bringing health problems to the attention of management or being denied permission to take a rest. It is possible that no matter how sick workers were, they feared losing their jobs if management realized they were not up to working a twelve-hour day. Moreover, many factories fine workers heavily for absences from the production line, even for illness, or deny them the end-of-month bonus for full attendance.

Two letters graphically describe toxic conditions:

> For a long time I haven't wanted to work in the paint-spraying department. I don't know what's wrong, whether it's because of the spray or that I have a cold, I have such painful headaches. The painkillers only helped for a while and the pain started again. I can't stand it. Every time father writes he tells me not to work in the spraying department. But it's not possible to switch. The other departments do not have work and do not need people. The only possibility is to change to another factory, but that's not easy. Here, they haven't paid our wages. No idea when we'll be paid.[45]

The second letter was written by a Zhili worker and was dated 8 March 1993. This worker and two friends had arrived in the Shenzhen area on 14 July and found work at three different toy factories. The toy and footwear industries are particularly hazardous because of toxic solvents in the spray paints and glues that are used.[46]

Aili got into Tianhe toy factory. Then she got boils on her face. On 28 July she went back home. She went in a Labor Bureau vehicle.[47]

Further down in the letter she wrote:

> Now let me tell you about my situation. When I first arrived, I worked at Yigangban factory [before coming to Zhili]. I was there for just over ten days. There was toxic gas in the factory. You must have heard of Li Yuxia's death? Yuxia died a horrible death. She got critically ill on July 18. Went to hospital. She died after having stayed there for only three days. I was scared. She's already been cremated.[48]

Aili and Li Yuxia seemed to have been victims of acute poisoning related to paint spraying. Yet instead of holding the factory responsible, the local Labor Bureau arranged to have Aili shipped quietly out of Shenzhen. Having shown symptoms of acute poisoning, she was disposed of as spoiled goods.[49] A similar fate befell survivors of the Zhili Toy Company fire, many of whom were severely burned. They were given rudimentary treatment at local hospitals for six months and practically forced back to their home villages with only small sums of compensation and with their burns and injuries far from properly healed. A report has been published on the broken lives of these survivors, living in disfigurement and shame and, in some cases, constant physical agony.[50]

## PHYSICAL ENTRAPMENT

Not a single letter indicated that the writer had ever made an individual or a collective complaint to management or to the local authorities.[51] Either they tolerated their factories as best they could and hoped conditions would improve, or they tried to find another factory. For many, looking for another factory was a consuming project. It was the second most frequent topic of the letter writers. There was always the hope that the grass was greener elsewhere, that the pay and job would be a bit more stable, that the working hours would be long only because it meant business was healthy and workers were paid on time. Their aspirations were modest. Short work hours were not desirable, portending low pay or no pay. To wish for better living conditions and better meals would be a luxury. But their desperation to escape from their current wretchedness explains the large number of entries (sixty-four) in which workers asked about, and reported on, work and pay conditions. Requests to get themselves, a relative, or friend into a factory, and discussions about job opportunities and job hopping appeared in almost all the letters.

The responses were frequently negative. For one, the labor market was tight, especially for male migrants, as reflected in references in ten letters to someone being unable to get into any factory. One male worker had two jobs, one after another, but neither paid anything: "I worked for five days and quit because it was a factory that didn't pay any wages." In the end he did not even have money to buys stamps to send a letter to his sister at the Zhili factory. He managed to get back to his home village, and only then could he send her a letter.[52] Unemployment befell women workers too:

> Dear Little Sister, actually our factory hired more than ten people to get the rush order out. But it was all casual work. They only worked for ten days, some even for only half a day. That is why I didn't dare ask you to come here. Mingxia came here because her factory is always idle. But she worked here for nine days and had to go. She is still a vagrant. She has not entered a new factory yet.[53]

Without a job, migrants could return home, but that was the last resort. The workers had invested capital in undertaking the long journey south, and some had borrowed to do so.[54] Back home, the financial situation was bad, as described in the letters—their families needed extra cash desperately. Parents revealed their concerns about unmarried daughters (and sons) who had embarked on the "dangerous" trip. To go back home without having made any money would mean plunging the family further into poverty. Finding a job that paid regular wages was imperative. But finding a place to stay while looking for work was a big problem. Often migrants had to hide in a factory's dormitory, squeezing into the bed space of a sibling or friend.[55]

The problem did not end there. Migrants who lacked jobs lived in constant fear of being deported from Guangdong. They were at the mercy of China's household registration system (the *hukou* system) that requires people to produce their ID card (*shenfen zheng*) and temporary residential permit when accosted by the authorities. Caught without these, the migrant could be sent back home:

> At our place in Shi'ai township, household registration inspection has been really tight in the last few days. Every day, load after load of people are being picked up and shipped out by truck. Therefore no one has dared to go outdoors recently.[56]

The prospect of finding a better job was not great. More often than not the situation in other factories was no better:

> I'm feeling discouraged. Since the year before last, after I left your place, every several months I've changed factories. Changed and changed again, and now I am back to an old one. I haven't been able to save a cent in the past two years. It's been a waste of my time. It's too late for regrets.[57]

> Shuniu, you talked about changing factories in your letter. Are you serious? It's better to stay put. Wherever you go it's the same. I now regret having changed factories. Sometimes when I read your letter I start to cry. Had we been in the same factory it would have been so good.[58]

The news occasionally could be encouraging: yes, the situation here is better; the factory is recruiting; come as soon as possible. But then there would be other hurdles. The main barrier was that the present employer would not give back the workers' ID cards, their deposit, and their unpaid wages. Sometimes the worker was simply too scared to travel to another locality to take up the job. Here is an example of someone who had just been informed of the good news but missed the chance:

> I was so happy to receive your telegram. But when I thought about it I didn't dare come by myself. . . . I asked so-and-so, but he didn't know where Bao'an is either [Bao'an is the county adjacent to Shenzhen]. . . . I hope you'll forgive me for not coming. Next time when there is another opportunity, please write down the exact instructions on how to get there. Besides, I can't get back my ID card. So I can't come anyway. When Xueqin and Shuhui left here, they didn't get back their ID cards. I wonder whether they've gotten into a factory. . . . As for the situation here, again there is not enough work this month. Many people have left the factory. I have gotten my April wages [the letter was written on 18 May], 114 yuan and 54 fen. But I had to repay someone ¥65. So I haven't sent money home.[59]

The household registration system has proven a boon for factory management. Even when a factory is not running at full capacity and not paying the workers, management can prevent the workers from leaving simply by withholding their ID cards. Fourteen letters discussed ID cards and other personal documents. Zhili was one such factory. A letter written by a Zhili worker intimated that quitting was difficult: "If I could resign that would be great," she wrote, implying she was not permitted to leave.[60] Amid the pile of letters there were also two short resignation letters written by two Zhili workers. One was dated about a month before the fire, written in a tone of abject deference:

> Dear Respectful Manager and Various Other Leaders,
> How are you? I have already been working here for three years. My contract has long expired. Now my family wants me to go home. May I request you to grant permission.
> Resignee: Yili
> October 4, 1993

Presumably permission was not granted, since she was still working in Zhili when the fire broke out. On the other hand, as we saw above, some workers were so desperate to get out that they left factories without getting their ID cards back. Without them their lives could only become even more precarious.

For females, there was yet one more personal document that was required—the unmarried-status certificate (*weihun zheng*). Without this, getting a job was difficult.

I've been away from home for more than a month. . . . I am writing for one particular reason—for the unmarried-status certificate. Please, younger brother, help me to get this done. . . . It's been so long already. Is it because there is a problem? By hook or by crook, you must try to get it for me. The faster, the better. I haven't gotten into a factory yet. Every day I can only hang around in the room sleeping. I dare not go out because once out, it's difficult to get back in. This is becoming really intolerable.[61]

It seems that she had been smuggled into a factory dormitory by a friend. Because security guards were stationed at the factory gate it was not possible for her to go in and out easily. She was trapped.

When the withholding of ID cards became widespread in Guangdong factories, people began borrowing IDs from other workers. This flourished because factory management and local governments were willing to turn a blind eye to the illegal practice. As can be seen from the following two letters, the borrowing of ID cards was widespread:

The fellow villager who came with me said her factory is about to recruit workers soon. She asked us to go. She said the factory is very good. The food's also good. She asked us to get our IDs ready. But my factory is keeping my ID. There's no time to get another one from home. Can I borrow yours? That factory doesn't keep IDs, so I can return it to you fast. Now we don't even have a cent. If you don't have an ID card, can you borrow one for me? You must get one for me. If you can't do it, then all I can do is die in this factory.[62]

I am operating a single-line machine; that's why I have wanted to leave for a long time. But I'm afraid the factory won't return the ID card, and the card is yours. No matter what, I don't want to leave your ID behind. Even if I change factories, I'll try my best to get back your ID card. But I'm afraid it is very difficult. I want so much to change factories. I can't stay here for another day![63]

The workers were in a no-win situation. At best, factories paid pitiful wages for very long working hours; at worst, there were no wages and they had to idle around in factory dormitories being fed two or three meals and, worse, worrying about not being able to send home the much needed cash, a highly dreaded situation. Yet even if they could get away, the new situation might be worse—and job hopping cost money. Leaving a factory probably meant losing their deposit and unpaid wages, or the ID card. Getting another job meant paying another deposit. Thus those who succeeded in changing factories sometimes gained nothing and regretted the move. Without having made or saved any money, going home was not an option either. The odds were stacked against them. The prospect was so bleak to the writer of the first letter quoted above that she was in utter despair. As she observed, she might as well be dead.

Nonetheless, workers often decided to leave despite all odds. My interviews with factory managers in South China in 1996 revealed that the turnover rate was quite high, at least from the perspective of the managers, who put it down to the "disloyalty" and "ungratefulness" of the workers.[64]

## MENTAL STATES AND SPIRITUAL SUSTENANCE

Suddenly thrust into a strange new environment, the first time away from home, young workers needed psychological and practical support to help them get through the initial period and over the months to come. For this reason, novices tended to leave home as a group. The best time to undertake the long journey was when a relative or a fellow villager returned home for Chinese New Year. The veteran could then "lead the way." This accounts for the annual flood of migrants into Guangdong province immediately after the Chinese New Year.

But they soon discovered that it was hard to stay together as a group. They often had to separate when they landed jobs in different factories or even in different cities. The young people had to confront factory life on their own. Letters became an important part of their lives: they were important sources of information about job opportunities and, more importantly, their only meaningful contact with the world beyond the factory and dormitory walls. Telephoning each other, even locally or in times of emergency, did not seem to be an option, since not even one letter mentioned telephoning. They could, if need be, resort to telegrams. But for the most part, in this part of China, where cellular phones had already become an indispensable plaything for businesspeople, workers had to depend on an unreliable postal service. Some of the letters expressed a palpable anxiety about letters, remittances, or documents getting lost in the mail or being intercepted by management.

The letters tell of a daily grind that quietly and steadily consumed workers' lives and spirits. They also reveal the inner feelings of these migrant workers. Among the sixty-nine letters written by workers, there were thirty separate entries expressing loneliness and feelings of isolation or misery, of sorely missing friends and relatives, of crying, and of yearning for letters.[65] They were voices crying out for human contact, comfort, and support. Most of the letters between women were filled with emotion and intimacy. More research will be needed to understand whether young peasant women are closer to their blood sisters and their peers of the same sex (also addressed as "sisters") than their urban counterparts are. Could this closeness be a romantic reaction to loneliness and isolation only after they had parted?

> Songying and Xiaojing, though we have only parted for just over ten days, it seems like several months. Perhaps it is because I am not familiar with this place. . . . While working I seem to hear you talking and laughing in my ears. The moment I wake up in the morning I think of you. I am just too lonely here.[66]

I sent you a letter a few days ago. Have you got it? I look forward to your letter every day but it never comes. I think of you very much.[67]

Exchanging photographs took on a new emotional significance. Visual images substituted for the physical distance:

Now the several of us are scattered all over. Oh, how difficult it is to get together again! What a shame! When I think of our innocent lives at school, how beautiful it was. I can't bear to think about it. . . . Now you and Wang Guangfang have come here [to the Shenzhen area] as well. Though we are so near, we can only see each other in our letters. Little sister, can you please send me a photo? I sent my photo to your home. Did you get it? I'll close off here. See you in a letter next time.[68]

I received your photograph. I looked and looked at it and felt so happy because I've wanted it for so long. I can't express how happy I am. But suddenly I felt lonely. So lonely.[69]

If they were lonely, why had they not made new friends among their fellow workers? In all the letters there was not even a single reference to someone having made a new friend or having attempted to do so. Did they not want to tell old friends for fear of being accused of having been disloyal? Or was the in-group feeling among those who had grown up in a tight community so strong that it was difficult to make new friends? Was this a characteristic of females of peasant origin? Here I can only pose these questions without providing answers.[70]

Two letters were written by a husband in a village to his wife who had left home and found work at Zhili.[71] The wife had left because the family was in debt. The letters were filled with endearments; they were romantic, intimate, and sad. Their daughter had been sent to stay with a relative. The husband was eager to know what kind of work the wife was doing in the factory. He had little idea of what production line work entailed, since in both letters he queried, "Do you carry heavy things? Do you carry loads on shoulder poles?" The wife, who was illiterate and whose letters had to be written by someone else, seemed reluctant to provide him with the details. Her main message was she was terribly sorry she could not send home any money for the time being.

Social relationships and responsibilities could be a source of psychological burden. There was an overwhelming sense that they had to send money home to help their impoverished families. A study Mobo Gao conducted of his ancestral village showed that each migrant worker sent home ¥100 a month and that this was a vital help to family finances.[72] The writers of these letters who were not getting paid or not able to save money from their meager earnings suffered great anxiety.[73] Out of a total of thirteen entries in which the topic of sending money home arose, only seven indicated that money was being sent.[74]

Friends and relatives could be a burden in another way. Because family and social circles were close, gossip among relatives and friends spread quickly despite the physical distance, causing ill feelings and bickering. The most destructive gossip was that so-and-so was not trying hard enough to help someone else find a "good" factory. No amount of explanation—that the job market was tight or the factory was not recruiting or a job there was not worthwhile—seemed to dampen suspicions that a villager or relative had let someone down. Fellow villagers back home desperate for factory jobs simply would not accept no for an answer. Here are two examples:

> Dear Shubi, Sorry, I really can't help aunty find a factory. I hope you understand my situation. Let me tell you what has been happening to me. During Chinese New Year quite a few fellow villagers came here. Up till now many of them still have not gotten into factories. . . . There is no way I can find a job for aunty. Shubi, perhaps you are feeling the same pressure because we know how it feels [in not being able to find jobs for others]. My younger cousin has also arrived. She left home on 25 January, has been here for two months, and still has not entered a factory. We are so anxious for her. Her family is even more worried. If people do not understand what the real situation is they'll say, "how come she has two cousins in Guangdong factories and they can't get a job for their cousin?" They think we're not willing to help. Well, if that's what they say, then let it be. . . . I really don't want my relatives to come here to become vagrants—no food, no shelter. Besides, public order is so chaotic here. What a miserable place this is.[75]

> Shuniu, now our factory wants to recruit eighty people. The manager told us to go home to bring some villagers out here. He said we could go by plane. But I don't want to go home. If it doesn't work out for them here, they will all blame me. I don't want to go. So I lied to the manager that I'd write home to ask.[76]

The fear of being responsible for the livelihood of a group of fellow villagers was too great to bear. They were caught in a bind. If they could not find jobs for others, they might be blamed. If there were openings, they worried that if the jobs were no good they would get blamed as well.


## THE MISSING TOPICS

Several major concerns stand out clearly in these letters as being foremost in the minds of the workers, but many other topics that we might have expected to appear do not. For example, it might be expected that the letters would contain at least some information on factory ownership. In Guangdong province many of the factories are owned and managed by Asian foreign investors, the majority of whom are Hong Kong and Taiwanese Chinese, and they mainly produce for the export market. Zhili was a typical factory of this type: a Hong Kong–managed compensation-trade factory and a supplier for a Western brand-name toy company. Yet, except for one brief reference to an umbrella factory that was

Japanese,[77] none of the letters gave any clues as to the nationalities of the managers or owners. The letters usually referred to "my factory" or "our factory" as if they were managed by invisible hands.

The workers mainly categorized factories into two types: "good factories" (*hao chang*) and "bad factories" (*buhao de chang*). But they apparently had not discerned any pattern about what made a factory good or bad, for instance, the good factories are usually managed by someone of a certain nationality and the bad factories by someone of another nationality. How do we explain this lack of generalization? My interpretation is that most factories appeared equivalently bad, either based on their own experiences or from knowledge acquired through shared information. Thus who owned or managed them was irrelevant. They hoped for a "good factory," but it was a mirage, an illusionary exit from hell to heaven.

Similarly, the letters betrayed no information on shop-floor conditions, the products they were making, or the number of workers on the job site. We know that several factories made toys only because one letter mentioned serious OHS problems with the spray-painting. The letters normally begin with a couple of lines of greeting and then plunge into a standard sentence: "Now let me tell you something about the conditions in my factory." But by "conditions" they mostly meant wages and work hours. There was almost nothing about the tasks or the workstations they were assigned to unless there was a problem. Production line supervisors were their immediate superiors, with whom they had the most contact, but there were only two complaints about them.[78] There were only two reports of incidents that involved conflicts with fellow workers from a different place of origin. Though academic studies have emphasized workers' place of origin as a major divisive factor in workplace relationships,[79] this problem did not preoccupy the writers of these letters. Nor did discrimination by locals either inside or outside the factory. Only one letter, from a male worker who had gotten into a fistfight with a local Guangdong worker, mentioned this problem.[80] Even though they were subjected to harsh and exploitative labor regimes, there were no complaints, anger, or hatred directed at factory managers. For example, there were no comments that a particular manager was horrible, had scolded them, or had docked their wages. How do we explain the absence of such issues in the letters?

I can only hypothesize. We should not conclude that these issues did not exist because they are not mentioned in the letters. After all, scholars studying such factories have verified their existence. What is obvious is that they were not important enough to be included in the short letters that the workers had time to write. The lack of comments about the production process can be explained by the fact that their tasks were so deskilled, so repetitive, so simple and meaningless, that whatever tasks or workstations they were assigned to made little difference to them. Nor did the difference in tasks have any meaningful correlation to the wages they ultimately received. Although they were theoretically paid at piece rates, in reality payments had little correlation with the speed and volume of work. The rates kept changing as new orders came in and new production processes were established. That they were paid irregularly, a month or several months later, rendered the kind of tasks and the piece rates even more irrelevant. Not even one of them mentioned informing management about a miscalculation in their wages.

Yet the total number of hours worked each day was important to them. The work was boring and tiring, and they eagerly looked forward to finishing. Whether it was eight, ten, twelve, or more hours of work a day at the production line made a difference in terms of rest and pay. If they only had to work for eight hours, it meant bad business—some rest but little money. If it was twelve hours for a long stretch of days, it meant good business and at least some money, but it also meant they would be extremely tired. That is why so much was written about work hours in the letters.

As to why they expressed no anger or bitterness, it could very well be that they were resigned to their treatment, since it was their choice to work in a factory in south China. They were aware they would be going back home after a few years because the household registration system prevented them from staying in Guangdong. Factory work was seen as an interim solution to family financial problems; no matter how intolerable the conditions, they would try to tolerate them because they would not last forever. They were not resigned to a life in the factories; seeking a short-term solution to their problems, they concentrated their energy on finding a better job. The sliver of hope that their friends and relatives would be able to get them into a better factory sustained them through the inhumane conditions in which they were temporarily trapped.

## THE "CULTURE OF SURVIVAL"

Believers in the perfection of the free market, especially classical economists, will undoubtedly challenge my descriptions of the horrific conditions of Chinese migrant workers, just as they have challenged previous exposés of such conditions. They base their skepticism on the following logic. If the migrant workers were experiencing such bad conditions, they would not have come in the first place. The very fact that migrant workers do not return home and that new waves of such workers keep coming into the cities is proof that working in the factories is better than their situations back home. Further, even if it is granted that their experiences in the factories really are that bad, it is a free labor market. It is their free choice.

Using the information extracted from these letters, I would like to put forward this counterargument. Trapped in a "culture of survival," as the letters reveal graphically, the workers and their families were very much aware of the harshness of factory life before the workers left their home villages and towns. The letters home, the erratic remittances, and the oral reports that accompanied the annual home visits all indicated that the streets of the south were not paved with gold. There was also the evidence of young people returning home with disfigurements (the survivors of the Zhili fire were a few of many) and strange illnesses. Still, teenagers and young adults, women and men alike, continued to surge into the coastal areas looking for work.[81] They were aware of the fate that awaited them, but there was no other way. Their families were trapped in poverty, owing not least to the heavy arbitrary taxes and fees levied on them.[82]

The two letters sent by a husband to his wife working in Zhili provides some idea of how important every yuan was to a poor peasant family.[83] By the end of the year, this family was burdened with debts and the wife had not yet been able to send back any money. This is her husband's report of their financial situation:

> Since you left, I got the cow sold on 10 January [Chinese calendar]. When I got the cash in hand, I immediately returned ¥100 to so-and-so, another ¥50 to so-and-so, and ¥10 to uncle. There were ¥40 left. I also finally sold the three pigs on 20 January for ¥130. I paid ¥80 for rent, and ¥30 to so-and-so for the meat. Then I had a wood-cutter cut down some trees for firewood, and it cost ¥40.[84]

Most of the money was used to repay debts. The family was about to start off a new financial year with little cash and most probably would have to borrow again soon. Every yuan of remittances was vital to maintain the family at subsistence level. The overall impression made by the letters is that the young people would not have gone to the factories had their families not been under such financial strain.

Their apparent freedom of choice needs to be set against the poverty trap they were in at home. No one chooses to be poor. The young migrant workers from rural families were immersed in a different form of poverty than they had experienced at home. They might have resorted to the "weapons of the weak," as described by James Scott, to alleviate their conditions, but the letters betrayed no preoccupation with this.[85] Whether the workers who wrote these letters had put up any form of resistance, covert or overt, is unknown. The workers were absorbed in survival. Poverty necessitates the creation of a culture of survival to confront everyday basic needs. In the villages, the need to survive pushed families to send their offspring into the factories despite the uncertainties of getting paid, the precarious employment, and the terrible conditions. The need to survive creates a false hope and a will that somehow the young people can tough it out for a few years. If only they could send home ¥100 a month, it could make a difference. What has been discounted and undervalued by all parties—the peasants, the migrant workers, and the free marketeers—is the human cost of sustaining this survival. The fatigue, the psychological isolation and anxiety, the spartan living conditions, and the occupational diseases cannot be given a monetary value or entered into account books.

The argument about free choice also ignores the elementary fact that, once inside the factory, the workers were at the mercy of management, which withheld their ID cards and deposits. Also, the workers were unwilling to abandon the back wages owed to them. Supporters of free markets also ignore the effect of "flexible" management on migrant workers who are placed at the mercy of a globalized chain of production. The vagaries, whims, and fashions of consumers in industrialized countries, the high and low production seasons, the increasingly short turnover time between the placement of orders and shipment, the lack of operating funds, especially among small manufacturers, and the wish to avoid overproduction all favor extreme flexibility in work hours and payment. The migrant workers are the ones who bear the risks.[86] From management's perspective, all that is needed is to provide for the workers' most basic needs, or perhaps a bit above that level to keep labor turnover down. This can be sustained when the production lines are idle for as little as ¥2 in food a day. This "largesse," as we have seen, allows management to lay claims to labor at short notice.

There are times when this level of minimum subsistence cannot hold workers, especially if they wish to go to a factory that actually pays some wages or offers slightly better working conditions. If withholding deposits, wages, and ID cards does not suffice to keep workers from leaving, even more heavy-handed methods are sometimes employed. The most common is the use of security guards to bar workers from leaving the factory compound.[87] All of these measures that entrap the workers are in blatant violation of the much admired free and flexible labor market.

As revealed in these letters, workers become consumed by the most primary concerns—a subsistence income, food, and health. They concentrate on the physical need to survive and the mental strength to tough it out. In the factories, the culture of survival inhabits a milieu that is very constricted. The young people have traveled long distances to get to these factories, but once inside, their physical world shrinks. When there is work in the factory, their days are divided between the shop floor and the dormitory. When there is no work, they have no use for their free time because they have no money to go anywhere.

Leisure and entertainment are not part of their lives.[88] The highlight of an occasional day off is no more than window shopping (not buying). Having a soft drink in a café is far beyond their financial capacity.[89] For the duration of their years in a factory, their physical and mental horizons barely extend beyond the compound. It is therefore not surprising that one of the workers at a Shenzhen factory, mentioned above, had no idea where neighboring Bao'an county was and was scared to go there by herself. Letters from home and from relatives and friends working in other factories is the only means by which factory workers maintain links with the outside world. Photographs become valuable memorabilia that can provide contact with the world beyond the factory walls. Their emotional life seemingly revolves around these letters and photographs. It is possible to see parallels between the situation of these migrants and that of soldiers trapped endlessly in battlefront trenches, longing for letters and photographs of their loved ones. Their emotional focus on a place far away from the factory, where the question of survival looms large, is what keeps the migrants going. The letters, which potentially carry news of other opportunities, also provide hope of escape from their present state. These escape routes are essentially illusory, but the workers prefer to live with hope rather than the despair that their circumstances seem to warrant.

The chance to visit close friends and relatives in other factories can alleviate the monotony of their existence. There is much excited discussion in the letters about the possibility of such visits. But this is easier said than done, and reunions seldom materialize. The correspondents are too far away, the journey is too expensive, they do not know the way, they are too afraid to venture out on their own, or their days off do not coincide. In the end they are left with little other than their decision to endure factory life and the hope that they can escape it.

## NOTES

My thanks go to Chang Kai for sharing these letters with me and for granting me permission to use them. Chang Kai is a researcher and teacher at China's Labor Movement Institute who normally writes under the pen name Yi Fu. I would also like to thank Jiang Kelin for typing out the letters; Eva Hung for helping categorize them; the staff of the Asian Monitor Resource Centre and the Hong Kong Industrial Christian Committee for supplying information on the fire and its victims; Tan Shen, Pun Ngai, Robert Senser, and the three editors of this volume for their encouragement, discussions, and various forms of assistance; Jonathan Unger for his critical editing; and Sarah Leeming for her meticulous copyediting. The funding for the project comes from an Australian Research Council Fellowship and Large Grant.

1. The Zhili Company is a compensation-trade enterprise. This type of enterprise differs from other forms of foreign-funded enterprises. While nominally owned by a local government, it is completely managed by the foreign investor. Factories tend to manufacture brand-name goods for export and do not produce for the domestic market. The Zhili toy factory manufactures for the Italian toy company Artsana/Chicco S.p.a. The Guangdong local government is basically a renter and a supplier of labor only marginally involved in the factory. It sends in a few officials to work as staff members, carrying the nominal titles of deputy managers. For a more detailed description of the organizational structure of such a compensation-trade enterprise see Robert Lambert and Anita Chan, "Global Dance: Factory Regimes, Asian Labour Standards and Corporate Restructuring," in *Globalisation and Labour Resistance,* ed. Jeremy Waddington (London: Mansell, 1999), 72–104. Also see Wu Jieh-min, "Strange Bedfellows: Dynamics of Government-Business Relations between Chinese Local Authorities and Taiwanese Investors," *Journal of Contemporary China* 6, no. 15 (1997): 319–46.

2. Yi Fu, "Feixu shang de pingdiao: Shenzhen '11.19' teda huozai shigu jishi yu fansi," *Zhongguo gongren* (Chinese workers) 5 (1994): 4–11; and no. 6 (1994): 8–11. For the English translation, see Yi Fu, "Toyland Inferno: A Journey through the Ruins," *Sociology*

and Anthropology, Summer 1998, 8–34. Through an international campaign launched by
Hong Kong, American, and European NGOs (nongovernmental organizations), the Italian toy company Artsana/Chicco S.p.a. (the main buyer of products made by Zhili) eventually agreed to compensate the injured Zhili survivors and the families of the deceased.
It would have been the first contracting transnational corporation to recognize its responsibility to the workers employed by its suppliers. As of the end of 1999, however, two
years after that pledge, the victims still had not received anything: the company had
reneged on its promise. At the time of writing, the NGOs had therefore renewed their
international campaign against the Italian toy company. See "Toy Campaign: Sixth
Anniversary of the Zhili Fire, Dossier no. 6, Special Issue," compiled by Asia Monitor
Resource Centre and the Coalition for the Charter on the Safe Production of Toys, Hong
Kong, November 1999.

   3. Siu-mi Tam, "Chinese Regional Sentiment in Graffiti," International Folklore
Review 9 (1993): 73–80; Emily Honig, "Regional Identity, Labor, and Ethnicity in Con-
temporary China," in Putting Class in Its Place: Worker Identities in East Asia, ed. Elizabeth
J. Perry (Berkeley: University of California, Institute of Asian Studies, 1996), 225–43.

   4. Tamara Jacka, "Working Sisters Answer Back: The Presentation and Self-Presen-
tation of Women in China's Floating Population," China Information, Summer 1998,
43–75; Lee Ching Kwan, Gender and the South China Miracle: The Worlds of Factory
Women (Berkeley: University of California Press, 1998), 14–35.

   5. Pun Ngai, "Becoming Dagongmei (Working Girls): The Politics of Identity and
Difference in Reform China," China Journal, July 1999, 1–18; Lee Ching Kwan, "Engen-
dering the Worlds of Labor: Women Workers, Labor Markets, and Production Politics in
the South China Economic Miracle," American Sociological Review, June 1995, 378–97.

   6. Dorothy J. Solinger, Contesting Citizenship in Urban China: Peasant Migrants, the
State, and the Logic of the Market (Berkeley: University of California Press, 1999).

   7. Anita Chan, "The Emerging Patterns of Industrial Relations in China and the
Rise of Two New Labor Movements," China Information 9, no 4 (1995): 36–59; "Labor
Standards and Human Rights: The Case of Chinese Workers under Market Socialism,"
Human Rights Quarterly 20, no. 4 (1998): 886–904.

   8. Thomas Scharping and Walter Schulze, "Labor and Income Developments in the
Pearl River Delta: A Migration Survey of Foshan and Shenzhen," in Floating Population
and Migration in China: The Impact of Economic Reforms, ed. Thomas Scharping (Ham-
burg: Mitteilungen Des Instituts Fur Asienkunde, 1997), 119–200; Scott Rozelle, Li Guo,
Minggao Shen, Amelia Hughart, and John Giles, "Leaving China's Farm: Survey Results
of New Paths and Remaining Hurdles to Rural Migration," China Quarterly, June 1999,
367–93.

   9. Tan Shen, Dagongmei de neibu huati: Dui Shenzhen yuan Zhili huanjuchang baiyufeng-
xin de fenxi (Internal communications among dagongmei: Analyses of more than one hundred letters of the former Zhili toy factory in Shenzhen), unpublished. Her paper uses a
set of letters from Zhili that partly overlaps the set used in this chapter, though the
emphasis of Tan Shen's analysis is quite different from the topics that are drawn out in
this chapter.

   10. Pun Ngai, "Opening a Minor Genre of Resistance in Reform China: Scream,
Dream, and Transgression in a Workplace," Positions, forthcoming.

   11. Other summary statistics of the letters are as follows: sixteen were from workers to

siblings working in Zhili, thirty-seven were from workers to relatives and friends working in Zhili, and three were from boyfriends or girlfriends of the Zhili workers.

12. In addition to these data, I have acquired a knowledge of the conditions of migrant workers from documentary research, yearly field visits to factories in China, a questionnaire survey of workers in fifty-four Chinese footwear factories, and personal interviews with workers, managers, trade unionists, and government officials.

13. Some of the letters have letterheads that include a city or name of a factory, identifying the senders' locations. The location of writers can be deduced from the context of the letter and place names referred to.

14. Wage issues appear in items 3, 9, 11, 12, 13, 14, 19, 26, 31, 32, 37, and 39 in table 7.1.

15. Issues related to job-seeking appear in items 1, 2, 15, 17, and 28.

16. Work hours and issues of overtime work appear in items 4, 5, 18, and 22.

17. References to physical existence are found in items 7, 8, 23, 27, 33, 34, 36, and 41.

18. References to loneliness and isolation appear in items 10, 20, 21, and 29.

19. Readers should be aware that the absence of references to a particular topic does not mean that it was not relevant to the letter writer. There could be many reasons why a topic was not mentioned. For example, there were twelve references to ailments such as rashes, headaches, and lethargy, and some could be symptoms of occupational health and safety diseases.

20. "Wages: After the Labor Law," *China News Analysis*, 1 October 1995, 3.

21. *Zhongguo laodong bao* (Chinese labor news), 3 December 1993.

22. For Shenzhen's regulations on minimum wage standards, see *Shenzhen tequ bao* (Shenzhen special economic zone news), 11 June 1994 and 6 November 1994. Also see the Asia Monitor Resource Centre report, *Zhujiang sanjiaozhou gongren quanli zhuangkuang* (The conditions of workers' rights in the Pearl River Delta), May 1995, 19. Because nationwide minimum wage standards are not gathered and published systematically, it is difficult to collect the hundreds and possibly thousands of locally set standards that are revised annually. Zhuhai city had the highest minimum wage in the country at ¥328 in 1993 and ¥380 in 1994. See Asia Monitor Resource Centre, *Zhujiang sanjiaozhou*, 18; *Zhuhai laodong bao* (Zhuhai labor news), 19 May 1995. In 1994, the minimum wage was ¥230 for Guangzhou city, ¥220 for Shanghai, and ¥200 for Beijing (*Change*, April 1994, 2).

23. The wages mentioned in the letters were reported in different ways. Some were given as the wage per month, some as the wage per day and some as the wage per hour. I converted these into a wage per month for a 11.8-hour workday. I arrived at this by averaging the numbers of hours worked per day provided by twenty-one of the letters. For the number of workdays per month, I used a twenty-eight-day work month. This is based on my own observations in the field, which indicated that most migrant workers in Guangdong get about two days off a month.

24. This figure is close to the eleven-hour workday obtained in a survey of fifty Chinese footwear factories that I conducted in 1996. The average workday of the letter writers is longer by about an hour, perhaps because the factories in my survey were not among the worst: we would not have been given permission by factory managers to enter factories where working conditions were unusually poor. For preliminary results from this survey, see Anita Chan, "Globalization, China's Free (Read Bonded) Labour Market, and the Chinese Trade Union," *Asia Pacific Business Review*, Spring-Summer 2000, 260–81.

25. The working conditions described by this letter writer may not have been entirely in keeping with the law in that the worker probably had only two days off a month, which violated the labor law. This extra work drags down the hourly rate to below the legal minimum.

26. Letter 2.

27. Letter 28.

28. Letter 5.

29. This fieldwork was conducted in August 1998 in Jinjiang county in Fujian, a county well-known for its privately owned footwear enterprises, which hire only migrant workers on the production line.

30. Letter 54.

31. Letter 49.

32. Letter 27.

33. For example, see Wang Ningde, "Yiming jizhe de shiwu tian dagong riji," *Gongren ribao* (Workers' daily), 27 April 1996, 3. A translation of this article is available in *Chinese Sociology and Anthropology*, Summer 1998, 62–76.

34. Letter 41.

35. Letter 19.

36. Letter 11.

37. Letter 49.

38. Letter 48.

39. Letter 57.

40. *Guangdong laodong bao* (Guangdong labor news), 13 January 1997. This OHS survey was carried out by the Shenzhen Labor Bureau Safety Protection Inspection Section and Tongji University's Industrial Hygiene Research Department.

41. Letter 7.

42. Letter 33.

43. Letter 70.

44. Letter 65.

45. Letter 9.

46. Jia Xiaodong and Jin Xipeng, "Woguo yourongji weihai de xianzhuang he yufang" (The damaging conditions and prevention of our country's organic solvents), *Zhonghua laodong weisheng zhiyebing zazhi* (Chinese journal of industrial hygiene and occupational diseases), April 2000, 65–67; *Shenzhen tequ bao* (Shenzhen special economic zone news), 2 May 1995; Asia Monitor Resource Centre, "The Working Conditions of the Toy Industry in China: Preliminary Report," November 1998; Chen Meei-Shia and Anita Chan, "China's 'Market Economics in Command': Workers' Health in Jeopardy," *International Journal of Health Services*, forthcoming. Another toxic labor-intensive industry is electronics. See Pun Ngai, "Opening a Minor."

47. Letter 6.

48. Letter 6.

49. Kevin Bales, "Modern Trade in Disposable People," *Guardian Weekly*, 20 June 1999, 25.

50. See Asia Monitor Resource Centre, "Toy Campaign."

51. In Letter 69 there was a one-line reference to a strike having taken place earlier: "Since the strike last time, our fellow companions have all left."

52. Letter 25.

53. Letter 23.

54. Before leaving home, they first needed to buy various personal documents—an identity card *(shenfen zheng)*, the unmarried-status certificate *(weihun zheng)* or birth control certificate *(jihua shengyu zheng)*, the permit to work elsewhere *(wugong zheng)*, and a border certificate *(bianfang zheng)*—if they were planning to enter the Shenzhen economic zone. They also needed a train or bus ticket and then enough money to cover expenses before they got their first pay, including enough money to buy a return ticket in case they could not find a job. These expenses would have been several hundred yuan.

55. See letter 27 below.

56. Letter 24.

57. Letter 52.

58. Letter 1.

59. Letter 26.

60. Letter 14.

61. Letter 27.

62. Letter 7.

63. Letter 32.

64. During my interviewing in the field in 1996, these were frequent complaints about workers by members of the Taiwanese Business Association in Dongguan city in Guangdong province and in Putian city in Fujian province.

65. In table 7.1, these are included as items 10, 20, 21, and 29.

66. Letter 48.

67. Letter 7.

68. Letter 11.

69. Letter 39.

70. According to my personal communication with Pun Ngai, who has worked as an ordinary worker with female migrants, coworkers do make friends with each other.

71. Letters 41 and 42.

72. Mobo Gao, "The Rural Situation in Post-Mao China and the Conditions of Migrant Workers: The Case of Gao Village," *Bulletin of Concerned Asian Scholars*, October-December 1998, 70–77.

73. I can only surmise why Gao migrant workers could send more money home than the workers who wrote the Zhili letters. The Gao migrants went to other parts of China, whereas the writers of the Zhili letters were all in Guangdong. Based on my own survey and field observations, migrant workers in the Shenzhen area actually make less than those in private enterprises in other parts of Guangdong province (see, e.g., Jonathan Unger and Anita Chan, "Inheritors of the Boom: Private Enterprise and the Role of Local Government in a Rural South China Township," *China Journal*, July 1999, 67). In my field research in 1998 I also discovered that migrants in Jingjiang county working for private enterprises made more than those in the Shenzhen area. When indexed against the local minimum wage, foreign-invested enterprises in Guangdong near Shenzhen paid less than four other cities elsewhere in the country (this information derives from a survey of fifty-four footwear factories in five cities that I conducted in 1996).

74. Nine entries gave the amounts of remittances home, but among these, five of the letters referred to two particular workers. The largest amount of money sent was ¥2,000

over a period of a few months. This case could be interpreted as an outlier statistically, as this was the only worker making more than ¥700 a month, well over double that made by other letter writers.

75. Letter 38.

76. Letter 53.

77. Letter 53.

78. One writer complained that her production line leader was Hunanese and there-fore incompetent. A complaint of another writer was that some group leaders and techni-cians were biased in work allocation (letter 10).

79. See Siu-mi Tam, "Chinese Regional"; and Pun Ngai, "Becoming *Dagongmei*."

80. Such antagonisms between different ethnic and regional groups reportedly show up much more frequently in restroom graffiti. On this, see Siu-mi Tam, "Chinese Regional."

81. Even for the relatively better-off rural families, the enormous urban-rural gap in living standards meant that the opportunity was too good to be missed.

82. Gao's article contains a breakdown of these levies, which in the end left a family of four with only ¥100 per person per year. For another report on the heavy burden imposed by local governments on peasants, see Thomas Bernstein, "Farmer Discontent and Regime Responses," in *The Paradox of China's Post-Mao Reforms*, ed. Merle Goldman and Roderick MacFarquhar (Cambridge: Harvard University Press, 1999), 197–219.

83. Letters 41 and 42.

84. Letter 41.

85. James Scott, *Weapons of the Weak: Everyday Forms of Peasant Resistance* (New Haven: Yale University Press, 1986).

86. This is generally the case throughout the developing world. Larry Elliott, "Globali-sation Will Lead to Moral Disorder Unless It Is Tamed," *Guardian Weekly*, 15 July 1999, 14.

87. See, for example, Liu Xinhuan, "Zhaojie xieye gonsi kedai yuangong shou chachu" (Zhaojie Footwear Company's mistreatment of workers under investigation), *Gongren ribao* (Workers' daily), 17 April 1996. For a translated version, see *Chinese Sociology and Anthropology*, Summer 1998, 58–61.

88. The normal Chinese word for a vacation is *fangjia*, but to the letter writers *fangjia* simply refers to any period when production line work has been suspended and they have involuntary free time.

89. Such an outing to a supermarket and café is vividly described by Pun Ngai, "Becoming *Dagongmei*."

# 8

---

# The Chinese Enterprising Self: Young, Educated Urbanites and the Search for Work

*Amy Hanser*

"Back in March [when I was looking for work], the feeling of competition *really* was strong—rows of tables squeezed together, all sorts of companies, all sorts of people looking for jobs," Han Suying, a recent college graduate in Harbin, told me as she mulled about her search for work at a Beijing job fair. Although Han eventually found a job, she "didn't expect that the standards would be so cut-throat."[1]

Han's description piqued my interest, and later I attended one of Beijing's many job fairs. People pressed in from all sides as I struggled down rows of exhibition booths, each filled with a potential employer and a listing of job openings. It was like being aboard a packed Beijing city bus, except that I had paid ¥10 for admission. Flashy posters introduced the operations of the more media-savvy companies; others had simply tacked handwritten signs to the walls of their booths. One company was playing a videotape on which a woman's voice intoned a seductive mantra about challenge, growth, and opportunity. Young people crowded around booths, reading job descriptions and presenting resumes for inspection. In the corners of the exhibition center others crouched or sat, leaning against walls and columns as they filled out forms.[2]

Completing school and entering the workforce—when work suddenly becomes a defining element in one's life—is an important transition in many societies. For young people in urban China, however, this stage is doubly difficult. In addition to the personal transition, *work itself* has been in rapid transfor-

189

mation because of the nation's economic reforms and the swift pace of its social change. The content of work experience has changed dramatically from what young people in urban China encountered just ten or fifteen years ago.

Hiring practices are also in flux, and many urban youths feel as if they have been thrust headlong into shifting circumstances. The pattern of twenty years ago—which rewarded the ability to maneuver for the best of government-allocated, guaranteed, lifetime jobs—has been replaced by a new form of competition in which, increasingly, free market mechanisms distribute jobs that people hardly expect to hold for life. "I feel like [my generation] is on the border of something," said Li Xiaoping, a twenty-four-year-old graduate student in Shenyang. "Between the old system and the new . . . I have to force myself to face competition, to be competitive."

Change has come both in the ideological terrain on which job aspirations and expectations are formed and in the daily-life contexts in which jobs are actually sought. Competition itself is hardly new, since government distribution of work in the old system was fraught with competition as well. But the paradigm has clearly shifted from one in which competition was characterized by an explicitly political, virtuocratic set of criteria to an increasingly profit-seeking framework in which success or failure is built on autonomous choices and individual ability, initiative, and effort.

This chapter examines youth work aspirations and expectations in the context of broader changes in China's urban labor market. By "aspirations and expectations" I mean individual hopes and preferences as well as perceptions of objective constraints.[3] Many of the questions raised here are empirical: How do young urban Chinese feel about work and the search for work after the major shifts in hiring practices? How do they see themselves within the broader economic and social changes in their environment? And what, in the end, do they search for?

## THE ENTERPRISING SELF

Labor market changes have enabled many young urbanites to view work not simply as their contribution to society or a political and economic necessity but as a newly available realm for autonomy and self-development. The ideas that young, educated urbanites espouse about work and their hopes for the future center on individual selves that are tested and tempered through market-based competition. An active, calculating self is often at the core of such notions of work. British sociologist Nikolas Rose, basing himself on Western European examples, has posited the "enterprising self." Rose argues that in Western societies governed "neoliberally" (i.e., through capitalist market mechanisms), "the self . . . is to aspire to autonomy, it is to strive for personal fulfillment in its earthly life, it is to interpret its reality and destiny as a matter of individual responsibility, it is to bind meaning in existence by shaping its life through acts of choice."[4] In the following discussion I draw on Rose to understand how the new market-driven competition in urban China both cultivates and tests young Chinese "enterprising selves."

The bulk of my data comes from twenty-two interviews with urban youth—ten men and twelve women aged nineteen to twenty-nine—that I conducted in summer 1998 when I visited Beijing, Shenyang, Harbin, and Qingdao in northern and northeastern China. The educational background of my interviewees ranged from high school to three years of graduate study.[5] This makes them relatively privileged within their contexts, yet much of what they told me fit well with more informal and wide-reaching observations I had made as an English teacher in China from 1994 to 1996. I found my interviewees largely through the network of personal connections that I maintained from that extended stay. I also visited job fairs in Harbin and Beijing, collected articles and advice manuals for young people looking for work, and had many informal conversations with both friends and strangers.[6] Sometimes conversations continued off and on over several days or turned into group discussions. Most conversations had at least one listener—usually a friend, sibling, or classmate of my interviewee. If this condition introduced certain inhibitions for some, there were compensating advantages as well, since third or fourth parties often contributed valuable information to the discussion or made comments that sparked lively debate.


## EMPLOYMENT AND COMPETITION IN
## SOCIALIST CHINA BEFORE REFORM

Prior to the introduction of economic reforms in 1978, participation in China's workforce was officially viewed as participation in revolution—in part, at least, a patriotic contribution and sacrifice for the people and the nation. In urban China, not having a job was nearly equivalent to nonexistence. The work unit (*danwei*) not only provided a means of distributing economic resources but also operated as an important governmental administrative unit, serving functions of both social welfare and governance.[7]

Work was subject to extensive government control. In the 1950s jobs began to be assigned through centralized mechanisms and government labor bureaus. By the early 1960s urban work units acted as mediators not only between the individual and the state but also—by guaranteeing basic food, housing, and other aspects of welfare—between the individual and the rest of society as well. Employment was a lifetime tie between a person and the work unit, and changing work units was almost unheard of.[8] For young urbanites entering the workforce for the first time, finding a job generally meant accepting a government job assignment (*gongzuo fenpei*) over which one had little or no control. Only rarely would the government make a second assignment if the first were rejected. From the 1950s until the early growth of the private sector in the late 1970s, there were virtually no other avenues for finding work in China's cities.[9]

Despite rhetoric about placing collective interests above individual ones, competition for resources in socialist China predated the era of economic reform. Susan Shirk's examination of urban secondary schools of the 1960s reveals that monolithic distribution of job positions "put students into face-to-face competition with one another for limited goods in one high-stakes game, with no alternative avenues to success."[10] Students took part in evaluating one another's political performance in a system in which political and moral criteria often trumped technical merit. Competition—which could take the form of self-criticism and self-disclosure—became a public performance in local contexts. Individual ambition certainly survived and was often intensified by the nebulousness and changeability of political criteria. Young people learned to be highly calculating about their futures. Shirk notes that "students' expectations about their futures were the dominant influence on their behavior. They adapted their behavior to the structure of opportunities and the rules of the game."[11]

## LABOR MARKET REFORMS AND EMPLOYMENT

Through the 1980s and 1990s market reforms led to a relaxation of government control of the hiring process in China's cities, and by the late 1990s the form and context of job-related competition had shifted considerably. As early as the late 1970s, high youth unemployment in the cities prompted the central government to encourage young people to seek alternatives to the standard system of job assignments, and since then new labor policies have reduced the scope of the system drastically.[12] By 1998 even university students were being encouraged to bypass official channels of job assignment.[13]

By the late 1990s interested employers could directly contact schools to recruit personnel, and such labor market reforms had a disproportionately powerful effect on the young. Because new labor market regulations often grandfathered existing arrangements, new workers or workers who switched jobs were the first to experience the differences.[14] For many urban youth, finding work on their own—through newspapers, job fairs (*zhaopinhui* or *rencai jiaoliuhui*), or phone calls to the personnel departments of potential employers, as well as private "connections"[15]—has become the only alternative and is increasingly the preferred alternative even among those who still have access to the job-assignment system. Among college students the traditional system is now widely regarded as a backup. Political criteria have been removed from most job hiring decisions, producing a new focus on a person's ability to compete in a freewheeling economic scene. As Anita Chan has noted, with reforms "the 'socialist man' ethos was abandoned in favor of notions of 'economic man.' "[16]

A new set of catchwords, invoked in official reports, the media, and everyday speech, reflects general shifts in how employment is conceived. A guidebook for young college graduates entering the labor market introduces such job-search jargon as *gongxu jianmian* (the coming together of supply and need) and *zizhu zeye* (autonomy in job choice). The term *shuangxiang xuanze* (double-sided choice) means that both employers and employees have a choice in job-hiring decisions. This phrase—unthinkable under the old centralized system of job allocation—came up frequently in my interviews.[17] The new competitive environment has required new strategies and, as I will show below, the perception that one now needs an "enterprising self." The effects are sometimes felt to be invigorating, especially when they lead to personal development and a sense of autonomy. But risks are high as well, and anxieties loom.

The well-established Chinese practice of "social connections" (*guanxi*) might seem to counter the emphasis I am placing on the "enterprising self." In fact the term *guanxi* seldom arose in my interviews, and when it did the method was usually attributed to someone else. But this is not to deny a continuing if diminished role for *guanxi* in actual Chinese practice. Indeed, some of the people I interviewed had plans for cultivating a network of professional contacts as their work experience grew. It can be argued that resourceful use of *guanxi*, far from contradicting the notion of an "enterprising self," is an integral part of it (in China as elsewhere).

## CONSTRUCTIVE COMPETITION: FORGING THE ENTERPRISING SELF

Many have observed that, in general, competition has been crucial to the reform of China's ailing and inefficient factories and businesses. My interviewees— especially the well-educated, well-trained, or well-connected ones—tended to concur. They saw competition as necessary, natural, and fair. When I asked Wang Anning—a talented twenty-four-year-old master's student studying in Shenyang—about competition, she answered with a peppery, "Whoever's best is most successful." Such confidence highlights the advantages and range of options that education is perceived to bring.[18]

But competition can have a variety of meanings. Among my interviewees the competitive labor market meant, variously, motivation, challenge, or unwanted pressure—but above all it altered the self. Young people in the late 1990s felt a pressing need to adapt or change themselves, and they felt that the seemingly "objective" labor market was what imposed this need. Such a feeling may not be unique to China, but, as already noted, it was *new* to China. Job seeking and work became important routes for defining and fulfilling oneself.

This is not to deny the importance of material considerations like salary and benefits. Although my interviewees did not always mention money first or rate it most important, material concerns were a consideration for all of them. Yan

Rongxi, whose work unit sponsored him as a master's student, said that "because you live in society and lots of things require money, you can't *not* think about this question. You can't just say that because you've found a job you really like, but they won't pay you a cent, you'll still do it—that's impossible." Even people who claimed to rate other things higher than money and material rewards had certain underlying expectations about acceptable pay.[19]

Yet there is much evidence that work for Chinese youth is not just about making money or supporting oneself. A 1988 survey conducted by the Chinese Academy of Social Sciences found that 52 percent of urban youth believed that "suitability to one's individual skills and strengths" (*fuhe geren de techang*) was the most important criterion in choosing a job. (Only 12 percent of respondents ranked salary first.)[20] In a 1990 survey 41 percent felt "giving full play to one's skills" was important, and the authors of the study conclude that "in the minds of young people, work already is not just for making a contribution to society or for supporting oneself, but is also a process by which to perfect and develop oneself. . . . That young people hope to realize their aspirations is an expression of professional, enterprising, career spirit."[21]

What is meant by a "professional, enterprising, career spirit"? My interviews suggest a number of factors, of which two pairs are especially important: autonomy and mobility and self-development and fulfillment.

## Autonomy and Mobility

During a boisterous reunion dinner, the husband of a friend was discussing his views about a "good" job. He was not afraid of unemployment—there were plenty of jobs to be had. He wanted to find a *satisfying* job, one that met his personal criteria. High salary and good benefits were important, but he spent most of his time talking about *zizhuquan* ("right to independence" or "autonomy"). The following exchange took place:

> "Before I went to graduate school in Chinese medicine, I worked in a hospital for two years. On one occasion I felt I knew better than my superior how to handle some patients' cases—but I had to do what I was told. I got my way on only one patient, and that one survived. The others all died. But I still was reported to the higher-ups for my insolence."
>
> "Couldn't that happen even at a good work unit?" someone asked.
>
> "Yeah, there's really no way around such things. So I'd rather go to a small hospital first, some place where I'll get more freedom to develop myself (*fahui wo ziji*). Once I've established my reputation, then I can move to a larger place."

Zhou Min, a confident young computer engineer in Beijing, wanted to leave his current job largely because he disliked the managerial style. "It's old-style management," he told me over a bowl of noodles. "They tell you what to do. I have no chance to be creative. . . . Maybe my expectations of what a job should be like are influenced by what I know of the United States and Europe. In China the 'old way' [state socialist way] makes it easy to be lazy and places too little emphasis on getting things done." Zhou suggested that people at his workplace are jealous of talented, hard-working people and that he himself had become frustrated.[22]

Young people who had confidence in their ability to compete tended to switch jobs often. They believed this would enhance their careers and promote personal improvement. Du Liming, an ambitious college graduate working for a Sino-foreign joint venture in Harbin, said, "I'll probably look for a new job after I get married. It's really important to switch jobs in order to get new and broader experience." He had changed jobs three times in two years.[23] In Beijing, twenty-seven-year-old Luo Anda, graduate of a technical college, talked about his four different workplaces in the three years since his graduation: "Every time I've changed jobs, I've felt like da-da-da [moving up steps]. . . . When I have the right skills, I'll go to an even better company." Work experience had helped Luo learn about himself and had given him "direction." Earlier, he said, "because I wasn't very mature, I didn't know in which direction to develop myself." He noted that "sometimes when I've been unsuccessful, I've felt hurt. But then I think about why . . . I was unsuccessful this time. . . . [and realize that in some ways] it was good for me to lose that opportunity." He explained that failure and self-reflection have enabled him to perfect his interview style to the extent that now "I'm sure I can control the interview . . . [and can sense] what the perfect answer is." Ding Haoran, a twenty-five-year-old college graduate from Guangdong province, had worked three or four different jobs in the past two years in Beijing and planned to spend another two years "working on my career" (ba shiye gaohao). He expressed great confidence in his ability to find work in Beijing's competitive labor market; his visit to a job fair that day had netted him four or five follow-up interviews. I pressed him on whether he felt comfortable with rapid job shifts and he said, "I'm used to it. After I left college, my ideas changed very quickly, so I'm able to adjust."

Correspondingly, job stability was sometimes portrayed as something that prevented people from reaching their full potential. One woman in Beijing had consciously chosen flexibility over stability. She rejected a work assignment in her hometown of Wuxi largely because it was with a state unit. "It would've been boring (mei yisi), don't you think?" For Xie Gang, a Harbin graduate student, mobility within a single workplace was important. He turned down an attractive job offer at a Shandong research institute because he believed the work unit was parochial and unprofessional. "Without connections I might work a whole lifetime at that unit and never be promoted very high," he said. Instead, he lobbied hard for a job at a joint venture company in freewheeling Shenzhen, where he felt he could expect both good pay and plenty of professional challenge.

The high school graduates I interviewed were generally not so enthusiastic about switching jobs, but twenty-three-year-old Ahong in Harbin was an exception: "In the past two years I haven't held a job for more than three months at a stretch. I've left jobs for lots of different reasons—sometimes I was fired because I didn't have the ability for the job, and sometimes I left because the wages were too low. Sometimes I work a job until I learn pretty much all there is to learn about it, and then it gets to be boring and I quit. . . . My future goals are pretty much to find jobs with higher salaries and to try different jobs. . . . With all the changes in China now, there are many, many different types of jobs I can try."[24] I asked her how it feels to be switching jobs all the time. "Oh, I'm used to it (*xiguan le*)," she shrugged.

Ahong thought autonomy in the labor market was important for success in work. But for others, especially people with more education and professional training, personal development was at least as important for work success.

### Self-development and Fulfillment

Zhou Min, who had been my student a few years earlier, believed that his three years of work experience in Beijing had transformed him into a mature, savvy, and confident young man and that work had taught him much about his own strengths and interests. "Do *you* think I'm the same?" he asked me. For Zhou, the notion of professional success had become so closely allied with that of personal fulfillment that work was seen as an important avenue to personal happiness. Many others of my interviewees echoed this thought. A job, they felt, should suit not only your skills but also your personality and even your choice of lifestyle. "The biggest issue facing China's young people," said Harbin college graduate Du Liming, "is the question of employment—not just finding a job but finding the *right* job."

Han Suying, an energetic and gregarious college graduate in Harbin, had found an accounting job with a state unit in Beijing that provided a satisfactory salary as well as housing. She felt very lucky to have gotten the job offer because only fifty people had been selected from among five hundred applicants. Her parents, classmates and friends all approved of the job. But it fell short of her ideals. "I feel it's a good job, too," she said, "but at the same time I was hoping to find something that would expose me to . . . more of the world . . . something more exciting. Personal interests are important. Of course money is something important too, but I feel my interests are even more important."

Han had not yet started work when I interviewed her. Yan Rongxi, by contrast, had been working three years, and he felt he had sacrificed too many personal interests to practical considerations. His views on work had changed, and he felt "the change can be divided into three stages. Before graduating and not having yet worked, while at college . . . your knowledge about work is very superficial . . . very naive . . . because you've never worked before. Then after working, you start to feel a bit like this isn't your favorite job, but now I still have to do this job well, still have to adjust to it. But now I also have a kind of . . . the third stage . . . it's a kind of idea . . . that I should still look for a job that I like, because that way I'll do [my job] even better." Not long thereafter Yan did indeed forgo the security of his state job in order to look for something more closely aligned with his personal interests and professional ambitions. The experiences of Han and Yan show that the enterprising self needs more than autonomy; it needs to use autonomy well, through acts of choice.

## THE IMPORTANCE OF CHOICE

There was little room for job selection in Mao's China, but by the 1990s youth in the big cities already faced many forks in the road before them. How will I go about looking for work? Should I stick with my specialization from school or strike out in a new direction? Should I accept a new job offer and quit my current job? But the alternatives that will be available cannot always be controlled. How difficult will it be to find another job? Will the salary be reasonable? Will it offer professional advancement? Will it be interesting?

Some of my interviewees said that an important factor in making good choices is knowing what kind of person you are. They felt their job choices were limited in part by their personalities. A young woman in Shenyang said "people now can find jobs to which they are better suited." Luo Anda said he wanted a "simple" work environment "because I feel I'm not very good at dealing with people [i.e., with office politics]." Self-help books designed to assist young people in finding the "right" job also stressed that one should begin with one's strengths and weaknesses, likes and dislikes. One such text includes an extensive section on personality, complete with various personality tests by which a job seeker might come to understand him- or herself more clearly and make better employment decisions; failure, it implied, is a consequence of bad decision making.[25] In a section called "Psychological Advice for Choosing an Occupation," the authors emphasize the importance of "choice," "self-knowledge," and "self-confidence" in making career decisions.[26] They stress that self-knowledge also leads to general well-being: "A young person with a healthy mind-set always maintains confidence in life."[27]

Correspondingly, bad decision making and a negative mind-set go hand in hand. One interviewee said, "I know that a lot of people, especially now in modern society, everybody is crazy about money. . . . If your mental state doesn't allow you to adjust to competition, and you don't have an accurate and healthy way of thinking . . . you'll lose your direction, won't know what to do, or you'll get extreme and make bad decisions."

Even guidebooks that champion the independent job seeker, however, acknowledge the limitations that China's conditions sometimes imposed. The handbook cited above lists the "big picture" of the whole nation as the first "principle for selecting an occupation. . . . When choosing an occupation, we need to take society's needs as our starting point, and when personal wishes and collective benefit are in conflict, we have to . . . obey the needs of society."[28] Passages such as this seem to carry traces of China's socialist history as well as a subtle acknowledgment that not all of China's young job seekers are equal.

## DISAPPOINTMENTS AND INEQUALITIES

The new "enterprising self" was not uniformly a happy proposition. Many people, even among the most skilled and educated, felt they had no choice *but* to adapt to labor market changes. And not all young people I interviewed anticipated a smooth transition into working adulthood. For many, the end of government job assignments and reliable lifetime employment loomed as a considerable worry.[29] In the late 1990s bookstores in Beijing stocked a plethora of self-help books that addressed issues like job instability and competition. One, entitled *Learn How to Console Yourself*, includes sections entitled "Don't Take Life Too Seriously" and "Say to Yourself, 'I'm OK.' "[30] One young man suggested that young people are interested in self-help guides partly because the reforms had created a general "sense of unsteadiness" in society. In Harbin, twenty-five-year-old Yan Rongxi explained that "in China there is more and more job switching now, but with frequent job changes there's a feeling of unsteadiness, so I worry about this a bit." His fear of job instability, he added, had prevented him from pursuing a potentially rewarding job in Guangzhou.

Reservations about employment often sprang from perceived or experienced barriers to autonomy and opportunity in work. Young people with less education or fewer skills, or groups perceived to be less able as workers, such as women, encountered serious barriers to securing their "ideal" jobs. Aware that they were more vulnerable to the vagaries of the labor market, these people were less ready to speak about fulfilling personal desires or ambitions through work. Their job-related considerations focused more on salary—both its size and its reliability—and on working conditions, including the degree to which bosses respected workers. What was "good" was often made clear by describing what was *not* good: long hours, boring work, few or no benefits, few or no regular days off, heavy-handed bosses.

Discomfort with labor market changes was often expressed as lack of confidence in one's ability or desire to compete. Zhao Jun, a twenty-five-year-old Harbin man, had been trained in computers in a small, local technical college. Despite his educational background he found it hard to stay employed, and this was true of many of the high school students I interviewed. When I asked him his idea of "a good job," he immediately replied, "A stable job. With the job I have now . . . well, I could get fired at any time. When my boss gets angry, I get really worried." Zhao already had a number of bad work experiences. In one case, he was hired at a job fair for one type of work but was assigned to something quite different when he showed up for work. The boss publicly scolded and criticized him, and after working a month and a half Zhao had only been paid ¥100 of the ¥300 in monthly salary he had been promised. He quit. He was fired from his next job, and his third job was a temporary summer position. His experience left him skeptical of job fairs ("It makes you think they're just out to cheat people") and highly conscious of his vulnerability at the hands of employers. Zhao acknowledged that competition provides people with "motivation" but saw his own situation as "a kind of forced adjustment." He saw the job market less as opportunity than as inescapable and sometimes treacherous reality. His perception was likely influenced by the experience of his parents as well; both were workers who had been laid off from state enterprises.[31]

The market seemed even harsher to eighteen-year-old high school graduate Li Ci, whose difficulty finding any work at all had eroded her confidence in her ability to compete. "A lot of my classmates had an easier time. . . . They applied for the same jobs and got offers, but I didn't, even if I was a stronger candidate," she explained while peddling foam puzzles at a local night market. Eventually she took a job as a saleswoman for a toy company in Harbin because the position—unlike many similar ones—provided a base monthly salary of ¥360 in addition to sales commissions. "At first the pressure was terrible," she said, noting that on her first day she sold only ¥5 of merchandise. She added that she had now grown "accustomed" to commission sales work, but the statement may have been partly a cover for inner insecurities. Her friend, who had introduced us, confided to me, "Looking for work has been a real blow to Li Ci's self-confidence."

Even Ahong, the high school graduate who claimed to be quite comfortable with her rapid job turnover, had experienced disappointments. "I had worked for almost three years doing accounting in a Sino-American joint venture company when it was decided that they would employ only people who had four-year college degrees or higher. So I stepped down. We all felt very bad about it. . . . I don't think the new policy was very fair. People should be hired on the basis of ability, not educational level."

A problem among the college-educated was that work situations often fell short of what they had anticipated. A young man in Qingdao told me, "When I was in college, I had everything planned out very clearly, but once I actually started working, everything was entirely different from what I had imagined." His job had not provided the opportunities and challenges that he expected. Yan Rongxi, thinking back on how he imagined work while still in college, said, "I didn't think about it all that much but thought it would be similar to college—very relaxed, harmonious relationships—you could say I thought about it in very idealistic terms. But after I started working, I discovered that it wasn't like I thought it would be, and I felt disillusioned."

## EMPLOYMENT AND GENDER

It is probably no accident that my more "enterprising" interviewees—confident, ambitious, independent, professional—were men. Women, even those who were highly educated, often faced sex discrimination that tempered their confidence in their ability to compete.[32]

One major barrier is society's perception of women as workers. An employment guidebook for young people explains that employers look for people with a good "work ethic" who "give full play to their talents, creating even greater value."[33] But for women in particular, it gives further advice: since women have strong psychological barriers to being active and enterprising, they should avoid "only seeking to pass life peacefully" instead of "pursuing the development of personality and ability."[34]

The young women I interviewed knew of many examples of discrimination and sometimes showed irritation that their male counterparts seemed so ignorant of the phenomenon. Master's student Li Xiaoping related the story of a female classmate who "was in touch with a work unit in Shenyang for about a year; for all that time the company wasn't quite willing to sign a contract with her despite the fact that she was a good student and suitably qualified. In the end they hired a male graduate student from the same school who wasn't even all that interested in the position and was far less qualified. We [Li and her female classmates] were very angry when we heard about this."

The women I spoke with considered such practices unfair but felt that there was little they could do to change things. Tan Huifang, a graduate student of pharmacology, remarked, "I know it's harder for women to find jobs. Work units expect young women to marry and have children right away. And there are some things that men can just do better. But in my field there are not so many men [so some work units will have to hire women]. The only way to deal with the situation is to try very hard and to look for work tirelessly. I am very determined."

Ironically, women nearer the bottom of the opportunity ladder—those with less education and fewer job skills—were the least likely to feel disadvantaged by gender. In Harbin I spoke with a group of high school graduates, all of whom were employed as restaurant wait staff, "greeters" in department stores and boutiques, shop clerks, and other service sector jobs that were strongly sex-typed as "women's work." These young women were more concerned with marketable job skills than with "personal development." When I asked them if it was more difficult for women than men to find jobs, the response was a resounding no. "Absolutely not," Ahong said. "There are lots more jobs open to women—in hotels, restaurants—and they often pay better." When I expressed surprise and began to explain what better-educated women had told me about discrimination, Zhao Hui interrupted with, "Well, maybe their requirements are too high."

For women, tensions between work and family life challenge the centrality of work and make the development of an "enterprising self" more difficult. For example, Zhang Huarong, a twenty-six-year-old woman, enrolled in graduate school solely to improve her chances of finding a job that would secure her a residency permit (hukou) in Beijing, where her long-time boyfriend lived and worked. Zhang explained that without a Beijing residency permit, children do not get immediate access to schools or child care facilities, and to purchase such services on the open market is prohibitively expensive.[35] Before we met, Zhang told a classmate that she was reluctant to meet with me because she was afraid that as a foreigner I "wouldn't understand" why she had sacrificed her former job—which would have given her a very good chance of studying abroad—in exchange for the chance to go to Beijing to be with her boyfriend. Besides reminding me of the pitfalls of field research, the comment illuminated Zhang's own ambivalence about the divergent pull of work and marriage.[36]

In contrast to Zhang, my male interviewees at all educational levels generally felt that residency permits were of virtually no significance any more. "The permits are no barrier to moving," a male college graduate in Harbin argued. A young man in Beijing needed to be pressed a bit in order to recall any advantages of a residency permit: "The permit is not important unless you have a child you want to send to school. Perhaps that is very expensive in Beijing." Young men did recognize that, as they married and began families, tensions between work and home could emerge. A young man in Beijing concluded that it was best not to have children. He said he had friends who worked long hours, left their children with relatives, and saw them only once a week. "What's the point?" The same young man, however, suggested that women who chose to find fulfillment solely in their work were the ones who had "lost at love" (shilian).

Further reforms may indeed make residency permits obsolete. But for now they stand, along with gender bias in hiring practices, as a major concern for China's urban working women.

## CONCLUSION

In this chapter I have employed Nikolas Rose's term "the enterprising self" to describe people primarily in their economic roles. The real analytical power in Rose's concept, however, is that the enterprising self is a political notion as much as an economic one. It accords, in Rose's words, "a certain *political* value to a certain image of the human being."[37] The image of the enterprising self leads young Chinese to recast their understanding of society and to see social situations as inhabited by autonomous, responsible individual actors. In a passage evocative of China during its economic reforms, Rose asserts that "the enterprising self" lies at the core of a political rationality in which "the well-being of both political and social existence is to be ensured not by centralized planning and bureaucracy, but through the 'enterprising' activities and choices of autonomous entities."[38]

Many urban young people in China cannot or will not view themselves as fully enterprising selves. Factors such as education, locality, lack of connections, inadequate skills or ability, personality, and even luck can be perceived as barriers to success in finding, landing, and keeping a good job. One young man who spoke of "realizing my personal value" (*shixian ziwo jiazhi*) was quick to add that "in reality . . . there are lots of limitations, imposed by society and so on." Encounters with such limitations could weaken young people's sense of *zizhuquan* and could lead them to reevaluate or dispense with job ideals altogether. As one study on Chinese youth concludes, "in the vast majority of cases, it is still the job that chooses the youth."[39]

Despite the disappointments, however, most of my interviewees held fast to their aspirations and rarely gave up on self-development, preferring to adapt rather than surrender. "I don't always feel capable of handling [competition]," one said, "but you have to face reality or be weeded out (*taotai*)." The faith that many young people had in what they saw as a new meritocracy led them to accept responsibility for their own success or failure in finding work and pursuing a career. Many viewed the assumption of this responsibility for themselves—without parental assistance—as an achievement in itself. "I've been to college," said a woman in Qingdao, "so I ought to be able to find a job on my own."

Some research suggests that where memories of state socialism remain fresh, Chinese people express less willingness to accept new models for the self and social organization. Lisa Rofel, for example, cites examples of older women factory workers who resist "modern" factory discipline by taking breaks and socializing during work hours as they did under the old system. Their memories of that system, Rofel says, "have taken on the hue of subversion in the context of economic reform."[40] In Shanghai Douglas Guthrie found enterprise managers who were reluctant to impose contracts and other new profit-oriented practices on older employees, citing socialist beliefs about proper treatment of workers to defend their position.[41]

The young people I interviewed, however, were not interested in challenging or criticizing the emerging employment system, and even the ones with relatively poor job prospects did not hanker for the "job assignment" system of state socialism. Especially in economically sluggish northeast China, they associated assigned jobs with financially troubled state work units, low wages, and tedious work. They preferred the genuine sense of autonomy and choice that the new system offered. They often felt confident that they could adapt to competitive pressures, and to change in general, better than other people could. A newly minted college graduate in Harbin was especially direct on this point. "What does competition mean?" he asked rhetorically. "Competition means someone is stronger than someone else. Well, I feel I am stronger." He then drove his point home by addressing me, his interviewer: "Could I, perhaps, offer *you* a job?" Susan Shirk's observation that Chinese young people in the 1960s "adapted their behavior to . . . the rules of the game"[42] seems equally true of the young people in the new game today.

## NOTES

1. Quotations are taken from interviews conducted in China by the author during the months of June, July, and August 1998. Respondents' names have been changed.

2. The large, two-day job fair, the '98 Beijing Summer Season Joint Talent Hiring Fair, was held in August 1998 at Beijing's International Exhibition Center. More than two hundred employers were represented and thousands of job seekers attended.

3. My understanding of aspirations and expectations in this sense owes much to Jay MacLeod's study of lower-class youths in the urban United States. Jay MacLeod, *Ain't No Makin It: Aspirations and Attainment in a Low-Income Neighborhood* (Boulder: Westview, 1995), 61, 137.

4. Nikolas Rose, *Inventing Our Selves: Psychology, Power, and Personhood* (Cambridge: Cambridge University Press, 1998), 151, 154. Rose's notion of the enterprising self grows out of his discussion of Michel Foucault's concept of "technologies of the self." Technologies, or techniques, of the self refer to a particular ethical relationship between a person and his or her self. These techniques involve practices for knowing and altering one's self. Rose argues that "the enterprising self" is a guiding principle for modern technologies of the self in the West and is "embodied in the very language that we use to make persons thinkable, and in our ideals as to what people should be" (151). Rose's conception of the enterprising self is complex, involving a detailed consideration of power relations, politics, and expert knowledge. I will not engage this concept theoretically in this paper but rather will use it as a conceptual tool for my observations and interview data.

5. Three had graduated from *zhongzhuan* (technical high school), five from *dazhuan* (two-year college), and six from *daxue* (four-year university). Eight were working on master's degrees, but five of these eight had looked for jobs after college and so are considered in both the "college" and "graduate student" categories in my study. In China's cities generally, in 1998, only 49 percent of people aged twenty to twenty-four, and 34 percent of people twenty-five to twenty-nine, had a high school (*gaozhong*) education or higher. *China Statistical Yearbook 1998* (Beijing: Zhongguo tongji chubanshe, 1998), 175.

6. Examples are Liu Jiaqi, Jiang Chunlong and Hu Yi, eds., *Dangdai daxuesheng zeye zhinan* (A contemporary college student guide to choosing an occupation) (Harbin: Harbin Gongye daxue chubanshe, 1995), 1–14; Wang Yongjiang, ed., *Bang ni xuanze zhiye* (Helping you choose an occupation) (Beijing: Zhongguo laodong chubanshe, 1994); and Ji Xinhua, ed., *Zhaopin yu yingpin: Qiuzhi chuangye zhinan* (Advertising jobs and accepting a job: A guide to seeking a job and creating a career) (Haikou: Hainan chuban gongsi, 1998).

7. Andrew G. Walder, *Communist Neo-Traditionalism: Work and Authority in Chinese Industry* (Berkeley: University of California Press, 1986); and Barry Naughton, "*Danwei*: The Economic Foundations of a Unique Institution," in *Danwei: The Changing Chinese Workplace in Historical and Comparative Perspective*, ed. Xiaobo Lü and Elizabeth Perry (London: Sharpe, 1997), 169–94.

8. Yanjie Bian, *Work and Inequality in Urban China* (Albany: State University of New York Press, 1994).

9. Bian, *Work and Inequality*, 60. For the group Yanjie Bian studied in Tianjin in 1988, 64.5 percent of those entering the workforce between 1949 and 1952 had gotten their first jobs through direct state work assignments (*guojia fenpei*). For the period between 1966 and 1976, 88.5 percent of those entering the workforce had used direct state assignments. On the rise of the private sector as an employment option, see Lora Sabin, "New Bosses in the Workers' State: The Growth of Non-State Sector Employment in China," *China Quarterly*, December 1994, 944–70; and Deborah S. Davis, "Self-employment in Shanghai: A Research Note," *China Quarterly*, March 1999, 22–43.

10. Susan L. Shirk, *Competitive Comrades: Career Incentives and Student Strategies in China* (Berkeley: University of California Press, 1982), 180. See also Walder, *Communist Neo-Traditionalism*, 162–89.

11. Shirk, *Competitive Comrades*, 2. See also Anita Chan, *Children of Mao: Personality Development and Political Activism in the Red Guard Generation* (Seattle: University of Washington Press, 1985); and Jonathan Unger, *Education under Mao: Class and Competition in Canton Schools, 1960–1980* (New York: Columbia University Press, 1982).

12. After 1983, only college students (two- and four-year) were guaranteed job assignments upon graduation. *Qingnian laodong jiuye fazhan baogao* (A report on the development of youth employment), in *Zhongguo qingnian fazhan baogao* (Reports on the development of youth), ed. Lu Jianhua and Shan Guangnai (Shenyang: Liaoning renmin chubanshe, 1994), 190; see also Charlotte Ikels, *The Return of the God of Wealth: The Transition to a Market Economy in Urban China* (Stanford, Calif.: Stanford University Press, 1996), 191.

13. For a detailed chronology of employment reforms affecting college graduates, see Davis, "Self-employment," 29–30.

14. *Qingnian laodong jiuye*; Ikels, *Return*, 217. Instituting a labor contract system and phasing out "permanent" employees starting in the mid-1980s is one example; see Douglas Guthrie, "Organizational Uncertainty and Labor Contracts in China's Economic Transition," *Sociological Forum* 13, no. 2 (1998): 457–94. Housing reform policies under which newly hired workers no longer receive housing benefits (at state work units especially) also affected the newly hired disproportionately.

15. See especially Yanjie Bian, "Bringing Strong Ties Back In "Indirect Ties, Network Bridges, and Job Searches in China," *American Sociological Review*, June 1997, 366–85.

16. Chan, "Chinese *Danwei* Reforms," 100. The nature of competition within the workplace just as surely has shifted, but these changes largely fall outside of the scope of this study. See also Shirk, *Competitive Comrades*, 186–97; Lisa Rofel, "Rethinking Modernity: Space and Factory Discipline in China," *Cultural Anthropology*, February 1992, 93–114; Anita Chan, "Chinese *Danwei* Reforms: Convergence with the Japanese Model?" in *Danwei*, 94–95; and Yang Yiyong et al., *Shiye chongjibo: Zhongguo jiuye fazhan baogao* (Tide of unemployment: A Report on the development of employment in China) (Beijing: Jinri zhongguo chubanshe, 1997).

17. Examples are from Liu Jiaqi et al., *Dangdai daxuesheng zeye zhinan*.

18. Official statistics do not allow for easy comparison of earnings between groups with varying levels of education. But one recent study argues that returns on higher education have been increasing since the introduction of economic reforms to urban China. *China*

2020: *Sharing Rising Incomes, Disparities in China* (Washington, D.C.: World Bank, 1997), 32–33.

19. This finding accords with other research on the attitudes of Chinese youth toward work. A 1985 study conducted in Shanghai found that "high income" was the top criterion in job hunting, with the young (aged twenty-nine and under) placing more emphasis on money than older people (aged fifty and over). See Godwin C. Chu and Yanan Ju, *The Great Wall in Ruins: Communication and Cultural Change in China* (Albany: State University of New York Press, 1993), 108–111. A more recent series of national-level surveys, conducted in 1988 and 1990 by a group in the Chinese Academy of Social Sciences in Beijing, revealed that salary was a consistently important consideration among urban youth and the primary reason for working hard. Yang Gang, Chen Fei and Long Jie, eds., *Zhongguo qingnian datoushi: guanyu yidai de jiazhiguan yanbian yanjiu* (An in-depth look at Chinese youth: Research on the evolution of a generation's values) (Beijing: Beijing chubanshe, 1993), 176.

20. Yang Gang et al., *Zhongguo qingnian*, 173–75.

21. Yang Gang et al., *Zhongguo qingnian*, 160–61, 173–75. From their 1985 Shanghai survey findings, Godwin Chu and Yanan Ju argue that money was the primary consideration for young Chinese seeking employment. Chu and Ju, *Great Wall*, 108–9. The gap between these two interpretations suggests that a shift in thinking about work among Chinese young people might indeed be taking place.

22. Zhou did indeed soon leave his state work unit.

23. Deborah Davis reports that in Shanghai recent graduates expected to change jobs often "until they found an 'ideal job.'" Davis, "Self-employment," 27 n. 21.

24. The use of trial, or intern, periods (*shiyongqi*) has increased job mobility. Usually lasting three months to a year, the trial period precedes the signing of labor contracts. This allows the worker to quit without incurring a penalty for breaking her contract, and it enables the employer to fire unsatisfactory workers easily. Wages paid during a trial period are lower than regular wages, and some people suspected that certain employers always fire workers after a three-month trial in order to keep labor costs low. On this point, see also Sally Sargeson, *Reworking China's Proletariat* (New York: St. Martin's, 1999), 99–101.

25. Liu Jiaqi et al., *Dangdai daxuesheng*, 53–107.

26. There are Western influences here (e.g., the authors invoke the Greek notion of humors to discuss four distinct temperaments), and it is possible that parts of this text are taken fairly directly from foreign texts. Liu Jiaqi et al., *Dangdai daxuesheng*, 53–60.

27. Liu Jiaqi et al., *Dangdai daxuesheng*, 49.

28. Liu Jiaqi et al., *Dangdai daxuesheng*, 42.

29. For evidence of general concern among Chinese urbanites about loss of stability, see Ikels, *The Return*. See also "Zhongguo shehui chengyuan de shehui xintai he xingwei quxiang" (The social mind-set and behavior of members of Chinese society), in *Zhongguo xin shiqi shehui fazhan baogao, 1991–1995* (Reports on the social development of China in the new period, 1991–1995), ed. Lu Xueyi and Lin Peilin (Shenyang: Liaoning renmin chubanshe, 1997), 577–79, 602–3.

30. Chen Rusong, *Xuehui anwei ziji* (Learn how to console yourself) (Beijing: Zhongguo jingji chubanshe, 1996). Another example is Tian Shude, *Shiji chongjibo: Xin shiji dui qingnian de liaozhan he huhuan* (Pounding waves of the century: The challenges and call for youths in the new century) (Fuzhou: Fujian renmin chubanshe, 1993).

31. Page 589 of Zhongguo laodong nianjian 1997 (China labor yearbook 1997) (Beijing: Zhongguo laodong chubanshe, 1997) lists unemployment in Harbin at 3.0 percent in 1996, but this official statistic seems too low. It apparently does not count more than 200,000 workers who were officially registered as xiagang, or laid off (Haerbin tongji nianjian 1998 [Statistical yearbook of Harbin] [Beijing: Zhongguo tongji chubanshe 1998], 92) and it does not square with general perceptions among the people of Harbin or with unemployment rates in other Chinese cities. See Yang Yongyi et al., Shiye chongjibo, 43, which estimated national unemployment rates for China at 4.2 percent in 1998 and predicted they would hit 5.0 percent by 2000. See also the discussion of official unemployment statistics in Davis, "Self-employment," 30.

32. On job-related sex discrimination in the 1980s, see Emily Honig and Gail Hershatter, Personal Voices: Chinese Women in the 1980s (Stanford, Calif.: Stanford University Press, 1988), 243–63; and Li Yinhe, Nüxing quanli de jueqi (The sudden emergence of women's rights) (Beijing: Zhongguo shehuikexue chubanshe, 1997), 160–67.

33. Liu Jiaqi et al., Dangdai daxuesheng, 30.

34. Liu Jiaqi et al., Dangdai daxuesheng, 140.

35. Concern about residency permits touches all social levels, especially for women, because a child's permit "follows" its mother's. On the continuing importance of the hukou system to employment for both men and women in Shanghai, see Davis, "Self-employment," 31; for Hangzhou, see Sargeson, Reworking, 79–86.

36. Deborah Davis provides compelling evidence that family duties—especially during the early years of motherhood—strongly influence women's job preferences and decision making in Shanghai. Davis, "Self-employment," 26.

37. Rose, Inventing Our Selves, 151.

38. Rose, Inventing Our Selves, 153.

39. "Qingnian shenghuo fangshi fazhan baogao," Zhongguo qingnian, 397.

40. Rofel, "Rethinking Modernity," 95.

41. Guthrie, "Organizational Uncertainty," 486–87.

42. Shirk, Competitive Comrades, 2.

# 9

# Beggars in the Socialist Market Economy

*Leila Fernández-Stembridge and Richard P. Madsen*

For Wei Jingsheng, it was a terrible epiphany, a moment that propelled him onto the path of dissidence. As a Red Guard in 1966, he took a train journey to western China.

> Leaving behind the city of Lanzhou . . . we came to a sudden stop at a small station. . . . The moment our express train came to a halt, a horde of beggars swarmed around nearly every car. In a crowd of youngsters begging below my window, I noticed a young woman, her face smeared with soot and her long hair covering her upper torso, who moved me to pity. . . . I began to lean out the window in order to put . . . cakes into their hands. No sooner had I stuck my hand out, however, when a sudden reflex made me pull it back in quickly, my arm still dangling in midair. In that brief instance, I had seen something that I could have never imagined or believed before: Other than the long hair spread over her upper torso, that young woman of about seventeen or eighteen years of age had absolutely nothing covering her body. From a distance, the soot and mud smeared all over her had looked like clothing, and among all the young unclothed boys who were begging, she had not been conspicuous. I had never been one to blink at reality, and I certainly knew that what I had seen was real, but there was simply no way that I could take this in. The girl and the other beggars didn't understand why I had withdrawn so suddenly and they begged even more loudly. I immediately realized that to them their hunger was the most pressing matter, so I quickly threw the cakes in my hand out and a great clamor arose by the rails as they fought over them. . . . For the remaining two days of the trip, I could not put the scene at that nameless little station out of my mind. Was this the "fruit" of socialism? Or was it the evil doings of a few bad local leaders? . . . At the same time, it dawned on me that in order to discern the true face of this society, it was not enough to understand the conditions existing in the cities and among the upper classes; one had to probe the situation at the lowest levels as well.[1]

In China today, it is not necessary to go to Lanzhou to see beggars. Right outside the immigration building in Shenzhen there are dirty, disheveled people who aggressively solicit money. A pedestrian who tries to avoid them may find that the beggars persistently walk alongside, pleading for money. Female teenagers with babies commonly use this method. Sometimes young girls carrying flowers walk next to couples, asking for a few yuan in exchange for a flower. If a couple refuses, a beggar often kneels on the pavement and holds the legs of the man so that he buys flowers for his companion. Sometimes beggars cling to the clothes of passersby, not letting go until they are given some money.

The Shenzhen beggars are the most aggressive we have seen in China. In other places, many beggars are more passive. They often sit or lie on blankets on street corners or (in Beijing and Shanghai) in subway entrances, sometimes displaying pieces of paper on which they have written their misfortunes, sometimes calling out and kowtowing but making no attempt to follow the passersby. They are usually dressed in dirty clothes and their faces are dark from hours in the sun—or sometimes from makeup designed to make them look dirtier and darker and thus more pitiable than they really are.

Sometimes an elderly man or woman or a young child will beg alone. Often such people display grotesque scars or amputated limbs. In other cases, adults are accompanied by small, listless children. Sometimes, there is a whole family of beggars, mother and father and several children, and even three-generational families, including the grandparents (photos 9.1 and 9.2).

The beggars in the large coastal cities today do not seem as utterly desperate as the ones Wei Jingsheng encountered three decades ago near Lanzhou. We have never seen any completely naked beggars, as Wei describes. But they are usually very dirty and they often project an appearance of total abjectness. And their numbers are increasing, at least in major coastal cities. As far as we know, there are no up-to-date statistics about the numbers of beggars in China. But there are some 1980s data that describe a trajectory of rapid increase, and casual observation in coastal cities today certainly suggests that this trajectory has extended into the 1990s. According to the *Zhongguo qigai shi* (A history of beggars in China, 1993) the number of beggars registered in government shelters in Guangzhou increased from more than 12,000 in 1985 to almost 30,000 in 1987. In 1986 there were ten times more beggars in Zhuhai than there had been in 1979.[2] There are more beggars today than there were during Wei Jingsheng's youth. They are much more prevalent in the prosperous coastal cities than they were then. Although they do not seem as desperately poor as the ones Wei encountered, their existence raises the same kinds of moral questions that troubled Wei.

The basic question concerns the ability of a modern society—and especially its representatives in government—to provide a life of dignity for all of its members, particularly the most vulnerable. The legitimacy of modern nation-states depends on their capacity to carry out such a social responsibility. At a mini-

*Photo 9.1    Child begging in the Beijing subway, August 1998. (Photograph by
Victor Manuel Benito Carrasco)*

mum, it would seem, such responsibility entails enabling all citizens to maintain
an adequate material standard of living without having to engage in behavior
that is considered morally degrading. The presence of significant numbers of beggars obviously challenges the claims of any modern society that it is meeting its
responsibilities.

But there are different moral frameworks for responding to such challenges. In
the socialist tradition, the government should provide jobs with an adequate

*Photo 9.2   A group of beggar women, August 1998. (Photograph by
Victor Manuel Benito Carrasco)*

income to all citizens. This tradition was the point of departure for Wei Jingsheng. He was shocked that in spite of its egalitarian rhetoric the Maoist state
failed to provide for many people in Lanzhou—excusing itself with the false
claim that these victims were "bad elements" and not really citizens. In liberal
capitalist societies (including the United States) a common view is that the government should simply provide the framework for a vigorous private economy
that will generate adequate jobs for everyone who chooses to work. Ideologues
for such a position justify the persistence of large numbers of beggars (rather than
a temporary presence caused by transitions to new forms of industries) by the
notion that the beggars have somehow chosen their lifestyle, either directly by
eschewing hard work or indirectly by allowing themselves to become unfit for
work, for instance, by abusing drugs and alcohol.

Depending on which of these broad moral frameworks one used, one would
look for different information about a society's beggars to argue whether the society was living up to its ideals of providing a decent life for all members. From
the socialist perspective, one would want to know if the beggars had been forced
into their condition by the government's failure to provide them with adequate
jobs or if they were truly noncitizens whose status was their own fault. From the
liberal capitalist perspective, one would want to know if the beggars had been
able to find jobs in the market economy as long as they made a good-faith effort,

if they had received enough of a "safety net" to sustain them through unavoidable fluctuations of the job market, and if they had taken adequate responsibility for keeping themselves fit for work.

Yet the actual experience of beggars in China—especially during the reform era, but also during the Maoist era—suggests that neither of these sets of questions touches on the most important features of Chinese beggars' existence. Many ordinary Chinese citizens, expert Chinese social scientists, and—most importantly—many Chinese beggars themselves commonly say that begging is a *zhiye*, a "profession." Like the English term "profession" or "vocation," the term *zhiye* connotes an occupation that is based on a body of systematized knowledge and skills, an organization that passes on and imparts such knowledge and skills, and the certification of the occupation by the state. The term also imparts a certain dignity to the profession, implying that it is not simply entered into out of desperate necessity but is a freely chosen way to develop oneself and to serve a wider community.

In this chapter, we use both quantitative and qualitative data—surveys and interviews conducted by Chinese social scientists and journalists as well as our own ethnographic observation—to make the case that, from the point of view of many of its practitioners at least, begging does indeed constitute a profession. Most beggars in China belong to organized groups that pass on skills needed to solicit money, allocate desirable places to beg, provide some mutual support, and regulate the conduct of beggars within the group. Faced with the practical impossibility of handling beggars in the way that official ideology and formal law says they should, agents of the state—such as the police and officials in civil affairs—unofficially recognize begging as a traditional profession by confirming the status of the leaders of beggar associations and giving beggar organizations an accepted sphere of activity. Although begging is indeed a lowly occupation, its members do not necessarily see themselves as pitiable victims driven into the occupation by sheer desperation. Rather, they often see their profession as a creative way to provide for families and communities under difficult circumstances, and as a way to feel "economically free," too.

If this is so, then begging with Chinese characteristics confounds the moral categories of both modern socialist and capitalist ideologies. The persistence of large numbers of professional beggars in China does not simply show that either socialism or capitalism has failed to fulfill its promises of providing an adequate standard of living for all Chinese citizens. It shows that both socialism and capitalism have failed to completely modernize China. (And it is thus one more rebuke to the assumptions of classical modernization theories that economics and perhaps politics determine the nature of all other aspects of society.) Professional begging in the People's Republic of China represents the persistence of a premodern tradition—not of course in a timeless, pre-twentieth century form, but in forms that have adapted themselves to modern political economies. This tradition has been adapted in different ways to Maoist socialism and to the reformist socialist market economy—ways that in each case have unfortunately tended to solidify the harshest aspects of the tradition. The challenge posed by the presence of professional beggars in China is not just about how to improve either the socialist or the market political economy. It is about how to modernize China's society and culture, and how to do so in a way that would be most humane toward the most vulnerable people in China.

## BEGGARS DURING THE MAOIST ERA

Let us first consider how the Maoist state tried and failed to eliminate the premodern practice of begging and how a new generation of socialist beggars revived traditional practices while adapting them to the constraints of state socialism.

In his 1939 essay entitled "The Chinese Revolution and the Chinese Communist Party," Mao Zedong had few kind words to say about the contribution of the "vagrant" class to the revolution.

> China's status as a colony and semi-colony has given rise to a multitude of rural and urban unemployed. Denied proper means of making a living, many of them are forced to resort to illegitimate ones, hence the robbers, gangsters, beggars and prostitutes and the numerous people who live on superstitious practices. This social stratum is unstable; while some are apt to be bought over by the revolutionary forces, others may join the revolution. These people lack constructive qualities and are given to destruction rather than construction; after joining the revolution, they become a source of roving-rebel and anarchist ideology in the revolutionary ranks. Therefore, we should know how to remold them and guard against their destructiveness.[3]

Beggars were thus lumped together with criminals and seen not as objects of socialist sympathy but as obstacles to the social control necessary in the new China.

After 1949 beggars were the kind of riffraff that tended to get swept into the category of "bad elements," which in turn was incorporated into the system of bad political types. If they were counted as workers, they were ranked among the lowest categories of workers. Thus in the 1950s the Ministry of Civil Affairs created three hundred centers for detaining and deporting beggars. Where possible, special industries were created within the framework of state socialism that offered a modern application to some of the beggars' traditional skills. For instance, it had been traditional in some places for beggars to be employed to carry the coffin at funerals (in order to gain karmic merit for the deceased by providing some work for the beggars). In these places, the new government organized such beggars into a "funeral trade union" (*gangye gonghui*), which gave them a fixed salary to be pall bearers within funeral parlors. When funeral rituals themselves were suppressed, or at least radically simplified, the former beggars were incorporated into other types of jobs, such as porters within organizations that transported heavy goods.[4] Political and occupational stigma thus being added to social stigma, beggars were then kept together in the lower strata of society by a Stalinist political system that provided them with a basic livelihood but inhibited all mobility.

But the government could not generate the wealth to provide even a minimal livelihood for people at the bottom of society. When the economy collapsed, especially after the Great Leap Forward, the government had to allow a resumption of begging. Indeed, it created its own class of professional beggars. In famine-stricken areas, government officials organized whole villages into beggar associations. These were given official letters of introduction, safe conduct passes, and official beggar identity cards to beg in approved urban areas. This was, in effect, a government-controlled way to collect taxes for direct poverty relief. Thus begging now became an officially sanctioned profession regulated by the state. People so organized developed a repertoire of skills based on the traditional beggars' craft. They took a certain pride in their work, and in some cases they continued doing it even when the Great Leap famine ceased.

We can get a glimpse of how these new socialist beggars understood their craft from an "eyewitness account" by a young intellectual, Zhai Yugui, during the Cultural Revolution. In 1974 Zhai Yugui, a former Red Guard who escaped to Hong Kong, published his two-part account in the periodical *Zhonghua yuebao*.[5] At the time, the article was denounced by leftist circles in Hong Kong for daring to suggest that there were large numbers of beggars in socialist China.[6] After the Cultural Revolution was launched, Zhai heard that there were many beggars throughout the country. Since there was no longer a famine, he wondered, why should there be any beggars? During his participation in the "linking up" (*chuanlian*) movement, he tried to find answers. He and fellow students at Sun Yat-sen University in Guangzhou talked to quite a few beggars and made the following generalizations, which are at variance with the impression of a disorganized mass of poor people that Wei Jingsheng had formed. All beggars that Zhai learned about had official permits. They all came from rural areas, mainly from northern China. They had the right to ride trains free of charge so that they could beg far away from home. For example, Zhai met a beggar in a Hunan train station, an old man from Henan who claimed to be the president of his community's Poor and Lower-Middle Peasant Association. He claimed that he felt a duty to beg in order to compensate for the losses caused by natural disasters in his home commune. He was in fact reviving an old occupation. He had also gone on begging expeditions during the Nationalist period. Then he had only begged close to home, but now the Communist government gave him train tickets so he could go all the way to Hunan. He had four children, and two of them begged with him. The other two sons were in Beijing, one in the PLA, and the other at a university. He was grateful for the Chinese Communist Party's policy of giving him an official begging permit. Besides, he said, if it were not for the Party, his son would not be at the university.

Originally, begging certificates were given to individuals, but by the late 1960s the government gave only one certificate to a chosen leader, who would be responsible for a beggar group. This was to enable the government more easily to track the movements of beggars and keep them under control. The efforts at control seemed to work. Once, when Zhai threw away the skin of a pear, a beggar immediately grabbed and ate it. Zhai suggested to the leader of the beggar gang that instead of eating garbage they should take the big sacks of food that were stocked in many train stations. But the leader refused, saying that such an act would be stealing from the state. As a result, Zhai concluded that beggars were tame, "more like dogs than wolves." In his outrage, he would have preferred them to be more like wolves. The difference in perspective was perhaps the difference between an intellectual disillusioned with the failed promises of socialism and poor people who had few illusions in the first place and were grateful that the government at least allowed them to resurrect a lowly but not dishonorable profession for meeting basic needs in hard times.

None of the beggars interviewed by Zhai belonged to the "five bad types"— landlords, rich peasants, rightists, counterrevolutionaries, or "bad elements." About 90 percent had the official status of poor peasants and the other 10 percent were middle peasants. This was puzzling to him because he had been told that beggars were part of the enemy classes. The answer to the puzzle came in a realization that the government had a hypocritical attitude toward beggars.

Having failed to provide adequate livelihoods for all its citizens, the government had to permit and even regularize the traditional profession of begging. One might even consider this a creative and compassionate way of dealing with the inadequacies of the socialist economy. Even as it organized beggars and regularized their traditional way of seeking welfare, however, the government kept them away from its biggest cities and told residents there that only a few "bad class" people were beggars. Beggars who ventured into Guangzhou, Shanghai, and Beijing were put into detention centers. The government was especially concerned to keep beggars away from foreign visitors. Once Zhai rescued a fifteen-year-old beggar from being beaten to death by policemen in Guangzhou. For doing this, Zhai's schoolteacher warned him that he could be labeled a counterrevolutionary because beggars were class enemies who should be eliminated and certainly not defended. The government could not admit to its more privileged citizens or to the outside world that it had failed to modernize the nation.

## BEGGARS IN THE REFORM ERA

The "four modernizations" and the various structural reforms that created the socialist market economy of the 1990s were supposed to produce a generalized prosperity that presumably would have eliminated the need for people to become beggars. Obviously they have not. Even though they may have diminished the degree of "absolute poverty" in China, the reforms have engendered great inequalities, as well as new opportunities for mobility. Incomes are so miserable at the lowest rungs of society that begging can actually provide a route to economic advancement. Under these circumstances, it is not surprising that poor, but entrepreneurial, people sometimes revive and adapt the traditional profession of mendicancy, which gives them a modicum of meaning and dignity even as they reject the work ethic at the basis of a modern market economy. Nor is it a surprise that the government would find this revival a blot on its image of modern China.

In the late 1990s, however, there seemed to be few "official beggars" in China. Beggars in postsocialist China are part of the huge "floating population" (*liudong renkou*) of unemployed or underemployed farmers who migrated to the cities during the reform era. Members of this population do not have urban residency permits and no guarantee of long-term employment. Most of them find reasonably steady work as unskilled construction workers, household servants, market peddlers, and so forth. One might suppose that beggars are those who have failed to find jobs. According to a survey of beggars in Beijing done in 1994 by Horizon Market Research Company,[7] however, this is not necessarily so. "In the case of Beijing, many of the beggars went there to beg, and did not even bother to look for a job."[8]

One reason for making begging a positive career choice is simply that beggars often make more money than other migrants. One quarter of the beggars in Beijing surveyed by Horizon Market made more than ¥600 per month, and the average income for all beggars was ¥15 per day. (As noted by Anita Chan in this volume, production line workers in Shenzhen often make less than ¥200 per month.) As summarized by the Horizon Market Research Company researchers, "Income sources [of beggars] are stable and the required work is very easy. Begging is therefore becoming a new form of profession (*zhiye*)."[9] Although some aspects of begging may be new, it is also in direct continuity with the past. Indeed, according to a Chinese journalist who has interviewed beggars in Shenzhen, many of the beggars there come from villages that had been given official permission to beg during the Maoist era, and they are now unofficially carrying on this tradition.[10]

Begging continues to be a profession with its own internally enforced rules of conduct and methods of organization. Begging is a kind of profession in which relatively low status is counterbalanced by relatively high pay. Like other migrants, beggars usually live together with others from the same native place—but only with other beggars, not with other *laoxiang* (people of the same native place) who have found a job in the city. This is partly because other migrant workers simply do not want to associate with beggars. For instance, in the words of the Horizon Market-Research Company report, "Mr. Wang, a beggar/garbage scavenger from Anhui, lives with nine other *laoxiang* in the Taiyan Hongbeikou neighborhood of Beijing. In the surrounding areas, there are other migrants from Hunan and Sichuan, but they do not have any relationship with him. This is not just because they come from different provinces or do different jobs. It is a pride issue."[11] To develop their own sense of pride in a world that looks down on them, beggars develop their own ways of giving one another mutual support and their own hierarchies of status.

Although they are rarely seen together while they are begging, at least 50 percent say that they live in groups of beggars. These groups vary in size and degree of organization. About 18 percent say they have a close working relationship with other beggars, and another 32 percent say that they maintain some kind of regular relationship. Most of these beggar groups have fewer than ten members, but at least one of the beggars keeps in contact with more than one hundred. Most beggar groups include only those who come from the same province. Only the best organized groups, with a longer history, accept beggars from other provinces.[12]

Sometimes a number of the smaller beggar groups confederate with a larger gang *(banghui)* directed by a strong leader, usually out of fear of being attacked by members of other gangs. The existence of these gangs is a very sensitive issue. "When beggars are asked about their relationship with the [gang] leader, their answer is: 'It is none of your business. Let me give you some advice: don't ask.' "[13] Nonetheless, about 10 percent admitted the existence of such gangs. We may presume that the real percentage is considerably higher. According to the responses received by the survey, gang leaders are men who are strong and clever and have a lot of experience. But the data are vague about exactly how gang leaders are chosen. Gang members have to pay a daily membership fee of one to five yuan to the gang leader. The leader wins the allegiance of gang members by teaching them the tricks of begging (e.g., how to pretend to be disabled), by protecting them from other beggars and perhaps from the police. But he also enforces his authority with threats of physical violence.

However lowly beggars are as a group, they maintain a strong hierarchy of status in their gangs. One interviewee said that he had never even met the leader of his gang, although he paid the leader ¥5 a day. He relied for daily help on his peers within the group, and the status of these "common beggars" was extremely low.

More than 60 percent of the beggars surveyed said that there is a lot of competition within their groups. Some of the stronger beggars try to rob the others, and this often provokes bloody fights. However, there is also an "occupational morality" *(zhiye daode).*[14] When one beggar has a serious problem, the others in the group will try to help. For instance, if one is sick, the others will beg even more money in order to get some food for that person. The leader of the gang is expected to settle conflicts and maintain cooperation among the gang members. About half of those surveyed said that they met regularly with members of their groups to enjoy each other's company (*yule*) and kill time (*xiaomo shijian*), as they generally felt lonely.[15]

From the common beggars' point of view, therefore, they are weak people in a world where the strong devour the weak (*ruorou qiangshi*). They can gain a little strength by seeking the protection of groups. However, they cannot trust anyone outside their gang, least of all members of rival groups. For a minimal level of security, it is probably best for smaller groups to affiliate with larger gangs. Failure to make this move threatens the survival of the group itself. In Beijing it is precisely the largest groups that have the longest history.

In a book published in 1999, the journalist Yu Xiu lets about twenty-five beggars from different parts of China tell their life stories in their own words.[16] Perhaps because she seems to have made a great effort to win their trust and has genuine empathy for them, her subjects express a sense of dignity in the practice of their profession. The dignity comes from the idea that they have freely chosen this occupation, even if, typically, the choices were among very limited options. It also derives from pride in the skillfulness of their begging performances. The strongest expression of quasi-professional autonomy comes from a group of teenage boys who sleep under bridges and spend their days begging in front of restaurants and shops in the business district of Chengdu in Sichuan province. Mostly runaways from families that rejected them (usually after their parents had divorced and remarried), they experience a kind of mutual support that they did not have in their abusive homes. They take pride in their cleverness in attracting handouts, and they teach each other the tricks of the trade. At the end of each day, the one who earns the most invites the rest to dinner. They claim that they are happy.[17]

The beggar's minimal experience of freedom makes sense only when contrasted with a background of tragic constraint. Consider the story of Lu Xiumei, who begs in front of the Beijing Zoo. At first the young woman does not want to speak with the journalist—not out of a sense of shame but for fear that Yu Xiu's presence will detract from the work of soliciting alms. Eventually the beggar invites the journalist to talk with her after hours in the small encampment of shanties where she lives. When the journalist meets her, Lu Xiumei has combed her hair and replaced her dirty clothes with a neat though faded dress. She has a tragic tale to tell. Coming from a modest but by no means desperately poor farming family, she had tested into upper middle school and hoped to go to university someday. But she was raped by an older unmarried man in her village and became pregnant. Responding to social pressure, her family forced her to abandon her schooling and marry the rapist. After the marriage and the birth of her child, she actually began to develop a feeling of commitment to her husband. But her husband became completely disabled in a farming accident. To gain money to help pay for her husband's medical bills as well as to provide for her daughter, Lu went to Beijing. To get work she had to go through a man from her local community who acted as a broker (*jingji ren*) for people from her region.

The job market was tight and he decided that she had the kind of appearance that could enable her to be very successful as a beggar. And thus she ended up on her mat in front of the Beijing zoo. Although there is plenty to be outraged about in this story, Lu does not see herself simply as a victim. In some ways she has more control over her destiny now than when she was in the village. She is making more money than she could have made in other unskilled jobs for migrant laborers. She is using the money not just for herself but to fulfill her responsibilities toward her family. She knows how to put on a good performance to attract alms, but she sees it as a performance and she is not really as abject as she appears to be on her begging mat.[18]

Such a sense of professional dignity has continuities with the beggars' craft during the Maoist era, when officially approved beggars, as already noted, could see their work as a creative way to fulfill responsibilities toward their communities. But the new socialist market economy has brought change to the social structure of the beggars' world, which renders different meanings to the practice of this profession at different levels. For example, Yu Xiu interviews a middle-aged beggar boss who works in Beijing but comes from Shaanxi, and who considers himself very successful. Although in the normal world people see him as "dirt under their feet," in the beggars' world he has enormous respect. He also makes a lot of money, which he displays by wagering tens of thousands of yuan on the gambling table.[19] He has so much swagger that he makes Yu Xiu, "this veteran journalist feel inferior (*zikui bu ru*)."[20] On the other hand, in the underpass near Beijing's Tongzhimen, Yu Xiu meets a beggar who said he became a beggar because he thought it was a "romantic" way of life, a way of being free and not under anybody's orders. However, he now realizes that this was an illusion. To be a beggar he has to belong to an organized gang and submit to the heavy-handed authority of its leader.

The competitive pressures of the modern Chinese city result in a stratification among winners and losers even in the world of beggars. It is a similar kind of stratification to that analyzed by Jean-Philippe Béja and his colleagues among Henan garbage scavengers in Beijing.[21]

Members of this stigmatized underclass occupation are organized into corporate groups with bosses who become quite rich, middle-level workers who make a decent living, and a rank and file who earn but a pittance doing extremely dirty and despised work. This stratification seems to become more significant among garbage collectors during the 1990s, and it has probably also increased among the beggars, for similar reasons. Because the boss's level of power and wealth comes more from the total number of people under him than from the average amount of money each of them earns, it is in the interest of beggar (and garbage collector) bosses to increase the size of their gangs even as their lowest-level members start finding their markets saturated. Even among the professional poor, the relatively rich get richer and the poor poorer.

Besides income and power, other kinds of social differentiation emerged among beggars in the reform era. During the Maoist era, almost all officially approved beggars were male. Women stayed at home to take care of the household while the men were sent out to beg. Now, however, female beggars are the most prevalent. As Yu Xiu's interviewee Lu Xiumei says, it is much easier for a female to elicit sympathy than a male. Bosses of the beggar gangs are almost exclusively male, however. And there have been ominous reports in the Chinese press suggesting sexual abuse of some of the females by male bosses.[22]

A final form of stratification is related to the methods used by beggars. Traditionally, *qigai* (beggars) encompassed a colorful variety of street performers, including singers, storytellers, snake handlers, sword swallowers, and acrobats. During the Maoist era, these vagrant entertainers were banned. Officially approved beggars simply performed the classic work of asking for alms. Now, however, many street performers have returned. Yu Xiu includes some in her book on beggars. They, however, do not consider themselves beggars. As one of them, a singer, puts it, he is not really begging, even though he asks for money in the streets, because he is using art. Moreover, he does not get something for nothing. His mission is to make pedestrians happy through his music, and they reward him accordingly. The same is true of garbage scavengers. In the past, they may have been lumped together with beggars. But the garbage pickers interviewed by Jean-Philippe Béja and his colleagues see themselves as different from beggars because they actually provide a social service for their money. In the new urban socialist market economy, the traditional beggar profession is thus splintering into a variety of subprofessions, which are themselves ranked in a hierarchical order of status.

Compared with the Maoist era, the reform era allows beggars a much more visible presence in large cities. This is because the system of social controls that was once able to keep beggars out of the major metropolitan areas has loosened. Yet they are still seen as pollution, a source of shame to a government that claims to be building a modern nation. Police periodically drive beggars out of the major cities, especially during such highly visible events as the celebration of the fiftieth anniversary of the People's Republic of China in 1999. In the weeks before that celebration, as an article in *Newsweek International* by Melinda Liu put it, "Around the country, police are rounding up anyone, from mentally ill beggars to an eighty-one-year-old Roman Catholic bishop, whose voice might dampen the party spirit." At that time, at least 100,000 rural migrants, including practically all beggars, were sent back to their province of origin.

Such efforts, of course, do little to address the underlying causes of begging. Government regulations specify that beggars are first sent to "detention repatriation stations" (*shourong qiansong zhan*), where they can be held up to a month before being sent back to their home provinces. They are supposed to be treated humanely and given political education at these centers. Care should be taken that "unusual deaths are prevented and for those who die while in custody, checks should be made to ascertain the causes of death and a legal death certificate made out."[23] When beggars are sent back, their local governments are to "resolutely resolve their work and life problems." This includes finding employment and housing for them. It is not clear, however, how local governments can get resources to do this. As soon as police controls are loosened, therefore, the beggars drift back to the big cities and resume their traditional profession.

## A PREMODERN PROFESSION IN THE MODERN WORLD

The modern socialist market economy is legitimated by the idea that the self-worth of Chinese citizens ought to be gauged in terms of how hard they work and how effectively they contribute to economic development. Beggars have been able to reject such ideas, we have suggested, because they can draw on a premodern belief system that provides a minimal dignity to the profession of begging and on premodern patterns of social organization that help beggars ply their craft. This belief system and these patterns of organization have not been eliminated by modernity but have been changed by it and have had to adapt. By analyzing the most important continuities and changes in the ways begging has been understood and organized from past to present, we can better understand why the practice of begging persists and better guess what might happen to it in the future.

Qigai—the formal, somewhat literary term for beggars, which is still used in the title of most publications on the subject—have existed from the beginnings of Chinese history. The ideographs qi ("to ask") and gai ("to give") are of ancient origin: gai is found on oracle bones of the Shang dynasty.[24] Qigai are mentioned explicitly in documents from the Warring States period, and the term is subsequently found in texts of every dynasty throughout Chinese history. The term qigai, however, has a range of meaning that differs from the English term "beggar," which is defined in terms of an action, soliciting alms. The term qigai has had somewhat different meanings in different periods of Chinese history. But even down to the present time, it seems to refer more to a status than an action—to a form of being rather than doing. When we discuss premodern mendicants, we will refer to them as qigai rather than "beggars" to convey a sense of their difference from the beggars of the modern West.

Many of the qigai mentioned in Chinese historical texts did of course beg for alms. But not all those who begged for alms were considered qigai. In some branches of Buddhism (still commonly found in Thailand, of course, but in the Tang and Song, at least, common also in China), there was a tradition of mendicant monks who supported themselves by begging for alms. However, they were not considered qigai.[25] Moreover, not all qigai made their living through asking passersby for handouts, although they were in fact the most common. (These qigai were further classified into a number of subcategories. For instance, the *hongxiang*, or "red type," grabbed hold of pedestrians' clothes; the *baixiang*, or "white type," attracted attention by screaming and crying.[26] The variety of terms undoubtedly reflects the wide prevalence and diversity of such beggars.) Some, as mentioned above, were street performers. Some peddled small items such as feather dusters. Others helped passersby carry heavy burdens. Others collected garbage. Still others were accessories at weddings and funerals. Giving money to *qigai* was considered an important way for people at such ceremonies to gain Buddhist merit. (This is still the case in Taiwan, although we do not have data to prove that it is common on the mainland. In contemporary Taiwan, the organizers of funerals sometimes give money to beggar organizations before the event. In return, the smelly, disheveled beggars stay away, but merit is accrued anyway.[27]) At some funerals, *qigai* also helped carry the coffin.

Unlike these more or less honest kinds of *qigai*, others took part in small swindles, like running rigged gambling games, selling patent medicines, or telling fortunes. Others spread fake blood over their bodies or told lies about sick parents or deaths in the family. Many *qigai* used varying degrees of coercion to get their money. Snake handlers, for example, threatened to turn their snakes on people if money was not forthcoming. Some *qigai* extorted money from shopkeepers by stationing a group of unsightly beggars in front of the shop door until proper payment was received. Sometimes *qigai* women performed prostitution,[28] and sometimes the men engaged in armed robbery. However, a distinction seems to have been made between prostitutes or robbers, who made such activity their sole occupation, and *qigai*, who only used it on an irregular basis.

*Qigai* were also considered different from famine victims or war refugees who temporarily had to beg for help but returned to families and villages once the crisis was over. To be a *qigai* was to be confined to a quasi-permanent status. In theory, some mobility out of this status was possible. According to David Schak,

> officially [*qigai*] status was not inherited. In traditional China, there were several categories of people regarded as *jianmin*, "mean people." People in categories so designated—prostitutes, actors, and criminals, to name a few—were not given full civil rights; they were not allowed to compete in the civil service examinations, and their status was passed on to their descendants. Beggars, however, were not "mean people" and were not so stigmatized. There are a number of tales and legends that point to figures, sometimes the same individuals, who experienced downward mobility into and upward mobility out of beggary. In some of these stories, the individuals mentioned were historical figures, without doubt the most famous of whom was Zhu Yuanzhang, who rose from beggar and bandit leader to overthrow the Mongols and establish the Ming Dynasty.[29]

But in practice the distinction between the "mean people" and *qigai* was vague, since *qigai* were stigmatized in a way that made it very difficult to get out of this status, and they were organized in a way that the status was passed on to their descendants. *Qigai* were people who did not have normal families, in a culture where the family was the irreplaceable center of social existence. The main cause of becoming a *qigai* was becoming an orphan, a widow, or an unmarriageable (perhaps because of disability or mental illness) bachelor.[30] There was no place for a person lacking a family in premodern China (unless the person joined a monastery or nunnery). *Qigai* gangs provided such unfortunate persons a quasi-familial life. According to the book *Zhongguo gaibang*, "In every town throughout [premodern] China, there were several *qigai* gangs." The members gave each other fictive kinship names. The relations among them were hierarchical and patriarchal, like those in extended Chinese families. Members of *qigai* groups would enter into quasi-marital relations with other *qigai* (although they commonly could not afford, or did not want to bother with, the ceremonies of a normal marriage), and they would raise their children to be *qigai*. Although these familistic arrangements were structurally similar to those in mainstream society, they did not have the legitimacy of proper family relations. Thus someone from a normal family probably would not marry a daughter into a *qigai* family, although in hard times a daughter might be sold or abandoned into the custody of a *qigai* group. Although it was theoretically possible to rise out of *qigai* status, in practice it was very difficult.[31] For practical purposes, the *qigai* almost formed a caste.

*Qigai* groups formed self-enclosed worlds. They had their traditions and customs and their own jargon, which of course varied by region. For instance, in Shanghai during the 1930s, beggars' jargon distinguished some of the following occupational specialties: *Dinggou* ("stubborn dogs," who chased after passersby), *Wanqinglong* ("players with green dragons," who handled snakes), *Sanjiao hama* ("three legged toads," who were missing an arm or leg, so they had to drag themselves on the ground), *Kai tianguang* ("skylights," who cut themselves on the head with a knife, so that they would be covered with blood), *Canji gai* (totally disabled, without arms or legs), or *Paixiong* (who hit themselves with a shoe until they were covered with wounds).[32] They also had their own religious rituals, often venerating Zhu Yuanzhang, the man who rose from being a beggar to founding the Ming dynasty, and Li Tieguai, "Iron Staff Li," one of the Daoist Eight Immortals, who is depicted as a beggar.[33]

Unlike early modern Europe, where beggars were confined in jails and poorhouses, *qigai* in imperial China constituted a legitimate occupational group, protected and supervised by the state. A virtuous emperor was supposed to have compassion for *qigai* and to provide for their basic needs.[34] Some emperors provided "compassion fields," which were places of refuge with basic food and shelter. Such provision, though, depended on the character of the emperor and his magistrates. More consistently, the imperial state integrated the *qigai* into its system of control.[35] In the Qing dynasty, at least, the local magistrates actually appointed the leaders of *qigai* gangs. The leader thus owed his power to the patronage of the government, not to the loyalty of those below him. He served the government by making sure that the beggars under his control did not disrupt public order, and he would be punished if any of his gang members committed a crime. In return, the magistrate gave him and his gang monopoly over a particular district. Backed up by the coercive power of the state, the *qigai* could apply coercive methods to get income within their districts. For instance, when the *qigai* extorted money from shopkeepers by threatening to stand outside the door and drive away customers, the shopkeeper could not complain to the magistrate because the magistrate had given the *qigai* implicit permission to do this.[36] Such practices could be viewed as a kind of taxation for social welfare purposes. It seems never to have occurred to imperial governments, however, to transform the living conditions of *qigai*, so that they would not have to engage in this occupation. It was a matter of giving them a secure (albeit lowly) place in society and keeping them under control.

Important aspects of the life situation of beggars in the China of the 1990s and today seem to reproduce this premodern *qigai* model. A first similarity is in people's paradoxical attitudes to beggars. People widely believe that most beggars are fakes. Even the Communist Party deputy secretary for Sichuan province remarked at the fifteenth Party Congress in 1997, "We even have beggars with gold rings and mobile phones!"[37] Yet many contemporary Chinese also consider beggars a normal part of society: "every country has them."[38]

Many of the premodern *qigai* were fakes, in that they made themselves out to be more desperately in need than they actually were. As suggested by the occupational jargon cited above, they were as much performers as supplicants, and they consciously developed a wide variety of bizarrely creative methods to make themselves appear as pitiable as possible. Yet people then—and even to some lesser degree today—were willing to support beggars despite the perception that they were at least partially fake. In the traditional Chinese worldview, *qigai* contributed to society by giving ordinary people occasions to acquire Buddhist merit by demonstrating compassion. Fake or not, *qigai* were a required presence at properly ordered weddings or funerals, and they were an expected presence in front of temples. And *qigai* also contributed by providing street entertainment and by performing odd jobs.[39] In a society conceived of as a system of interlocking roles, the *qigai* were permanently assigned to the socially necessary but unenviable role of "the poor." Absent a Puritan ethic and a modern capitalist system in which the nonproductive are simply a liability to an efficient economy, people in imperial China did not make a distinction between "deserving" and "undeserving" poor.

We can perhaps call this traditional model of begging the "Li Tieguai" model, after one of the Eight Immortals who is depicted as a beggar and is often considered the "patron saint" of beggars.[40] Li Tieguai is not depicted in Chinese legend as a pitiable, unfortunate person. He is rather an unconventional person who achieves Daoist ideals of carefree freedom by living as a *qigai*. Being a *qigai* in premodern China seems to have been a pretty miserable way to live. But the *qigai* did occupy a stable, if lowly, social niche that could be accepted with resignation as part of fate and perhaps even enjoyed at times for its freedom from convention. There were just enough redeeming features in the *qigai*'s life that knight errant (*wuxia*) novels could romanticize it.[41] And even a modern movie such as Wu Tianming's *The King of Masks* (Bianlian wang) can offer a positive (though undoubtedly unrealistic) portrait of this lifestyle.[42]

As we have argued above, the Li Tieguai model lives today. Today's beggars develop many of the same performance skills as *qigai* of old, and they work within organized groups similar to premodern gangs. At least one of the beggars interviewed by Yu Xiu saw himself as a free spirited romantic—a modern-day Li Tieguai—until he confronted the harsh discipline of his beggar gang. The structure of beggar group life today, with its semiautonomous organization led by a boss whose power depends to at least some degree on having a working relationship with the police, is more like premodern gangs than the groups officially organized by the Maoist state.

However, modern beggars do not necessarily belong to hereditary status groups. Few of the beggars interviewed by Yu Xiu came from families of beggars, and most of them did not plan to have their children follow in this profession. In some cases, their families did not know that they had become beggars and they were concerned to keep their profession secret. And yet precisely because they did not belong to a hereditary caste of beggars, it was important for them to think of their status as a result of their own free choice. This is perhaps a testimony to increased opportunities for mobility in reform era China. Viewed from this point of view, the growing presence of professional beggars does not result from the cruelties of capitalism but from the freedom that an emergent market economy creates for people to move around the country and to pursue a variety of occupations, even traditional occupations.

However, the modern market economy imparts a new harshness to this traditional profession. Beggars today are less like *qigai* in late imperial China and more like the early modern beggars of the first half of the twentieth century: more like early twentieth-century writer Lu Xun's character Ah Q than Li Tieguai.

As the Qing state collapsed, the systems through which the government protected and controlled *qigai* associations also collapsed. In reform-minded governments after the 1911 revolution, *qigai* became illegal, both because they were an embarrassment to governments that wanted to portray themselves as modern and because they threatened disorder in newly industrializing cities. At the same time, of course, the new governments lacked the capacity to police beggars and to give them an alternative way of life. Needing new sources of protection from rival gangs, from the general populace, and now from the government, beggars often had to rely on the criminal underworld of secret societies to give them protection and to mediate between their associations and the state. In return they helped the secret societies with menial tasks—retail drug peddling, debt collecting, and intelligence gathering. In the Shanghai red light district, for example, beggars helped protect the prostitutes from unruly customers and would threaten a commotion if customers tried to leave without paying their bills.[43]

At the same time, the general demoralization of society helped foment predatory relationships among beggars themselves and between beggars and the general population. Lu Xun's story of Ah Q reflects these realities in the "man-eating society" of the early twentieth century. Ah Q is, after all, a beggar. He is cynically abused by the leaders and respectable members of his village. At the same time, he cynically abuses fellow beggars—and himself. (When he slaps his own face and pounds his head on the ground, he is imitating actual beggars of the time, who tried to make themselves look as pitiable as possible.) He flirts with criminal organizations and is used and then discarded by them. He is so tied in to the traditional identity of a *qigai* that it seems completely normal and inevitable, even though it has now become a malignancy within a terminally sick society.

In an early modern society, the quasi-familistic relations through which beggar gangs had been organized became more exploitative than before. In Confucian ethics, the family is supposed to be based on authority and clear-cut gender difference, but ideally authority is supposed to be exercised for the good of subordinates and of the family as a whole. However, those in authority have often exploited those under them. Authors like Lu Xun condemned modern Chinese society as a place in which parents exploited their children, husbands exploited their wives, and in general the strong exploited the weak. Such relationships were seen to a strong degree in beggar gangs. There are well-documented accounts from the early part of this century of parents crippling their children— cutting off an arm or a foot—to make them better able to attract alms.[44] Even in Taiwan during the 1970s, as reported by the anthropologist David Schak, beggars spoke of their women and children as "implements."[45] An able-bodied man could not expect to be given alms, so he would employ a woman or child (or preferably a woman with child) as an implement to attract sympathy. The able-bodied man would then get a share of the money they collected. In the beggar gang studied by Schak, in the late 1970s, a girl who reached adolescence and became too old to attract pity was often contracted out to a brothel.[46] In our data from mainland China, we do not have any hard evidence of beggar girls being sold into brothels. But there is evidence in the survey data of able-bodied male members of beggar gangs using women and children as implements. And there is the chilling statement we heard from informants in Guangdong's Dongguan county that many of the young girls who beg on the streets are actually controlled by "evil men" (*huairen* or *huaidan*).[47]

In 1990s China, the harshness produced by the anomie and competitiveness of the emerging market economy was exacerbated by the remnants of state socialism. The residence permit (*hukou*) system is still partially enforced in the cities. Beggars, along with other members of the floating population who travel there, are like illegal immigrants in the United States or Europe, ineligible for the health and welfare benefits of urban citizens and vulnerable to arbitrary deportation. As mentioned above, beggars are periodically swept out of the cities when the government wants to put a modern face forward. Calling on the paternalistic ideology of socialism, the government claims that returning beggars to their homes is for their own good; the state will provide them with jobs so they do not have to beg on the streets. But now the ideology consists only of empty words. The dynamics of China's unevenly developing market economy continue to make it economically rational—albeit dangerous and painful—for some people in the lower reaches of the society to choose the profession of begging.

Thus beggars continued to proliferate throughout the 1990s. During the 1980s, some farms, factories, and technical schools were created for beggars. These are more institutions of control than rehabilitation. According to A History of Beggars in China, "beggars do not have the habit of being controlled, so they often escape from these centers and prefer to continue begging."[48]

It would be logical under these circumstances for beggars to seek protection from the criminal underworld. A History of Beggars in China cites documents from the Public Security Bureau and official newspapers to show connections between beggar gangs and criminal organizations. "From the 1950s, all the beggar gangs were eliminated. Nevertheless, from both an economic and a cultural point of view, the conditions from which these organizations arose have not changed with the new political regime. This is why there are some organizations that have been used for criminal activities."[49]

Meanwhile, the premodern values evoked by professional beggars no longer resonate with the modern values of most urban Chinese. A secularized public seems less willing to see giving alms to beggars as a means of gaining merit for the afterlife. Caught up in the pressure of life in the market socialist economy, people have less and less sympathy for beggars. Beggars now have to live in a modern urban environment in which they are seen as embarrassing losers in a dynamic competitive world, not a lowly part of a traditional hierarchy.

Thus, according to A History of Beggars in China, beggars are a "malignant tumor" (duliu) on society.[50] The criminal tendencies of beggars are increasing, the author argues. In 1986, 30 percent of all administered criminal cases in Harbin involved beggars. Beggars do not create any kind of economy that can have even indirect benefits for the rest of the population. Finally, beggars are dangerous because they have neither education nor possessions and thus do not fear risk. If one day they are able to join together with a large number of people, they may become a fearsome threat. Both the highest levels of society and the peasants are afraid of such people: the former fear social disturbances caused by beggars, and the latter are worried about being exploited.[51]

In the way of thinking represented by A History of Beggars in China, the problem with beggars today is not that they are poor but that they do not want to become rich in socially approved ways. "When beggars are asked if they feel ashamed of exercising this type of profession, they answer the following: 'If I do not eat anything, why should I keep face? If you want to keep face, you have to suffer hunger and cold, so when one is in such a situation, why should one keep face?!' "[52] With no feeling of shame to make them want to rise up in the world, they live for the present and never think of saving for the future. With little to lose, they are a danger to society. "Before," says the author of *A History of Beggars in China*, "begging was associated with poverty. . . . Now it is linked to public pollution *(gonghai).*"[53]

Professional beggars threaten both aspects of the socialist market economy. Because they are self-organized (perhaps with some help and protection from the criminal underworld), they undermine the socialist system of social and political control. Because they reject the ethic of rationalized work, they contradict the moral basis of the market economy.

## CONCLUSION: BEGGARS AND CHINA'S FUTURE

The persistence of professional beggars in China today is a reminder that China is not a fully modern society. (As China does become more modern, however—especially if it follows the neoliberal models of development favored by the United States and increasingly by European countries—it will probably continue to have homeless beggars. But these would not be traditional, professional beggars of the kind we have described here. They would be part of a less organized underclass of the sort that has been proliferating in the United States and Europe, consisting of losers in competitive market economies who have fallen through the increasingly tattered safety nets of what the French call "savage capitalist" societies.) But professional beggars do not simply represent the persistence of the premodern. Their changing status indicates that tradition and modernity are constantly interacting in a dynamic historical process. Different kinds of beggars have appeared during different phases of China's modernization. In motivation, lifestyle, culture, and modes of social organization, beggars in the early twentieth century were different from those in the high Qing. Beggars during the Maoist era were different from those in the early twentieth century. The beggars in the transitional society of today seem to be a mix of the old "Li Tieguai" *qigai* and their early-twentieth-century "Ah Q" variant—and of the refugees from botched social policy of the Mao Zedong era. How will beggars develop in the future? One might speculate that insofar as China remains a largely rural society with a sharp gap between city and countryside and with rising levels of economic inequality, the beggar's profession will continue, despite government attempts to discourage it. Denied the basic protections accorded to urban citizens, beggars will continue to rely on their own corporate groups. But given the increasing hostility directed against them, they may need to seek more protection, as they did in 1930s Shanghai, through at least a loose affiliation with the criminal underworld.

As to the style of begging, in the future, it may be influenced by the general ethos of China's changing culture. Around traditional temples and in parts of older cities like Beijing, many beggars still use the traditional styles. They make themselves look as pitiable as possible and abjectly kowtow in front of passersby, inspiring them to give a small donation in return for karmic merit. In Shenzhen, on the other hand, another style is prevalent: aggressive, intimidating, entrepreneurial. As the whole Chinese market economy becomes as intensely competitive as Shenzhen, the behavior of beggars may follow suit.

Even if China develops a more adequate social safety net, beggars will probably be part of its landscape for some time to come. In *A Chinese Beggar's Den*, David Schak documents traditionally organized beggar groups in 1970s Taibei. When Taiwan's economy took off in the 1980s, the beggar gang that Schak had studied began to decline. Until that point, the beggars' children had been socialized to carry on their parents' way of life. Because they were stigmatized by their occupation, they could not easily enter a mainstream occupation or marry into an ordinary family. By the 1980s, Taiwan's economy had developed to the point where there were fairly well-paying job opportunities for beggar children, and more and more beggar offspring were taking advantage of them, happy to avoid the stigma that had afflicted their parents.[54] It will take time for the mainland to achieve such comprehensive economic development. In the meantime, people from the inland areas will continue to be attracted by the beggar's life, and they will migrate to the coastal cities, where there will be more money trickling down than in the interior.

An understanding and evaluation of China's contradictory path toward modernization will—as Wei Jingsheng said—still need to be done from the perspective of those at the lowest strata of society. Perhaps we will need a new Lu Xun to write about a new sort of Ah Q in the early twenty-first century.

## NOTES

1. Wei Jingsheng, *The Courage to Stand Alone* (New York: Viking Penguin, 1997), 233–36.

2. Qu Yanbing, *Zhongguo qigai shi* (A history of beggars in China) (Shanghai: Shanghai wenyi chubanshe, 1993), 214.

3. Mao Zedong, "The Chinese Revolution and the Chinese Communist Party" [December 1939], in *Selected Works of Mao Tse-tung* (Beijing: Foreign Languages Press, 1967), 2:325–26.

4. Qu Yanbing, *Zhongguo qigai shi*, 95.

5. Zhai Yugui, "Qigai xianxiang mudu ji," *Zhonghua yuebao* 7 (1974): 75–82, 87–92.

6. Stanley Rosen, personal communication.

7. "Horizon Market-Research Company," whose original name in Chinese is Lingdian shichang diaocha gongsi, is a private company dedicated to market research, policy analysis, and public opinion polls. Its headquarters is located in Beijing, and there are two branches in Guangzhou and Shanghai. The company provided us with the raw data of a

survey carried out in Beijing in 1994, with a sample of 227 migrant beggars, using a questionnaire of thirty-six different questions. This type of research is original and particularly difficult, since the level of suspicion among beggars is fairly high and they rarely want to give information. It is quite old now, however, and we cannot entirely rely on these data, having encountered several shortcomings and mistaken inputs in our SPSS analysis. As a general description, we can confirm that almost 13 percent of the beggars were from Henan, 8 percent from Hebei, 7.5 percent from Shandong, 6.6 percent from Anhui, 2.6 percent from Beijing (presumably from the rural outskirts), 2.2 percent from Sichuan and Subei (northern Jiangsu), and the rest (almost 58 percent) from various areas of China. None of them were from Zhejiang. Most of the information gathered here also comes from Lingdian shichang diaocha gongsi, "Luoren," in *Guancha Zhongguo* (Beijing: Gongshang chubanshe, 1997), 165–261.

    8. Lingdian, "Luoren," 171.

    9. Lingdian, "Luoren," 171.

    10. Richard Madsen, personal communication.

    11. Lingdian, "Luoren," 172.

    12. Lingdian, "Luoren," 171.

    13. Lingdian, "Luoren," 171.

    14. Lingdian, "Luoren," 171.

    15. Lingdian, "Luoren," 172.

    16. Yu Xiu, *Zhongguo qigai diaocha* (Beijing: Zhonghua gongshang lianhe chubanshe, 1999).

    17. Yu Xiu, *Zhongguo qigai*, 58–71.

    18. Yu Xiu, *Zhongguo qigai*, 1–19.

    19. Yu Xiu, *Zhongguo qigai*, 27–44.

    20. Yu Xiu, *Zhongguo qigai*, 44.

    21. Jean-Philippe Béja, Michel Bonnin, Feng Xiaoshuang, and Tang Can, "How Social Strata Come to Be Formed: Social Differentiation among the Migrant Peasants of Henan Village in Peking," *China Perspectives* (Hong Kong), May 1999, 29–41; June 1999, 44–54.

    22. In newspapers collected by Leila Fernández-Stembridge in Dongguan county, Guangdong, in 1998.

    23. State Council notice concerning "trial method of detaining and repatriating the vagrant beggars in the cities" and Civil Administration, Public Security Ministry notice concerning the printing and distribution of "the implementation of detailed (trial) rules covering the methods of detention and repatriation of the vagrant beggars of the city," translated and quoted in Michael Dutton, *Streetlife China* (New York: Cambridge University Press, 1998), 120–23.

    24. Qu Yanbing, *Zhongguo qigai shi*, 6.

    25. Ren Jian and Lei Fang, *Zhongguo gaibang* (Nanjing: Jiangsu guji chubanshe, 1993), 1–5.

    26. Qu Yanbing, *Zhongguo qigai shi*, 11.

    27. David C. Schak, *A Chinese Beggars' Den: Poverty and Mobility in an Underclass Community* (Pittsburgh: University of Pittsburgh Press, 1988), 49–55, 91–92. Chapters 2–3 offer a thorough summary of all the Chinese and English literature on beggars in China. The two Chinese books we have been using here, *Zhongguo qigaishi* and *Zhongguo gaibang*, add some details but otherwise confirm the basic picture portrayed by Schak.

28. Ren Jian and Lei Fang, *Zhongguo gaibang*, 101–19.

29. Schak, *A Chinese Beggars' Den*, 37. See also Qu Yanbing, *Zhongguo qigai shi*, 228–30.

30. Ren Jian and Lei Fang, *Zhongguo gaibang*, 1–5.

31. Ren Jian and Lei Fang, *Zhongguo gaibang*, 4. See also Qu Yanbing, *Zhongguo qigai shi*, 74–110.

32. Qu Yanbing, *Zhongguo qigai shi*, 81. For more on beggar jargon, see also Ren Jian and Lei Fang, *Zhongguo gaibang*, 26–29; and Hanchao Lu, "Becoming Urban: Mendicancy and Vagrants in Modern Shanghai," *Journal of Social History*, Fall 1999, 7–36.

33. Ren Jian and Lei Fang, *Zhongguo gaibang*, 19–26; 209–14.

34. On the role of imperial compassion in the legitimization of the Chinese state, see Vivienne Shue, "Notes on Charity, Authority, and Legitimation" (paper presented at the University of California–Berkeley Center for Chinese Studies Workshop, May 7–9, 1999).

35. Qu Yanbing, *Zhongguo qigai shi*, 236.

36. This paragraph relies heavily on Schak, *Chinese Beggars' Den*, 20–25 and passim.

37. Steven Mufson, "Downsizing the Hero Worker," *Washington Post Foreign Service*, 18 September 1997, A23.

38. Fieldwork in Dongguan, Guangdong, July 1998.

39. Schak, *Chinese Beggars' Den*, 36–39, 49–55.

40. Schak, *Chinese Beggars' Den*, 24.

41. Ren Jian and Lei Fang, *Zhongguo gaibang*, 1–5.

42. *Bianlian wang* (The king of masks), dir. Wu Tianming (Xi'an: Xi'an Film Studios, 1996). Actors: Chu Yuk, Chao Yim-Yin, Zhang Riuyang, Zhao Zhigang.

43. Ren Jian and Lei Fang, *Zhongguo gaibang*, 215.

44. James W. Bennett, "China's Perennially Unemployed," *Asia*, 1931, 215–19, 268–69. Cited in Schak, *Chinese Beggars' Den*, 47. See also Ren Jian and Lei Fang, who refer to the practice in the late Qing of *caisheng shege* (to enslave a living person by cutting so as to damage), in which people would be kidnapped and crippled by beggar gangs so that they could be used as begging implements.

45. Schak, *Chinese Beggars' Den*, 47. The term in Taiwanese was *khit-ciaq e ke-si*, which means literally "begging implement." Although this, says Schak, was "a term that unfortunately connotes a mercenary and exploitative relationship . . . it was not necessarily that way, nor was it so regarded by the . . . beggars or others in the community." It seems to us that Schak has a little too sanguine view of relationships among his beggar informants. Relationships were not totally exploitative, but there was a strong mix of exploitation together with a sense of obligation arising from kinship and good "human feeling."

46. Schak, *Chinese Beggars' Den*, 47, 96–97, 166–69.

47. Fieldwork in Dongguan, Guangdong, July 1998.

48. Qu Yanbing, *Zhongguo qigai shi*, 238; 240–41.

49. Qu Yanbing, *Zhongguo qigai shi*, 97.

50. Qu Yanbing, *Zhongguo qigai shi*, 1.

51. Qu Yanbing, *Zhongguo qigai shi*, 214.

52. The interviewee literally said the following: "Mei you duzibao, hai gude shenme lianmian; yao lianmian jiude ai shoudong, rendao zhizhong dibu hai yao lian gan shenme!" See Qu Yanbing, *Zhongguo qigai shi*, 16.

53. Qu Yanbing, *Zhongguo qigai shi*, 18.

54. Schak, *Chinese Beggars' Den*, 203–6.

# 10

# When a House Becomes His Home

*Deborah S. Davis*

> In this connection it must be noted that the weight of private property
> rights as a factor in (determining) the status of women . . . is being drasti-
> cally reduced by the socialization of the Chinese economy. . . . By the end
> of 1958 . . . the people's communes replaced the agricultural producers coop-
> eratives as the national form of rural production. The individual or the fam-
> ily no longer owns land, business enterprise, or any other significant means
> of production, and private property is reduced mainly to personal articles
> with private ownership of houses in serious doubt.
>
> It is obvious that as private property ceases to be a major factor in status
> stratification, redistribution of property rights can serve only in a limited
> way in the alteration of the status of family members. It is the equalizing
> right to work outside the family, not property rights, that will serve that
> function."
>
> —C. K. Yang, *The Chinese Family in the Communist Revolution*

In December 1978, twenty years after Mao's Great Leap Forward, Deng Xiaoping
took the first steps to dismantle the people's communes and recommodify property relations throughout China. In the first decade of reform, privatization of
urban real estate was not a major objective, and even after twenty years of market
reform, only a third of urban homes were owner occupied.[1] Nevertheless, the
nationwide experiments to sell existing housing stock to sitting tenants begun
in the mid-1980s and the subsequent expansion of a private housing industry
after 1992 to stimulate the economy and attract foreign investment had a profound impact on contemporary urban society.[2]

Under Mao, private ownership had been stigmatized as antisocialist. In the
final years of Deng's leadership, the central government would look to private
real estate development as an engine of economic growth, and among the general population home ownership would come to signify social and financial suc-

cess.[3] In this environment, whether or not a family purchased its home, the new legitimacy of individual property rights granted all urban residents permission to dream of home ownership and to view their homes as a private space in which they could display family and individual prestige.

Previously, when historians of Western societies analyzed the role of the home during eras of rapid commercialization, they observed a marked feminization of domestic space as urban men ceded the home to wives and concentrated their own energies on the expanded opportunities for sociability in the public sphere of clubs and politics. Auslander even argues that as France built the republic in the second half of the nineteenth century there was an explicit dichotomy: "bourgeois men were (encouraged) to represent the family through the vote, and women to represent the family in their bodies and their homes."[4] In the United States Veblen also saw the home as the quintessential location in which wives "reworked" the economic success of their husbands into a heightened social prestige for all family members. Randall Collins described a similar feminization of domestic property among upper-middle-class American men after World War II.[5]

Yet it is not obvious that domestic space must be primarily the domain of women. In fact, the feminization observed in Europe and the United States is more likely the exception than the rule. Throughout the world, wives' claims to property are generally weaker than those of husbands. Also notable is the larger political environment in which citizens or subjects nurture unofficial sociability and associational life. In societies with longer traditions of democratic governments there is less control and censorship over public sociability and therefore less need for men to use the privacy of the home to socialize or nurture nonofficial social ties. By contrast in societies where leaders routinely censored public sociability, the home became a primary site for unofficial male associational life, and females were often restricted to certain locations within their own homes and denied control over the use or disposal of domestic property.[6]

In the case of imperial and even republican China, wives were identified as *neiren* (the person within) and to those unfamiliar with the history of China this designation may suggest that the Chinese home was traditionally a female domain while space outside the home was the domain of men. But as anyone familiar with Chinese history can attest, the *nei-wai* distinction rather than validating female claims over domestic property or space indicated the subordinate and excluded position of married women. Thus, for example, when Susan Mann wrote about the Jiangnan elite in "China's long eighteenth century" she not only rejected the equation of *nei* as female space and *wai* as male space but concluded that the women's chambers (*guige*) were actually "willed by men to be a refuge for men."[7]

My own earlier work on interior space and urban family life in Shanghai during the 1980s, however, found a clear departure from pre-Communist patterns as described by Mann for Ming-Qing China or by C. K. Yang for the republican era. When I interviewed one hundred women living in one residential estate north of Suzhou creek in 1987, I saw households in which wives' control over domestic space was equal to, or *even* greater than that of their husbands or coresident married sons.[8] Because the neighborhood in which I carried out interviews had been constructed with a uniform architecture, all flats had two rooms; because my sample required that each household have at least one women born between 1925 and 1935, the families were all at the stage in which adult children were launching careers and marrying. Among the interviewees the most typical household was a patrilocal home with a middle-aged couple, one married son, his wife, and one grandchild.[9] Typically the husband's employer had arranged the rental and the apartment was registered in the man's name. However, because the collectivization of urban real estate had transformed housing into a welfare benefit, husbands legally had had no greater claims of ownership than did their wives, and the sons' inheritance rights to the parental home were as weak as the daughters'. Although predominantly patrilocal in structure, tenancy claims did not privilege men for these families. Rather, the situation followed C. K. Yang, who "noted that the weight of private property rights as a factor in [determining] the status of women . . . [has been] drastically reduced by the socialization of the Chinese economy."[10]

When I looked closely at the way in which interior space had been decorated and asked respondents about daily routines, I discovered a gender "tilt" in accord with the Western European experience of feminization of domestic space. Because each room had multiple functions—bedroom, living room, dining room, study, and workspace—the apartments were crowded with things and furnished in the most utilitarian fashion. The possessions of women in their roles as housekeepers and mothers—sewing baskets, candy dishes, utensils for cleaning and cooking—filled the cabinets and covered the tables. Typically decorations were limited to a wall clock, a calendar, and family photos displayed under a glass tabletop. Awards from the workplace, souvenirs of business trips, chess sets, or artifacts of the masculine "scholars studio" such as calligraphy brushes, ink stones, or ceramic bowls, were generally invisible. Thus I hypothesized that collectivization of domestic property and transformation of housing into a welfare benefit had feminized or more specifically "maternalized" control over urban domestic space. Chinese urban homes of the 1980s were best described as "my mother's house" rather than "my father's house."[11] Or to use the vocabulary of Csikszentmihalyi and Rochberg-Halton, Shanghai men had apparently "cooled out their relationship to the home."[12]

Young and middle-aged Shanghainese whom I met that summer also seemed to emphasize the female character of city residences and routinely referred to their parents' homes, whether their fathers were alive or not, as their "mother's house" *(wo muqin de jia)*. Subsequently male friends from Shanghai have told me that they would probably refer to their natal home as *wo laojia*, and colleagues from northern China have reported that they never used nor heard other men use *wo muqin de jia*, suggesting that female-centered domestic space may be restricted to southern China or even to the city of Shanghai.[13]

Historian Hanchao Lu has also questioned my interpretation, but in a different way. Instead of denying that men might also call their parents' home their mother's house, Lu notes that because in pre-Communist years women used mother's house (*niangjia*) and not father's house to describe their natal home, it is not obvious that the use of *wo muqin de jia* is anything more than a modern translation of a traditional phrase. Therefore what is most intriguing to Lu about my respondents' language in 1987 is not a break from the past but a revealing continuity.[14] Next I discuss change and continuity, using materials gathered in the late 1990s to explore the possibility that reprivatization of home ownership has favored male over female claims to domestic space and property.

## MARKETING THE DREAM OF HOME OWNERSHIP

On June 4, 1999, a twenty-foot-high balloon soared above the reflecting pool of the Shanghai Exhibition Center to announce the opening of the seventh Shanghai Real Estate Exhibition. Inside, 189 development companies had rented space to showcase their commercial offerings. According to the evening newspaper of that day the apartments featured at the exhibition represented 60 percent of all available properties in greater Shanghai,[15] and indeed vendors featured a wide selection of apartments and villas in all districts of the city and surrounding counties.

In 1995 I had attended an auto show in the same venue. Admission was by ticket only, and the gleaming Porsches, Mercedes, and BMWs were priced beyond individual means. My colleague's husband, who was the vice president of a profitable instrument factory, was in the market for a secondhand motorcycle. After we left the exhibit, we posed in front of the reflecting pool to commemorate our outing and then pushed our way back to the street, where scalpers hawked tickets and the crowd spilling into the street blocked traffic.

In 1999 anyone could enter the exhibition hall and the sponsors were actually promoting a lottery to boost attendance. Inside the main entrance, employees of two local banks distributed application materials for individual loans for home purchase, home renovation, or real estate investment. I arrived at 10 A.M., one hour after the doors had opened, and already the long corridors were packed. That summer there was a glut of unsold space. Developers therefore courted customers and the socialist economy of shortage in which would-be tenants were "supplicants of the state" seemed a distant memory.[16] Of course it was impossible to gauge the actual intentions or financial resources of the milling crowds. Were they simply gawking at inaccessible luxury as we previously had gazed at the sports cars? Or were they serious buyers? Certainly the brochures from the banks documented practical steps for securing ownership. Equally incontrovertible was the professionalism of the exhibitors. They may have been marketing a dream, but they aggressively touted their good prices and methodically pushed the visitor-voyeurs to sign up for an afternoon van tour.

When historian David Fraser compared Shanghai housing advertisements in 1994 to those in 1997, he found that developers had increasingly sought customers through promises of exclusive lifestyle rather than simply the prospect of ownership. In Fraser's words the ideal of the home as a private "oasis (had) moved into the foreground."[17] In 1999 the advertisers continued to market luxury and exclusivity, but property values and affordability shared the foreground.

In their brochures and videos the developers advertising at the June 4 exhibition addressed an ungendered but upwardly mobile customer.[18] On the Friday morning when I visited, males slightly outnumbered females, but in the illustrated material from the Bank of Industry and Commerce the prototypical customer was more often a woman than a man. Generally the video clips of newly completed interiors excluded any resident and illustrations of the exteriors featured anonymous pedestrians of both sexes. To the extent that they had a targeted buyer, marketers wanted men and women of all ages to imagine themselves as potential owners.

Promotional materials from two of the most expensive complexes, however, did have explicitly gendered messages. In the brochure for Joffre Gardens (Dongfang Bali) under construction in the heart of the old French Settlement, the featured customer was a glamorous man in his thirties who carried a small boy on his shoulders as he strolled through a field of flowers. The large caption described him as "the New Age man who loves his family and home" (*xinshidai aijia de nanren*), and then in the smaller type the prospective customer reads that this "New Age man" was "the good father who is the first to send his child off to school, the good leader who is the first to arrive in the office, and the good husband who is the first to return home" (*diyige songhaizi de hao baba, diyige dao gongsi de hao lingdao, diyige huijia de haozhangfu*). None of the other flyers for upscale developments included a comparable profile of an ideal female customer. However, Kathleen Erwin, who has analyzed the speech in Shanghai radio shows,[19] has asked me whether the target here is an affluent woman for whom the New Age man is the ideal husband or a financially successful man eager to identify himself as the good leader.[20] In one housing advertisement that Fraser found, would-be buyers are enticed to "buy a home and become a boss!"[21] I would suggest that the agents for Joffre Gardens want to entice both men and women to buy a flat through identification with success. Not incidentally the graphic image of the success of the late 1990s is a handsome young businessman.

Advertisements for Hua'an apartments in the fashionable Jingan district in the old International Settlement made the most explicit pitch to a male buyer, designating a male as the targeted customer and the home as the female object. In this advertisement (which proclaimed in English "I love Jingan") there were no male persons, but the Chinese text explicitly described the housing complex as the beloved female whom the buyer loves for her incomparable taste. The word used for taste, *weidao*, connotes something tasty to eat; the word *pinwei* would denote refinement.²² Not surprisingly, none of these promotional brochures presented a home as the male object of female desire.

Overall, however, the exhibitors relied on a conjugal vocabulary that spoke simultaneously to husbands and wives. The message in the materials from the Shanghai branch of the Bank of Industry and Commerce was explicit. Above the bank's logo was a photo of a heavy golden door swinging open to a vista of three modern apartment towers. Printed over the photo was a list of eight types of personal loans, and below the photo the title: "A Compass to Mortgage Loans for Individual Purchase of a Home *[geren goufang anjie daikuan]*." On the left of the photo, the English phrase "Our Home" ran the entire length of the pamphlet. Here the bank represented the residential property of the 1990s as not only privatized and commodified but overtly centered around a couple strategizing to create a home of their own.

## A CONJUGAL HOME: RESULTS FROM A SURVEY

A conjugal profile also emerged during home interviews conducted in Shanghai in December 1998 as part of a project I designed with Yanjie Bian and Shaoguang Wang on urban consumption patterns. As part of this project our team interviewed one hundred Shanghai couples about their current household situation and their plans for the near future.²³ Although each member of the couple was interviewed separately, husbands and wives rarely disagreed about issues related to their home. For example, when asked about the necessity of homeownership, in only five cases did one spouse say home ownership was essential while the other said it was not.²⁴ They gave almost identical answers when asked about the value of the home, its size, and the amount they had spent refurbishing. These high levels of agreement about the need for home ownership and the financial details of their current home confirmed the general impression that homes of the 1990s were a shared marital property. Equally noteworthy, when asked to identify the names of all family members listed on a rental agreement, mortgage, or deed, less than 10 percent of couples listed a parent or an in-law as a coowner or householder.²⁵ In terms of property claims, these were homes of married men and women, not coresident sons or daughters or members of an extended family.

However, joint ownership or tenancy was exceptional and men were by far the most likely to be the sole name on the deed or rental agreement.²⁶ But would it be accurate to conclude that "my mother's house" (*wo muqin de jia*) of the 1980s had become "my husband's home" (*wo zhangfu de jia*)? During the interviews and casual conversations, I never heard this phrase. Rather like the design of the bank brochure, the more commonly used phrases were "our home" (*women de jia*) and "my home" (*wo de jia*). Nevertheless, discussions about home renovation among our December 1998 survey respondents suggested a tendency for the house to become *his* home when real estate property became the focus of major investment.

## FURNISHING AND RENOVATING THE CONJUGAL HOME

During the first decade of economic reform, urban families enthusiastically spent their savings on their first color television, first refrigerator, and first washing machine.[27] Some families repainted walls, installed tile flooring, or bought a new suite of bedroom furniture, but the main improvements were consumer durables that eased the drudgery of housework and retained their financial value. During my 1987 visits I noticed that prereform attitudes about appropriate display (as much as concerns about economizing) curbed expenditures and kept decorative improvements modest. Many people seemed to worry that neighbors would be critical—even hostile—if they discovered a family other than a recently married couple spending lavishly to make their home more comfortable than other homes in their community. Wallpaper or curtains were exceptional, and wooden floors so extravagant—perhaps even decadent—that I remember one respondent who went out of her way to hide the wooden blocks her son was using to lay a parquet floor to keep them from her neighbor's view. Over coffee one night with a university teacher who had just recently returned as a legal tenant to her family's house, the three guests marveled at the small English creamer, the only remaining piece of what had been a complete set of china at her marriage in 1956.

By the late 1990s, however, there had been a paradigm shift. Men and women of all ages felt free to use their homes to display economic success or cultural refinement. Large-circulation decorating magazines urged readers to leave behind the older simple styles and strive to furnish their homes in richer cultural taste (*gongfuyou wenhua pinwei*),[28] Even the educational channel controlled by the municipal government sponsored an evening show on home renovation. The male decorator who hosted the show prefaced his first demonstration by noting "that as soon as one enters an apartment, you know immediately whether the residents have taste (*you pinwei*)."[29]

Throughout the city, neighborhood shops sold the supplies needed to install parquet floors, recessed lighting, and upscale bathroom fixtures. Bookstores devoted entire sections to home improvement publications. New Web sites and television programs instructed viewers how to decorate their new home or renovate the old.[30] In 1987 household furnishings had been minimal and utilitarian; by the late 1990s merchandise was plentiful and styles were often indistinguishable from those found in North American or European magazines. Ikea was a popular destination of both young and middle-aged Shanghai residents and Toto,

American Standard, and Simmons advertised heavily on billboards throughout the city.

The impact of the new global styles is evident in the decorator magazines sold in state-run bookstores, small kiosks, and even the newly opened Shanghai library.[31] In these magazines the home is a happy nest, a warm and cozy place, in which residents *(zhuren)* display *(tixian)* their cultivation *(xiuyang)*, personality *(xingge)*, and economic power *(jingji shili)*.[32] Like the developers' brochures, the interior decorating magazines addressed a gender-neutral *zhuren* or *fangzhu*; the illustrations, like the real estate videos, omitted residents of either sex. In the bookstores I observed as many men as women reading the decorating magazines, and the targets of promotional materials seemed androgynous.

In December 1998 my colleagues and I asked the Shanghai couples in our consumer study who had renovated their apartment to identify the individuals who had participated in the process. We found that more husbands than wives had been active in finalizing plans, buying materials, supervising labor, and managing the finances (see table 10.1). Only in choosing furniture and interior decoration were wives as likely to be involved as husbands.

When I designed a 1997 pilot study about home renovation in Shanghai and Shenzhen, I also found that husbands were as deeply involved in renovating their homes as their wives and in many cases claimed to have taken the lead. When we observed customers in furniture stores that summer, men outnumbered women in the areas displaying couches, desks, and dining room tables. And when we took simple inventories of wall decorations in the living rooms, the husband's possessions and signs of distinction were more numerous than those of the wife. It appeared that the higher the income and the greater the authority of the husband in the workplace, the more clearly had the house become his home.[33] Subsequent interviews with working-class and professional men in 1998 and 1999 revealed that men wanted to claim a space distinct from the bedroom in which

**Table 10.1   Participation in Decisions about Home Renovation**

|  | Husbands (%) | Wives (%) |
|---|---|---|
| 1. Raised issue of renovation | 79 | 70 |
| 2. Discussed initial renovation plan | 79 | 71 |
| 3. Decided final renovation plan | 76 | 63[a] |
| 4. Bought materials | 72 | 41[c] |
| 5. Hired workers | 79 | 26[c] |
| 6. Supervised workers | 54 | 29[c] |
| 7. Chose furniture and decorations | 83 | 80 |
| 8. Managed renovation budget | 74 | 57[b] |
| 9. Personally did some renovation work | 26 | 19 |

*Source:* Consumer Project, December 1998.
[a]*p* ≤ .01; [b] *p* ≤ 0.05; [c]*p* ≤ 0.001

they could entertain friends or enjoy their hobbies. The following home interviews illustrate this pattern. They also document the remarkable improvement
in the quality of residential conditions since the Mao years as well as the impact
of home ownership on investments in a family home.

### Teacher Chen's Mao Button Collection

When we visited him in June 1999, Teacher Chen entertained my research
team enthusiastically in his bedroom/sitting room. He was a generous host and
served coffee accompanied by a rich array of cookies and chocolates purchased
to celebrate his daughter's recent wedding. The room of twelve square meters
was stuffed with furniture and memorabilia. A large double bed occupied one-
third of the floor while two chairs and a small table created a sitting space in
front of the veranda that faced the street. In one corner, as remote from the
kitchen as physically possible, stood a small refrigerator, on top of which were
displayed several dolls and an inflated plastic replica of a roll of Charms lifesav-
ers. All the remaining wall space was filled with bookshelves, cabinets, and tables
piled high with suitcases and boxes.

In many ways the room reminded me of the "mothers' homes" I had visited
in 1987. One entered the five-story, unpainted cement block apartment building
from a dark, dirty stairwell. Each apartment opened onto a narrow corridor,
jammed with old wicker baskets, rusted bikes, and wet mops. Inside the apartment the walls were green, the floors scuffed, and the furniture a mixture of a
few simple wooden stools, screened kitchen cupboards, and assorted pieces of a
bedroom suite. Over Teacher Chen's bed, there was a colorized, formal photo of
a couple standing shoulder to shoulder in their 1961 wedding suits. Beneath the
photo was a calendar with a red racing car and on the back of the door another
calendar with a traditional Chinese landscape painting.

But in many other ways the apartment was not at all like those "mothers'
houses" I had visited in 1987. First, the Chens were homeowners, not renters.
In 1995 they had purchased the home through the wife's unit for ¥9,000, and
Teacher Chen now holds the title—in his name alone—to a valuable property
in central Shanghai worth more than ¥200,000. Even before they bought the
flat, they had invested ¥5,000 to redecorate and he proclaims he would never
move, no matter how much money he was offered. He told us later that he and
his wife had offered the home to their daughter and her new husband and
planned to move to a larger flat that they had bought for ¥65,000 in eastern
Pudong with help from his old unit. But the son-in-law preferred to move into
an apartment that his mother had arranged in Hong Qiao district.

The commercialization and affluence of the 1990s distinguished this apartment also through the furnishings and decoration. Above the head of the Chens'
bed and on the opposite wall were two framed color photographs of their daughter posing as if for a fashion magazine. The English words "Happy to you" had

been embossed across a diaphanous yellow scarf she held under her chin. Across from the foot of the bed was a large-screen color television, a VCR, and a Karaoke microphone.

Finally, the apartment reflected the ways in which Teacher Chen wanted to relax and entertain his guests. The shelves displayed many different wine bottles to which he drew attention when he discussed how much he enjoyed socializing. When I asked what room he would add if he could have another room, he answered promptly, "I would add a big living room. We can sleep in any old small room, but if we had a big living room I would read, watch TV, and sing karaoke there. I like to drink wine and would like to invite guests here to have a good time."

And then Teacher Chen stood up from the folding chair on which he had been sitting opposite me and started to pull out twenty battered boxes from the drawers of a cabinet under his TV. For the next forty minutes we listened as he told with relish and pride how he had acquired his nearly 7,000 Mao buttons. The display was dazzling. He had them organized by size and then by material. In each box there were five or six layers of treasures, each pin carefully sewn onto a cloth or paper sheet. In one box there were only plastic circles of less than an inch in diameter, in another only ceramic ovals with the Great Helmsman gazing into the mountains or over the sea. He said that he had been offered hundreds of yuan for certain pins but had never sold one. He continues to build his collection, visiting markets to look for rare finds and occasionally trading with other collectors.

In 1987 he had already begun the button collection, and perhaps if I had asked then about his leisure time or hobbies he would have treated me to the same lavish display and hospitality. But in the homes I visited in 1987, husbands usually expressed no interest in joining the interview, and no one—male or female—offered to show me treasures that they had hidden away.

### Auntie Li's Dropped Ceiling

I first met Auntie Li in 1990 when she was a neighborhood cadre. We worked together on a daily basis for six weeks during one of Shanghai's severe heat waves, and I was forever grateful that I had been assigned a colleague of such unflagging goodwill. When I returned in 1995 to do a third follow-up study, she officially became part of the neighborhood sample and I began to learn more about her family history. In 1997 I missed a chance to visit because she was traveling, but in June 1999 I was able to spend a Saturday afternoon chatting with her husband, son, daughter-in-law, and grandson.

The recommodification of real estate and the keen interest in renovation had left an imprint on their home. Like Teacher Chen and perhaps the majority of Shanghainese now in their early sixties, Auntie Li had been born in the countryside. In 1947, when she was nine years old, she came to Shanghai for primary school. After her father became disabled, she took his place as a shift worker in a large textile mill. When I asked her to tell me about her earliest homes in the village and then in Shanghai, she uncharacteristically said she could remember nothing: "We, my mom and the three kids, just slept in a series of little rooms. My dad worked shifts; he only came home a few times each month."

In 1956, when she became a full-time worker, she too moved into a dorm at the mill. Four years later she married a man she met through an introduction by her sister's friend. When I asked about the size and neighborhood of her home after marriage, she refused to give details, saying that at first they had a small room of their own. In 1962, after the birth of her daughter, her mother-in-law came from the countryside. Between 1962 and 1970 they moved from one small room to another. I asked if it were not inconvenient to keep moving all the furniture and possessions. She replied, "What furniture? We had very little, we had my mother-in-law, two kids, and no money. So we really had nothing to move."

In 1970, as part of Mao's policy to build a third industrial front in remote areas, Auntie Li was transferred to work in a mountainous area of Fujian province. Her family stayed behind, and for the next fourteen years she only saw them once a year until she took retirement at age forty-six. In 1987, after her daughter married, she moved to their current apartment on the top floor of a six-story walk-up with her husband and son. The interior space is divided into two bed-sitting-rooms, a kitchen alcove, a toilet room, and a small balcony. Since 1989, when their son married, he and his wife have taken over the smaller bedroom as their own while Auntie Li and her husband claimed the larger room with its veranda as their bedroom/sitting room and the family living and dining room.

The impact of the economic changes of the 1990s on the home interior and the family's claims on the space is apparent. In 1994 they bought the apartment from the husband's steel factory for under ¥10,000, and today it is worth ten times as much. Like Teacher Chen, they do not expect to sell or move. They are happy with the location, and neither they nor their son and his wife have the resources to buy anything better. When I discussed her apartment in 1995, Auntie Li was singularly unenthusiastic and complained about the leaking roof and the drafty windows, saying to refurnish was really a waste of money. But four years later her husband had solved these problems by installing a dropped ceiling that allowed them to replace any section stained by mildew or rust. And on the dreary rainy day I visited, it was surprisingly bright and airy.

They had modified the entry and reconfigured the space outside the bedroom/sitting room. Just inside the front door they had laid a checkerboard of black and white tiles that echoed the squares of their bed-sitting-room and defined a small dining area. They had enclosed the kitchen sink and gas burners so that the kitchen could be closed off from the rest of the apartment. However, they could not afford to create a separate living room. Their large wooden bed still took up a third of the floor space, and the rest of the room was crowded with the sofa, a large chiffonier without a mirror, and the old screened kitchen cabinet that they had brought from their first apartment. Yet they had made some efforts to refurbish. In front of the sofa, they placed a low table that her husband had built and painted to match the white ceiling panels and a new large-screen television stood opposite. On the veranda her husbands kept a large cage for his homing pigeons, but we saw nothing as large and visible that was exclusively the focus of Auntie Li's hobbies.

When asked what room she would add if they had the money to relocate, she answered immediately: a room *(fangzi)* of our own. Both her son and husband nodded in agreement: "Ideally we would like our own *fangzi* with our own toilet and kitchen, and then my son and his family could have this apartment for themselves. Right now they have moved back to live with my daughter-in-law's mother because officially the household registration *(hukou)* of my daughter-in-law and my grandson are still with her mother and that is where he can go to primary school without paying extra fees. So during the week they live there, and then on the weekend they come back and stay with us. But probably we will all stay here forever because to move costs a lot of money (which we don't have). My son and daughter-in-law do not have good jobs and there is talk of layoffs."

Auntie Li's daughter has always lived in one small room with her mother-in-law. Now in addition to her husband, her mother-in-law, and her son, there is also a young niece. But Auntie Li is actually more optimistic that her daughter, unlike her son or herself, will eventually have a conjugal home because the home they share with her son-in-law's mother has been scheduled for demolition and by law the city is required to rehouse each adult generation in separate apartments. If they can afford to purchase ownership, they will become homeowners. In any case, the government guarantees that they will be able to rent a self-contained apartment in a new building.

## STAKING A CLAIM: OWNERSHIP AND GENDER

In the early 1990s the central leadership resolved to accelerate privatization of urban real estate. At the 1991 March Work Conference, Li Peng pushed leaders to design local initiatives to popularize ownership, and the State Council announced that home ownership should become the norm among the nonmigrant urban population.[34] Over the next two years, municipal leaders throughout China took steps to further monetize—if not necessarily privatize—residency claims on new real estate by recalculating rents to reflect market demand and require large deposits among new renters. Shanghai, under the leadership of Zhu Rongji, led the way by establishing the first provident fund for individual home purchases in May 1991. Guangzhou followed in April 1992.[35] In February 1995 the State Council launched the *Anju Gongcheng* program to establish provident funds as the primary means to promote home ownership among low- and middle-income families.[36] Subsequent banking reforms enabled an increasing number of families to take out home mortgages, with particular gains in fall 1996 and spring 1997.[37]

At the end of 1994 30 percent of non-migrant households held some type of ownership claim. Three years later ownership rates reached 33 percent.[38] Surveys conducted between 1997 and 1999 suggested that the desire for home ownership remained strong even after the slowdown in economic growth.[39] Overall, housing reforms of the 1990s launched a sustained recommercialization of urban real estate and popularized the ideal of home ownership.

In our Shanghai interviews, an overwhelming majority of men and women responded that home ownership was now a necessity for families and ownership generally improved the quality of housing.[40] When we compared attitudes of homeowners with those who were still renting, we discovered some noticeable and statistically significant differences between husbands and wives. First, in response to a global question about rating their overall life satisfaction, homeowners of both sexes were more likely to say they were satisfied than renters, but only among men was the difference statistically significant.[41] Second, ownership increased the likelihood of respondents' reporting that they had private space (*siren kongjian*) in their home, but among husbands the gain by owners over renters was larger than among wives.[42] Third, ownership increased the likelihood of respondents' saying that their name appeared on the title to the house; again, gains of male owners were greater than those of females. Because men were far more likely to hold the title, whether the home was owned or rented, ownership appeared to have intensified male control over family property.[43]

Clearly there is an interaction with class. Ownership levels are highest among the best-educated managerial and professional ranks, and thus what we may be seeing is that high-status men are more likely than lower-status men to assert dominance in the home. Or it may be a question of space. Because wealthier men have larger homes, they are able to claim space for their own use. Tellingly, however, in these larger homes, wives were no more likely to claim space of their own than were wives in the smaller rented apartments. A final case study of a middle-aged couple who for years had relied on the wife's employer to solve their housing problems illustrates how home ownership may strengthen male claims over domestic property and private space.

### The Calligrapher Cadre

The Yangs and their fifteen-year-old daughter live in a two-bedroom flat of eighty-five square meters purchased in 1996 through his unit and now registered exclusively in his name. Although both Mr. and Mrs. Yang both said they were unsure (*bu haoshuo*) if home ownership was definitely necessary for all families, it has been extremely important to Mr. Yang.

Like most Shanghai couples who married in the early 1980s, they began their married life in the household of his parents. It was a single room in Yang Pu district, where he had grown up with his two siblings. After their daughter was born, they became a household of six adults and a baby. Shortly thereafter Mrs. Yang's employer arranged for them to rent a tiny room near the old railroad station on the grounds of hardship. Three years later, her unit again helped the family by finding a four-room apartment in Hong Qiao, where they moved with his parents and (then) unmarried brother. The next year the brother married, and by 1990 they were a joint household of eight. Again Mrs. Yang's unit tried to solve their housing problem by renting them a second apartment for the exclusive use of the Yangs and their daughter. However, the second room could only be accessed through the first room, which meant the daughter slept on a folding bed next to her father's calligraphy table.

Finally in 1996 the hotel where Mr. Yang worked as a manager arranged for them to buy a ¥300,000 apartment for ¥40,000. The house is simply furnished and almost all the furniture is new. The walls are white, and the floors all gleaming light woods. The only decorations on the walls are paintings and calligraphy done by the husband. The second bedroom is set up as a calligrapher's studio. The daughter still sleeps on a folding cot, and she and her belongings seem to have left almost no impression on the house. The kitchen has not been modified, but the bathroom was renovated to resemble those in the husband's hotel.

Like Auntie Li, the Yangs would like to buy again. But Mrs. Yang, who is a well-paid accountant, is certain that the apartment is worth considerably less than when they bought it. Although both of them told a previous interviewer that neither had personal space of their own, during my visit Mrs. Yang said that "for sure" her husband has personal space. Mr. Yang not only was less willing to accept that the apartment had lost value, but he also disputed his wife's claim that he had personal space. He said, "I don't have enough space, and I still must share it when I am doing calligraphy. I really want my own space." When his wife asked him to compare the situation with their last rented place, however, he agreed that he did have space of his own. At the end of the visit, Mr. Yang volunteered, "My daughter will move out when she marries, so in any case I will be able to use that room exclusively for my calligraphy."

## CONCLUSION

The economic reforms launched by Deng Xiaoping created the most sustained urban housing boom in Chinese history. By 1995 more than half of all residential units were less than sixteen years old (see table 10.2), and average per capita living space was more than twice that of 1979.[44] Shanghai followed these national trends. In the late 1970s most of Shanghai's 6 million urban residents lived in crowded apartments with few amenities. A majority shared bathrooms and kitchens with neighbors, and many used public latrines. Three-generation households were typical. Even married couples who lived independently of their

**Table 10.2  Age of Urban Housing Stock by Units Built in Each Decade (%)**

|          | pre-1949 | 1950s | 1960s | 1970s | 1980s | 1990–1995 |
|----------|----------|-------|-------|-------|-------|-----------|
| National | 7        | 4     | 6     | 16    | 46    | 20        |
| Beijing  | 7        | 13    | 12    | 14    | 43    | 15        |
| Shanghai | 24       | 5     | 3     | 11    | 44    | 13        |
| Tianjin  | 13       | 5     | 5     | 13    | 52    | 12        |

Source: *1995 Quanguo renkou chouyang diaocha ziliao*, 630–32.

parents or in-laws rarely had the luxury of a private bedroom separate from their children. In the entire metropolis only five buildings exceeded twenty floors.[45]

The changes made in this built environment after 1978 were mind-boggling. Between 1979 and 1989, 830,000 households occupied new or renovated apartments,[46] and between 1992 and 1996 another 800,000 moved.[47] More than 4.5 million people changed address, and average space per capita doubled, in most cases a move guaranteeing a higher material standard of living.[48] By the late 1990s the norm for new construction was a three-room apartment (*liangshi yiting*) with its own kitchen and bathroom looking out over a skyline punctuated with high-rise towers in diverse international styles.[49]

Just as dramatic as the transformed physical conditions were the changes in popular expectations. One 1997 Xinhua article reported that 37.5 percent of city residents expected to buy an apartment through their unit and another 26 percent expected to buy on the market.[50] A 1998 Gallup poll in Chengdu, Beijing, Guangzhou, and Shanghai found that between 15 percent and 18 percent planned to buy a home within the next twelve months, and a follow-up survey in Guangzhou, Xi'an, and Wuhan indicated that 25 percent expected to purchase an apartment in 1999.[51]

New affluence and growing marketization of the urban economy have obliterated most communist certainties. In the prereform years, the claims of the collective trumped those of the individual and the public was always morally superior to the private. By the late 1990s, however, individual and personal preferences had gained a new legitimacy. Central to this cultural shift was the disappearance of the juxtaposition of proletariat and bourgeois that had structured everyday behavior for two decades. In the 1970s the ambitious as well as prudent person stood on the side of the proletariat not only in political discussions but even when selecting an appropriate hairstyle or ordering food at the market. Complaining in public about the lack of fresh fish could signal dangerous decadence.

Deng Xiaoping's decision to eschew class struggle and foster the hybrid of market socialism silenced the most vocal advocacy of proletariat fashion. Growing affluence and ever greater openness to the world beyond China even rehabilitated the previously odious lifestyle of the international bourgeoisie, but this time in the more politically correct form of the modern middle classes. China remained a communist polity throughout the 1990s. But in the material culture of the late 1990s, particularly within the confines of newly privatized residential settings, socialist lifestyles have been replaced by a transnational, global reference group, which at first glance looks suspiciously "bourgeois." Declining proletarian style and rising home ownership have been accompanied by a strong male investment in the domestic sphere.

In 1987 I relied on interviews with women in their fifties and early sixties to understand one strand of urban popular culture. In the 1990s I interviewed a more diverse group of residents. Consequently, the greater emphasis on the husband's role may simply reflect the fact that I was not listening exclusively to older mothers seated in their bedrooms. But in 1998 and 1999 my Shanghai colleagues and I also spent over four hundred hours interviewing women, and a third of the interviews took place in the single room that was the bedroom, as well as living room, dining room, and study. Thus the strong imprint of male investments and the strong views of male respondents did not result from the stilling of women's voices but from changes in the property regime.

In the late 1990s city residents of all economic strata wanted to become property owners, and the official endorsements to strive ambitiously for personal success spilled over to legitimize a more general desire to strive for distinction. In this new political economy both men and women saw their homes as an important place where they could legitimately compete for social recognition. In the mid-1980s homes had also been an important social terrain, but they were rarely private property. Greater affluence, reduced state censorship, and the popularization of home ownership—as an ideal and a reality—altered the equation and increased the individual and societal significance of domestic investments.

The possibility of property ownership and the increased legitimacy for indulging personal comfort and displaying social distinctions refocused the energies of both men and women on domestic space. But when—as in contemporary China—husbands have higher earnings than wives and there is a long tradition of patrilineal inheritance, increased investments in urban residences are unlikely to be gender neutral or to favor women. We need only look at contemporary Taiwan to see how high capitalism accommodates exclusive male property claims. To some extent, as C. K. Yang wrote in 1959, collectivization and proletarian culture made unequal claims to family property moot. Under the conditions of collective ownership and criminalization of private business and investment, household headship carried little power outside the home and Chinese families could cede domestic space to women and avoid the difficult task of putting legal equality into practice. However, once market reforms recapitalized domestic property and individuals could openly compete for status through conspicuous consumption, male attachments and investments in domestic space intensified. Most typically in both advertisements and home visits I observed a domestic space configured around the interests of a married couple who relished the opportunity to create a more comfortable and tasteful home for themselves and their single child. For these men and women, "my mother's house" of the 1980s had been succeeded by "a home of our own." But the greater impact of home ownership on male satisfaction and the higher percentage of male names on deeds suggest that conjugal property has a male tilt. Thus even as affluence and the single-child campaign have facilitated small nuclear households among urban families of all socioeconomic strata, privatization of real estate has strengthened male control over family property and thereby reversed the earlier tendency of collective ownership to neutralize traditional male advantages and feminize domestic space in Chinese cities.

## NOTES

1. "A New Look at Housing," *China News Analysis*, October 1, 1998, 6.

2. *China Daily*, 7 January 1991, 1; *Beijing Review*, 17 January 1991; *Renmin ribao* (hereafter *RMRB*), 26 May 1991, 8; *RMRB* 1 January 1992, 2.

3. David Fraser, " Inventing Oasis," in Deborah Davis, ed., *The Consumer Revolution in Urban China* (Berkeley: University of California Press, 2000), 25–53.

4. Leora Auslander, *Taste and Power: Furnishing Modern France* (Berkeley: University of California Press, 1996).

5. "Women and Men in the Class Structure," in Rae Blumberg, ed., *Gender, Family, and the Economy* (Newbury Park, Calif.: Sage Publications, 1991), 60.

6. The literature on women's subordination within their families is vast. One of the most comprehensive recent discussion was presented by Martha Nussbaum in the Seeley Lectures in Political theory at the University of Chicago in February 1999.

7. Susan Mann, *Precious Records* (Stanford, Calif.: Stanford University Press, 1997), 75.

8. Deborah Davis, "My Mother's House," in *Unofficial China*, ed. Perry Link, Richard Madsen, and Paul G. Pickowicz (Boulder: Westview, 1989), 88–100.

9. Eighty-four of the one hundred families had at least one married child, and of these fifty five shared a home with the married child. In 80 percent of the three-generation homes, the coresident married child was a son.

10. C. K. Yang, *The Chinese Family in the Communist Revolution* (Cambridge: MIT Press, 1959), 143.

11. Davis, "My Mother's House," p. 88.

12. Mihaly Csikszentmihalyi and Eugene Rochberg-Halton, *The Meaning of Things* (Cambridge: Cambridge University Press, 1981), 129.

13. This is was the observation of Columbia University political scientist Xiaobo Lu at the Columbia modern China seminar in January 2000.

14. Personal communication, January 31, 2000.

15. *Xinmin wanbao* (hereafter *XMWB*), 4 June 1999, 35.

16. Deborah Davis, "Urban Households: Supplicants to a Socialist State," *Chinese Families in the Post Mao Era*, ed. Deborah Davis and Stevan Harrell (Berkeley: University of California Press, 1993), 50–76.

17. Fraser, "Inventing Oasis: Luxury Housing Advertisements and Reconfiguring

Domestic Space in Shanghai," in *The Consumer Revolution in Urban China*, ed. Deborah Davis (Berkeley: University of California Press, 2000), 25–53.

18. This section draws on 35 brochures collected from 185 developers exhibiting in June 1999.

19. Kathleen Erwin, "Heart-to-Heart, Phone-to-Phone: Family Values, Sexuality, and the Politics of Shanghai's Advice Hotlines," in *Consumer Revolution*, 145–170.

20. Personal communication, February 10, 2000.

21. Advertisement for Yongde homes published in *Xinmin Wanbao*, 11 May 1994, 15.

22. When a colleague in Shanghai read this paper, he noted that this term could only be used for the taste of food and suggested that *pinwei* would be the better translation. In fact, I am simply quoting from the advertisement. The idea that it is the foodlike taste of the female that attracts the male customer confirms my argument about a "male tilt."

23. In 1998 we designed and implemented a longitudinal study of consumer behavior among four hundred couples in four cities to examine how the consumer revolution of the 1990s affected lifestyle among five occupational groups. In each city twenty-five families were randomly selected from residence committees in two to five different city districts from households headed by managers, professionals, blue-collar employees, or the self-employed. Over the year, each husband and wife was interviewed four times and in addition they twice filled out logs on one weeks socializing activities. In this chapter I will use only the interview results from Shanghai. For financial support for the project, we thank the Henry Luce Foundation.

24. Interviewers asked each husband and wife during a separate interview: "Do you think every family must own the property rights of their own home? (*Nin renwei meijia dou yinggai yongyou ziji zhufang de chanquan ma?*) The options were yes (*shi*), no (*bu*), and hard to say (*buhaoshuo*).

25. Seven percent listed husband's father, 2 percent wife's father, 5 percent husband's mother, 2 percent wife's mother, 2.5 percent husband's brother, 3 percent wife's brother, 2 percent husband's sister, 3 percent wife's sister, 2 percent sons, and 1 percent a daughter.

26. Sixty-three percent of husbands but only 23 percent of wives said the title or rental agreement listed their name.

27. A similar pattern of consumer purchases is found in all large cities between 1986 and 1990. State Statistical Bureau and the East West Population Center, *Survey of Income and Expenditure of Urban Households in China in 1986* (Honolulu: University of Hawaii Press, 1989), 242–45; 1990 *Zhongguo chengzhen shumin jiating shouzhu diaocha ziliao* (Beijing: Zhongguo tongji chubanshe, 1991), 225–28, 293–95.

28. Zhang Tianzhi, ed., *Shanghai jiating shinei zhuanghuang jingxuan* (Shanghai: Shanghai Sanlian Shudian, 1998), 3.

29. I heard this remark on Shanghai Education TV at 11 P.M. on 14 June 1999. The program featured a male decorator answering questions from a studio audience about how best to furnish a home. At the conclusion of this program, the shopping channel came on the air; the first product to be promoted was a heavy-duty cleaning liquid for kitchens.

30. One especially rich source is from the Web site of Rongxin Decorators, which advertised in the newspapers as well as on the Web at www.rxjtzh.online.sh.cn.

31. *Shanghai baijia zhuanghuang*, ed. Li Yang (Shanghai: Shanghai renmin meishu chubanshe, 1996); *Shanghai xinchao jiating zhuangshi* (Shanghai: Shanghai huabao chubanshe,

1996); *Xinbian Shanghai jiating buzhi yi baili* (Shanghai: Renmin meishu chubanshe, 1995); *Shanghai jiating shinei zhuanghuang jingxuan*, ed. Zhang Tianzhi (Shanghai: Zhongguo fang-zhi daxue chubanshe, 1999); *Shanghai jiating shinei zhuanghuang jingxuan*, ed. Zhang Tian-zhi (Shanghai: Sanlian, 1998); *Shanghai jiating zhuanghuang yishu*, ed. Chen Xuwei and Chen Guohong (Shanghai: Zhongguo fangzhi daxue chubanshe, 1999). I purchased eight other magazines in the same stores between July 1997 and June 1999, but they were not published in Shanghai and thus are not reviewed here.

32. *Shanghai jiating shinei zhuanghuang jingxuan*, ed. Zhang Tianzhi (Shanghai: Zhong-guo fangzhi daxue chubanshe, 1999), 5; *Shanghai jiating shinei zhuanghuang jingxuan*, ed. Zhang Tianzhi (Shanghai: Sanlian, 1998), 5.

33. Two friends who read this paper and whose families live in China remarked that before the reforms high-level cadre homes also tilted toward displaying men's status and achievements. One who had returned to attend the funeral of his grandmother noted that what struck him in his uncles' use of their homes was how the reforms has allowed them to "recapture their mother's house and turn it into a space for men's business."

34. *China Daily*, 7 January 1991, 1; *Beijing Review*, 17 January 1991; *RMRB*, 26 May 1991, 8; *RMRB*, 1 January 1992, 2.

35. Lau, Kwok-yu "Urban Housing Reform in China Amidst Property Boom" in Joseph Cheng and Lo Chi Kin, ed., *China Review 1993* (Hong Kong: Chinese University of Hong Kong Press, 1994), 24:1–35, 16.

36. *Guowuynan gongbao*, 1995, 70–73.

37. *Guowuynan gongbao*, 1997, 810.

38. *RMRB*, 14 September 195,1; *China News Analysis*, 1 October 1998, 6.

39. One 1997 Xinhua article reported that 37.5 percent of city residents expected to buy an apartment through their unit and another 26 percent expected to buy on the market. see *China News Analysis*, 1 October 1998, 5. A 1998 Gallup poll in Chengdu, Beijing, Guangzhou, and Shanghai found that between 15 percent and 18 percent planned to buy a home within the next twelve months. See Matthew Miller, "City Dwell-ers Hungry for Durables," *South China Morning Post* (hereafter SCMP), 14 January 1999. A follow-up survey in Guangzhou, Xian, and Wuhan indicated that 25 percent expected to purchase an apartment in 1999. CCTV, 7:30 P.M., June 21, 1999, as viewed in Shanghai.

40. Only 9 percent of husbands and 4 percent of wives answered in the negative to the following question: "Do you think every family must have ownership of their own dwell-ing? (*nin renwei meijia dou yinggai yongyou ziji zhufang de chanquan ma?*). When we com-pared the size, amenities, and number of rooms among families headed by each occupational category, owners did better. For example, among blue-collar men, owners averaged 2 rooms, renters 1.6; among professionals, owners averaged 3.0 room, renters, 2.1. Among managers owners averaged 2.5 rooms, renters 2.1. Similarly, among twenty-six owners, all but one had a private toilet while among the fifty-nine renters 34 percent shared a toilet with at least one other household.

41. Among men only 7 percent of renters but 24 percent of owners said they were very satisfied. Among women the gap was 9 percent versus 25 percent. Using a five-point scale, male differences were significant at a 0.07 level.

42. Among men, 13 percent of renters but 42 percent of owners said they had private space, among women 11 percent of renters and 31 percent of owners. Thus ownership significantly raised the likelihood, but the gain for men was greater.

43. Among owners, the percentage of men who said they were a legal leaseholder was 69 percent as opposed to 60 percent among renters. For women, ownership also raised the number claiming to be leaseholders from 21 percent among renters to 27 percent among owners, but women remained in a clear minority.

44. In 1979 it was 3.6 square meters; in 1995, 8.1 square meters. *Zhongguo tongji nianjian 1999*, 317.

45. *Shanghai tongji nianjian 1998* (Shenzhen: Zhongguo tongji chubanshe, 1998), 102. Hereafter *SHTJNJ*.

46. *Beijing Review*, 14 January 1991, 7.

47. *XMWB*, 24 August 1997, 1.

48. Between 1978 and 1998, the average square meters per resident rose from 4.5 to almost 10. *SHTJNJ 1999*, 85. By 1997 a majority of urban households (70 percent) had self-contained apartments with their own kitchen, bathroom, and private entrance (*XMWB*, 29 January 1999, 35).

49. By 1997 there were 861 buildings with between 20 and 29 floors, and 105 of more than 30. *SHTJNJ 1998*, 102.

50. *China News Analysis*, 1 October 1998, 5.

51. Matthew Miller, "City Dwellers Hungry for Durables," SCMP, 14 January 1999; CCTV 7:30 P.M., June 21, 1999, as viewed in Shanghai.

# 11

## In Love and Gay

*Robert Geyer*

"I'd always been very ignorant about sex and never thought people of the same sex could make love. I didn't even have any idea about how heterosexual people made love." So began an interview of Long Jianhua (not, as far as I know, his real name) by Hong Kong University sociologist Zhou Huashan in his 1996 *Beijing tongzhi gushi* (Stories of Beijing comrades). Long, twenty-nine years old, a college graduate and middle school teacher, became involved in a gay relationship for the first time when he was twenty-five. "When I was seventeen, alone and untaught, I learned to masturbate, each time feeling very nervous and guilty. The object of my fantasy was always a man, usually a famous singer from Hong Kong or Taiwan. I would quickly put my pants back on, afraid of being discovered. The thought of homosexuality never entered my mind.

"In junior middle school we male classmates used to pull down our pants, play with each other, and call each other 'rabbit.' Eight or nine out of ten guys played these games, which represented curiosity and awakening sexual interest at the time of puberty. But by the time we were sixteen or seventeen, we stopped this sort of thing. Once in class, when I was fifteen, I groped the classmate next to me. Annoyed, he blurted out to the teacher in front of our whole class that I was 'doing' homosexuality. I was severely scolded by the teacher, who said this was a strange, abnormal condition. That was the first time I'd ever heard this word. Two months later I read a blurb in the newspaper about a parade in the United States, describing a scene where 'tens of thousands of Americans, torsos naked, kissed others of the same sex on the street in broad daylight as if no one else were around.' After reading this I became even more disgusted by homosexuality, sure that it was a bad thing.

"My most important goal at the time was to study hard and get into college.

My grades were pretty good, I was considered an excellent student, and my parents had very high hopes for me. The pressure on me was quite heavy. I got into a key high school based on my test results, and my parents were really excited. Three years later I easily tested into Beijing University to study literature.

"Four years ago, in early summer, I read in the paper about gays gathering in a certain park. The word 'homosexuality' again penetrated my mind, and a kind of uneasy, sinful feeling welled up inside me. I struggled for a long time but finally, late one afternoon, following directions in the newspaper article, I walked into that park like a lone thoroughbred horse.

"Then, hey, the whole crowd started chattering, saying I was one in ten thousand, fortune's favorite, and so on, and I felt I was being accorded a heavenly reception. The scene remains in my mind's eye to this day: it was the first time I'd set foot in that park, casually strolling as if nothing were out of the ordinary, but unbelievably agitated and excited that there were *so many* gays. I no longer felt alone and knew I belonged there. I picked a stone bench and sat down. At a news board in front of me there was a crowd milling around, jostling in rows, shoulder to shoulder, leg to leg, very attentive—not to the newspapers spread before them but to the warm bodies rubbing against each other from top to bottom on all sides. Nearby, I felt a steady gaze fixed on me, as if someone were quietly spying on me. I lifted my head and looked in all directions, my line of sight passing the crowd and alighting on him. He was leaning lazily against a pine tree and smoking, light wisps of smoke floating upward from the edge of his mouth, curling about him, enveloping him like a thick fog. He flashed a beaming smile, his friendly face full of expectation. I hesitated. My gaze fixed on his face for three seconds, then moved away again as I pretended to lower my head. After a bit I looked at him again and, as our eyes met, I thought, 'I like him, and he likes me too.' He boldly but naturally walked over and said, 'Hi, can we chat?' and then, 'You're very nice-looking, pretty, and refined; are you still in school?' In fact, he was quite striking himself, more than a match for me, about 180 centimeters tall, strongly built, handsome, gentle, and showing those facial wrinkles that betray a hard life but are so attractive.

"We headed out of the park, walking shoulder to shoulder by the edge of the long lake. Rays of the late afternoon sun sparkled off the rippling water. All around the lake the sparrows were silent, and it was quiet as a hermitage. The moon was rising into the heavens from behind the darkening woods, quiet, secluded, and shadowy. We chatted as we walked, in a low tone of voice, not really saying very much. It was all very congenial; like-minded, we were getting along very well. For a first meeting it already seemed like old flames meeting again, using their minds and eyes to communicate and not needing much speech. When we did speak it seemed like a misty, evanescent fog—very enjoyable. His conversation had a refined, sophisticated flavor, and it sounded as if he were a very substantial and accomplished person. At this moment my emotional state was highly agitated. My body was open to him and I'd already surrendered my heart to him.

"He obviously was an old hand at this, leading me from the dark of the woods into the moonlit gleam of the lakeside. Walking stealthily, we slipped down a bank into an old, dried-out riverbed with tall grass on both sides. We staggered along a wall of reeds in the dark, and I tripped over a tree branch, losing my balance and nearly falling. With skillful hand- and footwork he caught me in his steady embrace from behind. We looked up at each other full of smiles, and in that instant there was a touching silence between us. He then gave me a warm, generous, long, slow, thorough, sweet kiss. He took off my pants and his own as well. His lips, bursting with desire, played swiftly over my torso as I lay on the ground. He swallowed me up, then thrust in and out, back and forth inside me I don't know how many times, gently sticking to me like glue. I grabbed tight onto his strong arms, letting him burn up and dissolve exhausted within me as my own body went limp, soft, and weak. I let out a soft sound of elation and saw his happy, contented face, like that of a handsome warrior returning triumphantly from battle. We fell asleep on the grass in a tight embrace.

"It began to rain. We got dressed awkwardly and fled the battlefield, waiting ten minutes before we could hail a cab. The rain didn't let up and left water dripping from roof eaves and tree branches. The cab wove slowly in and out of traffic on Beijing's rain-soaked streets, and because of the fine raindrops the scene was especially misty, showing indistinctly. Bumps and potholes in the streets tossed us back and forth in the cab. I sat by his side, my thoughts flying all over the place, as fuzzy as the scene outside, leaving me at a loss. I couldn't figure out what was fantasy and what reality.

"We didn't exchange phone numbers or addresses. I'd learned only that his name was Zhe as we said good-bye.

"It rained all night, the sound of the wind rustling through the trees mixed with that of the pattering rain. In bed I tossed and turned, sleeping fitfully. In the middle of the night the rain turned heavy and I clearly heard the sound of thunder and lightning. Feeling half dead, half alive, I slept for twelve hours. At noon I finally pulled myself out of bed, dripping with sweat and still very tired, and staggered out of my bedroom in a daze.

"That afternoon I went to the park hoping to run into him again. It was almost deserted, with the hillsides and stone pavilions still enveloped in misty rain. I waited three hours, didn't see him, and went home disappointed.

"I thought about him constantly. I frequently went to the park to look for him but always returned with my hopes dashed. This became a habit, a ritual. Like an idiot I waited, wanting to prove the depth of my affection and the reality of my romance. Just as I began to suspect that I loved him—or was it only that I was falling in love with this *idea* of love?—I finally ran into him again. He was just as dashing, striking, and refined as I remembered him; he was wearing a clean white Puma T-shirt and brand-new, tight-fitting jeans. He looked very happy, immediately pulled me to his side, asked how I was, and said he'd just come back from a business trip to Dalian.

"This time we didn't make love. We went to a nearby snack restaurant and chatted the whole evening, facing the steaming oven. It wasn't like last time— sparks flying in all directions, an intense surge of emotions and fantasies. Instead we chatted casually and looked ahead realistically. He was thirty, a hydraulic engineer, and married. We exchanged phone numbers and gently kissed good-bye on a dark street corner. I went with him to his bus stop. When the bus came and opened its doors, the crowd enveloped him immediately, leaving me calmly staring at the bus until it disappeared out of sight.

"We forged a stable relationship, seeing each other infrequently but trying to do so on a steady basis. Neither of us made any real pledges; instead, we put heart and soul into every moment, soon working out a delicate commitment of mutual trust and unswerving loyalty. I liked his bold generosity and emotional intensity, appreciated his work ethic and success, and even respected his feeling of respon-sibility toward his wife. He once said, 'You're the one I love, but my wife is the one I'll stay with for the rest of my life.' This actually made me feel more relaxed and lessened my guilt feeling. As for what he liked about me, I don't know! When with him I was relaxed and happy; he had the power to make me forget time and fatigue, just like love in novels. I learned a lot from him, and he changed all sorts of misunderstanding and bias I'd held toward homosexuality. For example, I thought I'd become gay only as a result of his leading me on. He said that if I weren't already attracted to men I'd only be more revolted as I did those deeds. Sex knowledge and skill could be taught, but not sexual orientation. And I'd always hated those sissy-type gay guys, but he said I'd been unable to get rid of my feudal ideas about male machismo. With him, I could see an amalgam of the petty demons and better angels of my own nature.

"Sadly, beautiful things don't last. A year later, his wife discovered our rela-tionship. Relations among the three of us had been quite good. I'd been going to their place once a week to help Zhe work on his English, which was actually just another excuse to be with him, and I never left until after dinner and conver-sation late into the evening. At first, his wife actually thought I was interested in her!

"One morning that summer, he and I lay naked in his bed making love. After ejaculating, we were both a little sleepy and dozed off in a tight embrace. With some emergency that unexpectedly brought her home from work, his wife by chance uncovered our sweet affair. Totally surprised, she murmured a horrified short sound and left the house in no time flat. On returning that evening, she said nothing about the matter, as if it had never happened, but her attitude was icy and severe. She wanted Zhe to come clean.

"He had always been mature and worldly-wise. He slept on the matter, then invited me out. That night a cold front and high wind seemed to freeze all my senses. We met in the park. As he raised his eyes and flashed me a smile, I could

clearly see the wrinkles on his face. His hair was uncombed and he looked generally disheveled. He seemed old, fragile, withered. Each of us felt the other's
embarrassment; it was a silent, desolate scene. After an eternity, he said, 'I guess
we'll have to break up!' This was the message I should clearly have expected, but
I still felt cut to the quick. Before my eyes was an expanse of white nothingness
as dusk fell. My heart skipped a beat, and tears forced their way from my eyes.
We were already deeply attached to each other and loath to part. I heard myself
saying, 'Maybe you won't believe this, but I'd never been involved in any way
like this and had told myself I'd stick around if the situation were agreeable and
leave if it weren't. I repeatedly tried denying it but had to admit it had happened.
I loved you from the start, and if we now have to part, I'll finally realize how
deeply I've loved you.' He said nothing, quietly looked up into the clouds, his
eyes moistening. I thought it was all going to end then and there and turned
around to leave. But he stopped me to say, 'There's something you asked me
twice, and I never answered you, but now I can say it: I love you, too.' He suddenly turned around and rushed away. I stood absolutely motionless until he had
disappeared in a crowd, cold wind and piercing raindrops beating against my
face. This word 'love' is too great a burden for me. The first time I'd said, 'I love
you,' in exchange for a chill wind, I trembled from the heartbreak.

"Our relationship underwent a tremendous change. We lost our previous blaz-
ing affection, which turned into a feeling of spiritual closeness. There was no
longer any lovemaking, kissing, or touching, as if all desire had deserted us, only
a pure, loving care. A year later they had a child, and he turned all his attention
there, which I perfectly understood. A person can't follow the dictates of his
heart forever; when young you can be flighty or crazy, but in middle age you have
to be docile and toe the conventional line.

"His wife ultimately was able to achieve peace with him. You know, for a
woman in China, it's better for her husband to be gay than to have a mistress.
He can't have kids with a gay partner, a gay relationship has no legal standing,
and the gay partner can't compete for much of a role in the husband's life. You
could say this is a variation on traditional society's theme of things being okay
as long as there's no threat to the wife's formal position. A gay husband can go
out for some kicks and the wife has to respect the male chauvinist principle,
giving him a little space. But she won't divorce him. Since his work unit (danwei)
provides their housing, if there were a divorce, she'd have no place to go and her
very identity would be at risk. They're a model couple in the eyes of the masses,
and absolutely no excuse for divorce exists.

"All that was three years ago. Since then I have not been involved with anyone else. Having lost the love of my life, I don't want anyone else. Other guys
don't seem to measure up. I'm in touch with him by phone, and we occasionally
get together. I'm quite okay with that and unable to imagine anything more.

"As for myself, there's no way out of getting married. China is just like that.
I'm now twenty-nine and constantly having to deal with girlfriends introduced

by a matchmaker—over ten already. Some women's qualifications have been quite good. Last month I met a pretty one—strikingly beautiful, in fact, even without being made up or dressed up—like a pearl shining in the dark. But striking beauty doesn't arouse me. We [gays] are just like that. We don't reject women; we just have no sexual interest in them.

"In the past I could say [as an excuse for rejecting women] I was focusing on work and just being picky. That's not working any more. Thirty and not married—my parents are starting to complain. Each time I meet someone and drop her, it's such a hassle with relatives, friends, and colleagues at work. They say I give the cold shoulder to outstanding prospects and heartlessly fail to give face to the matchmakers. I'm about to give in. The last two or three women introduced to me are pretty well qualified, so I'll probably pick one of them. There's no other way.

"One gets married to get housing. Without marriage, you aren't assigned housing, and that's just a fact. Right now I squeeze into a little room with three coworkers; it's very inconvenient. Thirty is an extreme limit, and it's just like that in our [gay] circle. You can go ask anybody over thirty—nine out of ten are already married and have kids. That's just the situation in China.

"Our kind is really pitiful, forever condemned to fake the life of a so-called normal person. When you run into one of our circle, you can't even greet him. Hearing colleagues or friends badmouthing homosexuality, you can't even rebut them. Even when you're so clearly unwilling, in the end you still have to marry out of fear of exposure. Even though in the last few years people in Beijing have a more liberal attitude toward marriage, being single is still subject to reproach. We gays are especially sensitive to that, so we use marriage as a protective umbrella. We even resort to divorce to try to assure that our private lives won't be upset. I have a friend who divorced six months after he got married; he asserted, 'I got married so I could get divorced' but still had to pretend to all around him that he'd been wounded deeply so that his parents and neighbors wouldn't dare introduce a new prospect. Of course, he also paid a heavy price—in divorcing he gratuitously sacrificed a woman—but in not divorcing he would have had to lie to her for a lifetime. How would you decide? Both choices are bad, and both would be really hard to bear. If I were bisexual, that would be a lot simpler. At least in making love with my wife, I wouldn't have to fantasize that she was a guy or find all sorts of excuses to avoid sex, and I could really get into loving her. That word 'love' again—how sweet!"[1]

The foregoing account is from Zhou Huashan's 1996 *Stories of Beijing Comrades*. Another story in the same collection tells of Feng Suzhen, a young professional woman and lesbian originally from the countryside of central China:

"My home is near Wuhan. When I was a child I was very close to a primary school classmate. She had light skin and a finely featured face. She also had a kind and open personality and was a sweet soul whom people fell in love with on sight. Our homes were not far apart, and every day we went to school and played together; we could talk endlessly about anything.

"In the third year of junior middle school a male classmate was pursuing her like mad, waiting for her at the door to finish her school day, writing her sappy love letters, and causing some misunderstanding between us. This boy was very handsome, tall and refined, also very studious and smart, and on top of all that a basketball star and school leader who totally snowed the girls. I feel she suffered some uncertainty, but, after all, our affection was as good as gold and she rebuffed this guy's advances, promising she'd share life's pleasures and pain with me forever and never marry. That day we were very excited and went to a nearby temple to make some mutual vows. All of a sudden, as we were offering incense, a pair of butterflies fluttered by, so moving us that we hugged each other right there in the temple. She said she'd never part with me. I embraced her tightly and, not knowing what I was saying, told her I loved her. That night we slept at her house, hugging each other and recalling the butterflies. We often slept together but had never thought about sex, instead having all-night heart-to-heart talks by candlelight. It was unspeakably sweet as she was holding me. I felt a kind of damp sensation in my crotch but dared think nothing of it.

"My parents of course didn't object to any of this, incapable as they were of thinking it had anything to do with homosexuality. In Chinese society it's only if I'm with a boy that there's a problem. People think it's natural for girlfriends to be publicly holding hands and rubbing shoulders, hugging and embracing, or sharing a bed. I saw the term 'homosexuality' in the newspaper once; two guys were having sex in the public toilets and were nabbed by public security. At the time I felt disgusted, believing homosexuality was abnormal. I even showed the newspaper reference to my girlfriend so we could both attack it. Ours was a case of beautiful and pure love, not homosexuality.

"The college entrance exam was the turning point in my life. Her grades had never been good, so she would fail the exam. After we took it, in July, we went on a two-week trip to Harbin, Jilin, Changchun, Dalian, and Beijing. We were aware we'd soon be going our separate ways, so we tried to enjoy ourselves as much as possible. We didn't bring up the future at all. In early August the exam results were announced, and my scores were outstanding. I would enter Beijing University to study literature. Holding my exam results, I cried. My mother thought I was just too excited and cried with me. But I really didn't want to go to Beida. I wanted nothing but my girlfriend.

"I was very conflicted. For many years getting into Beida had been my goal, or maybe I should say I'd wanted glory for our family. Only when faced with having to leave her did I realize I was willing to give up everything. But what could I do? Mom had already planned three days and nights of celebration, with neighbors, friends, and relatives falling over each other to come offer their congratulations. Of course I had to put on a brilliantly smiling face, pretending to look and feel so lucky. Back by her side, we were despondent, silently sitting by a tree in the fields, listening to the crickets, looking at the paddy fields, sadly passing our remaining time together.

"The night before we were to part, I was at home leafing through my diary of the past three years. Outside there was a fine rain falling. Tiny raindrops drifted by the dark yellow street lamps; the atmosphere was murky. I read the early pages of the diary, from three years ago, and was surprised that they were full of her. Not a single day had passed without my mentioning her: a wrinkled corner on the skirt she was wearing, a small dirty spot behind her ear, her pretty new pink stockings—every gesture I wrote down in great detail. If she were in a down mood and not speaking, it would hurt me all day; if she were all bubbly, my mood would also soar. Only in reviewing my diary did I realize that I'd always paid attention to her body. One day she had worn a tight tank top and a really short skirt that barely covered her tush, with every curvy line in her body showing up in minute detail, her breasts full and bouncy like two big pumpkins. I really had a special kind of desire to be close to her and wrote in my diary, 'It would be a real delight to make love with her.' That was a true and pure kind of love. At the time I thought, if my future husband is half as good as she is, that wouldn't be bad.

"Once at Beida, I immediately entered a very different space, a bright, riot-ously colorful new world. I switched majors to economics, and the pressure of homework was really tough. I participated in the student assembly, frequently losing sleep and missing meals to do homework and attend meetings. I lived hap-pily and worked hard, gladly trying to fulfill my potential. I couldn't forget her, but the distance between us kept growing. Her home didn't have a phone, so at first we secretly exchanged telegrams, but that stopped as my exam time approached. After the first year I returned home, as if in triumph. In seeing her again I was a little timid and ashamed, and both of us were very cautious. She said she was dating a guy. I was happy for her and couldn't conceal a slight sense of relief, as if a heavy burden had been lifted from my shoulders. How could I have known I would run into her holding hands with her boyfriend? Seeing that, I felt a sudden sense of loss, and a painful feeling welled up inside me. I was able to walk around them so they wouldn't see me and ran the twenty minutes home. My mother said I looked very pale and had a dull look in my eyes. I retreated to my room wailing. Fortunately I soon returned to Beida and once again had to devote full attention to my studies.

"In the new school year I roomed with three very close friends. One weekend two of them went on a trip, leaving only the other roommate and me. On that clear, bright night the sky was full of stars and a crescent moon. We lay on a stone bench outside the dorm sharing lots of stories of our childhood. Our mood was relaxed and happy, and only back in the room did we realize we'd talked for five hours. She said she wanted to sleep with me, and I very naturally embraced her, saying I'd been very content tonight. Unexpectedly, after hugging each other, she didn't let go and warmly massaged me from my shoulders and back down to my waist and thighs. Astonished, I didn't know how to respond, and I thought about asking her to stop. Embarrassed, I felt a slight, wet wave of wriggling pleasure down there. I was very, very scared and, holding her tight, asked her what had happened. She asked me if I didn't enjoy this as she continued to massage me lovingly. I was frightened to the point of panic. I started to cry and hopped over onto another bed, staring at that crescent moon and feeling very confused.

"Thinking back to the situation in my village and going over repeatedly the physiological reaction I'd just had, I started to wonder whether this wasn't abnormal. In the middle of the night, naked, she came over and hugged me. I shook with fear but hugged her back real tight. I said I was afraid but my body accepted her. By this time, emotionally, I gave in completely, began enjoying it and only then sensed her smooth, soft skin and white, glistening breasts with cherry-red nipples. I was totally transported, so excited just from the massage that I enjoyed my first sexual climax. Her skill was absolutely wonderful, and she gradually helped me abandon my fear and psychological burden. She excited me so much that she had to cover my mouth to keep me from crying out and alerting people in other rooms down the hall. My reaction also alarmed me because I'd completely lost control of my body. Around noon the next day, one of our roommates returned and found us naked in each other's embrace. Sensing what had transpired and knowing how to handle the situation, she silently retreated from the room.

"At the outset I still felt very awkward and wanted to hide this, but afterward I realized my other two roommates were both very thoughtful and open-minded, having picked up from me what was going on without my having to broadcast it.

"She was a very good student with a definite artistic bent, lively in her movements like a beauty of olden times, extremely well-read, a serious fan of Western culture from the Renaissance and Baroque down to the contemporary and popular—she knew it all like the palm of her hand. Being with her, I learned many things and for the first time read some Western lesbian novels, gradually accepting my identity. She was my first real teacher, but our personalities were really quite different and we occasionally quarreled. Neither of us knew how to handle that, so we suppressed things and let them go. A year later she graduated and went to the United States to study.

"I often think that without her I wouldn't have been able to comprehend these things. If I had remained in my hometown, I would especially never have understood this idea of lesbianism. I'd have continued to be with [my old girlfriend] and love her dearly, but our relationship wouldn't have reached the point of sex or had any such content at all. There wouldn't have been any self-awakening. This isn't a matter of what would have been good or bad but of discovering and developing my sense of self. A village has its own warm feeling, and at least everybody accepts women loving each other. As long as you get married, you can be with a woman your whole life. You wouldn't have to, as I do now, put a lesbian sign out on display for the rest of your life and risk exposure, and you wouldn't feel you had to come out to consider yourself liberated. In the countryside I could have been very natural and happy together with my old girlfriend, whereas here I have to be very stealthy and closeted to feel safe.

"When it came time to graduate, [my Beida girlfriend] tested first in all her classes, on top of which her mother was a high-ranking cadre. She easily got a scholarship to go to the United States to study, which had been her long-term dream, and we gradually lost touch. As for me, I went to work at a bank and later moved to an advertising firm where I've remained till now. About eighteen months ago, I met a woman over thirty, a client of my ad company, divorced and in business for herself, very capable, with a frank, open, honest personality. She is an outstanding person, but I admire her more than love her, and we are missing that certain spark, making us like an old married couple.

"Her experience had been quite unfortunate. I was the first lesbian she'd ever met. She'd realized from her childhood that she was attracted to women and totally accepted that about herself. It was the most natural and sincere thing about her. She'd never touched a lesbian but had always loved straight women, one after another, getting used to being hurt and each time expecting rejection. Her self-image suffered severely. When she was eighteen she fell in love with a naive, unspoiled young straight woman. They often hugged, embraced, and talked openly about love. The young woman misled her, and she allowed a glimmer of hope to dissipate her despair. The result? She suffered a crushing defeat, drank a cleaning agent in an effort to kill herself, and wound up in the hospital for three days. Fortunately she recovered, but her parents nearly finished the job by scolding her half to death, saying she had caused the family to lose face for three generations. She saw two psychiatrists who couldn't identify the source of her problem, indicating only that she had had too little contact with men and therefore become ill with homosexuality. That year she failed the college entrance exam. She also fared poorly the next year and wound up as a hostess in a restaurant. Fortunately she was attractive and refined, had a seductive body, and her personality was easygoing and candid, so at least her work went smoothly.

"By her parents' arrangement, she was introduced to many men, all of them admirable, outstanding, sharp, and capable, but none was able to move her. On the contrary, she constantly fell for women. She was convinced she was 100 percent lesbian, but her parents used every imaginable tactic, trotting out the hopes of her ancestors and the reputation of the clan to put pressure on her. Close friends also told her she was dabbling in lesbianism because she hadn't yet met the guy to pull her heartstrings. Facing her parents' blandishments over an extended period, her confidence wavered; she hated herself and detested her homosexuality. She again considered suicide, but to avoid hurting her parents she continued to endure the pressure and finally married a rich guy, divorced and old enough to be her father. She said on her wedding night that she wanted to run back home. She'd hoped she would change into a heterosexual. But nothing changed; she tolerated the arrangement for two years and wound up getting a divorce.

"She learned how to do business from her husband, setting up her own enterprise, traveling all over the country, and becoming quite successful. The house I live in with her she bought four years ago for only ¥190,000.

"As for myself, I don't feel any pressure. Other people don't suspect anything about two women living together. We have a living room and three bedrooms, and who would know we're sleeping in one bed? I always say she's renting a room to me, and, anyway, we're both professionals and there are plenty of excuses for marrying late. Contemporary housing units are all independent and neighbors don't bother about each other, so who's going to control us? When I travel out of town with her and we stay in the same room, nobody ever thinks it inappropriate. Only if I wanted a room with a guy would there be universal condemnation. My parents? They're not a big problem, either, since I left home when I was eighteen. When I go home I never bring up matters of the heart, in the past talking about school and now about work. In earlier years my parents had things to say, but after my older brother divorced three years ago, they learned a lesson, looking on marriage much less seriously and giving me lots more space. And, after all, people most often live in the here and now. Since I give my parents six hundred yuan a month, a lot more than my brother's monthly wage in Wuhan, maybe they actually prefer I not marry!

"My biggest problem now isn't any outside pressure, it's where to look for other lesbians. I've lived with [this woman] for a year, and I've become a little bored. We each know we're not the other's ideal partner, but, hey, even in Beijing you may very possibly encounter only two or three lesbians your entire life. You then can pick a lifetime partner from those two or three, or, if you don't, you stay single; you might as well get married. Up to now I've known exactly four lesbians, each of whom has known only me. What should I do? To be quite frank, I don't love her, but I need a partner. She doesn't love me, but she needs a woman. She's using her apartment to hang on to me, and I'm using my vanity to hold on to her. There's no love or special appeal there, but we're both satisfied and finding a way to meet our needs. We're both smart cookies and know what we need, so to spend our lives together like this isn't such a bad thing—at least no worse than most heterosexual marriages. I'm very practical: if you [Zhou] bump into any lesbians in your last two months here, please introduce them to me. My biggest problem now is I don't know where to seek out other lesbians. Don't laugh at my being so utilitarian. If I were in the United States and could meet several lesbians a day, I could look for my heart's true love, and we could shake heaven and earth loving each other. But this is China, and I don't have too many chances!"[2]

## THE HOMOSEXUAL TRADITION AND ITS
## MODERN FATE

As students of literature, Long and Feng may have been aware that they were part of a venerable tradition of homosexuality in China, even if it seemed far removed from their life in the contemporary period. The homosexual tradition in China may be as ancient as the history of Chinese culture itself. Sources that elucidate more familiar aspects of Chinese history and society from at least as early as the Zhou dynasty (1122 to 256 B.C.)—the *Book of Odes*, the *Han Fei Zi*, and the *Shuo yuan* of Liu Xiang, for example—also reveal a bit about this homosexual tradition. Stories of the emperors and their male favorites abound throughout the imperial period. But it is impossible, especially in contemporary China, to verify claims that many emperors were homosexual.[3]

Many if not most Chinese emperors had their favorites of both sexes. It is worth noting that classical Chinese has no term for a person who is homosexual—not, at least, in any sense commonly understood at the turn of the twenty-first century. Nevertheless, educated Chinese from the Zhou dynasty to the present, undoubtedly familiar with the stories, have recognized expressions such as *fentao* (dividing the peach) and *duanxiu* (cutting the sleeve) and names of such imperial male favorites as Mizi Xia and Dong Xian as clear references to homosexuality. In his *Passions of the Cut Sleeve* Bret Hinsch documents, over a period of many centuries, an extension of the homosexual tradition from the emperors, through the imperial court, down to the level of scholar-officials throughout Chinese society.[4] But it remains difficult to assess how prevalent homosexuality was among the *laobaixing* (general population), since sources on the topic are extremely rare. To extrapolate from contemporary times to conclude that it *was* common among average Chinese in the imperial period may seem reasonable but cannot easily be verified.

Chinese acceptance of homosexuality lasted into Ming and Qing times (A.D. 1368–1911), when several classic novels—including *Honglou meng* (Dream of the red chamber), *Jinping Mei* (The golden lotus), and *Pinhua baojian* (Mirror of theatrical life)—clearly acknowledged both male and female homosexuality. But in recent centuries an antihomosexual trend has taken root.

In the late 1700s, the Qing penal code began to reflect concern about homosexual rape, and authorities tried to crack down—not only on rape but implicitly on homosexuality as well. It is unclear how effective any crackdown on the *laobaixing* could have been in the late decades of the Qing (even, or especially, if homosexual behavior on the part of the emperors and court continued), as rebellion weakened the dynasty's control from within and foreign powers threatened it from without. But the very attempt at crackdown was an attack on homosexual tradition. Then, in the twentieth century, as moralistic Nationalist and Communist regimes fought their way to power, and as Western science (including its dubious assumption that homosexuality was a disease) gained influence, China's homosexual tradition was pushed into the closet. The Nationalist government considered homosexual behavior a "crime injurious to custom,"[5] although it is not clear to what extent the behavior was criminally prosecuted. We know little about homosexual life in China in the first half of the twentieth century, but we might speculate—based on such anecdotal evidence as Chen Kaige's depiction of Peking opera life in his 1993 film *Farewell My Concubine*—that the tradition struggled and survived at least in certain pockets of Chinese society.

After 1949, the People's Republic of China regarded homosexuality as "hooliganism."[6] During the Cultural Revolution years homosexuals were classified as "bad elements"—which, along with landlords, rich peasants, counterrevolutionaries, and rightists, was one of the "five black categories" of people who had no defense from abuse or attack. In the 1980s a pattern emerged—and survived into the 1990s—in which gay males were routinely harassed, detained, interrogated, and often arrested and jailed each time a political or social movement of virtually any kind was announced.[7] Lacking political clout, gays were easy targets for police and security authorities, and became sacrificial lambs to broader goals of government and society.

In the 1980s, scholarly and journalistic works purporting to have carried out surveys and other research among homosexuals began to appear in China. The authors, primarily medical and mental health professionals, did not necessarily treat gays or homosexuality objectively. In some cases, for example, they devoted much space to treatment of and "cures" for such a sexual orientation, while paying scant attention to research methods or rigorous rules of inference. Yet these works did break the long-standing taboo on public discussion of homosexuality and exploded the official myth that the phenomenon had never existed or had long since been stamped out in socialist China. Perhaps for these reasons, PRC government authorities opposed the circulation of such works and made efforts, largely unsuccessful, to suppress them. Around the same time the first glimmerings of gay consciousness began to emerge, and certain parks, street corners, public baths, and toilets became gathering places for small groups of gays, almost exclusively men. As early as the winter of 1978–1979, gay men are reported to have begun meeting in Beijing's Xidan area during the excitement surrounding Democracy Wall. A decade later, twenty hardy souls advocating gay rights were among the demonstrators on or near Tiananmen Square.[8]

In the 1990s the lot of gay men and lesbians in China began to improve. For those who could afford to go, a handful of bars, dance clubs, and restaurants catering to gays added to the kind and number of meeting places previously available. Homosexuality was addressed more dispassionately in newspapers, journals, television, and film. In 1992 a Men's World salon directed at gays appeared in Beijing and, though short-lived, for a few months provided a forum for discussing issues important to gays. A celebrated case of two lesbians living together in Anhui province ended inside the Ministry of Public Security with a decision that there was no law under which such an arrangement or the individuals involved could be prosecuted.

However, it may have been the AIDS crisis—abroad and, increasingly, in China itself—that provided the greatest impetus for a nascent gay "movement." The PRC government had emerged from a state of deep denial about AIDS among the Chinese people in the 1980s. Even though it still seemed to believe that HIV was "foreign" and an example of spiritual (as well as physical) pollution from the bourgeois West, the government began to realize in the early 1990s that it had to take steps to prevent the spread of AIDS. By this time it was clear that the population most affected by HIV and AIDS was drug users (many of them non-Han ethnic minorities) in Yunnan near the border with Burma, but the government acknowledged that gay men also were a high-risk group needing attention. Efforts by quasi-official and nongovernmental organizations to provide AIDS education to gays dovetailed with discussion of problems and issues of broader interest to gays. For example, an AIDS hotline was established in 1992 in Beijing by gay rights/AIDS activist Wan Yanhai under the aegis of the China Health Education Institute.[9] The hotline enabled gay callers to address their concerns, whether related to AIDS or not, but was suspended after six months because of fears in parts of the government about its human rights overtones.

## HOMOSEXUAL RELATIONSHIPS IN THE 1990s

Sources on this topic are difficult, and I begin with two preliminary notes. First, the most useful and credible sources for the 1990s focus overwhelmingly on gay males in urban settings, mostly Beijing. These are the above-mentioned *Stories of Beijing Comrades*, compiled by Zhou Huashan, and Chinese Academy of Social Sciences sociologist Li Yinhe's *Tongxinglian yawenhua* (The subculture of homosexuality).[10] Hence my own account necessarily reflects this bias. Second, although comparisons with the West are inevitable, I try to treat gay relationships in the Chinese context on their own terms, noting similarities but not assuming them.

The barriers to forming gay relationships in China loom large and are necessary background to understanding the relationships themselves. Many of the problems can be subsumed under the following four categories.

### Expectations about Marriage and Family

Social pressure to marry and raise a family remains strong in China, whether or not a person is gay or lesbian. Parents and grandparents, members of the extended as well as the nuclear family, friends, classmates, teachers and professors, coworkers and bosses, and societal and governmental institutions all expect a young man or woman, sooner (preferably) or later to observe this norm. This social pressure is so strong that many gays seem to have gone beyond resigning themselves to it and have actually internalized society's expectations. Most gay men and lesbians themselves expect to marry and have children, and for the small proportion disposed to fight the norm there is little support even from gay friends. Several respondents in the surveys by Li Yinhe and interviews by Zhou Huashan noted that it was their duty to society to marry and continue the family line, at the expense of their own fulfillment and happiness. The prospect of finding a compatible partner and entering a fulfilling, long-term relationship is daunting when partner and relationship will probably have to be abandoned in favor of marriage and child rearing in the mid- to late twenties. Even though the context of marriage in China retains its traditional scope for sexual and other kinds of relationships outside marriage (potentially with those of the same as well as the opposite sex), the practical difficulties of sustaining these are extraordinary. It is no coincidence or help (to gay men and lesbians) that social, security, and political institutions, not to mention a large proportion of members of the Communist Party and Chinese society at large, consider such extramarital relationships "feudal" and immoral.

### Social Attitudes about "Illness" or "Abnormality"

The Chinese view that homosexuality is "abnormal" *(buzhengchang)* appears to be grounded more in the strong Chinese bias toward heterosexual marriage and procreation than in the formal doctrine of Confucianism, Taoism, Buddhism, or other philosophical or religious belief—in the manner that Judeo-Christian tradition presumes homosexuality to have been treated in the Bible. In the last century the influence of Western medical and mental health science in China has bolstered the belief that homosexual orientation and behavior are abnormal. In the West this science was dynamic, with theories and results continually revised, but its development in China suffered the interruptions of war, revolution, and authoritarian politics beginning in the 1930s and lasting nearly half a century.

Since 1978 science in China has made enormous strides to repair the damage of these interruptions, but their effect was profound, and the continuing campaigns against such targets as "bourgeois liberalism" and "spiritual pollution" have interfered with recovery. Entire disciplines, such as cultural anthropology and sociology, were either abolished or cast into ill repute, and genuine research was nearly impossible for decades. Kinsey's monumental research on human sexuality in the late 1940s in the United States seemed to have no impact in China for at least thirty years, and the booming field of sexology in the PRC today is rife with outdated theoretical assumptions, not to mention a lamentable degree of hucksterism. In March 2001 the Chinese Psychiatry Association removed homosexuality from its list of mental illnesses *(biantai)*, a step the American Psychiatric Association took in 1974. Circumstantial evidence, in the form of their other efforts to limit space for gays, suggests that the Chinese Communist Party and government maintained pressure on the association not to "delist" homosexuality prior to 2001.

The published studies of gays and their behavior that appeared in the 1980s, while undermining the public taboo on discussion of the topic, did little to curtail the widespread belief that homosexuality is an illness and, as such, abnormal. Their discussion of a "cure" for homosexuality may, in some cases, actually have exacerbated prejudices. For example, one "study"—Fang Gang's *Homosexuality in China* (1995)—features the twenty-seven-year-old author (who, incidentally, published seven other books that year) masquerading as a physician in order to obtain information from his subjects and persuade them to accept his nostrums for their homosexuality.[11] Fang Gang's book had an initial print run of 70,000, and Zhou Huashan, who interviewed large numbers of Beijing gays around that time, estimates that 200,000 Chinese may have read it.[12] Li Yinhe, a University of Pittsburgh Ph.D. and senior scholar at the Chinese Academy of Social Sciences' Institute of Sociology, published with Wang Xiaobo the results of survey research in the early 1990s. They titled their book *Tamen de shijie* (Their world), suggesting that "they" (gays) are other, different, and perhaps not normal. Although such publications have helped lift the taboo on public discussion of homosexuality, they have done considerable harm in characterizing homosexuality as unhealthy for society and gays as mentally ill. A significant number of gay people themselves appear to accept this characterization.

**Political Rigidity**

Party and government policies constrict gay and lesbian life. The few gay bars, restaurants, and discos that exist in major cities operate at the whim of the security apparatus, which still exercises surveillance of public places where gay men are known to meet. Zhang Yuan's 1998 film *Donggong xigong* (East palace, west palace)—not yet released in China—portrays police harassment of and brutality toward gays in the neighborhood of the public toilets (the "palaces") near Tiananmen in Beijing. The portrayal is fairly realistic. As long as gay meeting places continue to be the focus of raids and occasional detentions by police, gays in search of kindred spirits will be less inclined to frequent them than might otherwise be the case. This is not to imply that many relationships are forged from sexual liaisons in public toilets, but at a time when the continuing existence of more "respectable" or possibly safer venues is still uncertain, many gays feel an ongoing need for the parks, street corners, and even toilets to seek *duixiang* (counterparts) for relationships as well as sexual gratification.

**Housing Scarcity**

The majority of urban Chinese still live in housing provided by the work unit of a family member, typically a husband. Young adults fresh out of school and/or new on the job tend to live at home or, if they are working far from home, in cramped, dormitory-type rooms until they marry and become eligible for an apartment for the two of them and the expected child. In either event there is scant opportunity for privacy for a young, single male or female who happens to be gay or, for that matter, for a married gay man or lesbian who may want to invite a friend home while his or her spouse is away. Since employer-provided housing generally cannot be secured outside of marriage, gays who might prefer some alternative housing arrangement to facilitate a nontraditional relationship are out of luck. And the longer they want to postpone the inevitability of marriage into their late twenties or beyond, the longer they may have to wait for a decent apartment once they become eligible. Needless to say, without housing of their own—and the privacy it would provide—gays are severely limited in their ability to develop same-sex relationships.

On the other hand, we should note that there are certain limited ways around the barriers just listed. First, with respect to the pressure to marry and raise children, traditionally there has been considerable leeway for husbands and fathers to have affairs outside the boundaries of home life. The PRC decades witnessed a partial whittling away of this leeway, but the prosperity of the reform era has provided a means for the nouveaux riches to keep mistresses, a practice that has reasserted itself recently. Increasingly, gay men can also maintain relationships outside marriage without raising undue suspicion as long as they provide material and emotional support for their wives and children and respond minimally to their wives' desire for sex.

Similar leeway was not available to women in traditional China and seems to have expanded little in recent years. Only to the extent that increased marketization in the Chinese economy has created new professional opportunities for women, including lesbians, have women been able to carve out extra space for relationships outside marriage, with men or with women. For both (gay) men and women, new opportunities in the job market and the new primacy of economics over politics have made it easier to postpone marriage. They can argue that establishing themselves in a career requires more time and psychic energy than in the old days of job assignment (*gongzuo fenpei*).[13] Moreover, whether due to the market economy, opening to the outside world, or other aspects of Chinese society, it has become less imperative to marry at an early age. This provides gay men and lesbians a wider window—from, say, their late teens to mid-thirties—in which to develop same-sex relationships before marriage and offers them some hope of being able to sustain those or enter new ones after marriage.

Second, a growing number of legitimate scholars and professionals in the fields of medicine, mental health, philosophy, ethics, and sociology, not to mention journalists and gay activists, have publicly challenged the conventional wisdom that homosexuality is a mental illness or an abnormality. They have done so primarily through research monographs, articles in the news media, small conferences, and lobbying efforts on the part of activists. Chinese gays in the PRC and overseas made a major push to have homosexuality removed from the Chinese Psychiatry Association's list of mental illnesses. It is unclear just how much impact these efforts are having, but the generations that reach adulthood in the 1980s and 1990s probably can be expected to have more open-minded views toward homosexuality than do their elders. There may be instructive precedent in the cases of Taiwan and Hong Kong, where, despite bumps in the road similar to those the PRC has experienced in the last twenty years, there are now considerably more relaxed and open-minded attitudes toward homosexuality than had been prevalent in earlier decades. In fall 1997, for example, the Taiwan writer Xu Yousheng married his Uruguayan partner in a civil ceremony in Taipei much ballyhooed by the local press, although Taipei mayor Chen Shuibian reneged on a promise to attend. Such a day in Beijing may not be far off.

As for continuing political rigidity in Beijing, the environment for gays who hope to forge relationships is far less restrictive than before, especially in large cities like Shanghai and Guangzhou. Reporting for the *New York Times* in 1997, Seth Faison highlighted a small restaurant on a Shanghai side street that was featuring a singer clad in a slinky black gown with curly, shoulder-length hair and Adam's apple on display. The restaurant was packed with gay customers in their twenties and thirties hooting with laughter at the suggestive lyrics and irreverent humor of the singer. Faison quotes one customer, "No one bothers about us anymore. As long as we're not disturbing anyone else, we can enjoy ourselves and the police will leave us alone." Faison himself concludes that "as official tolerance of gay men and lesbians quietly grows in China, they are taking their first steps toward openness, as the mere existence of this restaurant—run by two openly gay managers—testifies."[14] Faison does not say (and it would have been revealing to know) how many of the restaurant's gay patrons were married and how many, married or not, were in some kind of same-sex relationship. In any event, gays are far less frequently arrested for hooliganism or disturbing public order now than in the past. This is not because of any official decriminalization of homosexuality but because the Party is less concerned about gay activity than more serious threats to its control, such as political dissent or religious movements. As long as there are meeting places like the restaurant in Shanghai, where police raids are not a looming worry, there are a few safe spaces where same-sex relationships can germinate.

Finally, changes in housing policies could potentially facilitate the development of gay relationships. The increased marketization of housing would, in principle, go a long way toward enabling unmarried gay men and lesbians to find the private space to explore with new friends sexual compatibility, similarity in lifestyles, mutual interests of all sorts, and many other possible components of a love relationship. Such a development would facilitate same-sex partners' putting off marriage indefinitely. To be sure, gays who are already married will not enjoy equal benefit from a more open housing market, but even they might be more inclined to engage in relationships outside loveless marriages if their true love partners had their own apartments. We know nothing more about the lesbian couple living together in Anhui than that the Ministry of Public Security judged them not in violation of any law, but they must have had a housing arrangement that afforded them (for a while!) at least a modicum of privacy. It is not too difficult to imagine situations like that replicated all over China if the policy of allocating housing through the work unit is significantly eased, although cost will likely still be a serious deterrent to widespread advantages for gay Chinese in this regard. The very tight housing market in Hong Kong shows that young professionals and working people often live with their parents up to and even beyond marriage because apartments are so expensive.

The Internet too appears likely to play an increasingly important role in freeing China's gays and lesbians. John Pomfret has reported in the *Washington Post* that "hundreds of thousands of Chinese men and women, both homosexual and heterosexual," use a U.S.-based Web site and personal ad service to meet friends.[15] The burgeoning medium should contribute immensely to reducing isolation and making gay relationships much easier to establish.

## CONCLUSION

Given the difficulty of finding adequate sources on gay China, and given China's notorious variability in general, conclusions on the topic can be only tentative. But since tentative conclusions are better than none, I postulate the following five general characteristics of gay relationships.

### Gay Relations Start Early

Gay relationships in China tend to begin in a person's late teens or even earlier. Several persons interviewed by Li Yinhe and Zhou Huashan described relationships that began in junior or senior high school. These usually, although not always (especially in the case of young women), involved explicit sexual exploration. In the case of Feng profiled above, a close primary school friendship blossomed into a lesbian relationship. In another case a very young boy was befriended and mentored by an older neighborhood child; the mentoring went beyond help with schoolwork to skinny-dipping in a nearby river and sexual play. The two boys, who attended the same schools through high school, where the older one ultimately returned to teach, became fast friends and lovers until marriage and the birth of a child ended the relationship.[16]

The two most common patterns among males are the cementing of sexual and emotional bonds between school chums and the development of deep affection after a sexual encounter based on a chance meeting in a park or other cruising area (as in the case of Long and Zhe above). In the latter pattern, the parties tend to be older than in the former, since cruising parks and other public spaces is one of the few ways that gay married men have to meet kindred spirits. Given the early age at which many affairs begin, it is easy to conclude that they are merely cases of infatuation or "puppy love." However, in relationships that develop among schoolmates the depth of genuine affection and emotional commitment seems palpable and real. This is not surprising, since even in contemporary China "dating around" is not as common as it is in the West.

## Gay Relationships Do Not Last Long

Marriage and child rearing continue to constitute serious impediments to homosexual relationships. These hardy social institutions begin to affect the thinking and lives of gay men and lesbians at a young age, certainly by their mid-twenties. There is, therefore, a rather narrow window of opportunity for developing relationships into adulthood, even for people who get early starts. It is clear from the testimony of gays in Li's and Zhou's interviews that many, if not most, of them feel despair about involvement with a same-sex partner because they assume—often correctly—that they will have to end the involvement when one or both partners begin the forced march into marriage. Even relationships that manage to survive the marriage of one partner seem to continue on a more "spiritual" plane (like Long and Zhe's above), without most of the sexual or even emotional content that had existed before. As a practical matter, the arrival of a child in a marriage makes it even more difficult to maintain a longer-running same-sex relationship, not only because the parents are subject to increased demands but because genuine love for the child takes root and diverts attention.

One fairly common tactic is to marry and then quickly divorce; this can help bypass society's pressure and allow a gay relationship to continue or create space for developing one. But many gays express guilt over the approach, and social pressures to stay married and provide for children also remain strong. In a population of nearly 1.3 billion, there may be millions of long-term same-sex relationships, but evidence of them remains hidden. The evidence suggests that more gay men, if not also lesbians, are opting against marriage and preparing to endure the questions or disapproval of their families, friends, neighbors, and coworkers. Moreover, some—as the *New York Times'* Seth Faison found out on his visit to the Shanghai restaurant—find it possible to live their identities in public. A twenty-year-old singer told Faison that it was "now possible to live a psychologically healthy life as a gay man in China. 'There is no reason to hide it anymore,' he said. 'It's mostly about being honest with yourself. I've never been in trouble with the police. Why should I? I haven't done anything wrong.' "[17] Since this young man said nothing to Faison about being in a relationship or about whether he ever intended to marry, we are left to wonder whether he was ready for a long-term gay relationship.

## Gay Relationships Are Kept Secret

Homosexual relationships in China are hidden from not only family but also colleagues and bosses in the work unit, which is the source of important benefits, including housing. They are also hidden from neighbors, whose gossip is feared, and from nongay friends, who might abandon a friendship out of prejudice. Same-sex relationships are often hidden even from gay friends, since the gay and lesbian community in most cities is relatively closed, and jealousy, backstabbing, and blackmail are fairly common. For the married gay man or woman, a same-sex relationship outside the marriage also carries the danger of despoiling a marriage and family and the social respectability that goes with it. Li and Zhou found in their interviews that men especially can feel paranoia at being discovered in a gay relationship, and they are ready to express remorse and to abandon the relationship if caught.

## Gay Relationships Vary Dramatically in Emotional Content

The limited reliable data for this study suggest that homosexual relationships are disproportionately characterized by either their casual, sexual nature or by their intense emotional and spiritual quality. Neither kind of liaison seems to share much of its characteristic nature with the other, and few relationships appear to be "balanced" on the ground in between. For example, one respondent in Li's study met another man, a doctor, while cruising by a bridge in Beijing. After establishing telephone contact, the two had a torrid sexual affair lasting seventeen consecutive days, during which, we are told, the doctor achieved climax twenty times. Whether the doctor was insufficiently content with this level of intensity or perhaps just bored, he twice requested that his partner take him out "into society" for a look at other gay venues. The partner reluctantly agreed and, sure enough, the doctor met another man with whom he soon established a new sexual relationship, although he denied it to his original partner. With a third party now on the scene, the original relationship sputtered along at a lower degree of intensity until the doctor, trying to make yet another pickup, was trapped by a plainclothes policeman. The doctor appealed for help to his original partner, who used connections to persuade the local police station not to establish a case file in the matter and, in return, asked the doctor not to see the third party but to remain faithful to him. The doctor was unable to keep his part of the bargain, and the relationship ended, not more than three months after it began and not entirely without the respondent's feeling pain and sorrow. When the doctor eventually got married, his erstwhile partner sent him a set of woks as a wedding gift while reminding him that he had "continually cheated on me and toyed with my affections." The doctor responded remorsefully, agreeing that he owed his old partner a lot and promising to make amends in his next life by returning as a cow or horse.[18]

By contrast, another of Li's respondents had met the (older) man of his dreams, who spurned him after only two encounters, neither, as far as we are told, involving sex. The younger man then wrote his "partner" a series of letters—each more heart-rending and gut-wrenching than the last—over the following several weeks. The writer's tears flowed constantly and copiously, and the depth of his sorrow and grief was profound. None of the letters was answered, and he appeared to be at serious risk of suicide (most likely by drowning in the flood of his own tears). This was one of several examples in Li's and Zhou's studies of unrequited love—which sometimes involved pursuit, whether by gay men or lesbians, of heterosexual counterparts.[19]

The dichotomy in the emotional content of gay relationships seems to correlate most closely with age and marital status. Younger, unmarried gays typically become involved in relatively short-lived, casual, sexually oriented, and nonexclusive relationships. This may be a function of their youth, lack of maturity, inexperience, preference for experimentation, or fear of deep emotional attachments. But the generalization itself is far from perfect, since Li's and Zhou's interviews reveal numerous examples of younger gay men and lesbians for whom the sexual content of their relationship is not paramount and who do become heavily involved with their partner emotionally.

By contrast, older gays—mostly married men—seem less prepared to enter into a sexual relationship than an emotional one. They may feel that sexual relationships, especially with multiple partners, entail greater likelihood of discovery and thus constitute a more genuine threat to the stability of their marriage. Examples abound in the Li and Zhou studies of strong emotional bonds among gay men when at least one of whom is married. In these relationships the pain of the unmarried partner in the event of a breakup with the married one appears to run especially deep.

## Gay Relationships Appear Unaffected by Political and Social Realities

It can be striking how *disconnected* from social and political events homosexual relationships can be. This finding is all the more remarkable because most of the usable data for this study were collected in Beijing, where political controls are the tightest in the country. That gay men and lesbians pursue and enter into relationships, despite all the barriers, reflects a determination to carve out personal space for the kind of love, affection, and sex they prefer within a still hostile social and political order. In so doing, they are gradually succeeding in expanding that space in dynamic interaction with a society whose rules are gradually loosening. It is in this social space for relationships of their choice—rather than in the political arena—that gays in China are most likely to experience an improvement in the quality of their lives in years to come.

As the 1990s drew to a close, there were tentative signs of change for the better for gay and lesbian Chinese. For example, on 16 October 1999, a lesbian couple—Mingshui Xiushu and Wan Ru, who had met through the Internet—were married. Mingshui, a well-known thirty-year-old actress, has written a novel and a short story about homosexual love, neither of which has been approved for publication by China's censors. Wan, a twenty-four-year-old accountant, is out to her family, and her mother attended the wedding. The couple often spends weekends at her mother's suburban Shanghai apartment, but they have moved into their own cozy studio apartment nearer downtown. Mingshui has not told her parents this—or that she is lesbian. But she feels no pressure from them to marry in the conventional way, even though her marriage with Wan is not recognized under Chinese law.[20] Needless to say, one lesbian relationship consummated by marriage in freewheeling Shanghai does not by itself signal a trend. It does, however, reflect the reality that there was pressure for change on even this beleaguered edge of society as China entered the new millennium.

## NOTES

1. Zhou Huashan, *Beijing tongzhi gushi* (Stories of Beijing comrades) (Hong Kong: Comrade Research Society, 1996), 38–44.

2. Zhou Huashan, *Beijing tongzhi gushi*, 110–15.

3. Wan Yanhai, "When Will China Rehabilitate Gays?" *Taohong man tianxia*, 29 September 1997; www.csssm.org. Accessed 25 May 1999. *Taohong man tianxia* is the electronic bulletin of the Chinese Society for the Study of Sexual Minorities.

4. Bret Hinsch, *Passions of the Cut Sleeve: The Male Homosexual Tradition in China* (Berkeley: University of California Press, 1990), 20, 36, 53, and passim. Mizi Xia was a favorite of Duke Ling of Wei (534–493 B.C.). One day, while strolling with the ruler in an orchard, Mizi Xia bit into a peach and, finding it sweet, stopped eating and gave the remaining half to the ruler to enjoy. "How sincere is your love for me!" the ruler is reported (in the *Han Fei Zi*) to have exclaimed. Both the *Memoirs of the Historian (Shi ji)* by Sima Qian and *Records of the Han (Han shu)* report the celebrated love of the Han Emperor Ai (6 B.C.–1 A.D.) for his beloved Dong Xian. One day, Emperor Ai was napping with Dong Xian stretched out across his sleeve. When the emperor wanted to get up, Dong was still asleep. Rather than disturb him, the emperor cut off his own sleeve and got up, showing the extent of his love and thoughtfulness.

5. Jia Yicheng, "Should China Eliminate the Diagnosis of Homosexuality?" *Bulletin of Mental Health, Zhejiang Province*, 1 August 1997. Reprinted in *Taohong man tianxia*, 13 October 1997; www.csssm.org. Accessed 26 May 1999.

6. Jia Yicheng, "Should China Eliminate."

7. From personal observation I made when I worked in Beijing from 1985 to 1987.

8. Wan Yanhai, "Gay Rights in China in the 1990s" (address to the People's Summit of the APEC Conference, Vancouver, 21 November 1997). Reprinted in *Taohong man tianxia*, 24 November 1997; www.csssm.org. Accessed 21 May 1999.

9. Wan Yanhai, "Gay Rights."

10. Li Yinhe, *Tongxinglian yawenhua* (The subculture of homosexuality) (Beijing: Jinri Zhongguo chubanshe, 1998).

11. Zhou Huashan, *Beijing tongzhi gushi*, 26–32.

12. Zhou Huashan, *Beijing tongzhi gushi*, 26.

13. See Amy Hanser, "The Chinese Enterprising Self," chapter 8 in this volume.

14. Seth Faison, "Tolerance Grows for Homosexuals in China," *New York Times*; geocities.com/~nanfeng/news01.html. Accessed 17 March 1999.

15. John Pomfret, "Among Chinese, a Low-Key Gay Liberation," *Washington Post*, 24 January 2000, 1, 18.

16. Li Yinhe, *Tongxinglian*, 129–32.

17. Faison, "Tolerance Grows," 2.

18. Li Yinhe, *Tongxinglian*, 135–37.

19. Li Yinhe, *Tongxinglian*. Whether partnerships of such short duration, especially if the affection is not reciprocated, qualify as "relationships" is naturally a legitimate question.

20. Pomfret, "Among Chinese," 18.

# 12

# Urban Experiences and Social Belonging among Chinese Rural Migrants

*Li Zhang*

Since the beginning of the post-Mao economic reforms in the late 1970s, rapid commercialization, urban economic growth, and privatization have led to unceasing waves of labor migration in China. No longer tied permanently to farmland, some 100 million peasants have come to the cities in search of work and business opportunities. This unprecedented rural-to-urban mobility has created a newly differentiated urban mosaic and has significantly reconfigured the urban social landscape in reform-era China.

Most existing scholarship on China's reemerging migration (also known as the "floating population") tends to focus on its structural causes, the general profile of the migrant population, and migratory trends, supported by statistical data.[1] Few studies have examined rural migrants' everyday cultural experiences in the cities and such aspects of their emotional and mental worlds as their perceptions of themselves, their worries, and their sense of social belonging.

Today even though state policies have become much more relaxed than in the past, making it possible for peasants to work temporarily in urban areas, the household registration system *(hukou)* continues to play a powerful role in shaping rural migrants' experiences, social identity, and sense of belonging in the city. As scholars have shown, in socialist China, the *hukou* had divided the entire Chinese population into two distinct, hierarchical "nations"[2] or "caste-like" groups,[3] namely, the urban *hukou* holders versus the rural *hukou* holders. These two birth-ascribed groups, once mapped on two different kinds of places—the countryside and the city—are now brought together in the same urban space, leading to the formation of a new "two-class" urban society in the post-Mao era.[4]

It has become clear that the arrival of migrant peasants in the cities has not led to the breakdown of the household registration system or the dissolution of social divisions between urbanites and rural residents. Rather, the presence of migrants often exacerbates existing rural-urban differences and creates tensions between them as the two groups compete for limited urban space and resources. The *hukou* remains a salient mechanism that determines people's access to material resources, delegates people's rights to the city, and shapes migrants' lives and sense of self.

In her important study of the migrant population in China, Solinger describes city *hukou* as an emblem or a badge of (urban) citizenship because *hukou* registration virtually defines rural migrants in the cities as noncitizens and bars "the great lot of them from enjoying any of the welfare benefits and social services that urbanites received as their natural birthright."[5] Viewing *hukou* as a form of citizenship is important because it highlights the profound effects of this institution not solely in economic terms but also in political and cultural terms. Because Solinger's analysis is structurally based, it says relatively little about how rural migrants in different situations actually experience in their everyday lives the wide range of difficulties and dilemmas caused by the existing social structure. It says even less about how migrants themselves articulate their concerns, fears, and hopes as they live through this unstable, transitional period of time.

The aim of this chapter is to provide a detailed cultural account of Chinese migrants' experiences of urban life and their perceptions of identities and social belonging.[6] The main question addressed here is, given that they no longer farm or live in the countryside, yet are unable to obtain city *hukou* registration, how do rural migrants view themselves and their ambiguous relationship to urban society, while struggling to develop alternative modes of social life and cultural belonging? I explore this question not through abstract theoretical discussions but through in-depth ethnographic accounts of various intimate layers and aspects of migrant lives in the cities. The ethnographic materials on which this chapter is based derive from my extended field research on Beijing's migrant population from June 1995 to September 1996. Although I conducted research in three migrant communities, most of my time was spent in the Wenzhou migrant enclave known as "Zhejiang Village" (Zhejiang cun)—the largest migrant settlement in Beijing.[7] I interviewed more than one hundred migrants with diverse backgrounds and carried out field observation of migrants' domestic, social, and economic activities. Besides working in these three enclaves, I also interviewed and talked with numerous migrant workers and small traders scattered throughout the city. Further, roughly fifty short essays written by migrants themselves and published in a special column of the *Beijing wanbao* (Beijing Evening Daily) also provide additional information about their lives in the city and their understanding of their secondary status, the meaning of their home, and their uncertain future.[8]

The stories I present in the following sections focus on two groups of migrants:

wage workers (*dagong de*) and self-employed entrepreneurs and traders (*getihu*). I divide them into two parts because the two groups of migrants have quite different urban experiences and perceptions of self due to their different structural locations in the labor market and urban society. But I by no means imply that each of these groups is a homogeneous entity. Indeed, within each group there is a wide range of feelings, thought, and experiences.

## FLOATING WAGE WORKERS

My heart is like a piece of dry leaf in the fall season, floating in the wind and unable to find a place to settle. (interview with a migrant from rural Hubei who worked as a private security guard)

The majority of what constitutes the floating population are peasant workers (*mingong*), who perform various low-end, low-pay, sometimes dangerous manual or strenuous physical work in such urban economic sectors as construction, manufacturing, food services, street cleaning, and domestic work. These migrants are mostly young, unmarried men and women from the countryside who struggle to make a living by selling their labor. Unlike self-employed migrant entrepreneurs, wage workers do not own any means of production or small businesses and thus have to rely solely on their labor for limited cash income, forcing them to move frequently as they follow available jobs.[9] The lack of urban *hukou* and the temporary nature of migrant work have a significant impact on rural migrants' experience of the city and their sense of self and social belonging. Since most migrants cannot obtain permanent jobs and urban housing, they can easily become jobless and homeless, their temporary living quarters usually being provided by their employers. As a result, migrant workers share a strong sense of fear, temporality, and insecurity from the moment they leave their native place for the city—an unfamiliar world that is alienating and unpredictable.

### Departure and Arrival

Leaving home for the first time and entering the urban world can be a frightening experience mixed with excitement for young migrant workers. Many of the migrants I met started their migration journey in their teens and early twenties. They usually left home with a few friends or relatives and had some friends or relatives waiting for them at their destination. But even with such informal networks, migration for these young men and women, who have never been outside their villages before, is a challenge. Xiaomei is one of these tens of thousands of migrant workers who arrived in Beijing on the train. She left her small village home in rural Jiangsu with her best friend when she was sixteen because her uncle, who had worked in Beijing for several years, told her mother that he could arrange a job for her in the city. As she recalled, "I had nothing to do at home anyway. So my mother thought it would be good for me to earn some money for the family to support my younger brother's schooling. We heard that it was easy to make money in the city, but we had no idea what kind of work my uncle would get me." She continued: "My mother gave me the money to buy a train ticket and some change in case I needed it on the way. But just before I was about to step out of the door, my mother cried, saying that she did not want me to go anymore. I calmed her down but eventually left with my friend."

They took a bus to the train station in the city of Xuzhou. Neither of them had ever seen a real train before, let alone ridden on one. Because they did not know the procedure for taking a train, they got lost in the station and missed the train they had intended to take. This meant that Xiaomei's uncle would not be able to meet them at the Beijing train station later, and they would have to find their own way to his place. The two girls felt a bit scared and discouraged. After they finally got on the train to Beijing the next day and sat surrounded by strangers, Xiaomei began to miss her home and thought about her mother's words: "Always be careful outside. If you meet bad guys, fight with them or just jump off the train. Do not let them take advantage of you. Reputation is the most important thing for girls."

After they arrived in Beijing, finding her uncle was a difficult task because she did not have his exact address and only knew that he worked in a service division at Peking University. At the gate of the university, the guard stopped them, since their clothing style and demeanor easily identified them as "outsiders." "The guard refused to let us go in without telling us why. We didn't know what we were supposed to do. I almost cried because it was very cold and it was getting dark. You know what the winter is like in Beijing. We didn't have enough clothes on and didn't know where to go in this enormous city." They stood there for about an hour in the cold wind. Eventually another guard took pity on them and let them in after they filled out the entrance registration. They finally found the division in which Xiaomei's uncle worked. But when she told the men in the office her uncle's name, they said that there was nobody by that name working there. "My heart suddenly sank and I almost passed out. It was completely dark outside by then. If I couldn't find my uncle, nobody would take us in that night." She repeated his name several times. Still the men insisted that they did not know anyone by that name. Just when she was about to burst into tears, a man in the backroom heard them and came out. He said that he knew who they were looking for. It turned out that because of Xiaomei's heavy Jiangsu accent, the men could not recognize the name correctly.

Later Xiaomei found out that her uncle had not yet found a job for her even though he was trying very hard. She and her friend lived with his family and had to wait a month for jobs, feeling worried and depressed. "We ran out of money and had to depend on them completely. I was embarrassed and knew that his wife was not happy about the situation either." Finally he found a waitress position for her in a small restaurant on campus. The pay was ¥35 a month and she was required to work for about twelve hours a day, seven days a week. Her girlfriend could not find anything to do and eventually returned home.

Xiaomei's experience and anxieties are common among migrant workers who arrive in the city for the first time. Like her, most migrants I interviewed had some sort of connection with relatives or fellow villagers who had come to the city earlier. These informal social networks are extremely important for migrant newcomers as they settle in and find jobs. But the potential danger of long-distance traveling and the possibility of not finding the contact person or a job are always present. Young migrant women, without any legal protection in an unfamiliar world, are haunted by potential sexual assault. Other migrants are not as lucky as Xiaomei, since they have no relatives or friends in the city and thus have no place to stay upon arrival. They often sleep in the train station and are driven by the police from place to place every night. The next morning they go out to look for jobs in the "black" market spontaneously formed on the streets not far from the train station. For them, finding a job is the first crucial step because employers normally provide a place for workers to sleep, although the housing space is usually overcrowded and in terrible condition.

## Job Insecurity and Fear of Sickness

After making it to the city, most migrants live in the shadow of *hukou* regulation and are in a prolonged liminal state of being. Officially they are categorized as "temporary residents" (*zhanzhu renyuan*), but in reality they are treated as secondary citizens or aliens with fewer rights than permanent urban residents. In my conversations with migrant workers, they frequently used the following terms to describe their current situation: *piaoliu, piaobo,* or *liulang* (floating or wandering). These terms all convey a sense of rootlessness in a world that is not meant for them. No matter how long they have lived and worked in the city, migrants are treated as peasants and "outsiders" (*waidiren*) who should and will eventually return to their rural home. Most migrant workers are fully aware of their liminal and inferior positions in the city, and they have gradually internalized a low structural position in urban society. For example, the following reply from a young construction worker from Sichuan represents the common view of how migrants perceive themselves after working in Beijing for several years: "Of course I'm still a peasant. Just look at my *hukou* registration. It says clearly that I'm a peasant (*nongmin*). We'll always be peasants, no matter what we do in the city. Nothing can change that fact. Working in the city is temporary; as soon as state policies change or no more jobs are available, we'll all be forced out of the cities."

Unlike the majority of permanent urban residents who enjoy job security and state-subsidized housing, children's education, medical care, and so on, rural migrant workers have minimum job security and lack a stable place to live.[10]

Their survival is entirely tied to their jobs, but their jobs are highly unstable. Job loss often means the subsequent loss of shelter without any other recourse. Therefore, fear of illness is always the top concern of migrant workers not only because illness generates high costs in medical treatment but also because it can lead to the loss of wages and shelter. As one young migrant woman put it, "I feel that we're born to work without stop. If we're sick and can't work any more, we'll be gotten rid of immediately like trash. There is no alternative and no sympathy from city people." Almost all migrant workers told me that they could not afford to go to the hospital. If they were sick, they simply tried to get by without taking any medication and had to hide from their employers to avoid being fired. Only when absolutely necessary would they buy over-the-counter medicine. Illness that was chronic and serious could have other serious consequences.

Huimin was a seventeen-year-old girl from Hubei who worked as a maid in a Beijing household for several months. Later she fell ill, coughing frequently. As soon as the family found out that she had tuberculosis, they kicked her out immediately because they were afraid of being contaminated. She had no place to ask for help and became homeless. The service agency that had recruited her from the countryside temporarily put her up in a small makeshift shed on a construction site. It was a humid summer, and the shed was full of mosquitoes. Soon nearby construction workers heard that there was a girl living there and began to harass her from time to time. Huimin could not take it anymore and decided to go back home. But she had no money left by that time. Out of sympathy and guilt, the family she worked for offered to pay some of her medical bills and bought a train ticket for her to return home.

Another woman, Yang from Henan, related a similar story. After she turned sixteen, she left home and went to Zhuhai (a city in southern China) to work in a private factory. The work hours were long and averaged eighteen hours per day. After several months, her back started to hurt badly. Meanwhile, she was not used to the food and weather in the south. "I felt tired all day long and had no strength. I got really sick and could not afford to see a doctor. So I saved enough money to buy a train ticket and went back home," she told me. Two years later she left home for the second time. This time Yang worked in a factory producing penicillin in the city of Shijiazhuang in Hebei province for three months. But the boss only gave her ¥300 for three months' work instead of ¥1,200 as promised in the beginning. She was angry and quit the job because her earnings were not enough to pay for her daily expenses. She came to Beijing with another Henan girl whom she had met in the factory. At the time I met them, they had just been hired to operate an embroidery machine in a Wenzhou migrant entrepreneurial household in Zhejiang cun. The boss told them to work for a while and he would decide how much in wages to offer later. Yang had a sense that they might not get paid after working in vain for a month. But she and her friend accepted the offer because they needed a place to stay. Two months later, when I went to look for them at the same place, they had left and no one knew where they had gone.

Their words kept echoing in my head, "We are like fallen leaves in the wind. Who knows where the wind will take us tomorrow?"

## Migrant Expectations and Urban Prejudice

Many migrant workers come to the cities not only because they want to earn cash to support their families but also because they want to see the world (*jian shimian*). Prior to departure, they tend to hold romanticized visions and high expectations of modern, urban life as portrayed in movies and television shows. Yet almost as soon as they arrive in the city, their dreams are shattered by the harsh reality and urban prejudice against migrant outsiders. One young migrant, Zhao, explained to me his disappointment: "Before I thought that since Beijing is the capital, its people must be very polite, open-minded, and well educated. But now I can only say that Beijing people are parochial, arrogant, and intolerant towards outsiders like us." Derogatory terms such as "country bumpkins" (*xiangbalao* or *tubaozi*) and "stinky peasants" (*chou nongmin*) are typically used by urbanites to refer to migrants. In everyday life, migrant workers are subject to arbitrary questioning and personal searches by the police on the street. Such urban prejudice reinforces the migrants' sense of alienation and inferiority.

While fully aware of such negative images of migrants imposed by urbanites, some migrant workers also challenge urban prejudice and demand fair social treatment. For example, one migrant woman from Wuwei county in Anhui province wrote to the *Beijing Evening Daily*, "Every time I try to squeeze onto a crowded bus, I often hear city people complaining that there are too many *waidiren*. . . . But when you move into a brand-new apartment building, when you eat fresh vegetables, when you walk on clean streets, when your trash disappears, when your elderly and children are well taken care of, have you ever thought about us—migrant working brothers and sisters?" Likewise, many migrant workers point out that without their hard work and labor contribution, Beijing would not be the city it is today, and Beijing residents would not be able to live the lifestyle they enjoy today. They thus demand that urban society give them their deserved social space and better treatment. Yet the reality is largely dismal. Migrants as a whole are viewed by officials and urban residents as a social problem leading to overcrowding, crime, and other urban ills.

The low social position of migrant workers is clearly reflected in marriage choices. Due to the *hukou* barrier, most rural migrants have little contact with permanent urban residents in the realm of dating and marriage. They tend to find potential spouses within their own *laoxiang* circle (friends from the same native place). Only a small number of migrant women are married to urban Beijing *hukou* holders. But these men tend to have some sort of undesirable situation (*tiaojian buhao*), for example, they are disabled, are much older, are divorced with a child, lack a permanent job, or have little education. This kind of marriage is usually arranged through the introduction of a matchmaker, and love and mutual feelings are not considered important. Whether a man and woman match each other is often calculated according to their *hukou* status, physical ability, and appearance. Migrant women lacking permanent urban residential status are considered low on the social scale or socially disabled and thus only deserving of an urban man with a physical disability. Some migrant women who desperately wish to remain in the city and have a relatively stable place of their own are willing to enter this kind of marriage based on "rational choices." Others refuse to acquire a sense of security and stability at the expense of their youth and love.

Chenlin is a migrant woman in her early twenties from rural Sichuan. After she finished junior high school, her family decided not to send her to high school because it cost too much and they did not see much reward in it. She had her own ambition and did not want to stay in the countryside as a farmer for the rest of her life. So she followed a *laoxiang* to Beijing. This *laoxiang* worked in a Beijing hospital as a janitor and introduced Chenlin to the employer, who eventually hired her for the same job. Since Chenlin is good-looking and smart, several of her Beijing acquaintances at the workplace wanted to match her with some men. But each time she found out that there was something wrong with the man. She recalled for me what happened a few months before, when she was introduced to a man with a Beijing *hukou*:

> When we met at the introduction meeting arranged by the matchmaker, I realized that he had a hunchback and was very short. Also he was at least ten years older than me. I felt insulted and did not want to proceed further. But the matchmaker and my friends all thought that I was foolish and said, "If you marry him, you can stay in Beijing forever. So many other girls are dying for this kind of chance. How can you give it up?" But I just did not feel right. . . . Even though I'm poor and have no urban *hukou*, I have my own dignity and dreams. Why should I waste my youth on a strange older man?!

Young women working as maids (*baomu*) in urban households or as waitresses in restaurants, bars, and other service sectors are likely to encounter various forms of sexual harassment. Although the migrant women I interviewed said that they were not sexually assaulted by their employers, they had all heard of or knew someone who had experienced such disturbing assaults. Since the young women who work in individual households have little social contact with the outside world, they are in a vulnerable position in the event of an unwanted sexual advance. Domestic workers are strongly discouraged by the agencies that arrange their jobs from talking about or reporting any sexual harassment cases. If they disobey, the agencies will refuse to find new jobs for them in the future.

Besides the lack of legal protection, urban cultural perceptions and stereotypes of rural migrants also work against young domestic workers. Even though in most cases it is the man (the male head of a household, for example) who initiates the relationship or simply imposes himself on the migrant woman, it is the woman who often gets blamed. A young *baomu* explained to me why this is the case: "When things like this happen, most people do not believe us because we are migrant working sisters and outsiders. By contrast he [the man involved] is a local urban resident with a family. Due to our lower status, city people tend to conclude that he has no practical reason to seduce us and therefore it must be our fault." She further explained that sometimes different habits and norms of behavior in the countryside and the city also create misunderstandings and unwanted situations. She continued, "For example, back at home in the country-side, we tend to have a large undivided room where brothers and sisters and other relatives all stay together. But in an urban household one can't just lie down wherever one wants. Some of us may be used to the old way, which makes others assume that we're loose and intend to seduce men."

Women who work in the service sector report that they frequently encounter sexual jokes and remarks and unwanted physical advances from male customers in restaurants and bars. In such cases, young women have little power to change the situation. If they speak out and upset the customers, they are very likely to be fired by the business owner. Wang Yue was a young migrant woman from Hebei who worked in a restaurant in Beijing's east district. Over a period of time, some returning customers who got to know her well started to make explicit sexual jokes with her while she waited on them. Wang first pretended that she did not hear or did not understand the jokes. Later one of the men began to pat her derriere and touch her face, calling her to sit with them while they drank. Wang was very uncomfortable and frightened, so she told her boss what was going on. After hearing her story, however, the restaurant owner simply laughed and said that there was nothing to worry about. If the customers kept coming back, she should entertain them and "adapt" to the situation. Since she did not want to lose her job, all she could do was to try to avoid serving those particular customers. She lamented, "City men treat us like nobody. They think that we're poor and have no backing, therefore they can take advantage of us." Wang's experience is quite common among migrant women in the service industry whose choices are very limited: quit or accept the unpleasant treatment in order to keep their jobs.

### Homesickness and the Dilemma of Return

Homesickness (*xiangjia*) is a recurring theme in migrants' everyday conversa-tions and essays published in *Beijing Evening Daily*. As rural migrant workers encounter urban prejudice, they tend to develop a strong sense of nostalgia for home that is romanticized and idealized. This sweet image of the rural hometown and its associated warm and intimate social relationships are juxtaposed with the city, which migrants come to experience as an alienating and indifferent place. For example, a migrant worker from Heilongjiang province who made a living by washing dishes in a restaurant wrote: "Today is my birthday. There are no best wishes from my family around me or candlelight and birthday cake. My only company is the cold, indifferent full moon. Only me, a floating, outcoming working sister, can understand what it's like to taste such loneliness and bitterness." She then described her memory of the idealized village life she had left behind: the green willows and boundless golden wheat fields, the peaceful sunset, and the gentle haze from village cooking fires. Of course, such idealized images of home cannot simply be taken at face value. Migrants' longing for home does not necessarily mean that they all wish to return to their rural origins, but it expresses their yearning for a better and friendlier social environment in urban society. Migrants' nostalgia for their homes and the rural way of life is a reaction to and critique of urban xenophobic sentiments.

For married women who left family and children behind, homesickness is intensified by the physical separation from their children. Chen was one of those women I met at a spring outing organized by the Family of Working Sisters, founded by the editorial board of a popular journal called *Rural Women (Nongjia nü)*. Chen, in her mid-thirties, came from a poor village in Sichuan. When the local women's association went to recruit domestic workers in her village, she insisted on joining the girls who decided to work in the city because her family needed money to build a new house and support her son's schooling. She struck me as a capable and optimistic person who did not regret her choice. But later in our conversation, she told me that she often missed her family, especially her son, very much, and was torn between such feelings and the need to earn cash for her family. "Sometimes I feel weird because I'm here taking care of other people's children, while leaving my own son behind. My son is going to elementary school now. I wish I could just go back and cook for him every day. I often wonder what he does and thinks when he gets sick," Chen admitted to me. But she then rationalized her choice by saying that it was worth the pain because what she was doing would improve the well-being of her family and provide a better future for her son.

Almost all the migrant workers I interviewed said that they do not plan to stay and work in Beijing forever; ultimately they will return home. Some want to earn enough money to help their parents build a new house or support their brothers' schooling; some hope to accumulate more capital and learn certain business skills in order to start a small business of their own once they return to their hometowns. It is these dreams that support them as they endure various hardships and swallow the bitterness in a strange world during the years of migration. But things do not always work out as expected, and the dreams of migrants are not so easily fulfilled.

Having stayed in the city for a period of time, many young workers begin to change in different ways. Influenced by urban consumer culture, some of them begin to spend part of their savings on clothes, shoes, and makeup, rather than give every penny they have to their parents. Some of them may no longer wish to return to rural life. Others feel that their previously arranged engagement no longer fits their new expectations of marriage. Idealized images promoted by the mass media regarding urban ways of life and modern romantic love have significantly influenced young migrant workers' ideas about marriage and courtship. When some of them find new boyfriends or girlfriends among migrant workers they meet in the city, they want to break off existing engagements, decisions that often cause familial and interfamilial disputes in their home villages. Canceling the engagement *(tuiqing)* used to be a social taboo, but it is now accepted by more and more villages, according to my informants. Some migrants in this situation are not willing to go to such extremes because of their uncertain feelings about their future in the city, but at the same time they do not want to "just get married" yet. A common tactic is to delay marriage by extending their migration time in the city despite harsh working conditions. The spatial distance between them and their family members in the village makes this form of resistance possible, which would otherwise be crushed by direct pressure at home.

Another reason why returning home becomes more and more difficult is related to the notion of *mianzi* (face) and social expectations from friends and relatives. In some rural communities, a myth has formed that portrays rural-to-urban migration as the quickest and easiest way of "getting rich" for peasants. Villagers who stay behind expect to hear successful stories of migration and see nice clothing and gifts brought back by returning migrants.[11] An old Chinese saying highlights this kind of mentality: "to return to one's hometown in fancy silk robes" *(yijin huanxiang)*. Not being able to fulfill such expectations is considered shameful. But in reality migration does not always lead to wealth and success. Many migrant workers struggle to survive in the cities and cannot make the amount of money expected by others. Yet the myth persists because even though most migrant workers have not become rich, they feel it is necessary to perpetuate the myth in order to avoid losing face. As a result, many migrants decide to remain in the city in order to avoid the embarrassment of returning without the glory of success.

Li Hong is one of those migrant workers who struggles to survive in the city but fears going back home without being able to deliver what is expected by family members and peers. Li came from a Henan village and worked as a helper in a Wenzhou migrant household that produced leather jackets. She was only twenty years old but had been in several cities before coming to Beijing. When I met her, she had not been paid for three months and was tired of the floating way of life. So I asked her whether she was considering going back home. Li replied, "I'm thinking about it all the time, but it's not time for me to go back yet. I can't go back with nothing. That way I'll lose face and feel shamed in front of my friends. People in my village do not know how hard life is so far away from home. They assume that Beijing is like a heaven full of opportunities to make money." I asked her why she could not just tell them the truth. Li explained, "I can't because everyone else who goes back to visit tells lies to save their own face. If I tell the truth, people are going to think that I'm just incapable. They'll say: 'How come everyone can make a lot of money except for you?!' This is too embarrassing." Misguided by this picture, a lot of girls in the village who had never been outside envied Li and wanted her to bring them out also. I asked whether her parents knew what was going on. Li sighed, "I don't want to tell them how hard it is to work outside because I don't want to worry them. So every time when I go back to visit them, I also buy as many gifts as I can even though I have no money left for myself. I keep telling them that I'll do better and be able to save enough money."

The difficulty of returning home created a dilemma for these young workers and kept them in the city for much longer than they initially anticipated. After many years, some of them feel that they have become out-of-place strangers both in the city and at home. They begin to question where their home really is or whether they still have a place called "home."

## MIGRANT ENTREPRENEURS AND TRADERS

As long as we have money, Beijing is also a place for us. . . . I want to keep two homes—one in my *laojia*, Hongqiao, and one in Beijing—so that I can go back and forth and live in both places. (interview with a young migrant business owner from Wenzhou)

Unlike peasant workers who sell their labor for cash income, peasants-turned-petty traders and business owners enjoy a greater degree of personal freedom, flexibility, and economic power. Although this is also a heterogeneous group consisting of migrants with varying financial capacities and different types of businesses, self-employed migrant *getihu* (independent entrepreneurs) generally are less dependent on fluctuating labor markets and thus have more choices of residence than migrant workers. To illustrate alternative modes of cultural belonging and senses of self among migrant entrepreneurs, I will use Wenzhou migrants in the informal garment industry as a point of reference. There are about 100,000 migrants from the Wenzhou region of Zhejiang province living in their self-created migrant settlement—"Zhejiang Village" (Zhejiang cun), the largest such settlement in Beijing. This enclave is located in the Dahongmen area in Fengtai district, about five kilometers from Tiananmen Square. The majority of these migrants are engaged in family-based clothing manufacturing and trade and have been in Beijing for an extended period of time.[12] Because of their successful private business activities, Wenzhou migrants enjoy more economic capital and consumption power than other migrants and ordinary Beijing residents, and they have developed a new vision of social space and belonging that transcends a single fixed locality (i.e., hometown or urban destination).

## Spatial Mobility and Self-reliance

In everyday conversations, Wenzhou migrants frequently present themselves as a people with a long history of mobility. Most of them can tell stories about how early and how far their ancestors and fellow Wenzhou natives traveled or migrated for business purposes all over China as well as to many parts of the world (including Europe, Southeast Asia, and North America).[13] The story that they are most proud to tell is about Wenzhou sojourners in Paris who have established their own enclave based on family-run restaurants and garment manufacturing. It is common for Wenzhounese today to travel to Russia and eastern and western Europe as tradesmen. As one of them summed up, "Wherever there are markets, there are Wenzhou people." The self-fashioning of "floating" as a way of life constitutes an important part of their identity. Indeed, maximizing the use of different consumer markets through migration is deemed to be the secret of Wenzhou migrants' business success. For them, "floating" has become a necessary way of life and part of their mercantile-oriented identity.

Ai Lian is a migrant trader from Hongqiao township in the region of Wenzhou. She left home with her brother's family for the first time when she was eighteen. After staying in the cities of Xi'an and Taiyuan for about two years, they came to Zhejiang cun. Ai Lian worked in her elder brother's household-based garment factory sewing on buttons. A few years later, as she grew older and became more independent, she started her own business selling clothing produced by other Wenzhou migrants to retail stores in Beijing. The business was very profitable, although she often had to work day and night. Ai Lian told me that she liked being an independent entrepreneur even though it was unstable and required hard work: "I like it because I have freedom! With my own business, I don't have to go to work for other people on a fixed schedule or take orders daily from any officials or bosses."

This sense of self as mobile, flexible, and self-reliant is often juxtaposed with the static life of the majority of urbanites within the state-owned sectors. Another Wenzhou entrepreneur, Zhou, perceived this difference in the following terms: "The biggest difference between us and them (Beijingers) is this: they rely on the state; we rely on ourselves. As a result, they're afraid of losing benefits provided by the state and are tied to one place for the rest of their lives; but we have little to lose." Zhou's family owned a retailer stall in a trading building in Zhejiang cun, and the business was extremely successful. In 1995 his family made a profit of nearly ¥500,000 selling inexpensive fashion clothes. Small private businesses like Zhou's have few connections with state-owned economic sectors and do not receive any subsidies from the state. They rely heavily on the market and their own informal social networks. Since the market is often unpredictable, successful migrant entrepreneurs have to go wherever is best for business.

## Alternative Modes of Social Belonging

Over the years, Wenzhou migrant entrepreneurs have developed a different sense of identity and belonging, which is not based on a single geographic location as defined by the *hukou* system but is oriented simultaneously toward two or more locales. Let me illustrate this flexible, multilocale-based mode of place identity and social belonging with the following anecdote. One day, I was riding a minibus with several Wenzhou migrant entrepreneurs. For some reason, our conversation turned to the topic of "home." One of them said to me, "I miss my home a lot. You just can't imagine how beautiful and charming the landscape of my home province is. Walking along the misty West Lake in the morning and wandering in the jadelike green Yandang Mountains is like living in heaven. Although my village is small and remote, the hills are always green and the water is crystal clear *(shanqing shuixiu)*." I was touched by his homesickness and asked him why then he had decided to leave his hometown and stay in Beijing for so many years. He continued, "We left our homes not because we were poor and had to come to beg in the city, as many Beijingers imagine. We left our homes because we wanted to make more money, and making money required larger consumer markets. I can't help missing my hometown and I try to go back home once or twice a year. But this doesn't mean that I need to physically live there all the time. As private businesspeople, we must be able to go wherever is best for business."

For this man, as well as for many other migrant entrepreneurs, migration (as a strategy for capital accumulation) and the creation of their urban settlements do not necessarily indicate a diminishing of their emotional and practical ties to their places of origin.[14] They are able to reconcile a localized identity oriented toward their hometowns with a translocal identity based on frequent spatial mobility. While moving to different places for entrepreneurial activities throughout their lifetime, they also maintain close social and economic ties with their rural homes. For example, almost all rural migrants in China maintain their family land, which has been allocated to them by the state. They also build new houses back home even though they are physically absent from the village for most of the year. As they accumulate more savings, some of them use the money to establish small enterprises in their place of origin and many donate funds to rebuild ancestral halls, temples, and roads in their home village.[15] The migrant social world includes a larger social space that crosses multiple sites—their place of origin and their urban settlements.

In more recent years, improved transportation has reduced the time it takes to travel between locales, thus making it easier for some migrants to maintain contact with their native places. For example, the first airport in the Wenzhou region was completed in the early 1990s, and the first train station was opened in the mid-1990s. Because of their increased economic power, most Wenzhou migrants in Beijing can now afford to return home by air or train. During the Spring Festival, plane and train tickets are usually sold out completely. As a response to the increasing need for long-distance transportation, many family-run travel agencies have emerged in Zhejiang cun, offering chartered bus trips between Wenzhou and Beijing. During the special holiday season, villages and towns in Wenzhou become unusually crowded as migrants return home to hold wedding banquets, build new houses, and pay visits to relatives, friends, and ancestral tombs.

In February 1996 (the Chinese New Year occurred on February 19) I visited Wenzhou for half a month and stayed with a migrant family whose daughter, Jing, I had come to know very well during my fieldwork in Beijing. Jing's family was spread over several places at that time. Her father was the head of a village in a rural suburb of Yueqing, a county-level city in the Wenzhou region. He was the only one in the family who did not go to other places for business. Her mother, brother, and sister had migrated to a city in Hebei province and opened a store selling household electronic parts. Her mother came back to their hometown frequently to purchase the trading items in a nearby county-level city, Liushi, because the prices of products there were significantly lower than in other places. Jing, who had some basic medical training after junior high school, opened a small clinic in Zhejiang cun treating Wenzhou migrants. They all made very good money and had a nice three-story brick house built in the village. For most of the year, her father was the only one living in that house. Her mother made short visits for business reasons. Yet all of them stayed in close contact with one another and returned to celebrate the Chinese New Year for a month each year. This is a period of intense socializing activities. Besides getting together with immediate family members, people also visit friends and other kin. When I was in the village, almost every day we either went to visit others or had guests over for family banquets and mahjong games at Jing's home. But as soon as the holiday season was over, most migrants left home for wherever their business called them. The village became quiet again with mostly older men and women and children left behind.

Further, improvements in telecommunications in recent years have made it even more convenient for migrants to maintain everyday social contact with their friends and relatives in their place of origin. Most rural households in Wenzhou today have their own telephones. In the settlement in Beijing, it is common to see Wenzhou migrants carrying cellular phones and pagers because such services can be obtained more easily than regular residential phones and offer flexibility in conducting business. It is not unusual to see Wenzhou businesspeople paying phones bills that run over several hundred yuan or even a few thousand yuan. Public telephone booths run by private individuals can be found at almost every corner in the Wenzhou migrant community.

While maintaining close social ties with their rural homes, many migrant entrepreneurs have also developed multiple socioeconomic involvements in the cities: through both their private businesses and native place–based settlements and through material consumption. Although rural migrants are officially defined as nonurban citizens and thus have no access to state-sponsored goods and services, the recent development of a market economy has opened up new opportunities for them to acquire consumer goods outside the state's redistributive regime. Because of their remarkable business success, migrant entrepreneurs generally enjoy a high degree of consumer power. As their economic capital has increased, they have tended to develop new ways of thinking about their relationship to the city. This multilocale-oriented sense of social belonging constitutes the primary social space for many Chinese migrant entrepreneurs, challenging the officially defined social identity and fixed belonging to a single place, namely, one's *hukou* residence.

### Redefining Urban Membership through Consumption

My interviews with Wenzhou migrants frequently involved their perceptions of Beijing and the meaning of belonging to the city. What struck me most in their accounts was the ways in which they directly correlated urban belonging with economic status and the ability to consume goods and services in the city. This view was clearly articulated by Ruilan, a young migrant businesswoman: "Let me put it this way: If you have a lot of money, Beijing is a place of great fun; you can do whatever you want and dream. But if you don't have money, it is a hell; and you can hardly survive." I asked whether she would get a Beijing *hukou* so that she could stay in Beijing as long as she wanted. She continued:

> I don't need a Beijing *hukou* to stay in Beijing as long as I have money. Look at those arrogant Beijing *xiaojie* (ladies)—they work in state-owned units but make little money. They can't even afford to go to expensive restaurants or to shop at Saite and Guomao (the International Trade Center Mall) as we do. How can they be so proud? Just for the piece of *hukou* paper? . . . Don't they realize that today's society belongs to those of us who have money? As long as we have money, Beijing is also the place for us.

For many Wenzhou migrants like Ruilan, urban belonging in an era of rapid commodification and commercialization should no longer be defined by *hukou* status. Rather, migrants redefine social status and reclaim urban membership through flexible consumption practices. Some Wenzhou migrants reason that since they contribute to the city significantly through production, trade, and consumption, they are more entitled to be citizens of Beijing than the local people. This notion of membership challenges birth-ascribed *hukou* status by asserting achieved rights to a place through economic and consumer practices.

Reclaiming the rights to the city through business involvement and consumption is closely related to two specific characteristics of this particular group of migrants. First, Wenzhou migrants in Beijing are mostly fifteen to thirty-five years old, and they came of age in an emerging mass consumer culture during the reform years. It is no wonder that they, like their peers of the same generation, easily turn to material consumption as a way to acquire urbanity and modernity. Second, the consumer power that the majority of Wenzhou migrants in Beijing enjoy is ultimately determined by their position in the system of eco-nomic production. As small private business owners, Wenzhou migrants have the means to accumulate more wealth than other migrants and ordinary Beijing residents.[16] In sum, within the Wenzhou migrant community, wealth and consumption power are regarded as the primary components of social status. While "making money" (zhuanqian) and "doing business" (jingshang) have become popular mottoes for Chinese people in the reform era, this impulse is felt most clearly among migrant entrepreneurs because they are closest to the markets.

It is important to point out that migrant entrepreneurs' attempts to formulate new modes of identity and social belonging have not allowed them to move beyond the hukou barriers in everyday life, particularly when it comes to their children's future and education. Almost all migrant parents I spoke with said that their non-Beijing hukou status will negatively affect the lives of their children, who may not want to stay in private business and may prefer to pursue professional or other careers in the cities. Many of them believe that money alone cannot fully change their marginal position in society, but money and education together will help their children achieve a better social status and reduce urban discrimination.

So far I have highlighted the distinct sense of self and understanding of social belonging manifested among migrant Wenzhou garment traders in Beijing. In particular I have shown how these migrants maintain and perceive their relationships with their hometown and urban community in ways that are quite different from those of migrant laborers. Next I examine two issues that concern Wenzhou migrant entrepreneurs most: the fear of expulsion and the fear of crime.

### The Fear of Expulsion

Since the late 1980s, numerous large and small migrant enclaves have emerged in a number of Chinese cities. Beijing is no exception. But the existence of these newly emerged migrant enclaves does not necessarily indicate that enclave-based migrants have gained a stable and safer place of their own. On the contrary, migrant social spaces are highly politicized in Beijing, and migrants are subject to unpredictable expulsion due to government campaigns. As a result, these migrants (mostly self-employed small business owners) live in the constant shadow of periodic government campaigns to clean out their settlements.

In the 1980s, government policies toward migrants could be summarized as rejection and ejection. In Beijing almost every year officials carried out campaigns to drive migrants out of their own settlements. Migrants had to leave temporarily and went to hide in nearby villages outside Beijing. After the campaigns, they would return to the same place and resume their business.[17] Even though in the 1990s, government policies shifted from simple ejection to more tolerant practices focusing on regulation, "cleaning up" (qingli) campaigns—which targeted prominent migrant enclaves—took place from time to time, especially before and during important political and international events. Most Wenzhou migrants vividly recalled fleeing to towns and villages in Hebei province before the 1990 Asian Games and the 1995 World Women's Conference (both held in Beijing).

Liu Jinan and his wife came to Beijing in 1985. They manufactured wool coats in their small apartment in Haidian district and sold the products directly to stall owners in the downtown business district. "Every day we were worried about being kicked out by officials. Each relocation meant not only inconvenience and possible homelessness for a few days but also severe business loss," said Liu. In late 1989, in the name of preparing for the Asian Games, the Beijing government initiated a city-wide campaign to clean up migrant congregating zones in order to beautify the city. Liu recalled, "During that period of 'big expulsion' we closed down our business and my family was divided between two places. I went to work in the store owned by my sister-in-law in Xinjiang province, both to help out and gain some income, while my wife remained hiding in Beijing. This way we didn't have to give up all the sewing equipment and could resume the business as soon as the political cyclone was over."

The most devastating campaign that shattered Wenzhou migrants' lives occurred in late 1995, when the city government decided to significantly reduce the number of migrants in Zhejiang cun by demolishing all the housing compounds built and occupied by migrants. This migrant enclave was specifically targeted because it was perceived by officials and urbanites as a hotbed of disorder and the cradle of a nascent social force independent of state control. In the early 1980s, when Wenzhou migrants had just begun to arrive in the Dahongmen area, finding housing was not so difficult. They managed to rent extra rooms from local Beijing farmers and set up their garment manufacturing in their place of residence. But as the number of migrants in this area soared in the early 1990s, available housing space became scarce and rents also went up. As a result, some relatively wealthy migrants financed and built nearly fifty large housing compounds (locally known as *dayuan*) in Zhejiang cun and accommodated some 40,000 Wenzhou migrants and their workers. These privately owned and self-protected migrant compounds were deemed by city officials to be dangerous sites that could develop into bases for oppositional social forces. As a result of this official "clean-up," more than half of the migrants in this enclave were forced out, and all their residential compounds were flattened by government bulldozers. Tens of thousands of Wenzhou migrants and their workers suddenly lost their homes and many of them fled to Hebei province or hid in villages in remote Beijing counties.[18]

Xiuqin's family was among the displaced households that went to a small city in Hebei province just outside Beijing. When I met them in the new relocation site, her mother spoke to me in tears: "We lost everything. All the investment we put into that housing compound is now gone. We'll never be able to pay back the debt borrowed from friends and relatives." Her family had borrowed about

¥200,000 to invest in the construction of the largest housing compound in Zhe-jiang cun. Since the compound was brought down during the demolition cam-paign, only months after its completion, they did not make any profit and lost the principal. Xiuqin's family was desperate and felt that they had no face to return to their home village if they could not pay back the debt. Other ordinary families that were forced out of the compounds also encountered various kinds of hardship in everyday life and businesses, as well as stress and emotional insta-bility.

Three months later, most displaced Wenzhou migrants eventually returned to Zhejiang cun and began to rebuild their interrupted businesses and community life, but they continued to live in fear of being ejected again. As one of them said: "Government policies are precarious. That is the way it is. We don't know when another political cyclone will come."

### The Fear of Crime

Another issue that concerns Wenzhou migrants is their personal safety and public security (zhi'an). For example, a middle-aged garment trader expressed this sentiment in the following terms: "The thing that disturbs me most is the issue of personal safety and public security. Even if I'm all right today, who knows what will happen tomorrow. Every minute, we live in constant fear of being robbed or even killed. If we can't feel safe and settled, how can we focus on our production and business?" Another woman, owner and teacher of a family-run preschool, described similar concerns:

> Public security is what worries me most. Sojourning at a place so far away from home and with my personal safety in danger, this is the biggest problem. This feeling is like a hidden disease in one's vital organ [xinfu zhi huan]. When we first came to Beijing, we were afraid of Beijing hooligans [liumang] who were ferocious toward us. When they bullied us, we didn't dare say a word. Later, there were more and more of our Zhejiang people in this area, and we began to overpower Beijing hooligans. Now we're no longer afraid of Beijing hooligans, but we are afraid of Zhejiang hooligans.

My informants pointed out that because the local Beijing government was only interested in collecting regulation fees, it failed to provide any protection against crime. While people living in the housing compounds obtained a certain degree of protection from their patrons (housing bosses), those outside the com-pounds had none. To understand how robbery and extortion became a prevalent problem in this community, it is first necessary to examine the newly emerged drug culture, since the majority of robbery cases are directly or indirectly related to drug use. For this reason, Wenzhou migrants refer to robbers and other crimi-nals in two specific terms: chi dayan de (those who eat opium) or chou baifen de (those who smoke white powder—heroin).

Drugs did not become a major problem in Zhejiang cun until recent years. Due to the high concentration of private wealth and failed government control, drugs are smuggled into this community daily. Beginning in the early 1990s, narcotics—mostly heroin and opium—began to spread among Wenzhou migrant youngsters aged sixteen to twenty-five. According to Xiang's account (1994–1995), there were four to six underground drug trafficking spots and 2,000 drug addicts in this settlement by 1995. During the period of my fieldwork (1995–1996), the number of drug users had increased steadily, as did the drug price. One gram of heroin cost over ¥1,000, making it more expensive than a gram of gold. Since drugs are so expensive, those who become addicted can barely afford them after a while. Like a dark abyss, drugs drain away the addict's money, energy, and consciousness.

The effects of drugs on the social fabric of the community are profound. First, drug consumption creates tensions and conflicts between young drug users and their parents. When they discover that their children are addicted, some angry parents deny financial support to them or cut off their access to family businesses. Some parents manage to put their addicted children into a forced rehabilitation center in their hometown. But many parents are simply too busy with their business to pay enough attention to their children's problems. Unable to bear criticism and humiliation from family members, some youngsters simply run away from their families and live with peers in similar situations. Struggling with destitution, some of them turn to robbery in order to meet their increased craving for drugs. Others find secret places to continue to smoke heroin behind their parents' backs. Parents whose children are addicted to drugs feel ashamed, desperate, and helpless. But when their children are caught by the police, these parents will try to bribe officials to let their children off. Torn between feelings of love and resentment, one mother said about her son, "No matter how terrible his behavior is, after all he is my own child, my flesh and blood. How can I see him being locked in jail without giving him help?!" Given such mixed feelings, some parents end up helping perpetuate the problem.

Second, drugs can lead to the loss of family business and wealth, and to the disintegration of marriage and family ties. Some people begin with occasional use of a small amount of drugs and think that they can control how much they use. But soon they realize that they have entered a world ruled by uncontrollable cravings. The addiction only strengthens as time goes on. Meanwhile, addicts begin to lose interest in their own businesses and squander all of their savings on drugs. Using heroin two to three times a day, about thirty minutes each time, can cost ¥300–400. That adds up to over ¥100,000 a year! In the cases I knew of, young wives demanded divorces from their addicted husbands and assumed responsibility for raising their children on their own. In one case, the wife became a drug addict and lost custody of her two young children after the divorce. If both parents become addicted to drugs and leave their children unattended, their parents or relatives have to take custody of the children. These children are often abused by their parents and suffer from depression.

The twin of drugs is robbery and extortion. A commonly held view by Wenzhou migrants is that the predators responsible for most robberies and extortions include three kinds of people: young drug addicts, those who have lost their fortune in market competition, and convicted criminals who have escaped from jail. These people are seen as a hedonistic social group that "loves ease and despises work" (haoyi wulao), a new by-product of a consumption-oriented society. Unlike the migrant patron–client networks I described earlier, the primary goal of small criminal gangs is not self-protection but obtaining other people's wealth through violent acts. Most robbery victims are middle-income migrant families living outside the housing compounds. They have the money to pay the predators' demands, but at the same time they have little protection from patrons. The very wealthy households usually have more clout and their own followers for protection; those living in the housing compounds are under the patronage of powerful housing bosses.

Robbery takes place in both private and public spaces. Street robberies are mostly random, involving not only cash but also more visible items such as expensive leather jackets, furs, and items of apparel. Preplanned indoor robberies are more serious. The victims are carefully chosen and the timing of the robbery is well arranged. The robbers usually know the financial situation and business operation of the victim's family. While some cases are direct, face-to-face extortion combined with physical threat, others are carried out by masked and thus unidentifiable robbers who may well be acquaintances of the victim. "You know they are out there. They even say hello to you every day. But you never know when you will become their next target. . . . This is frightening," a migrant explained.

The "20 March case" reflects the experiences of many Wenzhou migrant families.[19] The home of Wenzhou migrant Kong, who lived in Zhejiang cun, was raided on the night of 20 March. The day before the incident, Kong went to the bank to take out ¥40,000 to buy more leather for his family business. Kong was a quiet person who never showed off his wealth. It turned out that the robber, Song, was his neighbor, a fellow Wenzhounese who had become addicted to heroin. With his increasingly strong addiction, Song had run out of money and had to rely on robbery to satisfy his craving for drugs.

One day he happened to hear from his two neighbors that Kong's leather garment factory was very profitable and Kong had just withdrawn a large amount of cash from the bank to buy more leather the next day. Song was secretly delighted and thought that his chance to get rich had finally arrived. He went to talk to his uncle, who was also in desperate need of cash. A robbery plan took shape. Song first appeared at Kong's residence at about seven in the evening for a casual chat and visit. He tried to memorize how things were arranged in the house and then left. At about 3:00 A.M., when Kong's household members and workers were still working in front of their sewing machines, several masked robbers suddenly broke into the house. They ordered everyone to keep silent and demanded that Kong hand over his money. When Kong refused to do so, one of the robbers hit him on the head and he fell to the ground. Then the robbers searched the house and found the ¥40,000, as well as an additional ¥48,900 that Kong's brother-in-law had temporarily left with him for a planned trip.

From the migrants' point of view, emergent crime in their community is closely related to the incompetence and corruption of the local police. For many years, the police failed to extend effective crime control into migrant enclaves. In recent years, the local police have become more interested in handling criminal cases related to Wenzhou migrants because these relatively wealthy migrants can provide a great opportunity for generating extra income. Clientelist ties have formed between corrupt policemen and local thugs, which allow the latter to buy freedom and bypass law. For many migrants, the new "regulation" now offered by the local police is an unofficial way of creating side income for underpaid policemen than an effort to keep good public order and restore justice for migrants.

## CONCLUSION

In this chapter I have sought to capture a wide range of migrant urban experiences, perceptions of self, and sense of cultural belonging as migrants encounter both socialist legacies and new market forces. As my ethnographic accounts and migrant voices show, the floating population is by no means a homogeneous social body. Their lives and perceptions of their homes and selves are not uniform but depend on their specific social and economic locations. Migrants rarely see themselves as constituting a homogeneous group with a shared identity and coherent experiences. Differences in economic status, place of origin, gender, ethnic background, and residential or settlement pattern all play a salient role in reshaping the self and group identities among diversely situated Chinese migrants.

Despite such diversity, certain common themes of thought and experience can be identified among migrant workers scattered in the city and among migrant entrepreneurs living in enclaves that are formed on the basis of native-place networks. For migrant workers, job availability, job security, and physical health are the top concerns. Although kinship and native-place networks are the primary means through which workers migrate and enter the urban labor market, these informal social networks are limited in scale and have not developed into visible associations that most migrants can rely on. Further, migrant workers have little economic capital; their choices are largely constrained by the urban labor market and their *hukou* status. By contrast, migrant entrepreneurs have gained economic power and better control over their own life and work trajectories. Their kinship and native-place networks have developed into their own communities and business centers. Although migrant entrepreneurs are not able to escape urban prejudice and discrimination, some of them create alternative modes of cultural belonging and self-identity beyond their officially designated place in society. Some enclave-based migrant groups are afflicted by increased crime because of the lack of local and official protection. At the same time, they are also the targets of systematic expulsion by the government. Therefore, migrant life is unstable for both wage workers and entrepreneurs, although in quite different ways.

Finally, I would like to speculate on how the mixture of such socialist legacies as the *hukou* on the one hand and emerging market forces on the other are reshaping the future of rural migrants and urban society in China. The *hukou* registration, buttressed by the state-controlled "urban public goods regime," had long divided the Chinese population into two distinct kinds of subjects fixed in rural and urban spaces.[20] In the reform era, characterized by global capital, partial privatization, and market forces, the *hukou* continues to play an important role in reconfiguring social differences and inequality, and in shaping the migrants' life, self, and social belonging. Migrants' lower social status in the cities and the diverse difficulties and dilemmas that they face in their daily lives are largely derived from the *hukou* system, which historically created urban prejudice against outsiders.[21] Yet, as I have also shown in this chapter, migrants' uneven possession of economic capital and relationship to the means of production figure their perceptions of self and their relationships to the city in dissimilar ways. Some migrants such as Wenzhou traders are able to attain a higher economic position through market-based economic practices and can create a space of their own in the city. Their alternative modes of belonging that cross different places thereby challenge the officially designated *hukou* identity. But for others, the ultimate return to the countryside seems inevitable. Given these multiple differences, what is emerging in urban China today is not just a two-class social system based on *hukou* status (urbanites versus migrants), but a much more complicated social configuration shaped not only by the *hukou* classification but also by gender, family background, economic position, and place of origin.

## NOTES

The ethnographic materials presented in this chapter were collected during my fieldwork on Beijing's "floating population" from June 1995 to September 1996. The project was sponsored by a Fulbright-Hays Doctoral Dissertation Research Abroad Fellowship, the Committee of Scholarly Communication with China, the Wenner-Gren Anthropological Foundation, and the President's Council of Cornell Women. Cornell's East Asia Program, the Center for International Studies, and the Peace Studies Program also provided supplementary funding for preliminary research. I am also grateful to the following colleagues and friends who offered useful comments and suggestions in the process of writing this essay: Leila Fernández-Stembridge, Sara Friedman, Jennifer Hubbert, Perry Link,

Mark Miller, Andrew Morris, Paul Pickowicz, and the participants of a conference on popular thought in postsocialist China held at Princeton University, October 1999.

1. See the following works for examples: Sidney Goldstein and Alice Goldstein, *Population Mobility in the People's Republic of China* (Honolulu: East-West Population Institute, 1985); Xiushi Yang, "Household Registration, Economic Reform, and Migration," *International Migration Review* 27, no. 4 (1993): 796–818; Hein Mallee, "Rural–Urban Migration Control in the People's Republic of China: Effects of the Recent Reform," *China Information* 11, no. 4 (1988): 12–22; Zai Liang and M. J. White, "Internal Migration in China: 1950–1988," *Demography* 33, no. 3 (1996): 375–84; Delia Davin, *Internal Migration in Contemporary China* (New York: St. Martin's, 1999); Yi Dangsheng and Shao Qing, eds., *Zhongguo renkou liudong taishi yu guanli* (The floating pattern and regulation of China's population) (Beijing: Zhongguo renkouxue chubanshe, 1995).

2. Anita Chan, Richard Madsen, and Jonathan Unger, *Chen Village under Mao and Deng* (Berkeley: University of California Press, 1984), 299.

3. Sulamith Heins Potter and Jack M. Potter, *China's Peasants: The Anthropology of a Revolution* (Cambridge: Cambridge University Press, 1990), 296.

4. Kam Wing Chan, "Post-Mao China: A Two-Class Urban Society in the Making," *International Journal of Urban and Regional Research* 20, no. 1 (1996): 134–50.

5. Dorothy Solinger, *Contesting Citizenship in Urban China: Peasant Migrants, the State, and the Logic of the Market* (Berkeley: University of California Press, 1999), 5.

6. My approach here is influenced by Ong's notion of "cultural citizenship," which focuses on immigrants' cultural experiences rather than legalistic aspects of citizenship in the context of the United States. Aihwa Ong, "Citizenship as Subject Making: New Immigrants Negotiate Racial and Ethnic Boundaries," *Cultural Anthropology* 37, no. 5 (1996): 737–62.

7. For detailed accounts of the spatial distribution and basic features of migrant enclaves in Beijing, see Laurence Ma and Xiang Biao, "Native Place, Migration, and the Emergence of Peasant Enclaves in Beijing," *China Quarterly*, September 1998, 546–81.

8. This special column was called "I Work Temporarily in Beijing" (Wo zai Beijing dagong) and ran for several months in 1996. It was intended to serve as a public forum for migrants who wished to talk about their experiences and personal feelings in the city.

9. The migrant workers I focus on are those scattered in urban service sectors and family-based businesses rather than the factory workers discussed by Anita Chan in this volume and by Lee Ching Kwan in *Gender and the South China Miracle: Two Worlds of Factory Women* (Berkeley: University of California Press, 1998).

10. Since the early 1990s, however, the accelerated reform of state-owned enterprises has eroded the job security previously enjoyed by most urbanites as more and more urban workers are laid off in the process of privatization.

11. That Chinese migrants are expected to display their wealth and success when they return to their native place is widely found in many parts of China. See Li Minghuan, " 'To Get Rich Quickly in Europe!': Reflections on Migration Motivation in Wenzhou," in *Internal and International Migration: Chinese Perspectives*, ed. Frank N. Pieke and Hein Mallee (Surrey, U.K.: Curzon, 1999), 181–98.

12. For a detailed account of this migrant group's social and economic activities and community development, see my book: Li Zhang, *Strangers in the City: Reconfigurations of Space, Power, and Social Networks within China's "Floating Population"* (Stanford, Calif.: Stanford University Press, forthcoming).

13. For detailed accounts of Zhejiang people's migration to and lives in Europe, see Pieke and Mallee, *Internal and International Migration*.

14. Similar phenomena whereby migrants simultaneously maintain important social and economic ties with their home communities while developing new involvements in other places are also observed by other scholars in both international and internal migration contexts. See Leo Chavez, *Shadowed Lives: Undocumented Immigrants in American Society* (Fort Worth, Tex.: Harcourt Brace Jovanovich, 1992); James Ferguson, "The Country and the City on the Copperbelt," *Cultural Anthropology* 7, no. 1 (1992): 80–92; Roger Rouse, "Mexican Migration and the Social Space of Postmodernism," *Diaspora*, Spring 1991, 8–23; James L. Watson, *Emigration and the Chinese Lineage: The Mans in Hong Kong and London* (Berkeley: University of California Press, 1975).

15. Mayfair Mei-hui Yang, "Tradition, Traveling Anthropology, and the Discourse of Modernity in China," in *The Future of Anthropological Knowledge*, ed. Henrietta Moore (London: Routledge, 1996), 93–114.

16. The average household income of Wenzhou migrants is very high. Eighty percent of the households that I interviewed claimed an annual income above ¥200,000, about twenty times the annual income of a middle-class Beijing household.

17. Xiang Biao, "Zhejiang Village in Beijing: Creating a Visible Non-State Space through Migration and Marketized Networks," in *Internal and International Migration*, 215–50.

18. Detailed accounts of this campaign, multiple social conflicts, and its impact on migrant lives can be found in my forthcoming book. Li Zhang, *Strangers in the City*.

19. This case was reported in *Beijing wanbao* (Beijing evening daily), 9 June 1996.

20. Dorothy Solinger, "China's Urban Transients in the Transition from Socialism and the Collapse of the Communist 'Urban Public Goods Regime,' " *Comparative Politics*, January 1995, 127–46.

21. For a historical comparison, see Emily Honig, *Creating Chinese Ethnicity: Subei People in Shanghai, 1850–1980* (New Haven: Yale University Press, 1992).

# Chinese Glossary

p. 90    日没胭脂红，无雨必有风。

未吃端午粽，寒衣不可送。

人勤地不赖。

桂林山水甲天下。

关东有三宝，人参貂皮乌拉草。

穷在闹市无人问，富在深山有远亲。

p. 91    害人之心不可有，防人之心不可无。

一任清知县，十万雪花银。

p. 92    百万雄师下大江。

百万雄鸡下江南。

p. 94    章子不如筷子，筷子不如面子，面子不如
辫子。

p. 95    存好的，烂坏的，卖烂的，坏好的。
crosspiece: 推旧存新。

301

p. 95        假酒假药贾省长，官道官商关书记。

吹牛皮象驴叫一样；巴结领导像哈巴狗一样；
训斥下级像老虎一样；公款吃喝像恶狼一样；
见便宜跑得像兔子一样；干工作像猴子一样；
遇见困难像泥鳅一样。

p. 97        五十年代人都人，六十年代人整人，七十年代
人哄人，八十年代个人顾个人，九十年代见人
就宰人。

干部拿钱引，群众为钱干，一切向钱看，离钱
玩不转。

p. 98        烟搭话，酒搭桥，解决问题大炒勺。

不吃不喝，经济不活。

财政是爹，银行是娘，工商税务大灰狼。电老
虎，水霸王，人民教育黑心肠。

小车嘀嘀喇叭响，来了一车共产党，追得鸡鸭
满天飞，碰得酒杯叮当响。

p. 99        下来一群瞌睡的，回去一群喝醉的。

党员不党员，只差几块钱；除了缴党费，其他
一个味。

工资基本不用，烟酒基本靠送，老婆基本不碰
，工作基本不作。

p. 100       喝酒两三瓶不醉，跳舞四五晚不睡，玩女人七
八个不累，问业务啥也不会，原来全是第三梯
队。

青春献给党，老了没人养，说是靠儿孙，儿孙
下了岗。

p. 100　　毛主席要我们下乡，邓小平要我们下海，江泽民要我们下岗。

民要我们下岗。

毛主席象太阳，照到哪里哪里亮；邓小平象月亮，初一十五不一样。

p. 101　　辛辛苦苦四十年，一朝回到解放前。既然回到解放前，当年革命又为谁？

贪污腐化成系统（陈希同），反腐倡廉未见行（尉健行），家事国事理难清（李岚清），满朝文武无官正（吴官正），厄尔尼诺江泽民（江泽民），平民百姓容易忍（荣毅仁）。

不反腐败亡国，反腐败亡党。

干部全枪毙，肯定有冤枉，隔着一个杀，肯定有漏网。

p. 102　　广东人什麽都敢吃，上海人什麽都敢穿，北京人什麽都敢骂，农民什麽都敢卖。

不到东北不知道自己胆小，不到北京不知道自己官小，不到关东不知道自己钱少，不到海南不知道自己身体小。

p. 103　　结婚是错误，生孩子是失误，离婚是觉悟，独生是大彻大悟，没有情人是废物。

男人有钱就学坏，女人学坏就有钱。

三陪小姐自述：
　一不偷，二不抢，怀里抱着个共产党。

p. 104　　鼓了勤劳人的劲，治了懒惰人的病。

包产到了户，管他干部不干部。

p. 104　摆个小摊，赛过县官；办个小厂，赛过省长；全家作生意，赛过总书记。

农民苦，面朝苍天背朝土；农民悲，四方摊派八方催；农民愁，孩子无钱把书读。

p. 105　六月工资十月发，领导仍坐桑塔纳；工资发不了，领导买蓝鸟；工资发一半，领导有皇冠。

工人劳，干部富，厂长拿钱没有数。

老大下岗，老二赚钱，老九光着屁股坐花轿。

p. 106　拿手术刀的不如拿剃刀的，弹钢琴的不如搬钢琴的，搞导弹的不如卖鸡蛋的。
老师就象盐，吃著有点咸，家家离不了，就是不值钱。

辛辛苦苦三十年，一夜回到解放钱。

技术干部是南瓜，越老越甜；政工干部是丝瓜，越老越空。

# Index

Adidas, 20
Ah Q, 225, 227, 228
AIDS, 264
Ai Lian, 287
*Anju Gongcheng* program, 242
*Arts and Life* (*Meishu shenghuo*), 139, 141
Asian Games of 1990, 292
Auntie Li, 240–42, 244
Auslander, Leora, 232
*Auto Fan* (*Che mi*), 115
autonomy (*zizhuquan*), 194–96, 202

Bank of Industry and Commerce, 235, 236
Baoyuan Shoes, 23
Barkley, Charles, 26
basketball culture, 4, 9–38, 93; and banning of NBA playoffs, 30; and capitalist market system, 15–20; centrality of to lives of Chinese youth, 24–25; and foreign players, 28–31; historical use of by PRC state, 13, 27, 28; history of in China, 12–14, 33n15; and the individual, 20–26; and the nation, 26–31, 37n72; and types of basketball shoes, 17–18, 20; and women, 37n71
*Basketball* (*Lanqiu*) magazine, 9, 14–15, 17, 18, 20, 23, 32n3; and Chineseness of CBA, 28; and foreign players, 29; and the nation, 27; popularity of, 34n24; and *Slam Dunk*, 26

beggars, 6, 207–30; and ability of modern society to provide life of dignity, 208–10; as a group process, 215–17; and Ah Q, 224, 225; as a profession, 211, 215; and autonomy or freedom, 217; and Buddhism, 220, 221, 223; changing nature of, 227–28; and criminal tendencies, 224–26; and detention reparation stations, 219; during the Maoist era, 212–14; exploitation of family by, 225; as fakes, 223; and funerals and weddings, 212–13, 221, 223; and gang leaders, 216–17, 218, 222–23; history of as *qigai*, 220–27; illegality of after 1911 revolution, 224–25; increase in numbers of, 208, 226; in the late 1990s, 215; Li Tieguai model of, 222, 223–24, 227; and Mao Zedong, 212; and "mean people" (*jianmin*), 221; methods of, 208; as officially sanctioned group, 213–14; periodic forcing of out of major cities, 219–20, 226; premodern tradition of and continuity with, 211–12, 215, 220–27; and professional dignity, 217–18; in the reform era, 214–20; and religious mendicants, 220; and socialist vs. liberal capitalist moral frameworks, 209–11; and swindles, 221; traditional occupational specialties of, 222

305

# About the Contributors

**Julia F. Andrews** is Bliss M. and Mildred A. Wiant Professor of Chinese Literature and Culture in the Department of History of Art at The Ohio State University.

**Anita Chan** is Senior Research Fellow at the Australian National University.

**Deborah S. Davis** is Professor of Sociology at Yale University and Director of Academic Programs, Yale University Center for the Study of Globalization.

**Leila Fernández-Stembridge** is Associate Professor of Chinese Economy and History at the Universidad Autónoma de Madrid, Spain.

**Robert Geyer,** former Director of the National Academy of Sciences' Committee on Scholarly Communication with China, is an independent researcher in Arlington, Virginia.

**Amy Hanser** is a Ph.D. student in Sociology at the University of California, Berkeley. She is currently researching a dissertation on marketplaces and consumption in urban China.

**Richard Levy** is Professor of Political Science at Salem State College.

**Perry Link** is Professor of East Asian Studies at Princeton University.

**Richard P. Madsen** is Professor of Sociology and Chinese Studies at the University of California, San Diego.

**Andrew Morris** is Assistant Professor of History at California Polytechnic State University, San Luis Obispo.

**Paul G. Pickowicz** is Professor of History and Chinese Studies at the University of California, San Diego.

**Kuiyi Shen** is Assistant Professor of Art History at Ohio University.

**Liping Wang** is Assistant Professor of History at the University of Minnesota.

**Li Zhang** is Assistant Professor of Anthropology at the University of California, Davis.

**Yuezhi Zhao** is Assistant Professor of Communication at Simon Fraser University.

**Kate Zhou** is Associate Professor of Political Science at University of Hawaii.

LIBRARY OF CONGRESS CATALOGING-IN-PUBLICATION DATA

Archer, Richard, 1941–

Fissures in the rock: New England in the seventeenth century /
Richard Archer.

p.   cm. — (Revisiting New England)

Includes bibliographical references and index.

ISBN 1-58465-084-2 (alk. paper) — ISBN 1-58465-085-0 (pbk. : alk.
paper)

1. New England—Civilization—17th century.   2. New England—Social
conditions—17th century.   3. New England—Biography.   I. Title.
II. Series.

F7.A74 2001

974'.02—dc21

00-011600